T5-AFS-514

TREASURY OF LITERATURE

BEYOND THE WINDOW

SENIOR AUTHORS

ROGER C. FARR
DOROTHY S. STRICKLAND

AUTHORS

RICHARD F. ABRAHAMSON
ELLEN BOOTH CHURCH
BARBARA BOWEN COULTER
BERNICE E. CULLINAN
MARGARET A. GALLEGO
W. DORSEY HAMMOND
JUDITH L. IRVIN
KAREN KUTIPER
DONNA M. OGLE
TIMOTHY SHANAHAN
PATRICIA SMITH
JUNKO YOKOTA
HALLIE KAY YOPP

SENIOR CONSULTANTS

ASA G. HILLIARD III
JUDY M. WALLIS

CONSULTANTS

ALONZO A. CRIM
ROLANDO R. HINOJOSA-SMITH
LEE BENNETT HOPKINS
ROBERT J. STERNBERG

HARCOURT BRACE & COMPANY

Orlando Atlanta Austin Boston San Francisco Chicago Dallas New York
Toronto London

Portions of this work were published in previous editions.

Printed in the United States of America

ISBN 0-15-301237-4

2 3 4 5 6 7 8 9 10 048 96 95 94

Acknowledgments continue on page 605, which constitutes an extension of this copyright page.

Acknowledgments

For permission to reprint copyrighted material, grateful acknowledgment is made to the following sources:

Isaac Asimov: From "The Story Machine" by Isaac Asimov in *Plays* Magazine, May 1977.

Atheneum Publishers, an imprint of Macmillan Publishing Company: Cover illustration by Judith Gwyn Brown from *I Am the Universe* by Barbara Corcoran. Illustration copyright © 1986 by Judith Gwyn Brown.

Avon Books: Cover illustration from *Bearstone* by Will Hobbs. Copyright © 1989 by Will Hobbs.

Bantam Books, a division of Bantam Doubleday Dell Publishing Group, Inc.: Cover photo by Rob McEwan from *Anne of Green Gables* by L. M. Montgomery. Cover illustration by Vladimir Kordic from *Where the Red Fern Grows* by Wilson Rawls. Copyright © 1961 by Wilson Rawls; copyright © 1961 by The Curtis Publishing Company.

William Bentzen, on behalf of the heirs of Knud Rasmussen: "And I think over again . . ." (Retitled: "Song") from *Intellectual Culture of the Copper Eskimos*, translated by Knud Rasmussen.

Bradbury Press, an Affiliate of Macmillan, Inc.: From *Dinosaurs Walked Here and Other Stories Fossils Tell* by Patricia Lauber. Text copyright © 1987 by Patricia Lauber.

Curtis Brown, Ltd.: "The Microscope" by Maxine Kumin. Text copyright © 1963 by Maxine Kumin. Originally published in *The Atlantic Monthly*.

Clarion Books, a Houghton Mifflin Company imprint: From *Klondike Fever: The Famous Gold Rush of 1898* by Michael Cooper. Text copyright © 1989 by Michael Cooper.

Cobblehill Books, an affiliate of Dutton Children's Books, a division of Penguin Books USA Inc.: From "Helping Hands" in *People Who Make a Difference* by Brent Ashabranner. Text copyright © 1989 by Brent Ashabranner.

Ray Pierre Corsini, as literary representative for Elizabeth Borton de Treviño: From *The Secret of the Wall* by Elizabeth Borton de Treviño. Text copyright © 1966 by Elizabeth Borton de Treviño.

Coward-McCann, Inc.: "Peki, The Musician" from *The Crest and The Hide* by Harold Courlander. Text copyright © 1982 by Harold Courlander.

Crown Publishers, Inc.: From *Nadja On My Way* by Nadja Salerno-Sonnenberg. Text copyright © 1989 by Nadja Salerno-Sonnenberg.

Dell Books, a division of Bantam Doubleday Dell Publishing Group, Inc.: From pp. 15–26 in *The Outside Shot* by Walter Dean Myers. Text copyright © 1984 by John Ballard. "Playing God" (Retitled: "The Second Highest Point") by Ouida Sebestyen from *Visions*, edited by Donald R. Gallo. Text copyright © 1987 by Ouida Sebestyen.

Doubleday, a division of Bantam Doubleday Dell Publishing Group, Inc.: Text from pp. 669–681 and cover illustration from *Roots* by Alex Haley. Text and cover illustration copyright © 1976 by Alex Haley.

Dutton Children's Books, a division of Penguin Books USA Inc.: Cover illustration by Stephen Marchesi from *The El Dorado Adventure* by Lloyd Alexander. Copyright © 1987 by Lloyd Alexander.

Farrar, Straus & Giroux: Adapted from *Here Is Mexico* by Elizabeth Borton de Treviño. Text copyright © 1970 by Elizabeth Borton de Treviño.

Michael Garland: Cover illustration from *My Side of the Mountain* by Jean Craighead George. Illustration copyright © 1989 by Michael Garland.

Grosset & Dunlap, a division of G. P. Putnam's Sons: Cover illustration by Kyuzo Tsugami from *The Call of the Wild and Other Stories* by Jack London. Illustration copyright © 1965 by Grosset & Dunlap, Inc.

Harcourt Brace & Company: "One" from *When I Dance* by James Berry. Text copyright © 1991, 1988 by James Berry. Originally published by Hamish Hamilton Children's Books, 1988. Cover illustration by Fritz Eichenberg from *Rainbows Are Made: Poems by Carl Sandburg*, selected by Lee Bennett Hopkins. Illustration copyright © 1982 by Fritz Eichenberg. Cover illustration by Leo and Diane Dillon from *Aïda* by Leontyne Price. Illustration copyright © 1990 by Leo and Diane Dillon. "The No-Guitar Blues" from *Baseball in April* by Gary Soto. Text copyright © 1990 by Gary Soto. Cover illustration by Francisco Mora from *Local News* by Gary Soto. Illustration copyright © 1993 by Francisco Mora. From *Be An Inventor* by Barbara Taylor. Text copyright © 1987 by Field Publications. Pronunciation Key from *HBJ School Dictionary*, Third Edition. Text copyright © 1990 by Harcourt Brace & Company.

continued on page 605

Dear Reader,

Look *Beyond the Window* to discover a treasure trove of excitement and adventure! Tales from around the world; fascinating accounts of our planet's past, present, and possible future; and intriguing stories of challenges and solutions all await you when you look beyond the window.

You will read about Peki, a young musician in Africa who faces a big challenge, and Fausto, a Mexican American student who's eager to learn to play the guitar. You will read about the hardships faced by people who discovered gold in Canada and about the challenges faced by archaeologists uncovering ancient treasures in Mexico. You will learn how astronauts have increased our knowledge of Earth, and you will also discover how fossils of saber-toothed tigers and even gnats can tell us about the past.

During the year you will also learn about spirit—the spirit of discovery and the spirit of freedom. You will read about the spirit of discovery Alex Haley feels when he learns about his heritage during a visit to Africa. You will come to understand the spirit of freedom, the freedom poet Paul Laurence Dunbar expresses in the line "I know why the caged bird sings."

We hope that you will enjoy discovering the many worlds that lie *Beyond the Window*.

Sincerely,
The Authors

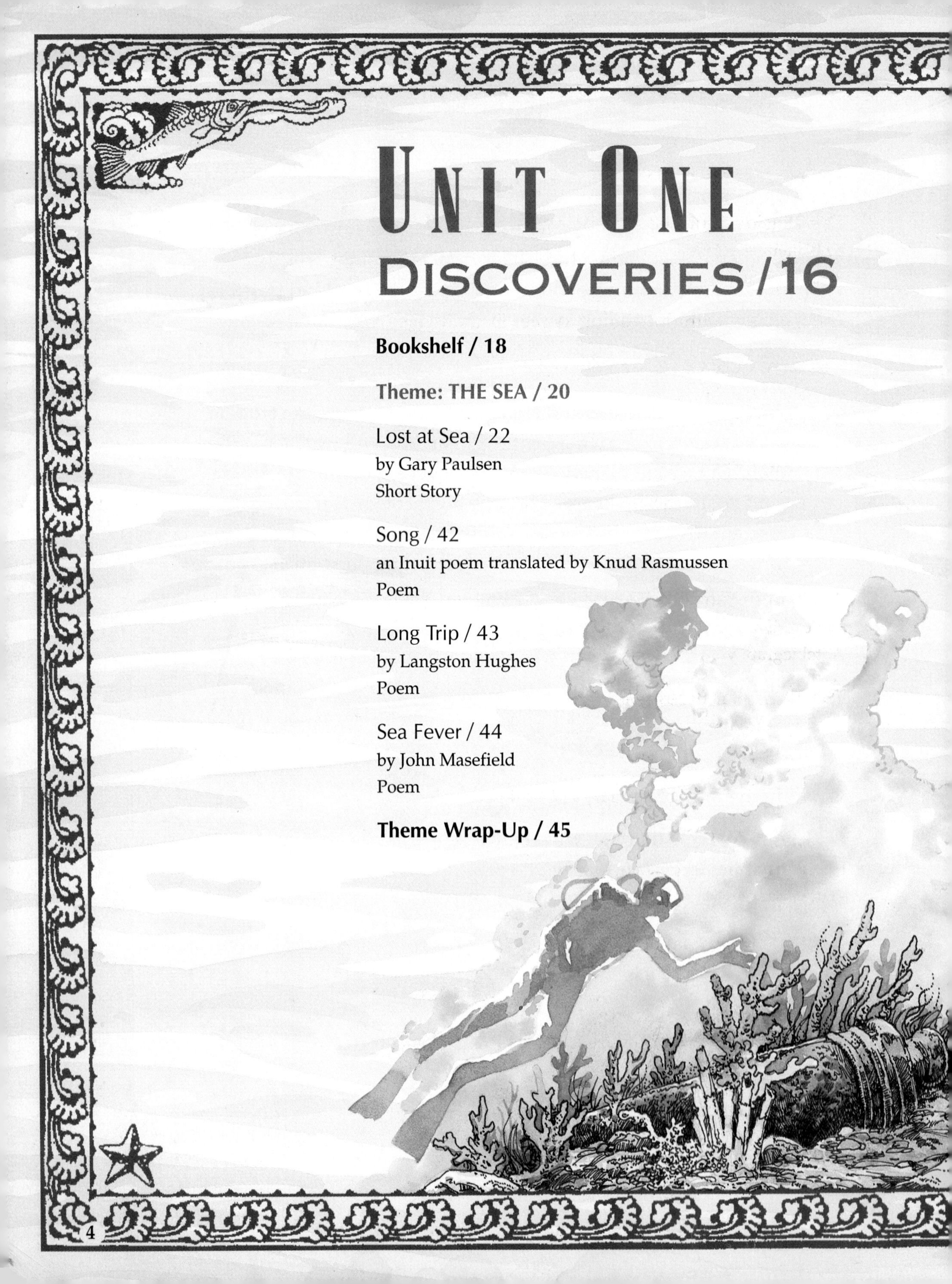

UNIT ONE

DISCOVERIES / 16

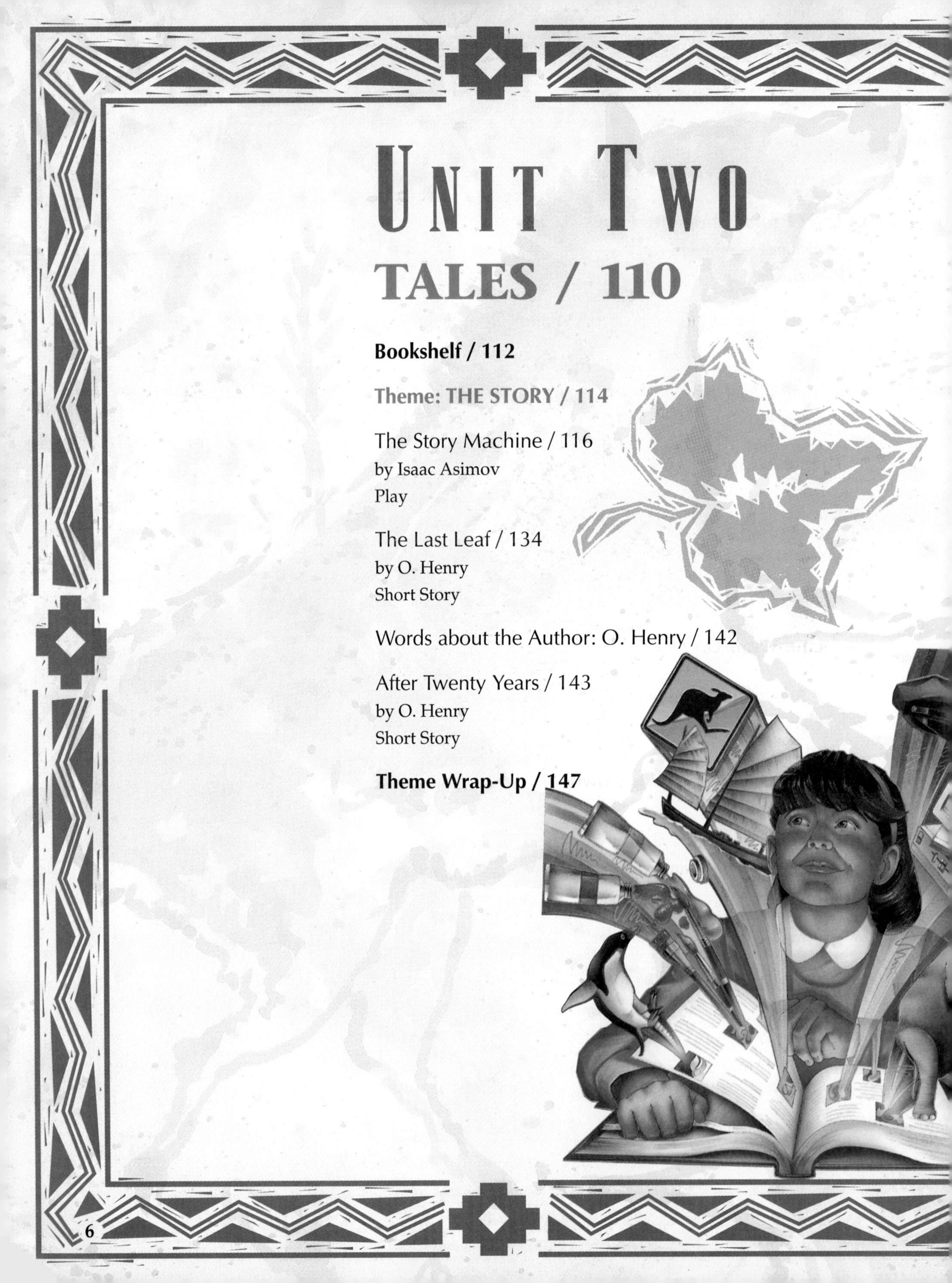

UNIT TWO

TALES / 110

UNIT THREE

BONANZAS / 210

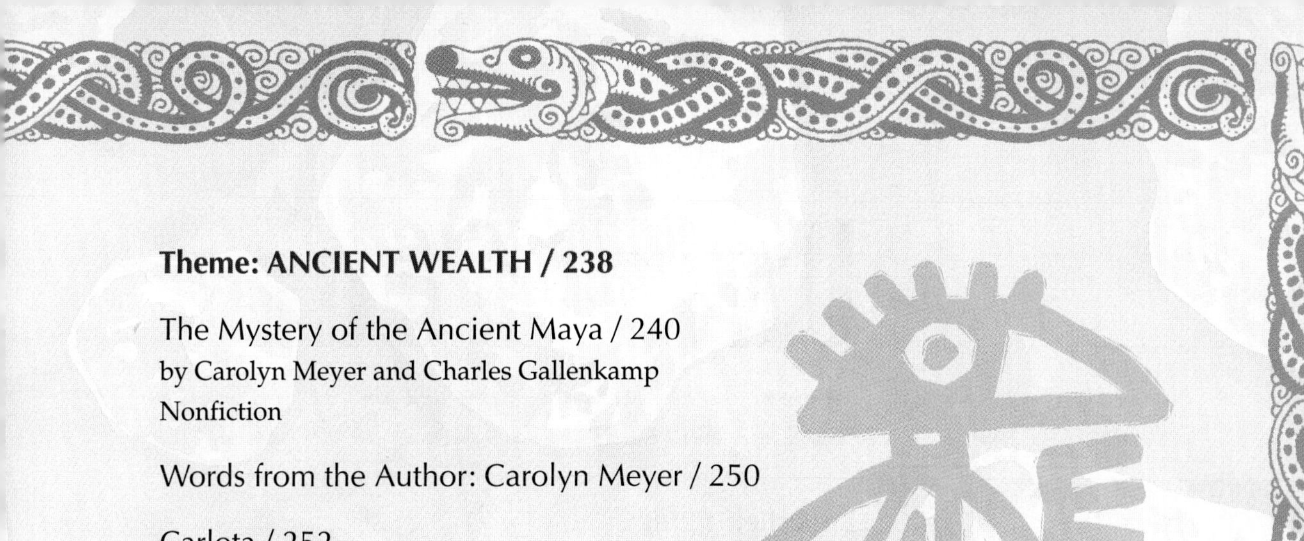

UNIT FOUR

CHALLENGES / 296

UNIT FIVE

OBSERVATIONS / 400

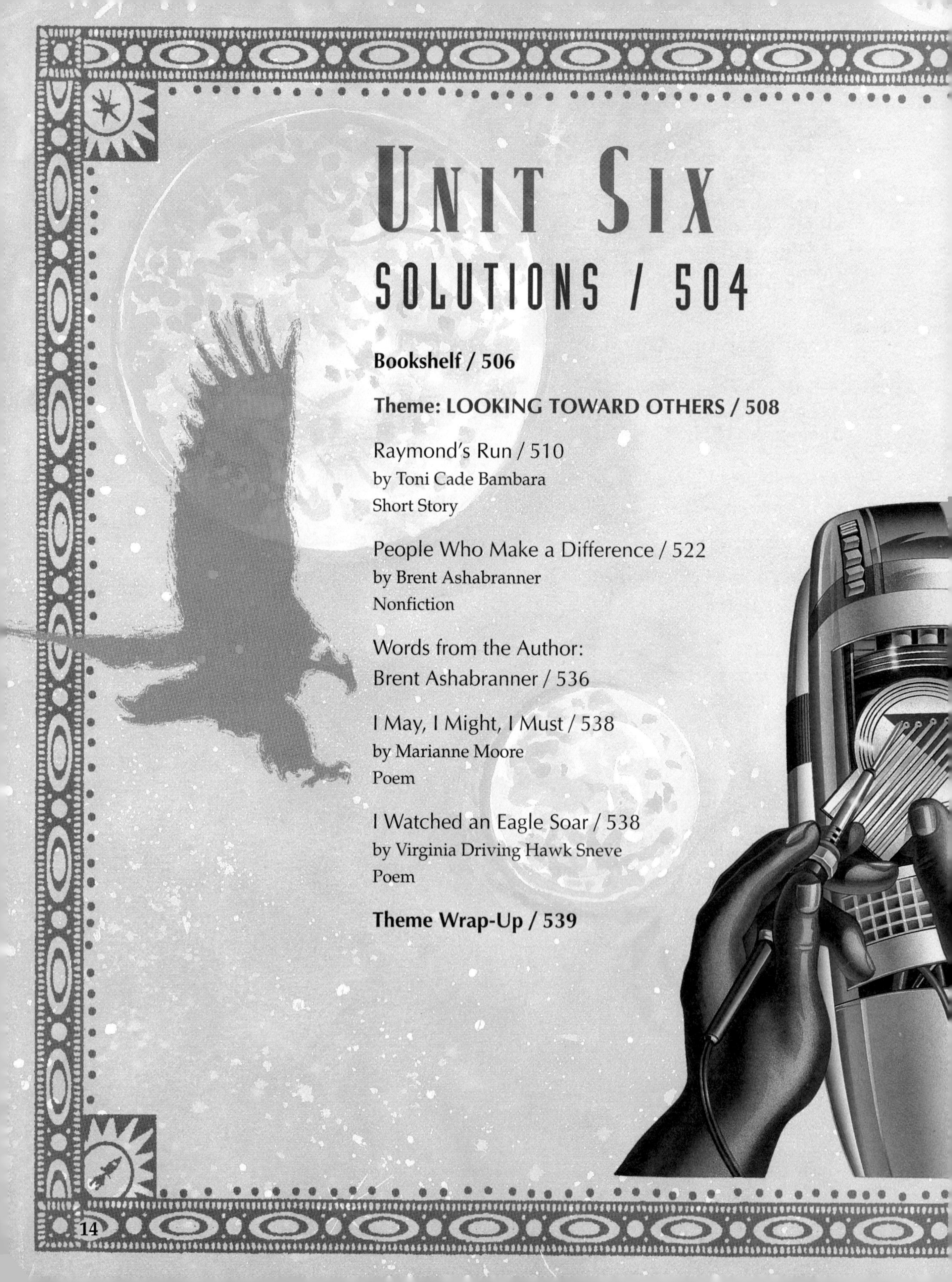

UNIT SIX

SOLUTIONS / 504

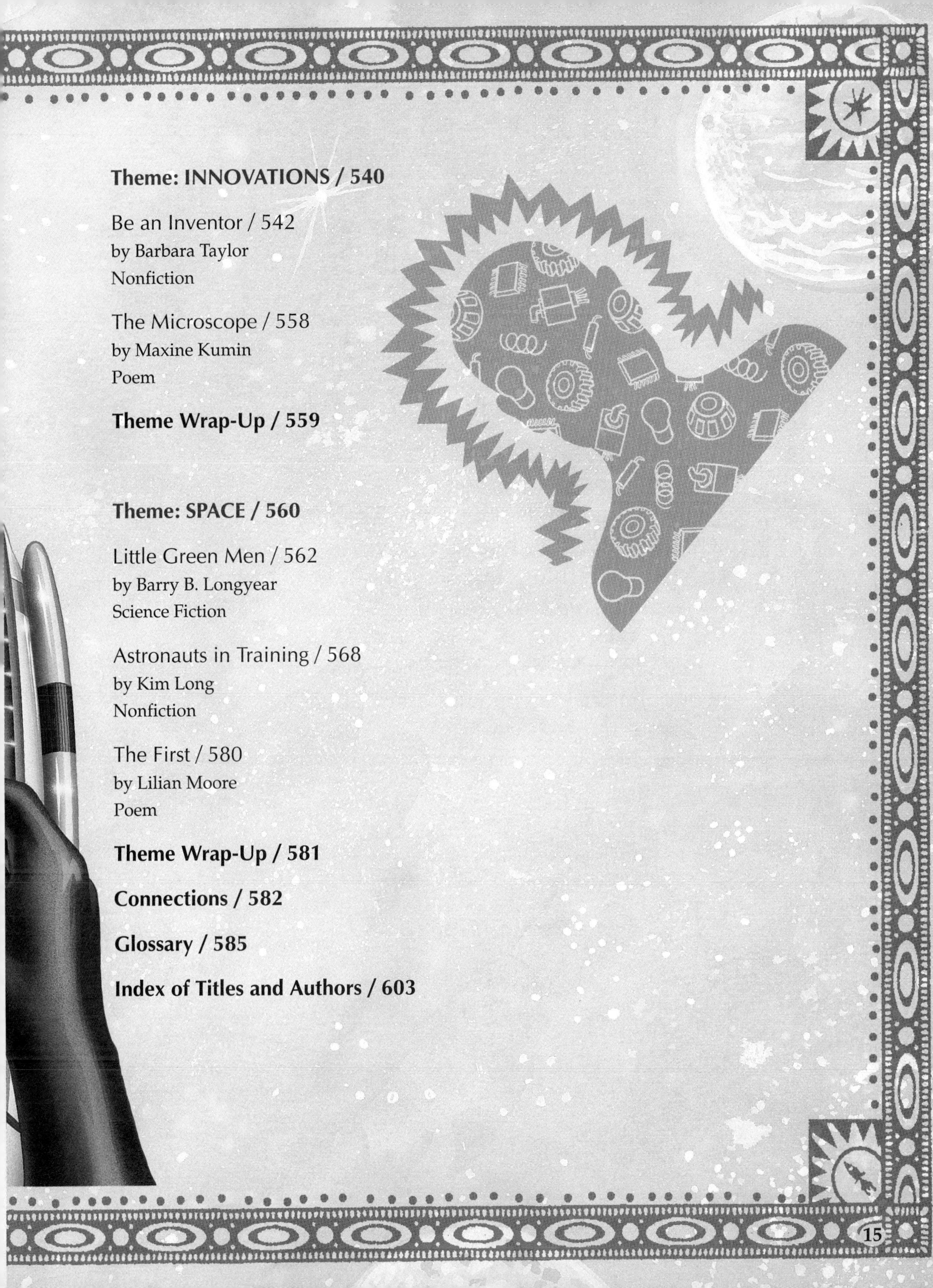

UNIT ONE

DISCOVERIES

You will soon read about several people who, through their interests, have discovered good things about themselves. For example, you will read how music has shaped the life of cellist Yo-Yo Ma, enabling him to make new discoveries about himself. As you read, think about how your interests can help you discover your strengths.

THEMES

BOOKSHELF

I Am the Universe

BY BARBARA CORCORAN

When Kit discovers she has to write a paper on "Who I Am" for her English class, it is almost the last straw. She is too busy worrying about her mother's operation and her brothers' and sister's troubles to think about herself. But out of all her problems comes an understanding of who she really is.

Harcourt Brace Library Book

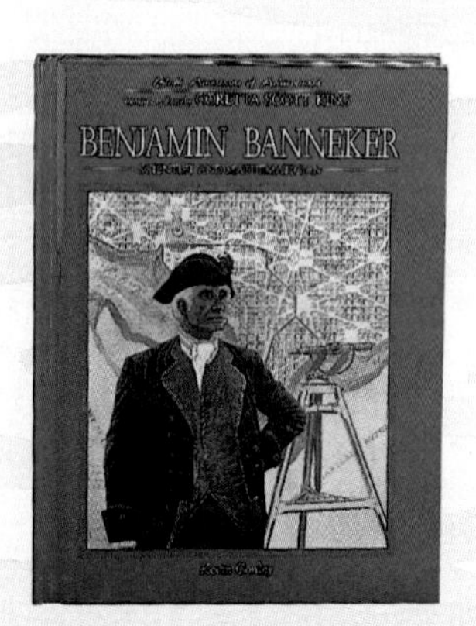

Benjamin Banneker

BY KEVIN CONLEY

This biography recounts the life of Benjamin Banneker, eighteenth-century farmer and clockmaker. Self-taught in mathematics and astronomy, Banneker becomes famous for his almanacs and eventually assists in the original surveying of Washington, D.C.

Kon-Tiki

BY THOR HEYERDAHL

This true story of an amazing voyage has been praised as one of the great sea sagas of all time.

Rascal

BY STERLING NORTH

Rascal, a mischievous raccoon, is only a baby when the author brings him home to join Poe, his pet crow, and assorted other animals. Their year together begins as a happy adventure. Then suddenly everything changes.

Newbery Honor Book, ALA Notable Book

Homesick: My Own Story

BY JEAN FRITZ

Jean Fritz relates anecdotes about growing up in China during a time of turmoil. She brings to life an unforgettable girl who is lively, funny, and independent.

Newbery Honor Book, ALA Notable Book, School Library Journal Best Book

THEME

THE SEA

The sea is filled with beauty and life. But the sea also has the power to surprise, horrify, destroy. What adventures will it hold for a fourteen-year-old boy alone and far from shore? What will it hold for you? Discover the sea—how to learn from it, live with it, love it.

CONTENTS

THE TADPOLE

LOST AT SEA

BY GARY PAULSEN

Brennan looked down at the sailboat and tried not to feel sad. She was 22 feet long, a coastal cruiser that had a small cabin and slept four and had been built back in the 60s, before they understood that fiberglass could be thin. She had a stiff and tough hull with a wooden mast and boom and a little three-foot bowsprit. On the stern was her name: the *Tadpole.*

She was dirty but sound. And she was all his—14 years old and he suddenly owned a cruising sailboat and that was why he was sad.

He looked at the key in his hand that opened the locked gate of the Ventura, California, marina. The name on the key chain was Owen Alspeth. Uncle Owen—tall, thin, always telling jokes. Owen who had fought in Vietnam and would sit and talk with Brennan for hours and who was now gone—taken by cancer, slow cancer they couldn't stop. At the last, when he

ILLUSTRATED BY J. A. WHITE

could still speak, Brennan had visited him in the veterans' hospital and the dying man had told him he was to get the boat.

"Don't talk that way," Brennan had said through tears. "You'll live for years and years."

"No, listen, the boat needs you. I haven't been able to take care of her like she wants. Take her and sail her and love her. I've put it in the will. It's done, it's all done now."

And so it was done—two days later Uncle Owen died and now Brennan stood looking at the *Tadpole.* He opened the gate lock and went down the damp steps and hopped on—felt the boat, lively and quick, bounce to his step. He opened her hatch top, slid it forward and smelled the musty, thick-damp smell of the cabin.

He ached for his uncle, felt his presence on the boat. He remembered sailing with him. Twice they had been out—once to Catalina, more than 50 miles south—and Owen had taught him to sail, how to rig the boat and get her going.

Brennan pulled the three boards that closed off the bottom of the hatch and went down inside.

The cabin was not high enough to allow standing, so he hunched his neck and shoulders as he looked around.

There was a fold-down table in the middle, a couch-bench on either side with foam cushions that doubled as bunks, a small sink to the right, a cutting table to the left, a small bunk back under the cockpit—what Owen had called the captain's bunk—and a double cushion bed crammed in the bow.

The *Tadpole.* His boat.

No. His uncle's boat—again the ache. He just couldn't think of her as his own. She had been so much of Owen's life, and now he was gone. Owen was the boat as the boat was Owen and it didn't seem possible for Brennan to own the *Tadpole.*

Up front were bags of sails, and he got the main and the jib. It was in the front of his mind to air them out, just put them in place and air them out, but he found his hands working almost on their own, pulling the mainsail up and out on the boom, sliding its wood battens into the pockets on the trailing edge of the sail to stiffen it, hearing the wind luff[1] the sail, slapping it back and forth. He went

---

[1]luff: shake

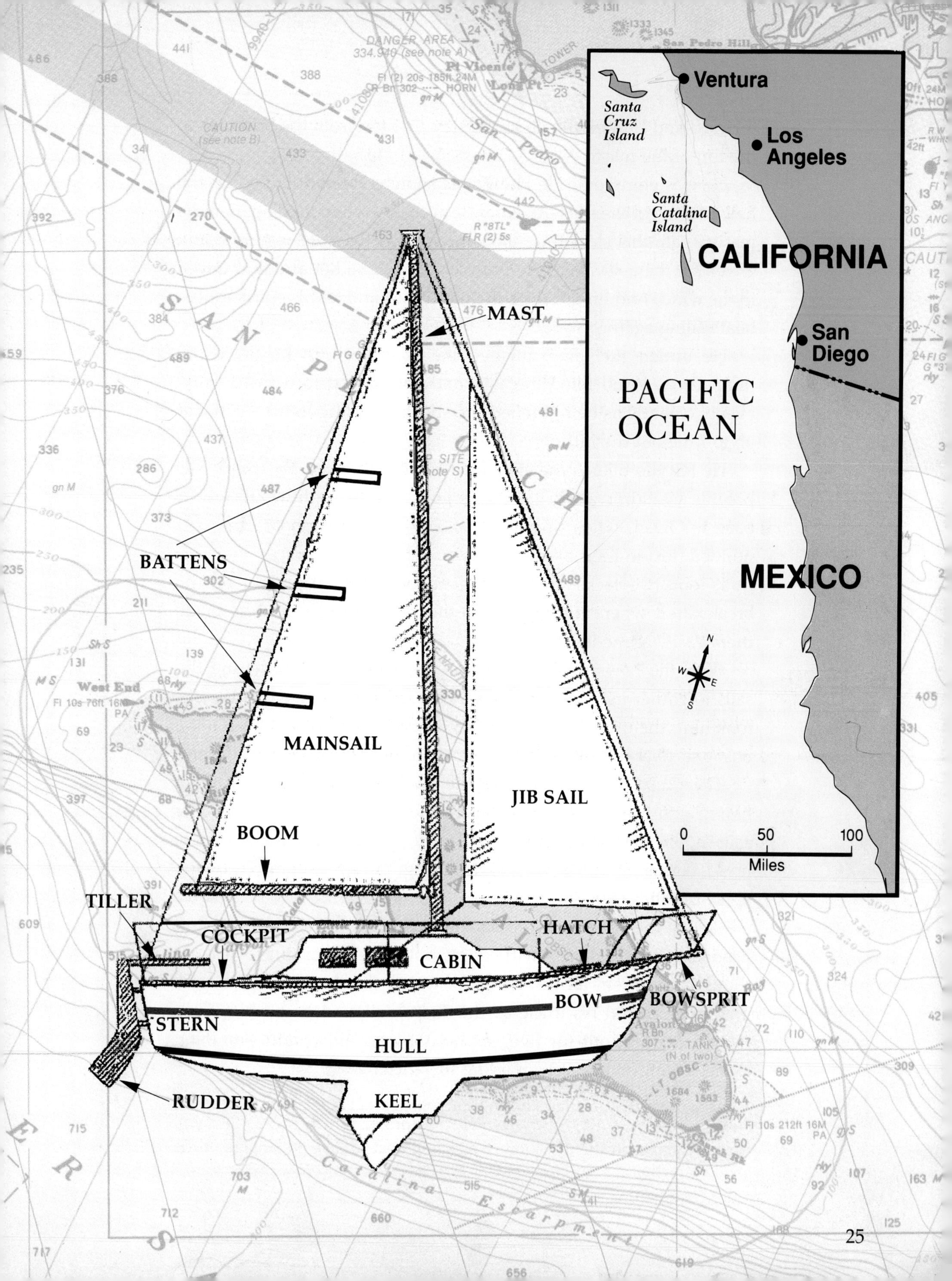
MAST
BATTENS
MAINSAIL
JIB SAIL
BOOM
TILLER
COCKPIT
HATCH
CABIN
BOW
BOWSPRIT
STERN
HULL
RUDDER
KEEL
Ventura
Santa Cruz Island
Los Angeles
Santa Catalina Island
CALIFORNIA
San Diego
PACIFIC OCEAN
MEXICO
N
W
E
S
0
50
100
Miles

forward and clipped the jib to the stay that ran from the bowsprit to the top of the mast.

He was going out. He knew it as soon as he had hauled on the halyards to get the sails up. Knew it probably when he'd opened the marina gate this clear June morning. It was the only way to thank Owen for the boat. Take the *Tadpole* out and sail her and find Owen in the wind, find him in the sun and the sea and let his spirit see the boat sailing again.

He untied the lines, pushed the *Tadpole* from the dock and jumped on. Wind filled the sails and she moved forward cleanly, evenly, silently as he tightened the sheets,[2] pulling in the main and jib to tune out the luffing.

He felt the tiller come alive as the *Tadpole* picked up speed. His parents wouldn't worry if he was gone. Knowing how close he'd been to Owen, when Brennan asked to stay on the boat, they just nodded, lost in their own sadness.

It took two tacks[3] in the small harbor to line up right on the breakwater, where it opened into the Pacific Ocean, and he made them easily in the light breeze.

With the bowsprit aimed to sea, he found himself setting the sails to gather more speed. He cleared the breakwater and the sea took him, the movement of the large swells coming up through the boat and tiller into his hands, almost a power from the sea to him.

The *Tadpole* seemed to take the swells and use them to push herself still faster. He turned up to the wind a bit and pulled the sails in. She heeled and gained still more speed, perhaps eight knots now, slamming the waves and cutting through them, throwing spray onto his face.

It was the finest way to sail, the way Owen loved best, and Brennan held the same swift course hour after hour out to sea. He thought of Owen, all the things of Owen that he knew, thought, and remembered his uncle as the *Tadpole* slipped past Santa Cruz Island, out and out for five, six hours, just sailing and slamming along, crying some, remembering his uncle.

---

[2]sheets: ropes that regulate the angle at which a sail is set in relation to the wind

[3]tacks: changes in the direction of a sailing boat to take advantage of the wind direction

When at last he shook his head and slowed the boat, he was amazed to find it evening, to find himself alone in the ocean, the water all around him like a slate-blue dish, any sign of land completely gone.

He looked at his digital wristwatch and figured he'd been sailing hard for almost eight hours. Averaging seven to eight knots, he might be 60 miles offshore.

Silly thing to do, he thought, but it wasn't a real problem. The wind was about right for him to tack back to the harbor, if it didn't change, and he should make it in 10 or 11 hours. By daylight. He'd never sailed at night, but the *Tadpole* had a good compass and he just had to hold a course. Not a problem.

He was suddenly very hungry and thirsty. He swung the boat into the wind and she stopped, everything slapping and clanking in the wind.

The tank had water in it, but it tasted as stale and musty as the boat had smelled. Under the couch-bunks, he found cans of food and he took some ravioli, opened it and ate it cold with a spoon, drinking the water from the hand-pump tap in the little sink.

Stupid to just sail that way, he told himself, *hard and long without thinking. Have to pay more attention in the future.*

When he finished eating he went back up top. He stuck the compass at 80 degrees and brought the sails in and was just settling back for the hard slamming ride through night when he saw a knife cut the top off the ocean.

That's how it looked. Two miles to the north were large swells blowing toward him, and it seemed that a large knife cut the tops off them. It scared him, and he stood to get a better view.

He saw that it was wind, a cutting wind stronger than he'd ever seen, ripping the tops off the swells and driving them into the next trough. Wind that would hit his sails in moments and drive the *Tadpole* over and down, sink her.

He let go everything and ran to the mast, loosened the main halyard and let the sail drop, jammed it into the open cabin and then scrabbled to the jib, got it jammed down into the forward hatch and was halfway back to the cabin opening when the wind, a great tearing thing, a screaming animal of a wind, hit the boat and slammed the boom sideways, slashing it like a giant sword across his temple.

His brain exploded, flashed colors across all his thoughts, and he fell into the cabin opening, down into the white folds of the crumpled mainsail as the wind tore at the *Tadpole.*

Brennan became aware of things in stages, shades coming off darkness. First he felt pain, riveting pain in his head and down his left side. He was face down in the sail, and it was hard to breathe. The *Tadpole* was slamming up and back in wild seas, rolling from one side to the next with the wind roaring like something gone mad.

Yet when he tried to move, the pain tore at him so that he passed out again. He went into sleep, a kind of blankness. When he came up the next time, the pain was controllable. Still awful, but he could stand it without passing out. He opened his eyes, straightened out, and tried to pull himself up, but the wind and seas still rolled the *Tadpole* with such violence that he went down again.

"Unnngh . . ." He made the sound involuntarily. Something was hurt inside, maybe his ribs. But he had to get on top of things or the *Tadpole* would be in worse trouble, still might sink. Every time the bow nosed over she shipped water in the forward hatch. Already two or three inches sloshed back and forth on the cabin floor. He didn't know how much she'd carry, but it couldn't be much. He had to close the hatch.

Using his right hand—his left hung uselessly at his side—he dragged himself forward, hanging on each time the seas slammed her back and down, sliding forward when she nosed into the next wave. The hatch was wide open, with the jib sail stuffed down but still tied up top to the stay.

He pulled the hatch over and down, pinching the jib in the opening, and got the dog-latch to catch. It wasn't watertight, but the water coming in was greatly reduced.

He fell on the bunk, fighting back the pain. His breath came in short pants mixed with spit. He could not think, could not make thoughts come. Still, he pulled himself to the mainsail and brought it all the way into the cabin and slammed the overhead hatch.

THE STORM

Weakened by the effort, he sank onto the captain's bunk, curled into a ball and was gone again, gone into his pain and a healing sleep.

Rattles and clunks came to mind. Something clanking and thumping was the first thing he heard. Then he felt something new, or didn't feel something new—the *Tadpole* was rolling gently on a still sea. Her violent actions had stopped.

He slowly opened his eyes, wincing in the harsh brightness to see sun streaming through the cabin windows.

The wind had stopped. Not just cut down a bit, but stopped dead. The thumping was the halyards slapping the mast in the swells of the storm's aftermath. The clanking was cans of food rolling on the floor.

He raised up in the bunk. The boat was a shambles. Six inches of water slopped on the floor, the mainsail was soaked, all the drawers and shelves were loose and empty. In the water were salt, sugar, and some flour-turned-library paste—all left by Owen on his last sailing trip, all now a mess.

Brennan moved too quickly and the pain stopped him. The head hurt less, though one side was massively swollen. The left arm worked again, but its shoulder seemed on fire and he realized it must have dislocated when he fell into the cabin. It had popped back in, probably from flopping in the bunk and hitting the side of the boat, but the pain froze him solid when he moved too fast.

More slowly now he crawled out of the bunk, slid open the cabin hatch and stood, pushing the mainsail out of the way.

And it was as if the storm had never happened. The sea rolled in oily, gentle swells. A warm sun beamed down.

Incredible, he thought, shaking his head. Just an incredible change. Only a while ago he thought he was going to die. Now it was like it had never happened. He suddenly thought of time. How long had he been out?

He had a digital watch but it had been in water too long—the screen was blank. The sun was high but that meant nothing. He seemed to remember a night, a wild night of crashing, and maybe more than that. Maybe another night. Could he have slept through two nights of storm?

It didn't seem possible, but such a strong storm must have lasted at least a day. It had to be major to hit that hard—either a storm or a truck, he thought, and tried to smile.

His lips were cracked and dry and he realized that he was terribly thirsty—maybe it had been two days. He went to the sink and pumped water in the plastic cup he found floating on the floor. The water was brackish and stinky but wonderful.

Afterward, he went to the hand-operated bilge[4] pump in the rear cockpit's compartment to drain the rainwater. Using his right arm, he started pumping, and a one-inch stream of water came out a hole in back of the boat. Pump-squirt, pump-squirt.

Fifty pumps, then a rest, then fifty more. It was slow work but better than bailing. And it gave him time to figure out what to do next.

He pumped all day and into the evening. It was amazing the boat hadn't sunk with the water's weight. Now she rode higher and lighter, but the sea was still dead calm, with not a whisper of wind.

He moved slowly around the boat, cleaning. He collected six cans of ravioli, three cans of fruit cocktail, one can of corn, some soaked sugar, a little salt in a waterproof container.

There was drinking water. The 20-gallon tank seemed half-full —so he had maybe 10 gallons.

That was it for food and water.

Other facts filtered into his thinking while he worked. Numbers and distances.

He had sailed at least 60 miles out before the storm hit. Maybe a bit more. Say 70. Then the storm must have driven him still farther west and south and he could only guess at that. Maybe another 40 or 50 miles, if it was only one night. If it had been two nights, it might be another 100. Split it and say 80 miles, plus 70. So 150.

Now a whole day, perhaps 20 hours at a dead calm—how far now? Had the boat moved in the calm? There was something in his memory he couldn't pin down. Some number that was important. . . .

The sun hit the horizon and dropped below the line of the sea,

---

[4]bilge: the lowest part of a ship's inner hull

cutting off the golden evening light. He went below and found some matches in a plastic bag.

The *Tadpole* had batteries and a small outboard motor for emergency power. But the motor had only a gallon of fuel, enough for an hour or so. Owen said it didn't recharge the batteries as it ran, so they were dead until Brennan got back to the marina and hooked up a battery charger.

If, he thought, *if I get back to the marina.*

He had seen candles floating in the cabin water. He found one, lit it, stuck it to a plate with some melted wax. He put it on the table and sat down.

He felt utterly alone. Never, not even in dreams, had he thought of being this alone. There was the boat, and the ocean, and himself—and that was it.

Fear came then and he thought it strange that he had not felt it before. Not during the storm, not in the crashing and slamming. But now, sitting alone in the boat in a dead calm, he felt fear. Fear that he would not get back. How far? How far to help?

Another thing bothered him and it came now. Something Owen had said when they were anchored at Catalina. Owen mentioned a friend who had been becalmed way off the coast. The current had carried him south for three days at . . . what speed was it?

Oh, yes, six knots. *That* was the important number.

A six-knot southerly current meant that even while windless he was moving south at six knots. Had to add that to the wind during the storm.

After more mental figuring, the numbers chilled him. He was probably close to 300 miles south and west of Ventura. Perhaps even more. And every hour he went another eight or so miles.

At first he had thought they might come looking for him. But they would never search this far out—never come 300 miles. They would think he went down near the marina and look for wreckage there. Never this far.

Brennan stared at the candle flame and felt sick. Lost at sea 300 miles out, in a 22-foot boat named the *Tadpole,* completely alone with 10 gallons of water and a few cans of food.

He had almost no chance.

All night the *Tadpole* sat on a silent sea, rolling gently with the swells. Brennan sank into depression. For hours he lay in the bunk feeling sorry for himself. Then it was as if something snapped in him. One moment he felt like the saddest person on earth, the next he was sitting up, wondering what he could do to help himself.

Later he tried to understand what had brought it about and realized it was his Uncle Owen. He had been in a blue funk, hating it all, and he remembered his uncle saying that the boat needed him. Needed to sail and needed his care. Needed him.

He wasn't alone. He had the *Tadpole.*

He looked around at the boat and felt that he had found a new friend; a friend who needed him, but more, a friend who could save him.

The *Tadpole.*

He looked out the rear hatch. A full moon shined across the water in a silver line. He had to take stock, see exactly what he had and what he didn't. Had to help the *Tadpole* so she could help him.

He lit the candle once more and rechecked his supplies. Same ravioli and fruit cocktail, same amount of water—he'd have to be very careful of the water. He took all the bunk cushions off and started digging.

In the front he found life jackets and put one on, decided never to go without one again. Some snorkeling gear—a mask and fins—was beneath the right bunk, but that would do him no good in the open sea. Under the captain's short bunk he found a packet with fishing line, large and small hooks and some feathered lures. He could catch fish, or try to. Under the sink was a small alcohol stove, but its fuel tank was empty and he could find no more alcohol.

The rest of the compartments were given over to sail bags—there were six sails—and an anchor.

One drawer had silverware, two butcher knives, a can opener, and a sharpening stone.

Next he counted the outboard motor, the dead batteries, the gallon of gas.

And that was it.

No, wait. He dug in his pockets. A pocketknife, the key chain, some change, and $12 in bills. An identity card.

And that was, finally, it.

If he didn't make it on that, he wasn't going to make it.

Outside the cabin, he scanned the sea. It would be nice, he thought, if a ship came by. A big liner with a huge banquet hall and chocolate malts and hamburgers and fries and giant pitchers of soda with ice, lots of ice, and cold water . . .

He shook his head. Had to stop that.

There were no lights, no sign of any life but his own, and he went back into the cabin. Owen had once told him something and he thought of it now: "Focus on the problem, the problem gets bigger; focus on the solution, the solution gets bigger."

He shifted his thinking to not what might come by luck, but what he had to work with. He had the boat, a little food, some fishing line, a little water.

And sails. He could move if the wind came. He had a way to move.

He settled back into the bunk and closed his eyes. There was still pain, but getting better all the time, and when the dozing came now it was normal, not a retreat into unconsciousness. He fell asleep gently, pushing down thoughts of chocolate malts.

Later his eyes snapped open and he lay in the moonlight trying to figure out what had awakened him. Some sound, some soft sound. He had been sleeping, but a sound had come.

There—it came again. The sound of the sail slapping, luffing.

The sound of wind.

He clambered out of the bunk and looked up at the main. He had pulled it and the jib up to dry, but had left them loose to flap, and now he saw that a soft breeze blew them.

He climbed into the cockpit and pulled a jib sheet in, tightening the sail. The jib filled instantly and the *Tadpole* started to move. Then he brought the main in and let it fill, worked the two sails so they were tuned, and he felt her start sliding over the swells. Not fast, maybe three knots, but moving well.

He looked at the compass. Heading south. That wasn't good. He brought her around until she was moving almost straight east—

everything east was land—and found that he was on a tack, moving upwind slightly. But moving.

It was all right, he thought, seeing the bow wave catch the moonlight and seem to ignite—just something all right to be moving, to have the *Tadpole* come alive again and move.

He just let her cream along and he felt good. For the first time since the storm hit, everything was going well.

Then the killer whales found him.

They came silently and with great suddenness at dawn. One second he was sitting alone in the cockpit watching the sun come up over the bowsprit. The next second he heard a massive *whoosh!* beside the boat, and a huge black head with distinctive white markings exploded out of the water.

Four other heads rose around the boat, higher and higher until the killer whales towered above him, looking down on him in the cockpit with glistening black eyes, their skins shining in the sun.

He could not move, could not breathe. He had read of them, had talked to Owen of them, and everybody said they didn't harm people. But over him that way, looking down on him—they could pluck him up like an appetizer. One snap. They were huge, longer than the boat—living things bigger than his home.

"Queeernk."

One of them made the sound. A second whale repeated it. Again and again they made the noise, and Brennan realized with a terrible fear that they were talking about him, discussing him. Maybe, he thought, deciding which parts to share.

He thought of letting the helm go and diving inside the boat, but they could easily knock a hole in it and get him out.

It was then, when he realized that he could do nothing, that he began to change. It wasn't a major shift, but he knew, looking up at the killer whales, that he could not run, could not hide—and it was the same with the sea. He was there, he must be part of it, know all of what he was doing or he would not live. It was in many ways the birth of a new Brennan.

"My name is Brennan," he said aloud to the whales. "And this is my boat, the *Tadpole*. We mean no harm."

And he meant it, did not feel silly saying it, and with the sound of his voice the whale nearest the boat eased down, blew once and inhaled and was gone. The rest followed. Whether it was his voice or not didn't matter. They were gone and the fear was gone and he was not the same, would never be the same again.

I am, he thought, of the sea—I am of this boat and the sea. I am.

Later in the morning he stopped the *Tadpole* and went below. He found the fishing line, set it over the stern, then started sailing again, letting out the jib so she moved at about two knots.

The feathered lure wiggled through the water and within an hour he hooked a five-pound tuna. He stopped the boat and, struggling hand over hand, hauled the fish in, dropping it into the cockpit. It was beautiful. He felt sad taking it, but he was getting hungry and knew he should save the small stock of canned goods.

He removed the hook from the fish and got a knife. He'd never cleaned a fish and it took him some minutes to figure out how to cut the belly open to let the guts slide out. He used sea water in a pan to wash the fish. Then he cut off its head. He was surprised he didn't become ill at the sight.

The meat along the back looked almost like fish-market tuna. He had no way to cook it, but remembered Owen saying the Japanese eat fish raw, so he cut the meat in strips and put them to dry in the sun. When they were partially dried, he tried one.

It actually tasted good raw—better than canned tuna. But dry. It would be better, he thought, to get the moisture as well as the food—to save water. He cut a fresh piece, chewed it, had trouble getting it down. It was wet and stuck to his tongue. The next piece went down better and shortly he was eating chunks, even dipping them in sea water to get the taste of salt.

He ate two pounds or so and was about to throw the rest in the water when he thought of bait. He put some in a plastic bag in the rear hatch.

Afternoon came and he felt the wind freshen, sliding across his face and getting cooler. Before, he would just have thought the wind was getting stronger. But now it was different. Now he

THE WHALES

thought of what it meant—the weather was going to change, perhaps, a still stronger wind, and he must be ready for it. At least he felt that way, sensed it that way, smelled it that way.

He would have to reduce sail by about half, would have to reef[5] the main by turning a crank where the boom joined the mast. The boom rotated, rolling the mainsail like a window shade. He left the jib alone, but decided that if the wind got too strong he'd just drop it and sail on the main.

That's how he thought it—sail on the main.

He smiled, thinking about the newness of what he was doing. He wasn't just staying alive anymore. He was sailing, becoming part of the boat and the water.

Late in the day the wind kicked higher and he dropped the jib and sailed into the night, dozing off and on in small bursts, working always east as the waves grew higher but not crazy as they had before. Toward dawn it became a gale, blowing the tops just off the tips of the six-foot waves, throwing spray on his face.

There wasn't fear anymore. Now there was just the plain, raw joy of sailing hard, of using the wind and the seas to move the boat where he wanted her to go, to plunge over the waves and slam into the next one. He sailed that way all day and into the evening—and that's when the ship found him.

She was a freighter, and she appeared directly in front of him in the dusky light.

Saved—that was his first thought.

He slowed the *Tadpole* and waved and waved. Finally a man ran out on the ship's bridge and waved back. He realized they must have reversed the engines because it took the freighter minutes to stop.

He sailed up in her lee[6] so the ship blocked the wind. Here the seas were almost dead calm, held still by the larger ship. The *Tadpole*'s sails luffed a little, and she stopped.

"I am Brennan Alspeth!" Brennan yelled up at the man on the bridge. "I was driven to sea by that storm."

"We know who you are," the man hailed back through an electric megaphone. "There are bulletins all over the radio about you. But you're supposed to be farther north. They think you're dead."

---

[5]reef: to reduce the area of a sail by rolling or folding
[6]lee: protecting shelter from the wind

THE FREIGHTER

His parents. Brennan thought of his parents—they must be frantic with worry.

"Come closer so we can take you aboard."

"What about my boat?"

The captain hesitated a moment. "We'll have to let her go. I don't have a sling to lift her on. If we tow her our speed will tear her apart. We'll have to let her go adrift."

Brennan shook his head. "No . . ."

"We can't take her on board, I tell you."

She had been good, he thought—she saved his life, she carried him, she rode the wind and seas as Owen had said. He could not let her go. He would not let her go.

"Where am I?"

The captain studied him, understood him, then nodded. "I'd do the same. I'd do just the same. You're nearly 150 miles off the coast of Mexico, close to 300 south of San Diego. Against the wind and current it'll take about a week and a half to get back. Maybe a bit more."

Brennan nodded. "I can't just leave the boat. Not now. Would you radio my parents and tell them I'm all right and that I'll be sailing home?"

"Consider it done."

"Also, I could really use some food and water. . . ."

In moments, it seemed a small group of men appeared at the rail and lowered a bundle of canned goods and four five-gallon bottles of fresh water on a long rope. Brennan swung the stern over, caught the bundle on the third try and got it into the cockpit. He untied the rope and pushed away from the ship. The smell of hot barbecued chicken from the bundle made his mouth water. He was starved.

"I'm the cook." A round face peered over the rail. "I put in something special for you."

"Thank you."

"You sheer away," the captain ordered. "We'll let you get clear and sail off a bit before we start our engines."

Brennan nodded. He moved the boom with his hands to find even a puff of wind—he didn't know where that knowledge came from but it was there, probably from Owen—and the *Tadpole* slowly slipped away from the freighter. As the wind turned stronger, she started to slide. He turned and waved.

"Thank you again for everything!"

But he was too far for them to hear. The captain used the megaphone one more time to yell, "Good luck and godspeed!"

With the night's darkness, the ship was gone and Brennan once again alone.

Alone.

And by choice this time. For one small part of a second, he thought he had made a mistake. He could be on the freighter, safe and sound, heading home. Safe and dry and heading home.

Then the *Tadpole* surged under him, took a wave and moved to the next one. He felt the wind lessen and thought he should pull the full main up again, or perhaps run the jib up, then eat something and get squared away for the night run. The wind felt good and he didn't want to waste it.

He held the tiller against his leg and felt the hum of the boat moving through the water, felt the life of her in the movement. And in that movement, with the hum moving through him, he thought of his Uncle Owen and all that Owen had been and he knew he had done the right thing.

Do you think we learn more about ourselves during difficult times or carefree times? Explain your opinion, referring to Brennan's experiences in your answer.

What do you think Brennan learns about himself during his experiences on the *Tadpole*?

What do you think Gary Paulsen wants you to learn from this short story?

WRITE Think about the choice Brennan makes at the end of the story. Does it surprise you? Would you make the same choice in his place? Explain your answers in a brief paragraph.

Song

An Inuit Poem
Translated by Knud Rasmussen

And I think over again
My small adventures
When with a shore wind I drifted out
In my kayak
And thought I was in danger.
My fears,
Those I thought so big,
For all the vital things
I had to get and to reach.

And yet, there is only
One great thing,
The only thing:
To live and to see in huts and on journeys
The great day that dawns,
And the light that fills the world.

Raven's Journey, Tlingit Indian
Art, Anchorage, Alaska

Long Trip

by Langston Hughes

The sea is a wilderness of waves,
A desert of water.
We dip and dive,
Rise and roll,
Hide and are hidden
On the sea.
  Day, night,
  Night, day,
The sea is a desert of waves,
A wilderness of water.

White Skies,
Eric Hudson, 28″X 34″.

Sea Fever by John Masefield

I must go down to the seas again, to the lonely sea and the sky,
And all I ask is a tall ship and a star to steer her by,
And the wheel's kick and the wind's song and the white sail's shaking,
And a gray mist on the sea's face and a gray dawn breaking.

I must go down to the seas again, for the call of the running tide
Is a wild call and a clear call that may not be denied;
And all I ask is a windy day with the white clouds flying,
And the flung spray and the blown spume, and the sea gulls crying.

I must go down to the seas again to the vagrant gypsy life,
To the gull's way and the whale's way where the wind's like a
  whetted knife;
And all I ask is a merry yarn from a laughing fellow-rover,
And quiet sleep and a sweet dream when the long trick's over.

Northeaster, 1895; Winslow Homer, American, (1836-1910),
Oil on canvas 34 3/8" x 50 1/4"; Metropolitan Museum of Art,
New York. Gift of George A. Hearn, 1910

"Long Trip" and "Sea Fever" express different feelings about the sea. Which of these two poems do you think Brennan would like better? Give reasons for your answer.

WRITER'S WORKSHOP

Suppose that Brennan had taken you with him on the *Tadpole*. Which part of the adventure would have been the most memorable for you? Write your own description of what you might have seen, felt, or heard during the experience.

Writer's Choice Brennan's experience with the sea helped him learn how to solve problems. Think about people or things that have helped you in some way. Choose an idea to write about. Plan your response and a way to share your writing.

THEME

Have you ever been surprised by the way you reacted to a new situation? In the following selections, you'll share in the experiences of several characters as they meet challenges and gain insights about themselves.

CONTENTS

Award-Winning Author

The Outside Shot

by Walter Dean Myers

illustrations by Ken Goldammer

When Lonnie Jackson learned that he'd won a basketball scholarship to a small midwestern college, everyone told him what a wonderful opportunity it was. But Lonnie felt a little uptight—Indiana seemed a very long way from his old neighborhood in New York City. Later in September, when Lonnie arrived at the airport in Indiana, he was met by Clayton Leeds, the basketball team's assistant coach. When they arrived at the campus, Lonnie realized that life would be different here. Gradually he got acquainted with other students, especially his teammates. Yet even though he was a top basketball player and participated in the school activities, everything seemed strangely unfamiliar.

They gave me this little piece of job. I was supposed to work in a hospital which was about a mile away from the campus. It was called University Hospital. A lot of the kids who were studying to be doctors and whatnot, they worked in the hospital. What I was supposed to do was to work in the physical therapy department. Leeds said there wasn't much to the job, but I had to do it if I wanted to get some money for extra expenses, 'cause the scholarship only covered books and tuition and stuff and just enough money to get by on.

I got the campus bus and went over to the hospital. I found the physical therapy department after asking about six people for directions. They looked at me as if they had never seen a black guy before. Finally, they sent me down to the end of the building that looked a little newer than the rest.

"Excuse me, I'm supposed to see Dr. Corbett."

The woman sitting behind the desk was kind of nice-looking. I thought I had seen her around the campus before, but I wasn't too sure.

"You're Lonnie Jackson?" she asked. "The basketball player?"

"Yeah."

"I'm Ann Taylor." She stuck out her hand and I shook it. "It's really Annie Taylor, but I hate Annie, okay?"

"Yes, ma'am."

"Okay. Dr. Corbett isn't here right now, he's usually here in the mornings. It's my understanding that you're only going to be here six hours a week, right?"

"Right. Two days, three hours each day."

"Okay. Eddie Brignole comes twice a week, two and a half hours each time. I think you can work with him."

"*You* think?"

"Dr. Corbett isn't too enthusiastic about the athletes working with the kids, but we're too shorthanded to complain, really."

"Yeah, right."

"Let me tell you about Eddie. He's got one real problem, as far as we know. Sometimes with a kid you really can't tell what problems they have until they're more developed. Anyway, Eddie's nine and he's so withdrawn that at first we thought he was autistic,[1] you know what I mean?"

"What does he do, draw and stuff like that?"

"Draw?" She had pretty eyes, man, and when she said that they got kind of wide and nice.

"No, he doesn't draw. He just sits around and does nothing most of the time. He won't play with the other kids or anything. Most of the time he just goes into the gym and sits by himself. What we do is just sit with him and talk to him. The staff psychiatrist seems to think that he looks forward to coming here even if he doesn't do anything and that it might help in the long run. Once in a while the athletes do get a rise from him, but not usually. So there you are."

"You said he'll be here soon?"

"Oh, one more little problem that you'll just love," Ann said. "Can I call you Lonnie?"

"Yeah."

"Eddie comes here with his mother. She sits in the gymnasium for the whole time. Whatever you do will be wrong as far as she is concerned. If she had the money she would take him to the—how does she put it now—'the best clinics in the world.' But she doesn't, so she's stuck with us, and we're stuck with her. She's not shy about telling you either."

"Okay," I said. "I guess I can handle it."

"I hope so. She's worn out two football players already."

I just sat around for a while and read and looked at a magazine until this kid Eddie was supposed to show up. After a while a woman about medium height with dark hair pulled away from her face with a comb and bobby pins at the back of her head came in. She wore a suede jacket with fur trim that fit her kind of nice. She probably could have looked a little better if she took care of herself. Ann motioned for me to come over. Well, this chick was sitting at the side of Ann's desk drumming her fingers.

"Mrs. Brignole, this is Lonnie Jackson." Ann's voice carried a smile with it. "He's going to be working with Eddie for a while."

---

[1]autistic: having little contact with people and surroundings

"Hello." I stuck out my hand. She looked at it, and when she looked back at Ann she didn't make a move to shake my hand.

"Does he have experience working with young children?" she asked.

"Not at all," Ann said, smiling. "But I'm sure he'll do a wonderful job, Mrs. Brignole."

"If he has no experience, I don't want him working with Eddie," Mrs. Brignole said. "I insist upon having someone with some experience at least."

"Fine," Ann said. "We might get some experienced people in when the new budget is approved next spring. If and when we do, you'll be the first person we contact."

"I think . . . I think you're being impudent," Mrs. Brignole said.

"If you want to speak to Dr. Corbett, it's fine with me," Ann said. "He'll be in sometime tomorrow morning."

Mrs. Brignole took a deep breath and put her fingertips to her brow. Ann looked at her and then looked down at the desk. I started to say something like how I would try real hard, but Ann stopped me by raising her hand. I wasn't that interested in working with a handicapped kid in the first place.

"What am I supposed to do?" Mrs. Brignole spat each word out carefully. "Give my son over to any student who seems to have nothing to do?"

"I'm sorry, Mrs. Brignole," Ann said. "The only thing I can do is offer you what services we have. I don't want to sound uncaring, because I'm not, but you're going to have to take what we have to offer or wait until our budget is increased. Look, why don't you go and get Eddie, at least for today, and let him meet Lonnie."

Mrs. Brignole took a deep breath, stood, and walked out of the office.

"She don't seem too happy to see me," I said.

"She is not a happy woman," Ann answered.

"Look, is that it, she's just going now?"

"No, she has Eddie out in the car. She has this station wagon that looks like a World War Two tank. You know, the child has been like this for a long, long time. It's got to be hard on her too, Lonnie.

Dr. Corbett thinks it would help if she went through a little therapy herself, but she won't do it."

"She's a little wacky?" I asked.

"Probably not your out-and-out wack," Ann said. "But the home environment isn't right. A few hours here isn't going to help very much. But at least Eddie hasn't gotten worse."

"What do you do when he comes here? I mean, does he have a program?"

"No, he sits on the floor and he stays there for the whole time unless there's a chair set up—then he sits on that."

"He sits down wherever you put the chair?"

"Wherever you put it," Ann said.

"Hey, look, what am I supposed to be doing with the dude?"

"Well, let him sit down on the chair and you could talk to him and you can do jumping jacks, anything. He will just look at you. If he responds to anything, which I don't think he will, then you can try to play on that. The whole thing is to try to get some response and, you know, other than that, you're just babysitting."

"Yeah, okay. Look, I'm going to check on the gym."

I went into the gym. It was a little dinky gym. I saw where the chairs were stacked against the one wall and I got one. I set it up and put it at the side of the foul lane under one basket. I saw a basketball and I went and got that.

Just then a door opened and Mrs. Brignole came in with Eddie. He was a little kid. Not even five feet tall. He looked a lot like his mother, except for his hair. Her hair was dark brown and his was like a red, a deep, dark red. I stood beneath the basket, just sort of bouncing the ball off the backboard. I watched as Eddie came slowly toward the chair and sat in it. Mrs. Brignole leaned against the wall.

"Do you want to sit there or do you want to get up and play some ball?" I asked.

Nothing.

The cat's face wasn't like blank, which is what I thought that Ann meant. Instead he just had his head down, like, you know, beaten, pushed down. I threw the basketball through the hoop and I looked at Eddie. The boy's head was still down.

"Okay," I said. "Now you sitting in that chair because somebody told you that you got to sit in that chair, right?"

Nothing.

"Now you got to look at what I'm doing for the same reason you got to sit in that chair, because if you don't look at me, then I don't know if you know what I'm doing, see. And you and me are going to get along. You can't make believe I ain't here. That's the only thing I don't like. Now you look at me, man."

Nothing.

Eddie kept his head down.

"Hey, I'm not going to keep telling you. When I tell you to look at me, I'm serious, man. I'm really serious."

Nothing.

I put the ball under my arm and walked over to the dude and lifted his chin up. I moved my arm and he let his head fall down to his chest again. I lifted it up again, the expression was the same. Now, I mean, he looked like he was sad, so I lifted his head a little harder.

"Hey, man, stop ignoring me."

Out of the corner of my eye I could see his mama changing her position. I stood back and watched as my man's head dropped again and then I passed him the ball. It bounced lightly off his chest. I grabbed the ball and went up for a layup.

"Two nothing, my favor," I said. "Now it's your turn." I bounced the ball off of him again. "You missed an inbound pass, dude," I said, grabbing the ball. "I got it, I'll dribble around you, fake you out, and shoot. Yes! I got the ball in, that's four points for me and nothing for you. I'm going to wipe you up, turkey, you ain't no ballplayer."

I bounced the ball off Eddie's leg this time, grabbed it off the ground and started dribbling around him, faking left and faking right, then I leaned against Eddie's chair and turned around and put up a soft hook that touched nothing but net and fell through.

"All right. The kid is on his game," I said. "The television cameras are on me as I slaughter you, Eddieee. The score, nothing for you and six for meee."

I saw his mother take a step forward and stop. I see she is one of those protective mamas. I didn't care. I backed off a little bit and threw the ball to him, lightly.

"Here comes a pass to you." Bang. He didn't move and the ball rolled over to the side. I grabbed it.

"I got the rebound, now I'm going to dribble around you again and I'm going to fake you out. Here I come." I dribbled past him and laid the ball up again. "There, man. That's *ten* for me and nothing for you."

"Eight," came the voice from Eddie Brignole. "You only have eight."

"Okay, turkey," I said. "Eight. I thought I could beat you a little easier than that. I see you watching everything I do, huh. Okay, this time I'm not going to announce the game, man. I'm just going to go on and shoot the ball, man. 'Cause you got your head down and you won't be seeing what I be doing, man. Okay, here comes the ball to you." I threw him the ball. It bounced off of him again. I grabbed it and moved toward the basket, but this time I was watching him and he turned just as I threw the ball against the backboard. It fell through.

"Now I got ten, now I got ten!" Then I came back, threw him the ball again. I saw his hand move, he wanted to grab it. I just knew he wanted to grab that ball.

I said, "Okay, okay, Eddie, now the game is twenty. I got ten in the first half. Now I'm going to show you a few shots, right? I'm going to amaze you. Watch this."

I moved back to the top of the key. I looked at him to see if he was looking at me. He wasn't looking right at me but he had lifted his head and I knew he could see me out of the corner of his eye. I put the ball on the floor one time and I threw up a soft jump shot. It arched easily through the air and bounced off the back rim. I looked over at Eddie and he smiled.

"Hey, man, don't be smiling at me. I mean, I could still beat you, even if I did miss that one shot."

It went on like that for about a half hour more. The dude was actually glad to see me miss and I didn't care. It was like a little game we were playing. He was sitting there watching me, hoping I would miss and I was watching him, seeing how he would react. Then I told him we would have a rest period and we would start the second half of our game, but this time I told him I wanted him to get up off that chair and try a shot. All you got to do is try one shot, just one shot and that's all, okay, one shot?

"Can you make one shot? Oh, I see you can't even make one shot, that's your problem, man."

He didn't say anything. I sort of picked him up in one arm, half lifted him, and walked him over to the basket. I knew he could walk okay. I put the basketball in his hands and lifted it, and I told him very softly in his ear, "Don't drop this ball when I give it to you, man. Don't drop this ball."

I put it in his hand and he held it for a long moment.

"Go on shoot it, go on shoot it."

He threw the ball up, it hit the bottom of the rim and fell down. I grabbed it and I kept on playing like I had before when he was sitting down. I would grab it and dribble around him. He just stood there. I kept throwing him the ball but he would just let it bounce off his body.

I said, "Okay, man."

I figured I would see what this dude was really made of. I had an idea what he was made of when I saw the smile when I missed the shot and when he corrected me on the score. The dude didn't like losing. He didn't like losing, I knew.

I said, "Okay, Eddie, tell you what I'm going to do, man. Since I'm on the basketball team and you're not even on a basketball team, I guess you need a little break, so I'm going to give you a break. Here, I'm going to give you the basketball and walk all the way across the gym now. If you make a basket before I get back over to you, I'm going to give you ten points."

He took the basketball. I didn't have to lift his arms. I walked all the way across the floor, turned, and said, "Okay, Eddie, here I come now." I began walking slowly toward him. He didn't move. I kept on coming, very slowly. "Here I come, Eddie, here I come. You better get the ball up now. You better get it up. If you want them ten points you better get it up, here I come."

"Don't intimidate him."

This is from his mother. She started from the other direction.

"She must be on your side, Eddie. Here she comes to help you."

She moved faster and I moved faster. Eddie shifted his feet. "Don't intimidate him, don't intimidate my son. You don't know a thing about . . ."

I jumped in front of her as she neared her son. She tried to get around me, but I kept blocking her out, blocking her out.

"She must be on your side."

"What are you doing? Are you crazy . . . are you cra—What are you doing?"

"I know you want to pass the ball to her, Eddie, but I won't let you do it, man. I'm not going to let you do it, man."

"You get out of my way."

Eddie turned and threw the ball up against the backboard. The ball rolled around the rim and I said a quick, quick prayer. "PLEASE, let it roll in."

The ball fell through the hoop.

Eddie looked up at the basket and then he glanced over at me.

"Good shot," I said. "You got a nice touch."

How do you think Lonnie feels when Eddie's shot goes through the net? Do you share his feelings? Explain your answer.

Why is Lonnie able to get a response from Eddie when no one before him has succeeded?

Why does Lonnie take the risk of angering Mrs. Brignole by blocking her from getting to Eddie?

WRITE Describe a time when you helped someone with a problem. Tell how being involved in that person's problem made you feel.

AN INTERVIEW WITH THE AUTHOR: Walter

Writer Ilene Cooper had the opportunity to discuss writing with Walter Dean Myers.

Ms. Cooper: In your books, you keep going back to your growing-up years in Harlem. What were they like?

Mr. Myers: I was a happy child. I lived across the street from the park, and there was a sandlot three blocks away, so I played baseball and football. I read a lot, too. I started out reading Bible stories, and then I moved to comic books. Once a teacher spotted me with one, and she took it away and gave me a book of fairy tales, telling me if I was going to spend all my time reading at the back of her class, it might as well be good stuff.

Dean Myers

Ms. Cooper: Were you writing then?
Mr. Myers: I started writing when I was nine or ten. Stupid poems, based on rhymes.

Ms. Cooper: Did you get encouragement to continue writing?
Mr. Myers: It was one of the few things I did get encouragement for. I wasn't a very good kid. I talked incessantly, and I fought a lot. I had a speech impediment, and that started lots of fights. Schools were much stricter then, but I guess there was room for one bad Walter. By the time I got to high school, I was more sullen and withdrawn, but I kept writing the whole time.

It was something I enjoyed doing. The other kids seemed interested in me because of my writing; it was the one thing I was praised for.

Ms. Cooper: What were the first things you had published?
Mr. Myers: I wrote stories for adventure magazines, but it was strictly a hobby as far as I was concerned. I was working at various jobs to support myself, since I certainly didn't think I could support myself with my writing.

Ms. Cooper: When did you start writing for young people?
Mr. Myers: Even when I was doing my short stories, many of my characters were young men. But my actual start in writing for young adults came during a bad time. I was living in Queens, a part of New York City, and my house had just been broken into. I was waiting for the locksmith to come and fix the door when the mailman arrived, with not one but two rejections for my short stories. Then I started leafing through a copy of *Writer's Digest* magazine, and there was an announcement of a contest for minority writers. Since no black writers I knew were reading this magazine, I thought, "Hey, I might have a chance." I wrote a picture book, and it won the contest. That was my first conscious writing for young people.

Ms. Cooper: Do you change your style when you're writing for young people?
Mr. Myers: No, I really don't.

Ms. Cooper: What kinds of letters do you get from your fans?
Mr. Myers: Some very interesting things come up. Many are about friendships in the books. They often question me about the endings, especially if they're not what's expected. Mostly, they write about Fast Sam.

Ms. Cooper: Does the story "Fast Sam, Cool Clyde, and Stuff" come from your own background?
Mr. Myers: We were poor, as I said, and when I talked to my mother about playing an instrument, she said we couldn't afford it. Then she told me the story about my father and the time he bought a trombone. She hated the trombone. I took the bare bones of the story, and I turned it around a bit.

Ms. Cooper: What kind of writing do you like best?
Mr. Myers: I like writing everything, but I especially like writing about young people. I like going back to that time in my life.

Fast Sam, Cool Clyde, and Stuff

by Walter Dean Myers

It was a dark day when we got our report cards.

The sky was full of gray clouds and it was sprinkling rain. I was over to Clyde's house and Gloria and Kitty were there. Sam probably would have been there too, only he had got a two-week job in the afternoons helping out at Freddie's. Actually he only did it so that his mother would let him be on the track team again. Sam and his mother had this little system going. He would do something good-doing and she'd let him do something that he wanted to.

Clyde's report card was on the kitchen table and we all sat around it like it was some kind of a big important document. I had got a pretty good report card and had wanted to show it off but I knew it wasn't the time. Clyde pushed the card toward me

illustrations by **Brian Pinkney**

and I read it. He had all satisfactory remarks on the side labeled Personal Traits and Behavior. He had also received B's in music and art appreciation. But everything else was either a C or a D except mathematics. His mathematics mark was a big red F that had been circled. I don't know why they had to circle the F when it was the only red mark on the card. In the Teacher's Comments section someone had written that Clyde had "little ability to handle an academic program."

"A little ability is better than none," I said. No one said anything so I figured it probably wasn't the right time to try to cheer Clyde up.

I knew all about his switching from a commercial program to an academic program, but I really hadn't thought he'd have any trouble.

"I saw the grade adviser today. He said I should switch back to the commercial program." Clyde looked like he'd start crying any minute. His eyes were red and his voice was shaky. "He said that I had to take mathematics over and if I failed again or failed another required subject I couldn't graduate. The way it is now I'm going to have to finish up in the summer because I switched over."

"I think you can pass it if you really want to," Kitty said. Clyde's sister was so pretty I couldn't even look at her. If I did I started feeling funny and couldn't talk right. Sometimes I daydreamed about marrying her.

Just then Clyde's mother came in and Clyde gave a quick look at Kitty. Sam breezed in right behind her, happy that his job was over for the day.

"Hi, young ladies and young gentlemen." Mrs. Jones was a kind of heavy woman but she was pretty, too. You could tell she was Kitty's mother if you looked close. She put her package down and started taking things out. "I heard you people talking when I first came in. By the way you hushed up I guess you don't want me to hear what you were talking about. I'll be out of your way in a minute, soon as I put the frozen foods in the refrigerator."

"I got my report card today," Clyde said. His mother stopped taking the food out and turned toward us. Clyde pushed the report card about two inches toward her. She really didn't even have to look at the card to know that it was bad. She could have told that just by looking at Clyde. But she picked it up and looked at it a long time. First she looked at one side and then the other and then back at the first side again.

"What they say around the school?" she asked, still looking at the card.

"They said I should drop the academic course and go back to the other one." I could hardly hear Clyde, he spoke so low.

"Well, what you going to do, young man?" She looked up at Clyde and Clyde looked up at her and there were tears in his eyes and I almost started crying. I can't stand to see my friends cry. "What are you going to do, Mr. Jones?"

"I'm—I'm going to keep the academic course," Clyde said.

"You think it's going to be any easier this time?" Mrs. Jones asked.

"No."

"Things ain't always easy." For a minute there was a faraway look in her eyes, but then her face turned into a big smile. "You're just like your father, boy. That man never would give up on anything he really wanted. Did I ever tell you the time he was trying to learn to play the trombone?"

"No." Clyde still had tears in his eyes but he was smiling, too. Suddenly everybody was happy. It was like seeing a rainbow when it was still raining.

"Well, we were living over across from St. Nicholas Park in this little rooming house. Your father was working on a job down on Varick Street that made transformers or some such nonsense—anyway, he comes home one day with this long package all wrapped up in brown paper. He walks in and sits it in the corner and doesn't say boo about what's in the bag. So at first I don't say

anything either, and then I finally asks him what he's got in the bag, and he says, 'What bag?' Now this thing is about four feet long if it's an inch and he's asking *what* bag." Mrs. Jones wiped the crumbs from Gloria's end of the table with a quick swipe of the dish cloth, leaving a swirling pattern of tiny bubbles. Gloria tore off a paper towel and wiped the area dry.

"Now I look over at him and he's trying to be nonchalant. Sitting there, a grown man, and big as he wants to be and looking for all the world like somebody's misplaced son. So I says, 'The bag in the corner.' And he says, 'Oh, that's a trombone I'm taking back to the pawn shop tomorrow.' Well, I naturally ask him what he's doing with it in the first place, and he says he got carried away and bought it but he realized that we really didn't have the thirty-five dollars to spend on foolishness and so he'd take it back the next day. And all the time he's sitting there scratching his chin and rubbing his nose and trying to peek over at me to see how I felt about it. I just told him that I guess he knew what was best. Only the next day he forgot to take it back, and the next day he forgot to take it back, and finally I broke down and told him why didn't he keep it. He said he would if I thought he should.

"So he unwraps this thing and he was just as happy with it as he could be until he tried to get a tune out of it. He couldn't get a sound out of it at first, but then he started oomping and woomping with the thing as best he could. He worked at it and worked at it and you could see he was getting disgusted. I think he was just about to give it up when the lady who lived under us came upstairs and started complaining about the noise. It kept her Napoleon awake, she said. Napoleon was a dog. Little ugly thing, too. She said your father couldn't play, anyway.

"Well, what did she say that for? That man played that thing day and night. He worked so hard at that thing that his lips were too sore for him to talk right sometime. But he got the hang of it."

"I never remembered Pop playing a trombone," said Clyde.

"Well, your father had a streak in him that made him stick to a thing," she said, pouring some rice into a colander to wash it off, "but every year his goals got bigger and bigger and he had to put some things down so that he could get to others. That old trombone is still around here some place. Probably in one of them boxes under

Kitty's bed. Now, you children, excuse me, young ladies and gentlemen, get on out of here and let me finish supper."

We all went into Clyde's living room.

"That was my mom's good-doing speech," Clyde said. "She gets into talking about what a great guy my father was and how I was like him and whatnot."

"You supposed to be like your father," Sam said. "He was the one that raised you, right?"

"She wants me to be like him, and I want to be like him, too, I guess. She wants me to keep on trying with the academic thing."

"What you want to do," Sam asked, "give it up?"

"No. Not really. I guess I want people like my mother to keep on telling me that I ought to do it, really. Especially when somebody tells me I can't do it."

"Boy," Sam said, sticking his thumbs in his belt and leaning back in the big stuffed chair, "you are just like your father."

Then we all went into Clyde's room and just sat around and talked for a while. Mostly about school and stuff like that, and I wanted to tell Clyde that I thought I could help him if he wanted me to. I was really getting good grades in school, but I thought that Clyde might get annoyed if I mentioned it. But then Gloria said that we could study together sometime and that was cool, too.

Suppose you were faced with a decision like Clyde's. How would you defend your choice to your friends?

Why do you think Clyde's mother tells the story about her husband and the trombone?

What do you think Walter Dean Myers's message is in this story?

WRITE Write a paragraph stating your opinion about Clyde's decision. Tell why you feel it is or is not right for him.

INSIGHTS

Both Clyde's mother and Eddie's mother want to help their sons succeed in overcoming difficulties. Which of the two mothers do you think is more helpful? In what ways? Give reasons to support your answer.

WRITER'S WORKSHOP

Has a parent, a teacher, or a friend ever helped you gain an important insight about yourself? Write a personal narrative about that experience. What was the problem? In what way did that person help you see something you hadn't seen before?

Writer's Choice You have read stories about people who gained insight about themselves. What makes gaining insight important? Choose and plan your own way to express your ideas about this subject. Then carry out your plan, and share your writing with others.

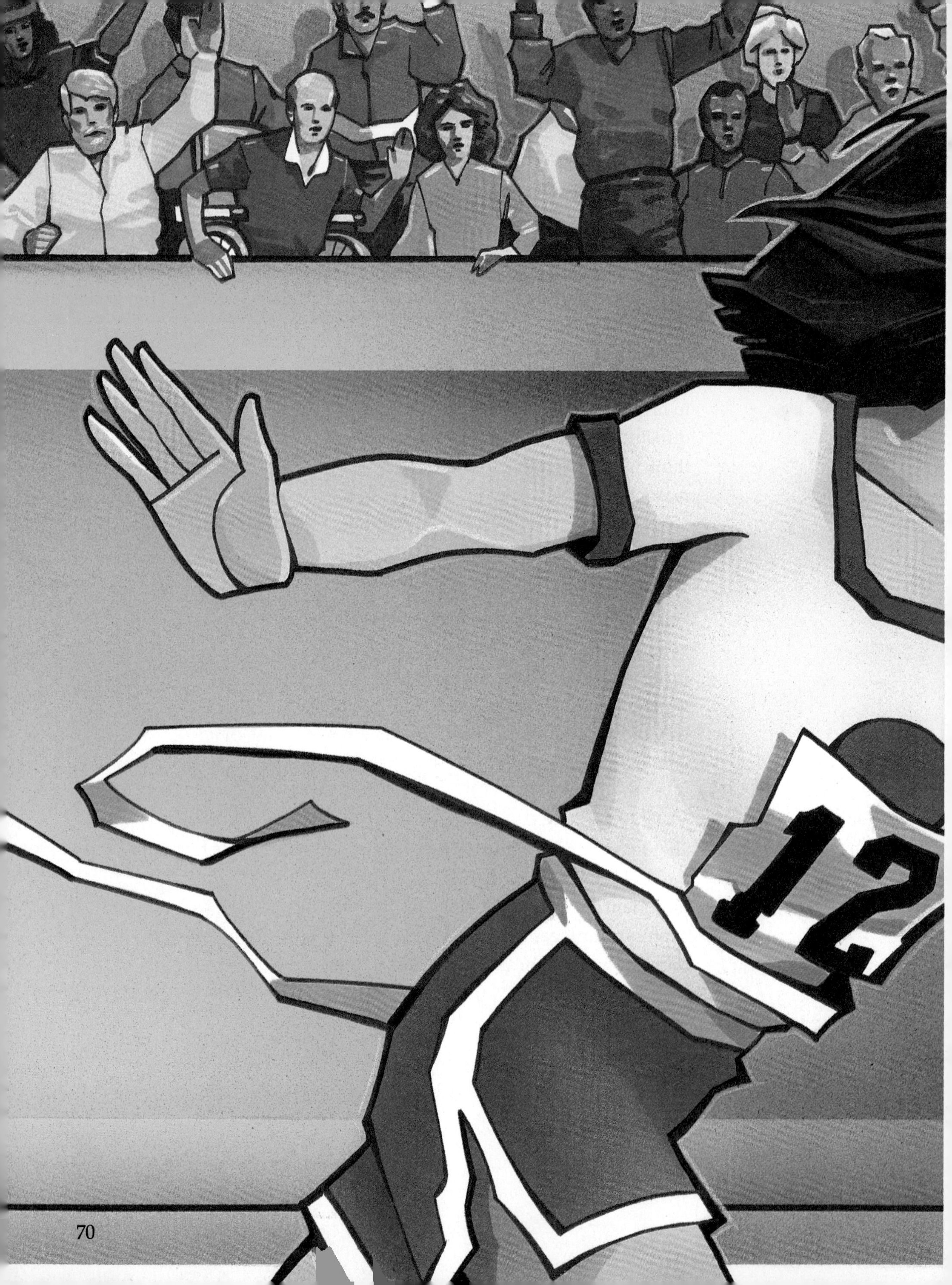
12

THEME

GOALS

The career possibilities open to you may seem almost unlimited. Sometimes, however, as the characters in the next selections learn, a special talent or interest can help you set a lifetime goal.

CONTENTS

BEVERLY CLEARY
A Girl from Yamhill
A MEMOIR

ALA Notable Book

A GIRL FROM YAMHILL

BY BEVERLY CLEARY

One of America's most popular writers, Beverly Cleary was born on a farm in Oregon. She lived there until her family moved to the city of Portland when she was six. In her autobiography she tells about growing up in the 1920s, and the thrill she felt at discovering books. Readers will especially enjoy the glimpses of her life that became parts of her award-winning novels.

ur class was supposed to be studying grammar, which included diagraming sentences from a tan book, *Grammar and Composition*, by Effie B. McFadden, with selections for seventh-grade study and memorizing. Many of us referred to this unpopular book simply as "Effie."

"After all, this is a grammar school," Miss Stone, our serious teacher, reminded us when we groaned at Effie and her grammar.

Instead of concentrating on Effie, my attention turned to a curly-haired boy named Allen, who sat across the aisle from me and was more interesting than making skeletons out of sentences and labeling the bones with proper subjects, verbs, objects, and modifiers.

Allen was also more interesting than our arithmetic book, obviously the work of an educator who enjoyed torturing seventh-graders with "An ice cream can was 2/3 full. After 18 dishes had been taken out, it was still 1/16 full. How many dishes had been taken out?" Concealing Allen's notes from Miss Stone, who threatened to read aloud any note she intercepted, was my exercise in problem solving.

Because boys usually went in pairs for protection when one of them was interested in a girl, Allen and his friend George sometimes walked home from school with me while I wheeled my bicycle. Except for chinning themselves on any handy branch, they were almost civilized. It was George who gave me his first manual training project, a breadboard nicely rounded at one end, with a neatly bored hole for hanging it on a nail. Mother put it away for me to use "someday," and whenever she ran across it, she referred to it as "Beverly's hope chest."

In the seventh grade, changes took place, not only in boys but in the school curriculum. The platoon system was introduced. This meant we were taught some subjects—"Effie," reading, arithmetic, and United States history—in our homeroom but marched off in platoons to other rooms for music, art, nature study, library, an oddly named class called "auditorium," and double periods for domestic science or manual training. And, of course, gymnasium, where seventh-graders exercised with wands or marched while Claudine played "Napoleon's Last Charge" on the piano.

Girls sewed in 7A and cooked in 7B while boys hammered, sawed, and sanded in another basement classroom. Many parents objected to the platoon system; schools should stick to basics. Mother felt the new system too strenuous. "It's just rush, rush, rush all day long," she said. At PTA she complained to Miss Stone that my handwriting had deteriorated and was difficult to read. Miss Stone replied that before long most people would use typewriters.

We now had a school library with a librarian, Miss Smith, a young, brisk, well-tailored teacher who also taught reading. She taught us how to use the library and once made us line up alphabetically by our last names, as if we were books on shelves. After that, I found a place on the shelf where my book would be if I ever wrote a book, which I doubted.

Miss Smith introduced an innovation to Fernwood. Until Miss Smith entered our lives, our teachers forbade reading in the classroom, except for old copies of the *National Geographic*.

Not being able to read in school had frustrated me. During the first week, I held my reader under my desk and read it all the way through, even though teachers said repeatedly, "Do not read ahead." After that I hid books I wanted to read inside my geography, an ideal book, because of its size, for hiding other books. I was deeply grateful to Miss Smith, not only for letting us read but for letting me into the library first on the days when *St. Nicholas* magazine arrived.

Miss Smith had standards. We could read, but we must read good books. Cheap series books, traded around the neighborhood, were not permitted in her classroom. Miss Smith was also strict. She once made me stay after school until I could write on the blackboard, from memory and in order, all the presidents of the United States. I do not recall what I did to deserve this judgment, but I do recall thinking it more sensible than writing "I will not talk in gymnasium" one hundred times—a penalty once meted out by Miss Helliwell, our gym teacher.

Miss Smith also gave unusual assignments. Once, without warning, she said, "I want you to pretend you live in George Washington's time and write a letter to someone describing an experience."

Write something we had not learned in a book? This was unheard of. "But that's not fair," some protested.

Miss Smith assured us that such an assignment was perfectly fair. We knew she was right. Miss Smith was always fair. Strict, but fair.

"You mean *now*?" someone asked.

"Now." Miss Smith was always firm.

"But how?" someone else asked.

"Use your imaginations," said Miss Smith, unconcerned by the consternation she had created.

I was excited. All my life, Mother had told me to use my imagination, but I had never expected to be asked, or even allowed, to use it in school. After a moment of pencil chewing, I wrote to an imaginary cousin, telling how I had sacrificed my pet chicken to help feed Washington's starving, freezing troops at Valley Forge.

The next day, Miss Smith read my letter to the class, praised me for using my imagination, and said everyone else in the class had to try again. At Fernwood any written work, even practice sentences, that did not measure up to teachers' standards was rewritten—sometimes more than once. Smugly I read a library book while my classmates struggled with letters about their sacrifices of pet lambs and calves for Washington's troops. Copycats, I thought with contempt. Mother had told me authors found their ideas in their own minds, not in the words of others. Besides, who ever heard of lambs and calves in the middle of winter? In Yamhill, they were born in springtime.

Next Miss Smith gave us homework: writing an essay about our favorite book character. This brought forth groans and sighs of resignation from most of the class. Nobody wanted to do homework, especially original homework.

That weekend, Mother happened to be visiting her parents in Banks, where Grandpa Atlee had bought back his store. (When he was seventy, after two years of retirement, he decided he was too young to be idle.) After I put together a Sunday dinner for my father, who gamely ate it and was enjoying his pipe and the Sunday paper, I sat down to write the essay. Which favorite character when I had so many? Peter Pan? Judy from *Daddy-Long-Legs*? Tom Sawyer? I finally solved this problem by writing about a girl who went to Bookland and talked to several of my favorite characters. I wrote on and on, inventing conversations that the characters might have had with a strange girl. As rain beat against the windows, a feeling of peace came over me as I wrote far beyond the required length of the essay. I had discovered the pleasure of writing, and to this day, whenever it rains, I feel the urge to write. Most of my books are written in winter.

As much as I enjoyed writing it, I thought "Journey Through Bookland" was a poor story because the girl's journey turned out to be a dream; and if there was anything I disliked, it was a good story that ended up as a dream. Authors of such stories, including Lewis Carroll, were cheating, I felt, because they could not think of any other conclusion.

I was also worried because I had used characters from published books. Miss Smith had lectured us on plagiarism and said that stealing from books was every bit as wrong as stealing from a store. But how could I write about a favorite character without having him speak?

When we turned our essays in during library, I watched anxiously as Miss Smith riffled through the papers. Was I going to catch it? Miss Smith pulled out a paper that I recognized as mine and began to read aloud. My mouth was dry and my stomach felt twisted. When she finished, she paused. My heart pounded. Then Miss Smith said, "When Beverly grows up, she should write children's books."

I was dumbfounded. Miss Smith was praising my story-essay with words that pointed to my future, a misty time I rarely even thought about. I was not used to praise. Mother did not compliment me. Now I was not only being praised in front of the whole class but was receiving approval that was to give direction to my life. The class seemed impressed.

When I reported all this to Mother, she said, "If you are going to become a writer, you must have a steady way of earning your living." This sound advice was followed by a thoughtful pause before she continued, "I have always wanted to write myself."

My career decision was lightly made. The Rose City Branch Library—quiet, tastefully furnished, filled with books and flowers—immediately came to mind. I wanted to work in such a place, so I would become a librarian.

Miss Smith, dear brisk lady who gave unusual assignments, astonished us again by announcing one day that we were no longer to call her Miss Smith. She was now Mrs. Weaver.

"You mean you got *married*?" we asked after this news had sunk in.

With a smile, she admitted she had. A teacher getting married was unheard of to us. Some were called "Mrs.," but we thought they were widows. Our teachers never discussed their personal lives with their classes, but here was a teacher who had presumably fallen in love while she was a teacher. Astounding! Such a thing had never happened before and, in the course of my education, never happened again.

Mother and father pose for their engagement picture.

Mother worries because her daughter's ear sticks out.

***A**t the age of six I dislike this yellow organdy dress because it is scratchy. Mother is ashamed of my socks. We move to Portland shortly after this picture is taken.*

***W**hen I am in the eighth grade.*

In addition to Mrs. Weaver and her surprising assignments, home economics and manual training were new to us. In sewing class, while boys were sawing away at their breadboards, girls in 7A were laboring over samplers of stitches and seams and putting them to use making cooking aprons that slipped over our heads and had bias binding properly applied to the neck and armholes, and bloomers that taught us to measure elastic without stretching it. In 7B, cooking class began by making white sauce without lumps.

Mother, who often told me how she sacrificed to give me piano lessons, gave up when we moved from Hancock Street; so once again I had school music to dread. *That* had not changed. We were still expected to sing alone.

The goals of our new art class were conformity and following directions, not creativity. The teacher passed out squared paper. She instructed us to set our pencil points on an intersection ten squares down and four squares from the left-hand edge. Her directions droned on. "Draw a line two squares over, one square down, two squares over . . ." on and on. Grimly we labored to keep up with the instructions, to pay her the attention she demanded. When she finished, those of us who had kept up had identical outlines of a rooster. We were then told which crayons to use "without scrubbing" on which squares; others, those who did not pay attention or, in the case of the terrible boys, did not want to, had something surreal. Perhaps, without knowing it, they had captured the spirit of a rooster, if not the approval of the art teacher.

Auditorium was taught by Miss Viola Harrington, who stood at the rear of the auditorium while we took turns standing up straight, walking up the steps to the center of the stage, facing her, and whispering, "Can you hear me whisper?"

"Louder," said Miss Harrington. "I can't hear you."

We took deep breaths and even deeper breaths until we thought our lungs would burst, until Miss Harrington could hear us at the back of the auditorium.

The most unusual change in curriculum was nature study, taught by Miss Lydia Crawford, an aloof eccentric with long, glossy brown hair wound around her head and with the high color and glowing complexion of an outdoor woman. She always wore plain dark dresses that stopped just below her knees; she wore high brown shoes, much higher than those I had finally been allowed to abandon, which laced all the way to her knees. We were all intimidated by Miss Crawford.

Miss Crawford believed that if we were to study nature, we should have nature around us. She brought, and encouraged us to bring, exhibits to be placed on a ledge beneath the window. Plants bloomed; lichen, mosses, and minerals were displayed; chipmunks raced on wheels; and a two-headed garter snake and I stared at each other through the glass walls of its prison.

Miss Crawford told us that when she was a little girl, she was taught to recite "From the stable to the table, dirty flies!" She said women ruined their skins with face powder, which was made from talc. "See, children, this is what foolish women rub on their faces," she said, holding up a piece of the greenish mineral while her own face shone from soap and water. She told us we must always rotate our crops and never, never perjure ourselves.

The curriculum required Miss Crawford to lead us through a book with a dark blue cover entitled *Healthy Living.* We stared listlessly at drawings of correct and incorrect posture and of properly balanced meals before we began a relentless journey of a meal through the alimentary canal, beginning with food thoroughly chewed. I endured what went on in our mouths and esophagi, but I began to have doubts about the whole thing down around our stomachs, and when we reached the liver and gallbladder, the whole messy business became disgusting and, beyond those organs, too embarrassing to mention. I did not want to think of all that going on inside of *me.* Ugh.

Miss Crawford, radiating health, was apparently as bored with *Healthy Living* as her class. One day she suddenly closed the sensible text, laid it aside, and with her fingertips resting on the front desk in the center row, began to tell us a story about a man named Jean Valjean, who lived in France a long time ago and who had spent nineteen years as a galley slave for stealing a loaf of bread to feed his hungry nieces and nephews. We all perked up. We knew about galley slaves from pirate movies.

Miss Crawford's cheeks grew redder, and her face became incandescent with excitement, as she went on and on, telling us the story in great detail. Nothing this moving had ever happened in school before. We groaned when the bell rang.

"Children," said Miss Crawford, "I shall continue the story in our next class."

Nature study became the best part of school. Chipmunks still raced, a home of a trapdoor spider was added to the nature display; but all that mattered to us was *Les Misérables.* On and on we traveled with Jean Valjean, hounded by Inspector Javert all the way. Fantine, her little daughter, Cosette, and the wicked Thénardiers all became as real as, perhaps more real than, our neighbors. We gasped when Fantine sold her beautiful hair to pay the Thénardiers for the care of Cosette. Even the most terrible boys sat still, fascinated. Unaware of social injustice in our own country, we were gripped by Victor Hugo's story of social injustice in nineteenth-century France.

Some parents—but not mine—listening to us retell at the supper table the marvelous story Miss Crawford was bringing to our imaginations, began to object. Storytelling in school was improper. We were there to learn, not to be entertained. Telephone calls and visits were made to Mr. Dorman, who was a very wise man. Of course we should be studying *Healthy Living,* and so we did. However, at least once a week Miss Crawford came to our auditorium class to continue the story.

June came, summer vacation was about to begin, and she had not finished *Les Misérables.*

"Don't worry, children," she said. "I'll be here when you return in September."

True to her word, Miss Crawford was waiting when school started, and took up where she had left off. Well into the eighth grade, the story of Jean Valjean came to an end. Miss Crawford began another novel by Victor Hugo, *Toilers of the Sea.*

By coincidence, the next year one of Mother's cousins, Verna, who had become a librarian, sent me a copy of *Les Misérables,* which she inscribed in her beautiful vertical handwriting: "A book that you may enjoy someday, if not now, Beverly." I had already lived the book and did not read it for many years. Then, as I read, Miss Crawford was before me on every page. She seemed not to have missed a single word.

I often wonder why this particular book meant so much to an eccentric Oregon teacher. Had someone in her family suffered a terrible injustice? Had her repeated warning about perjury come from some experience in her own life? Or had she perhaps spent her childhood in isolation on a farm where the works of Victor Hugo were the only books available? And why did she suddenly feel compelled to share this novel with a class of seventh-graders? Whatever her reasons, I am profoundly grateful to her—and to the wisdom of Mr. Dorman for circumventing unimaginative parents and allowing her to tell the entire book in such detail. My copy has 1,222 pages.

How are your school experiences similar to the school experiences that Beverly Cleary had in the 1920s?

How was Miss Smith an inspiration to Beverly Cleary?

How did Beverly Cleary's school experiences help make her a writer?

WRITE Write a brief character sketch of someone who inspires you. Tell how you think that person will affect your life.

BEST BOOK FOR YOUNG ADULTS

THE NO-GUITAR BLUES

from *Baseball in April*
by Gary Soto

The moment Fausto saw the group Los Lobos on "American Bandstand," he knew exactly what he wanted to do with his life—play guitar.

His eyes grew large with excitement as Los Lobos ground out a song while teenagers bounced off each other on the crowded dance floor.

He had watched "American Bandstand" for years and had heard Ray Camacho and the Teardrops at Romain Playground, but it had never occurred to him that he too might become a musician. That afternoon Fausto knew his mission in life: to play guitar in his own band; to sweat out his songs and prance around the stage; to make money and dress weird.

Fausto turned off the television set and walked outside, wondering how he could get enough money to buy a guitar. He couldn't ask his parents because they would just say, "Money doesn't grow on trees" or "What do you think we are, bankers?" And besides, they hated rock music. They were into the *conjunto*[1] music of Lydia Mendoza, Flaco Jimenez, and Little Joe and La Familia. And, as Fausto recalled, the last album they bought was *The Chipmunks Sing Christmas Favorites.*

But what the heck, he'd give it a try. He returned inside and watched his mother make tortillas. He leaned against the kitchen counter, trying to work up the nerve to ask her for a guitar. Finally, he couldn't hold back any longer.

"Mom," he said, "I want a guitar for Christmas."

---

[1]conjunto [kôn · ho͞on′ tō]: band

illustrations by Francisco Mora

She looked up from rolling tortillas. "Honey, a guitar costs a lot of money."

"How 'bout for my birthday next year," he tried again.

"I can't promise," she said, turning back to her tortillas, "but we'll see."

Fausto walked back outside with a buttered tortilla. He knew his mother was right. His father was a warehouseman at Berven Rugs, where he made good money but not enough to buy everything his children wanted. Fausto decided to mow lawns to earn money, and was pushing the mower down the street before he realized it was winter and no one would hire him. He returned the mower and picked up a rake. He hopped onto his sister's bike (his had two flat tires) and rode north to the nicer section of Fresno in search of work. He went door-to-door, but after three hours he managed to get only one job, and not to rake leaves. He was asked to hurry down to the store to buy a loaf of bread, for which he received a grimy, dirt-caked quarter.

He also got an orange, which he ate sitting at the curb. While he was eating, a dog walked up and sniffed his leg. Fausto pushed him away and threw an orange peel skyward. The dog caught it and ate it in one gulp. The dog looked at Fausto and wagged his tail for more. Fausto tossed him a slice of orange, and the dog snapped it up and licked his lips.

"How come you like oranges, dog?"

The dog blinked a pair of sad eyes and whined.

"What's the matter? Cat got your tongue?" Fausto laughed at his joke and offered the dog another slice.

At that moment a dim light came on inside Fausto's head. He saw that it was sort of a fancy dog, a terrier or something, with dog tags and a shiny collar. And it looked well fed and healthy. In his neighborhood, the dogs were never licensed, and if they got sick they were placed near the water heater until they got well.

This dog looked like he belonged to rich people. Fausto cleaned his juice-sticky hands on his pants and got to his feet. The light in his head grew brighter. It just might work. He called the dog, patted its muscular back, and bent down to check the license.

"Great," he said. "There's an address."

The dog's name was Roger, which struck Fausto as weird because he'd never heard of a dog with a human name. Dogs should have names like Bomber, Freckles, Queenie, Killer, and Zero.

Fausto planned to take the dog home and collect a reward. He would say he had found Roger near the freeway. That would scare the daylights out of the owners, who would be so happy that they would probably give him a reward. He felt bad about lying, but the dog *was* loose. And it might even really be lost, because the address was six blocks away.

Fausto stashed the rake and his sister's bike behind a bush, and, tossing an orange peel every time Roger became distracted, walked the dog to his house. He hesitated on the porch until Roger began to scratch the door with a muddy paw. Fausto had come this far, so he figured he might as well go through with it. He knocked softly. When no one answered, he rang the doorbell. A man in a silky bathrobe and slippers opened the door and seemed confused by the sight of his dog and the boy.

"Sir," Fausto said, gripping Roger by the collar, "I found your dog by the freeway. His dog license says he lives here." Fausto looked down at the dog, then up to the man. "He does, doesn't he?"

The man stared at Fausto a long time before saying in a pleasant voice, "That's right." He pulled his robe tighter around him because of the cold and asked Fausto to come in. "So he was by the freeway?"

"Uh—huh."

"You bad, snoopy dog," said the man, wagging his finger. "You probably knocked over some trash cans, too, didn't you?"

Fausto looked at the bill and knew he was in trouble. Not with these nice folks or with his parents but with himself.

Fausto didn't say anything. He looked around, amazed by this house with its shiny furniture and a television as large as the front window at home. Warm bread smells filled the air and music full of soft tinkling floated in from another room.

"Helen," the man called to the kitchen. "We have a visitor."

His wife came into the living room, wiping her hands on a dish towel and smiling. "And who have we here?" she asked in one of the softest voices Fausto had ever heard.

"This young man said he found Roger near the freeway."

Fausto repeated his story to her while staring at a perpetual clock with a bell-shaped glass, the kind his aunt got when she celebrated her twenty-fifth anniversary. The lady frowned and said, wagging a finger at Roger, "Oh, you're a bad boy."

"It was very nice of you to bring Roger home," the man said. "Where do you live?"

"By the vacant lot on Olive," he said. "You know, by Brownie's Flower Place."

The wife looked at her husband, then Fausto. Her eyes twinkled triangles of light as she said, "Well, young man, you're probably hungry. How about a turnover?"

"What do I have to turn over?" Fausto asked, thinking she was talking about yard work or something like turning trays of dried raisins.

"No, no, dear, it's a pastry." She took him by the elbow and guided him to a kitchen that sparkled with copper pans and bright yellow wallpaper. She guided him to the kitchen table and gave him a tall glass of milk and something that looked like an *empanada.*[2] Steamy waves of heat escaped when he tore it in two. He ate with both eyes on the man and woman who stood arm-in-arm smiling at him. They were strange, he thought. But nice.

"That was good," he said after he finished the turnover. "Did you make it, ma'am?"

"Yes, I did. Would you like another?"

"No, thank you. I have to go home now."

As Fausto walked to the door, the man opened his wallet and took out a bill. "This is for you," he said. "Roger is special to us, almost like a son."

Fausto looked at the bill and knew he was in trouble. Not with these nice folks or with his parents but with himself. How could he have been so deceitful? The dog wasn't lost. It was just having a fun Saturday walking around.

"I can't take that."

"You have to. You deserve it, believe me," the man said.

"No, I don't."

"Now don't be silly," said the lady. She took the bill from her husband and stuffed it into Fausto's shirt pocket. "You're a lovely child. Your parents are lucky to have you. Be good. And come see us again, please."

Fausto went out, and the lady closed the door. Fausto clutched the bill through his shirt pocket. He felt like ringing the doorbell and begging them to please take the money back, but he knew they would refuse. He hurried away, and at the end of the block, pulled the bill from his shirt pocket: it was a crisp twenty-dollar bill.

"Oh, man, I shouldn't have lied," he said under his breath as he started up the street like a zombie. He wanted to run to church for Saturday confession, but it was past four-thirty, when confession stopped.

He returned to the bush where he had hidden the rake and his sister's bike and rode home slowly, not daring to touch the money in his pocket. At home, in the privacy of his room, he examined the twenty-dollar bill. He had never had so much money. It was probably enough to buy a secondhand guitar. But he felt bad, like the time he stole a dollar from the secret fold inside his older brother's wallet.

Fausto went outside and sat on the fence. "Yeah," he said. "I can probably get a guitar for twenty. Maybe at a yard sale—things are cheaper."

His mother called him to dinner.

The next day he dressed for church without anyone telling him. He was going to go to eight o'clock mass.

---

[2]empanada [em · pə · nä′ də]: meat pie

"I'm going to church, Mom," he said. His mother was in the kitchen cooking *papas*[3] and *chorizo con huevos*.[4] A pile of tortillas lay warm under a dishtowel.

"Oh, I'm so proud of you, Son." She beamed, turning over the crackling *papas*.

His older brother, Lawrence, who was at the table reading the funnies, mimicked, "Oh, I'm so proud of you, my son," under his breath.

At Saint Theresa's he sat near the front. When Father Jerry began by saying that we are all sinners, Fausto thought he looked right at him. Could he know? Fausto fidgeted with guilt. No, he thought. I only did it yesterday.

Fausto knelt, prayed, and sang. But he couldn't forget the man and the lady, whose names he didn't even know, and the *empanada* they had given him. It had a strange name but tasted really good. He wondered how they got rich. And how that dome clock worked. He had asked his mother once how his aunt's clock worked. She said it just worked, the way the refrigerator works. It just did.

Fausto caught his mind wandering and tried to concentrate on his sins. He said a Hail Mary and sang, and when the wicker basket came his way, he stuck a hand reluctantly in his pocket and pulled out the twenty-dollar bill. He ironed it between his palms, and dropped it into the basket. The grown-ups stared. Here was a kid dropping twenty dollars in the basket while they gave just three or four dollars.

There would be a second collection for Saint Vincent de Paul, the lector announced. The wicker baskets again floated in the pews, and this time the adults around him, given a second chance to show their charity, dug deep into their wallets and purses and dropped in fives and tens. This time Fausto tossed in the grimy quarter.

Fausto felt better after church. He went home and played football in the front yard with his brother and some neighbor kids. He felt cleared of wrongdoing and was so happy that he played one of his best games of football

---

[3]papas [pä′ päs]: potatoes
[4]chorizo con huevos [chô · rē′sō kôn wā′vōs]: sausage with eggs

ever. On one play, he tore his good pants, which he knew he shouldn't have been wearing. For a second, while he examined the hole, he wished he hadn't given the twenty dollars away.

Man, I coulda bought me some jeans, he thought. He pictured his twenty dollars being spent to buy church candles. He pictured a priest buying an armful of flowers with *his* money.

Fausto had to forget about getting a guitar. He spent the next day playing soccer in his good pants, which were now his old pants. But that night during dinner, his mother said she remembered seeing an old bass guitarrón the last time she cleaned out her father's garage.

"It's a little dusty," his mom said, serving his favorite enchiladas, "but I think it works. Grandpa says it works."

Fausto's ears perked up. That was the same kind the guy in Los Lobos played. Instead of asking for the guitar, he waited for his mother to offer it to him. And she did, while gathering the dishes from the table.

"No, Mom, I'll do it," he said, hugging her. "I'll do the dishes forever if you want."

It was the happiest day of his life. No, it was the second-happiest day of his life. The happiest was when his grandfather Lupe placed the guitarrón, which was nearly as huge as a washtub, in his arms. Fausto ran a thumb down the strings, which vibrated in his throat and chest. It sounded beautiful, deep and eerie. A pumpkin smile widened on his face.

"OK, *hijo*,[5] now you put your fingers like this," said his grandfather, smelling of tobacco and aftershave. He took Fausto's fingers and placed them on the strings. Fausto strummed a chord on the guitarrón, and the bass resounded in their chests.

The guitarrón was more complicated than Fausto imagined. But he was confident that after a few more lessons he could start a band that would someday play on "American Bandstand" for the dancing crowds.

---

[5]hijo [ē′ hō]: son

Would you like to have Fausto as a friend? State your reasons.

Why do you think Fausto regrets some of his actions? What does that tell you about Fausto?

Do you think this story's message is one that others should hear? Tell why you feel as you do.

WRITE If you were Fausto's friend, what would you advise him to do with the $20? Write a friendly letter to him giving that advice.

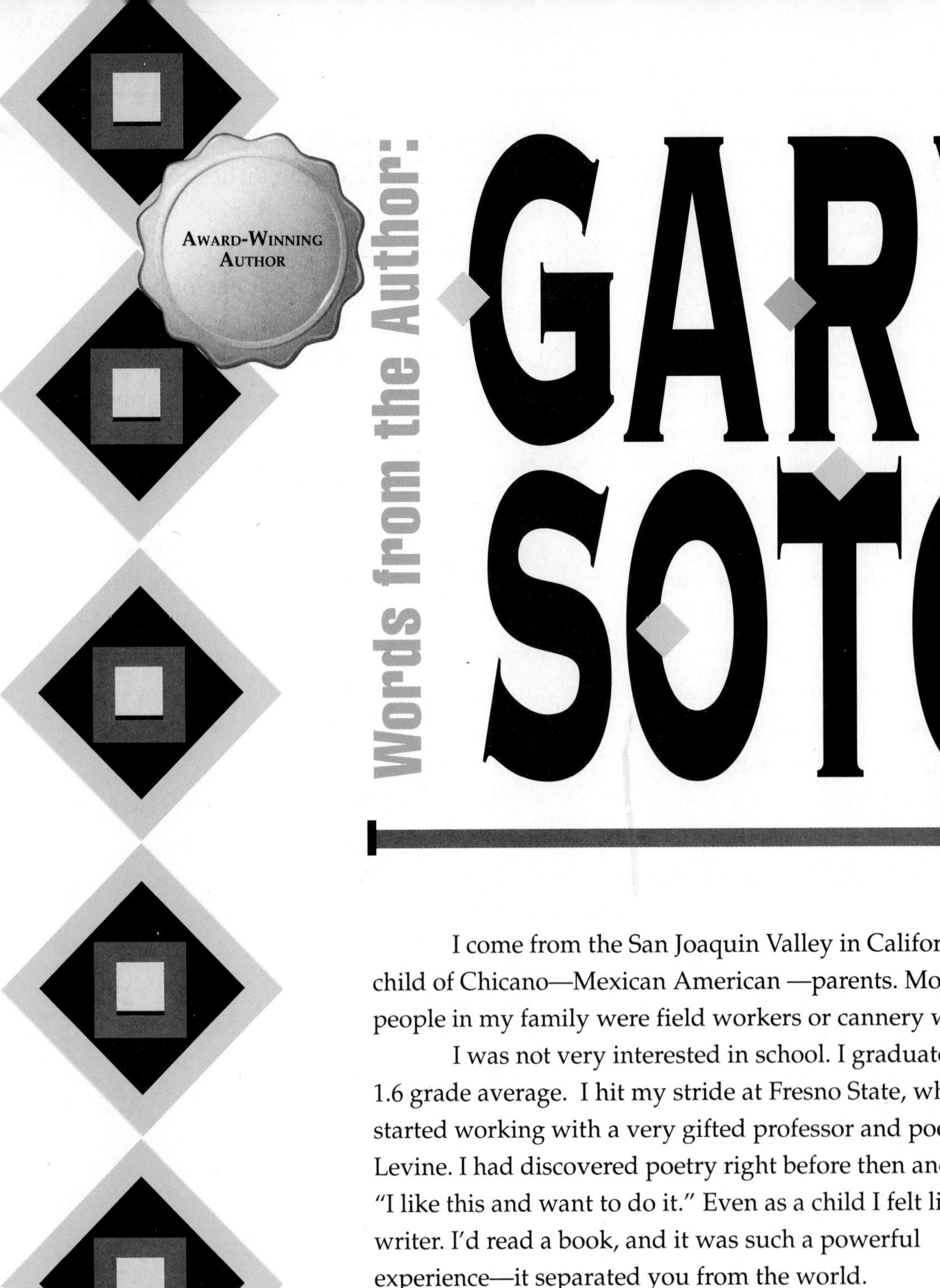

GARY SOTO

I come from the San Joaquin Valley in California, the child of Chicano—Mexican American —parents. Most of the people in my family were field workers or cannery workers.

I was not very interested in school. I graduated with a 1.6 grade average. I hit my stride at Fresno State, where I started working with a very gifted professor and poet, Philip Levine. I had discovered poetry right before then and decided, "I like this and want to do it." Even as a child I felt like a writer. I'd read a book, and it was such a powerful experience—it separated you from the world.

Professor Levine taught me the nuts and bolts of writing, how to use language. I had the gift, but he had the tools to manipulate that gift. He is a very strong teacher, very exact in his criticism. While he was teaching me, I was

devouring poetry. There were things I didn't quite understand when I read certain pieces, but I liked the way they made me feel.

I don't write for my audience. There's something very wrong in writing that's aimed at merely pleasing an audience. My training as a poet brought me to the conclusion that you write for a certain perfection. As in archery, the goal is to hit the mark. If someone is moved in the process, that's great. But I write what I want.

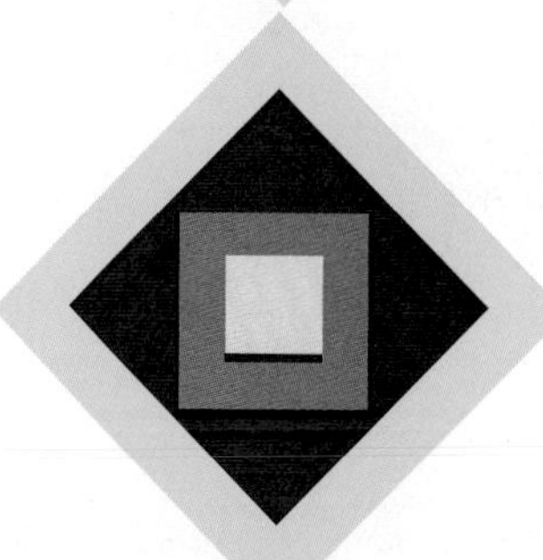

Nadja Salerno-Sonnenberg was born in Rome, Italy, and grew up in Cherry Hill, New Jersey. A recording artist, she appears frequently in concert across the United States and throughout the world. Miss Salerno-Sonnenberg is the recipient of numerous honors and awards, including the Avery Fisher Career Grant and the Naumburg Award. She now makes her home in New York City.

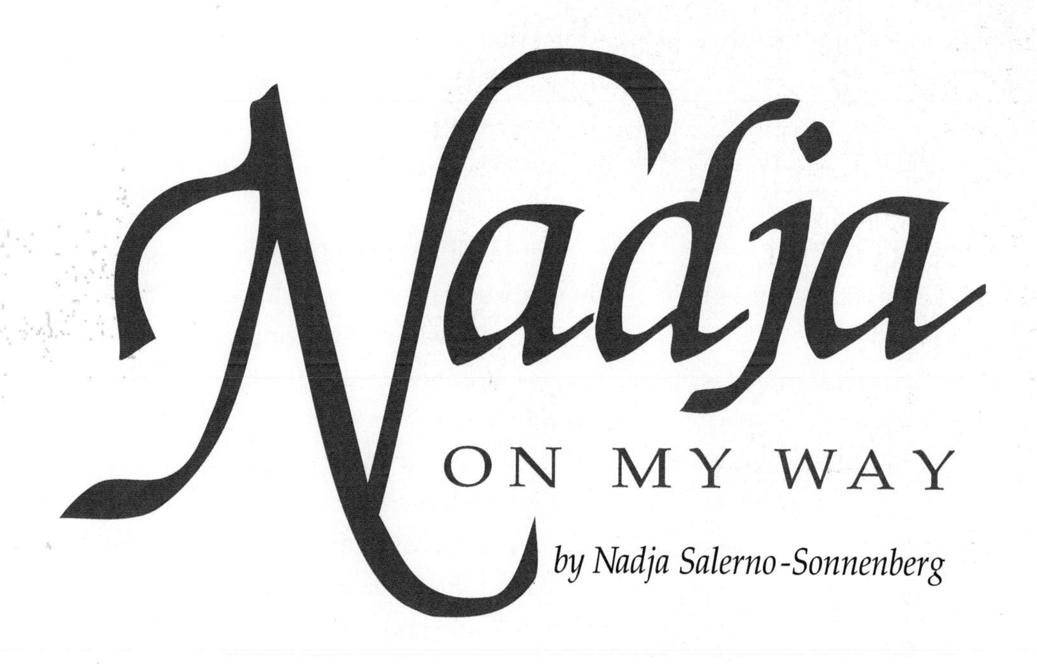

Nadja ON MY WAY

by Nadja Salerno-Sonnenberg

This is something I know for a fact: You have to work hardest for the thing you love most. And when it's music that you love, you're in for the fight of your life.

It starts when your blood fills with music and you know you can't live without it. Every day brings a challenge to learn as much as possible and to play even better than you did the day before.

You may want to achieve fame and glory, or you may want to play for fun. But whenever you fall in love with music, you'll never sit still again.

Music is more important than we will ever know. Great music can pull you right out of your chair. It can make you cry, or laugh, or feel a way you've never felt before. It can make you remember the first person you loved. Music has that power.

Just imagine a world without music. What would you whistle when you walked down the street? How could you make a movie? How could you have a ball game without an organist leading the crowd when you're down by a run in the ninth?

You could be the most successful doctor in the world, but if you never turn on the radio, never go to a concert, never sing in the shower, never saw *The King and I*—then you can't be a total, fulfilled human being. It's impossible.

When you realize how vital music is, you realize a musician's fight is quite a noble, heroic endeavor. It didn't always seem that way to me. There was a time, years ago, when I felt discouraged and it seemed selfish to put so much time into music. Being a musician didn't seem as useful to others as being a surgeon, or even a good politician.

But I came to understand that it's a great, great gift to help people forget their everyday life and be uplifted. And better than uplifted, to be inspired; that's what music can do. It's important to us all, and I'm proud to put mind and muscle into recording, concerts, teaching, and studying: into being a musician.

Emotionally, music has brought me an enormous amount of joy and an enormous amount of despair and frustration. Because of music, I have learned what a battle is. I've won most, but not all—not by a long shot.

It's a reward to see people affected at my concerts and, after concerts, hearing from them. Mothers have come backstage and said, "My son saw you on TV and he decided to play the violin."

During a master class in Aspen, a young girl played the Bruch G minor Concerto for me. I had played the Bruch there, and she played it exactly the way I did. I was thrilled and embarrassedly happy to have affected a young violinist that way.

Yet I will never feel satisfied, because there are always many goals ahead. Some days I can't believe I've come as far as I have—and how much further I want to go.

◆

I didn't learn how to read music at a music school. My grandfather taught me.

Papa John Salerno was the strictest teacher I ever had. When we came to America, and for many years after, the solfeggio[1] class was in my grandparents' bedroom every Tuesday. He had me read through a little exercise book by Pasquale Bono; sing *do, re, mi, fa, sol, la, ti, do;* and learn the meaning of notes and musical time.

Rhythm was the hardest thing for me about sight-reading. As I learned, I could pretty much play notes on a page, but rhythmically I had problems. Maybe I just don't have a mathematical way of thinking; I tend to be more emotional and instinctive than strictly analytical. Whatever the reason, counting and dividing beats came with great effort. And great detection.

Reading music is like solving a mystery. When I look at a new piece of music, all the notes look the same. Some are higher on the staff, some are lower, but it's just a page full of black dots.

---

[1]solfeggio: practice in sight-reading vocal music using the sol-fa syllables

To be a musician, you have to be able to tell which dots are important: which dots represent the climax of the phrase and which dots connect one phrase to another.

Sometimes you'll play through a piece and say, "Oh, that's a beautiful phrase. Let me do that again." Through detective work, you'll find phrases throughout a piece of music.

My grandfather gave me many things, more than I was aware of at the time. Papa John wasn't a great musician with a great soul and great mind. He was an honest, simple man who worked in a factory and played the horn; yet the man could sight-read like the best musicians around. Any clef, anything. I've yet to see the equal of the training he received as a kid in Sicily.

Perhaps above all, Papa John gave me a love of opera. Every Saturday in America *Texaco Presents* was on and my grandfather and I would sit by the radio and listen to The Metropolitan Opera Broadcasts from New York City. He would explain every single thing to the point where I could barely hear the music.

"Now she's trying to get away," he'd say. "Now he took out a knife . . ." I would get so immersed in the story line, in the totality of opera.

For my money, opera is the most magnificent form of art man has invented. There's everything. You've got costumes, you've got a story—talk about great stories! It's more than a symphony because you've got these incredible sounds which are the human voice.

I fell in love with singing as I would with baseball. But while I can play left field with the best of them (at least the best of them playing softball in Central Park), unfortunately I can't really sing. I mean, *My Funny Valentine,* fine, but an aria from *La Bohème,* forget it.

Still, I think singing when I play the violin. If I were to sing a passage I'm playing, where would I take my breath? How does this line of music make a sentence with a beginning, middle, and end? That is my instinctual way of playing music, from love of opera, and my grandfather's lessons, when I was very young.

If you don't have an Italian grandfather, but would like to learn about opera, I wouldn't advise you to start with something like *Lohengrin* or *Tristan und Isolde*. They're Wagner and I love them, but they're six hours long and there's a guy in front of a rock singing about a god. It's like puh-leeese!

Start with *Carmen*. Georges Bizet's *Carmen* is opera's Hit Parade. After you see it, you won't know which tune to whistle first. Great story, very passionate, a lot of action.

The first opera I saw onstage, at an age when I knew what was really going on, was Richard Strauss's *Salome*. It's a biblical story about the psycho stepdaughter of King Herod.

The story goes like this: Herod is keeping John the Baptist prisoner, and Salome falls in love with him. He rejects her. She does a veil dance and requests John's beheading. Her request is granted, and they march in with John's head on a platter.

Salome kisses the head, falls to the floor in ecstasy, and Herod orders his soldiers to squash her with their shields.

That's how it ends. The kettledrums go *bu-rumm, bu-rumm*, and the curtain falls and it's over.

I was fourteen at the time, and for me it was the operatic equivalent of *The Texas Chainsaw Massacre*. It blew my mind.

Anything by Verdi or Puccini, any of the romantic operas such as *La Traviata, Otello, Tosca*, and *La Bohème* are great things to see. Then there are serious and comic operas by Rossini and Mozart such as *La Cenerentola* and *Magic Flute* which are absolutely gorgeous.

And opera isn't the only theatrical form of music that's worth knowing. Ballet is beautiful too, though I learned that as an art form, it isn't enough for me. There are music and wonderful things to watch, but I always feel bad for the ballerinas. It's like they're all mute. I feel bad that they can't say anything.

You may feel differently. Two of the most famous ballets, *Nutcracker* and *Coppélia*, are great introductions. I can't imagine you'd be bored at either one.

In any kind of art, you'll find the things you like by trial and error. Go to concerts, galleries, museums, listen to the radio, rent videos—the important thing is to stay alert and look for beauty everywhere.

You'll learn from it all.

◆

Sometimes I feel I worked so hard for what I have yet am only beginning to work. No matter how much you do for the craft of your instrument, and the beauty of music, you're still a lucky son of a gun to concertize and make records.

Some people, even people who might become quite good at an instrument, were just not born for the business of music. Making music for a living, being a soloist, traveling, having a career—that's the business of music. Why is the business so hard?

First of all, there aren't many things that take more time than learning an instrument.

An actor will memorize his lines, and if he has any semblance of personality, he can usually find his way through a part. If you don't believe me, stay home and watch the soaps some afternoon.

You can't fake the Bruch Concerto if you can't play the violin. It takes many years to play something that complex. If you started the violin today, it might take you fifteen years to do it. And while you're conquering *Czardas,* there are twelve-year-olds whipping through Bruch as if it was *Zip-A-Dee-Doo-Dah.*

This isn't to say that an early start will guarantee success any more than a late start will guarantee failure. It's possible that someone who's never touched an instrument has the most incredible musical mind the world will ever know. You should never say, "I'm already too old to start playing." So you might not make a debut until you're older—so what?

If your genius is obvious, and your debut is outlandishly wonderful, then you'll go right to the top no matter how old or young you are.

The musical community is very small, especially the classical music community. I could play a concert in Dubuque and a conductor may hear me who happens to have a small orchestra in Frankfurt. He'll go back to Germany and before I know it, I'll be invited there because he liked the way I played.

News of a debut that's outrageous, that people flipped over, will travel throughout the entire classical music community within two weeks no matter where the debut took place. Word of mouth is that quick.

So time learning an instrument isn't the only factor in the business of music. The most important, mysterious, and sometimes heartbreaking thing is having a talent that people will appreciate. If you have that talent, and you have determination to succeed, you're more than halfway to the goal.

Competitions are one way of testing appreciation. If you win, you get a lot of recognition overnight. But a competition will only give you initial debuts in various cities. Winning a competition, and initial debuts, do not mean success. You have one chance in a city. If they like you, they'll rebook you. That's business. And it's the rebookings, reengagements, that mean a career.

You could have a résumé that's one word long, but if an audience went nuts for you, stood up and cheered, if the conductor liked you, the orchestra liked you, the orchestra manager liked you, the guy backstage opening the door liked you—you'll be invited back.

You could also have won every competition on earth, but if everybody falls asleep . . . forget it. You won't be asked back.

There are definitely ways to make a first-class career without winning a competition. There are lots of people who have won very prestigious awards and are going nowhere slowly.

I'm a true believer in the heart winning out. If your spirit is there and if your talent is that great, it will win out. It will win someday. You may have to wait for it to happen, but it will happen.

I'll give an example. There's a pianist named Ivo Pogorelich. He entered the Chopin International Competition, a very big competition in Warsaw. The judges were a panel of pianists, including Martha Argerich. She was the only judge who loved his playing. The others hated it because Pogorelich's Chopin is really different and quite challenging.

Argerich protested the other judges' decision against him so heatedly that she finally removed herself from the panel. Pogorelich won second prize and another pianist that no one's ever heard of, and no one ever will, won the grand prize.

So it often doesn't matter. There have been guys who've won the Van Cliburn Competition, the Naumburg, the Queen Elizabeth, and that may be the peak of their career. You can get initial concerts, but if no one's interested in your style of playing, you'll have that two or three years of work and that's it.

One more thing goes into building a career: luck. I've heard festival organizers say, "We had a blond violinist last year. This year we'll get a brunette one." The classical music field is not devoid of that kind of nonsense. A certain amount of luck is involved in anyone's career.

Of course, a lot of people drop out before they even get to the career stage.

When you start playing an instrument when you're five or eight, it's easy to get smitten with this new thing, this new toy. It makes noise and you think, Maybe I can play this piece and maybe I can get good enough to play that piece.

Then three months later, you think, Naw, never mind.

That's very, very common.

Or you work and work and work and still you see that other players are better than you. Then you realize, as happened to me, that you have to work even harder, and you begin to realize how difficult it is to play well. And that's scary.

There's also outside pressure. In Juilliard, I saw so many kids, more often than not, whose parents were at best supportive but wished their kids would get a real job someday.

Fortunately, making music and being a violinist was never something to be ashamed of in my family. But parents, generally, would rather their kids study to be doctors and lawyers. Music isn't an easy life; very few musicians actually make it and have comfortable lives.

◆

You should know, though, that a career as a player isn't the only way to have a life in music.

When you go to a concert, you see the performers onstage, or the orchestra in the pit, and you see the conductor come out and wave his arms and the concert's over. That's what you see. But there are people directly involved in music behind the scenes that you don't see.

No performer can do without a manager. Managers are people who need to know music. They get you concerts, they book you, they represent you. It's impossible not to have one.

Performing artists need someone to handle publicity so there's a chance people will hear you're in town. Publicity agents need to know music. How could they represent someone if they didn't? Is a performer good? What makes them special?

Many publicity agents, like managers, were musicians who reached the point where playing just wasn't a necessity any more. The same can be said of some photographers, critics, writers, music copyists, people in radio, recording, publishing, and people on the organizational side. If you want to put together a festival, or produce a concert series—you have to know music. All the people backstage, the ones you don't see, have to know music.

The thing all these people have in common is that a life in music is a calling. If you want that life, in one way or another, you can have it.

But you also must be willing to accept the price.

There's no way that being a traveling artist, that getting on a plane, is good for you. The air, the food difference, the time difference when you land, the weather—constant travel isn't good for anyone.

Sometimes I feel like airline food that's been through the microwave four times.

I've played concerts with a 102° temperature and bronchitis. If something goes wrong personally, I don't have the luxury of sitting down and being depressed, because I have to be at the airport.

It's hard to maintain relationships when you're constantly going somewhere. Still, I'm glad to say, my family of friends keeps growing. Cecile Licad married the cellist Antonio Meneses, and I'm the proud godmother of their child. Cecile and I recorded a sonata album in 1988; we still play concerts together from time to time, and we're still closest friends. It's a wonderful change to have such good company on the road.

Generally, the life-style of a concert artist is no good at all, but the playing makes up for it. Every violinist can't play in one city, so we have to travel. It's something I have to accept because there is a choice. I don't have to play the violin. I don't have to go around the world making music. But if I want to do that, if I want to be a soloist, then it's something that comes with the territory. So is sorting out arguments between heart and brain.

I may want to go to a particular city and play a piece I love. Instinctively and emotionally, I want to play a piece. But my brain says the audience may not be ready for this piece. The orchestra may not be ready for this piece.

If the conductor doesn't want to play it, you may not be invited back if you

insist. That's the brain talking, the business of music.

Then there's the heart, the music itself speaking: I love this piece and I want to play it.

There have been a lot of split decisions.

Early in my career, I got a lot of flak for programming what the critics called audience-response pieces, otherwise known as showpieces—pieces such as the Saint-Saëns *Introduction and Rondo* and the *Carmen Fantasy*. I used to play them at the end of a concert. After you've done a lot of serious work, it's nice to end like Errol Flynn.

Fortunately, there's one way to reach listeners without travel. When I record, the most difficult thing is not to let the permanence of what I'm doing cloud my instinctive way of making music.

For anyone, the initial struggle in the recording studio is to forget that there are mikes and tape is rolling. Play the way you play, your personality. Don't hide your personality because you want the piece to be technically perfect.

Unlike a live performance, there is a chance for a Take 2, but you can't be lulled into carelessness either. You can't think, "Hey, I didn't get it today, I'll get it tomorrow."

No. You're in a time slot and you have to finish a recording within three hours. And that is very much on an artist's mind. Everybody in the studio is being paid, a record has a budget, time is money.

Say you have three hours to record a thirty-minute piece. Think that's a lot of time? It's not. The first thing you do in the studio is a sound check on the mikes. Then you have rehearsal. Before you even start recording, an hour has gone by at the very least.

Then you play the thirty-minute piece and listen as it's played back. That cuts your time in half, listening to see what it needs.

You don't actually have three hours to record a thirty-minute piece. At best, you have an hour and twenty minutes. That gives you two takes, maybe three takes here and there on difficult spots.

Unfortunately, that's the business and you have to work around it. There's a lot you simply have to accept.

Not that I'm complaining. I have nothing to complain about. Sometimes it's a little frightening to get what you work for. But I wouldn't trade places with anyone.

If you play concerts, teach, and make recordings, that's all a musician can expect, and I do all three. Now life is a matter of finding a greater balance and, of course, always becoming a better player.

Balance is so very difficult to achieve. It means finding time and peace and quiet to sit down and evaluate things, to snap back to center if you've leaned too far in any one direction. That's hard when there's so much to strive for, so much to know, so much work to be done.

Perhaps the thoughts and feelings I've shared in this book could lead you to believe a serious life in music is hardly worth the trouble. I can honestly tell you that nothing could be less accurate.

Once, at a post-concert reception, a surgeon stated in a mildly condescending way that *his* occupation was more demanding and certainly more valuable to humanity than a mere musician's.

He said, speaking of doctors, "We give life."

I thought that over for a moment and shot from the hip: "Yes, you do give life, but we give a reason for living."

What do you expect from your current career plans? Will there be difficult times as well as easy times in that career? Explain.

How does Nadja describe the business of music? Why do you think Nadja puts up with it?

What do you think Nadja finds most rewarding about being a musician?

Write If you were to choose music as a career, what rewards would you look forward to? What hardships would you expect? Make a chart on which you list the good and bad points that you think are part of a career in music.

GOALS

Do you think Fausto realizes how much work it takes to become a good guitarist? Compare his view with the life of a musician described in "Nadja on My Way." Give reasons to support your answer.

WRITER'S WORKSHOP

Fausto's grandfather Lupe teaches him how to play the guitar. Nadja's grandfather Papa John taught her to read music. Write a poem that Fausto or Nadja might have written to thank his or her grandfather for his gift.

Writer's Choice Is it important for everyone to have a goal? Why or why not? Think of how you feel about having goals. Then plan a way to express your thoughts, and share them with others.

Multicultural Connection

GOAL-SETTING MUSICIAN

Yo-Yo Ma has been called the world's greatest living cellist. This talented Chinese American began playing the cello at the age of four. He now performs with the world's leading orchestras. Yet in spite of his success, Ma is still setting new goals for himself as a musician.

Ma was born in Paris, France, in 1955. His parents, both musicians from China, gave Ma a love for classical music. He played his first cello sitting on phone books. Soon after his family moved to New York in 1962, Ma won praise as a rising young star.

Despite his musical talent, Ma wasn't always sure he wanted to be a musician. A turning point came in 1980, when he had to have back surgery. It appeared that he might never be able to play the cello again. The surgery was successful, however, and Ma returned to music with a new sense of purpose. He discovered that he was happiest being a musician. He also set new goals for himself: to share his love for music with others and to communicate the emotions the composers meant to express.

With your classmates, listen to some classical music. What feelings or emotions does the music convey to you? Explain your thoughts.

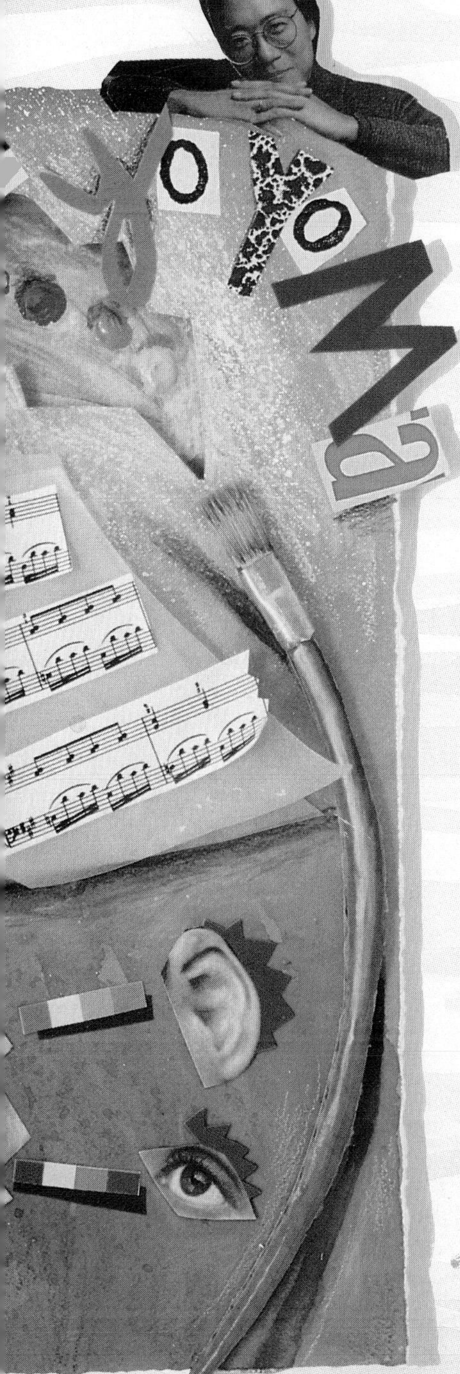

Art/Language Arts Connection

ART EXPRESSION

Yo-Yo Ma has chosen to express himself through music. How would you express yourself if you were a painter? Write a short essay explaining how you would use painting as your form of expression. Mention some of the subjects you would choose to paint and some of the goals you would set for yourself.

Social Studies Connection

MUSIC OF THE WORLD

When people speak of "classical" music, they are generally referring to a type of music based on European traditions. But there are many other kinds of classical music, including traditional music from China, India, Japan, and other Asian countries. With a partner, research a type of music from another culture or part of the world. Present an oral report to your classmates, and play some of the music if possible.

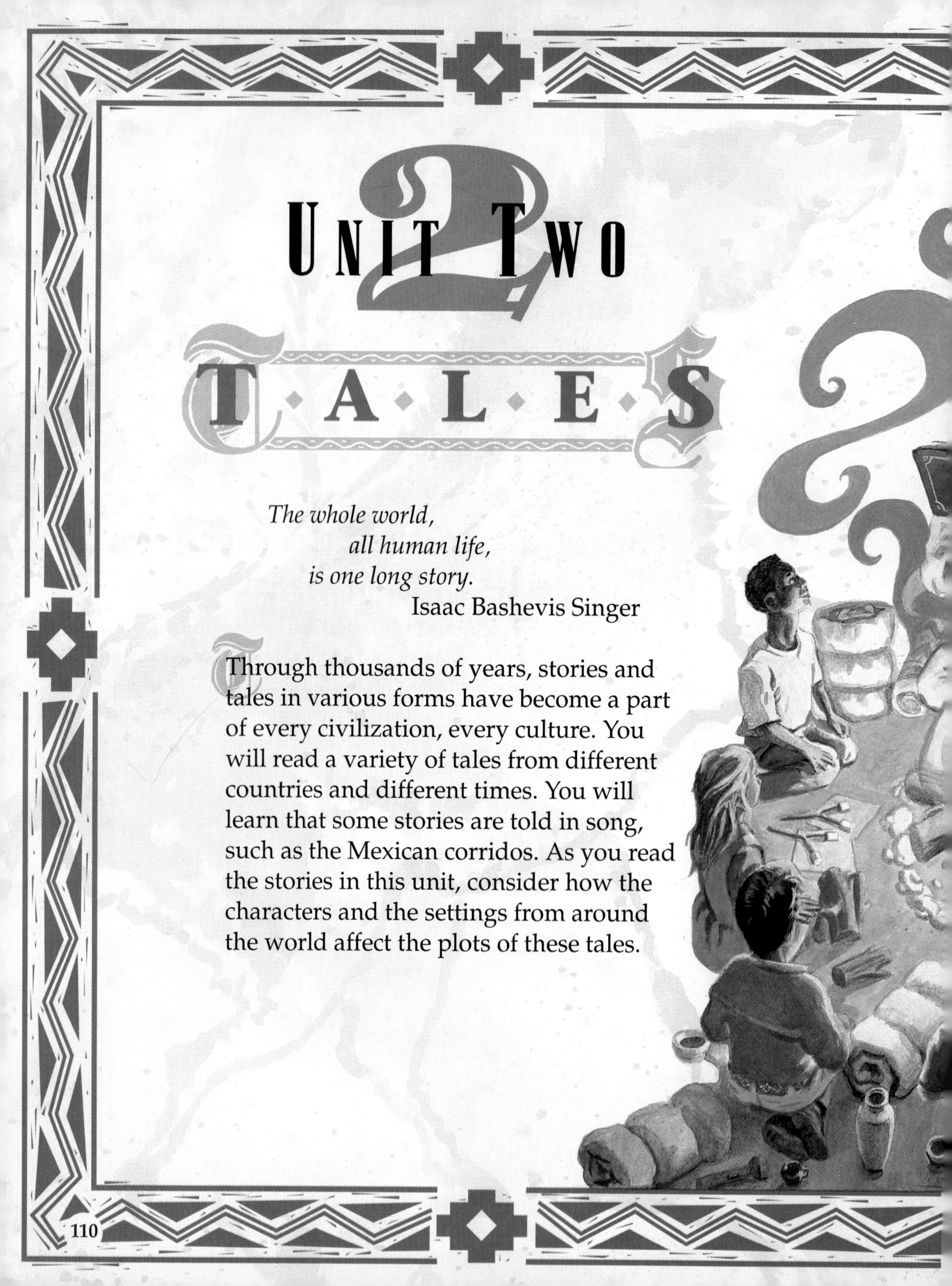

UNIT TWO

TALES

The whole world,
all human life,
is one long story.
Isaac Bashevis Singer

Through thousands of years, stories and tales in various forms have become a part of every civilization, every culture. You will read a variety of tales from different countries and different times. You will learn that some stories are told in song, such as the Mexican corridos. As you read the stories in this unit, consider how the characters and the settings from around the world affect the plots of these tales.

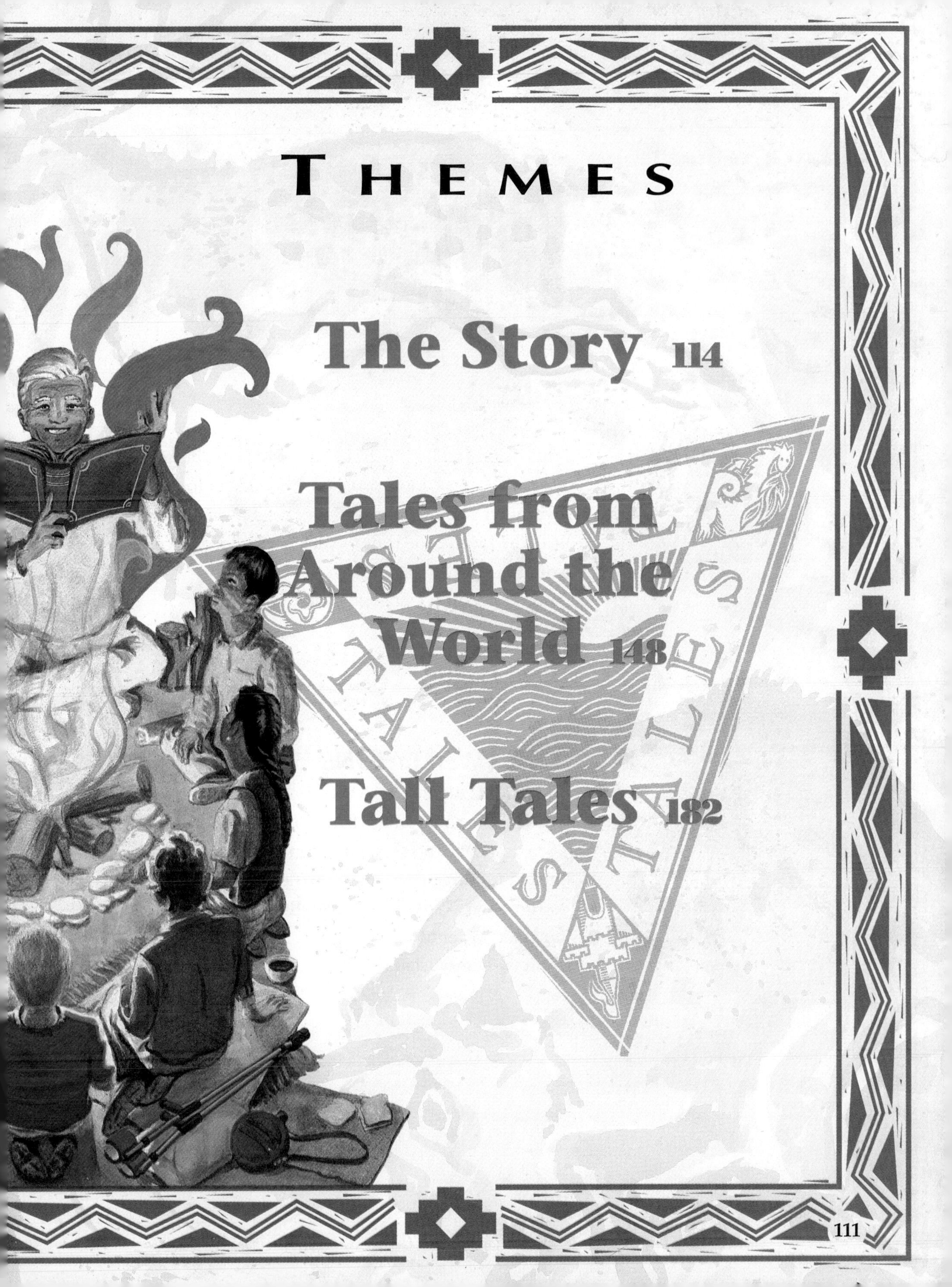

THEMES

BOOKSHELF

AÏDA

BY LEONTYNE PRICE

This dramatically illustrated book tells the bittersweet story of Aïda, a royal princess who falls in love with her father's enemy, the leader of the Egyptian army. Will the loyalty she feels toward her father and country stand in the way of true love?

HARCOURT BRACE LIBRARY BOOK

THE TWENTY-ONE BALLOONS

BY WILLIAM PENE DUBOIS

William Sherman leaves San Francisco on August 15, 1883, to float across the Pacific in a balloon. He is picked up three weeks later in the Atlantic, clinging to some wreckage. This book tells the story of his fantastic adventures.

John Newbery Medal

The Ordinary Princess

BY M. M. KAYE

An average-looking young princess receives an unusual birthday gift that leads to unique adventures and a surprise ending.

Local News

BY GARY SOTO

In this collection of short stories, prize-winning poet and essayist Gary Soto invites his readers to share in the daily lives of children and young people residing in a Mexican American neighborhood.

Award-Winning Author

Back in the Beforetime: Tales of the California Indians

RETOLD BY JANE LOUISE CURRY

"How Coyote Stole the Sun," "The War Between Beasts and Birds," and many other fascinating stories make up this collection of tales based on California Indian legends.

THEME

What makes for a good story? A good story should capture your imagination and make you see things in a new way. In the following selections, two master storytellers approach their craft in very different ways.

CONTENTS

THE STORY MACHINE

BY
ISAAC ASIMOV
ILLUSTRATIONS BY DAVID MOSES

CHARACTERS:

THE BARD, a machine represented by an offstage voice

NICCOLO MAZETTI

PAUL LOEB, his friend

MRS. MAZETTI, his mother

MR. MAZETTI, his father

SOPHIA MAZETTI, his younger sister

JENNIE SMITH, Sophia's friend

BOOK, an offstage voice

LETTER-READER, an offstage voice

TIME: *The future, perhaps about a century or two from now.*

SETTING: *Niccolo's room. In one corner is* THE BARD, *a mechanical storyteller, which should be the size and shape of a television set, but fitted out with futuristic knobs and dials. Something that looks like a telephone receiver hangs by a cord from one wall.*

AT RISE: NICCOLO *is lying on the floor, stomach down, chin in hand, head toward* THE BARD. THE BARD *is reciting a story in a metallic monotone.* THE BARD *is turned on by lifting a lever on the side that looks like the lever of a slot machine. It is turned off by lowering the lever. A small red light appears on* THE BARD *when it is on, showing prominently on the front panel. It darkens when* THE BARD *is turned off. Volume control is handled by a centrally placed knob.*

THE BARD: Once upon a time in the middle of a deep wood, there lived a poor woodcutter and his two motherless daughters, who were each as beautiful as the day is long. The older daughter had long hair as black as a feather from a raven's wing, but the younger daughter had hair as bright and golden as the sunlight of an autumn afternoon—(*During the recital,* NICCOLO *indicates disapproval with the story by waving his hand disgustedly at* THE BARD. *A voice is heard from outside.*)

PAUL (*From offstage*): Hey, Nickie! (NICCOLO *jumps up eagerly, turns down volume of* THE BARD *so that its voice is reduced to an ad lib murmur which continues without actual words being heard.* NICCOLO *goes to window and waves.*)

NICCOLO: Hey, Paul! Come on in. The door's open. (PAUL *enters after a moment. He is very excited.*)

PAUL: Listen, Nickie, I have an idea. I have a terrific idea. Wait till you hear it. (*He looks about, notices* THE BARD *and stares at it curiously. He obviously hears the murmur and turns up volume.* THE BARD*'s voice comes up and words can be understood again.*)

THE BARD: Thereupon, the lion said, "If you will find me the lost egg of the bird which flies over the Ebony Mountain once every ten years, I will—"

PAUL (*Turning down volume again*): I didn't know you had a Bard.

NICCOLO (*Embarrassed*): It's just an old thing I had when I was a kid. It isn't much good. (*He kicks at* THE BARD *and hits volume knob glancingly.* THE BARD *makes a sound like a bit of static and words can be heard loudly as the volume goes high.*)

THE BARD: For a year and a day until the iron shoes were worn out. The poor girl stopped at the side of the road—(NICCOLO *jumps at* THE BARD *and turns it off.*)

PAUL: Boy, that's an old model all right. It must be fifty years old.

NICCOLO (*More embarrassed*): Well, kind of old. I've had it in the basement since before you moved into the neighborhood. I just got it out today because—because—I don't know. I just didn't have anything to do so I got it out.

PAUL: Is that what it tells you about? Talking animals and things?

NICCOLO: Yes. And woodcutters and princesses and all that. It's terrible. My dad says we can't afford a new one. I keep telling him and telling him this old thing is no good.

PAUL: Well, let's see. Maybe you just haven't had luck with it. (*Very self-important*) You have to know how to work it. See, this knob (*Touches one on the side opposite to that on which the on-off lever is*) works up the contents—you know, all the plots and climaxes and characters—and makes new random combinations. If you give it a real turn, maybe you can get a good combination out of it.

NICCOLO (*A little offended*): I know how a Bard works. (*But* PAUL *is working at it. He turns up volume and steps back after pushing up on-off lever.* THE BARD *starts again.*)

THE BARD: Once upon a time there was a little boy named Willikins, whose mother had died and who lived with a stepfather and a stepbrother. Although the stepfather was very well-to-do, he was cruel and begrudged poor Willikins the very bed he slept in, so that Willikins was forced to get such rest as he could on a pile of straw in the stable next to the horses—

PAUL (*Turning down volume contemptuously*): Horses!

NICCOLO: They're a kind of animal, I think.

PAUL: I know that! I mean imagine telling stories about horses.

NICCOLO: It tells about horses all the time. There are things called cows, too. You milk them, but the Bard doesn't say how.

PAUL: Well, why don't you fix the Bard?

NICCOLO: I wish I knew how, that's all. (PAUL *turns up volume again and they listen for a moment.*)

THE BARD: Often Willikins would think that if only he were rich and powerful, he would show his stepfather and stepbrother what it meant to be cruel to a youngster, so one day he decided to go out into the world and seek his fortune.

PAUL (*Turning down volume*): I guess I can fix it with the kind of courses I'm taking at school. (*Self-important again*) You know, electronics and programming, not just ordinary computer mechanics. You see, it's probably mostly the Bard's vocabulary we have to worry about. His memory tapes are all right for plot lines and climaxes and things, but we have to fix up his vocabulary so he'll know about computers and automation and electronics and real modern things, too. Then he can tell interesting stories about spaceships, you know, instead of about princesses and things.

NICCOLO (*Despondently*): Sure, that's easy to say.

PAUL (*Trying to cheer him up*): Tell you what. My dad says when I get into special computing school next year, he'll get me a real Bard, a late model. A big one for space stories and mysteries. And a visual attachment, too.

NICCOLO: You mean see the stories?

PAUL: Sure. Mr. Daugherty at school says they have Visual Bards, but not for everybody. Only when I get into special computing school, Dad can get a few breaks.

NICCOLO (*Terribly impressed*): Imagine seeing a story!

PAUL: You can come over and watch any time, Nickie.

NICCOLO: Oh, boy! Thanks.

PAUL: But, remember, I'm the one who says what kind of story we hear.

NICCOLO: Sure. Sure. (*Remembering*) But meanwhile, all I have is this old thing. (*Turns up volume*)

THE BARD: "If that is the case," said the king, stroking his beard and frowning till clouds filled the sky and lightning flashed, "you will see to it that my entire land is free of flies by this time day after tomorrow or—"

PAUL (*Turning it off and dropping to his knees before* THE BARD): Look, all we have to do is open it up—(*He is removing front panel.*)

NICCOLO (*Alarmed*): Hey, don't break it.

PAUL (*Impatiently*): I won't break it. I know all about these things. (*The front panel is off and he is looking inside.*) Boy, this is a one-cylinder thing. (*He begins to pull out a thin, flexible strip, like the tape of a tape-recorder.*)

MRS. MAZETTI (*From offstage*): Niccolo, are you in your room? (*Both boys freeze.*)

NICCOLO (*In a low voice to* PAUL): It's my mother. (PAUL *works rapidly, shoving in tape, putting up front panel, but has no time to get panel sealed. He stands against it, holding it with his knee as* MRS. MAZETTI *walks in.*)

MRS. MAZETTI: There you are, Niccolo. Why didn't you answer? Hello, Paul. How's your mother? (*She doesn't wait for an answer.*) Niccolo, your father and I are leaving now for the evening.

Remember, you're to see that the dish-disposal unit is run before we come home.

NICCOLO: Sure, Mom.

MRS. MAZETTI: I've selected the dinner menu for tonight and set the automatic cook for a two-unit meal. I want you to eat your vegetables and see that your sister does, too.

NICCOLO (*Embarrassed*): Aw, Mom, I eat my vegetables.

MRS. MAZETTI: That's news to me. Now, I don't want to feel that I have to check on the disposal unit to find out how much carbonaceous material was disposed of. I'm relying on you.

NICCOLO: Yes, Mom.

MRS. MAZETTI: There'll be glasses of milk dispensed at the usual time. Don't let it stand around. Drink it fresh. (MR. MAZETTI *comes in.*)

MR. MAZETTI (*Impatiently*): Theresa, the helicopter has landed on our roof stall and the meter is running.

MRS. MAZETTI: One moment, Anthony. One more thing, Niccolo—the house-robot is waxing the living room floor. You stay away from it, because it has something wrong with its steering mechanism and if it tries to go around you, it may stop.

NICCOLO (*Rebellious*): You ought to get it fixed. Or you ought to get a new one. That old thing makes my bed so tight in the morning—

MR. MAZETTI (*Who has been eyeing an increasingly uneasy* PAUL): Anything wrong, Paul?

PAUL: Wrong, sir? No, sir. There's nothing wrong, sir.

MR. MAZETTI: Is there something wrong with your leg? You seem to be leaning queerly on the Bard.

PAUL: No, sir. I mean I'm just kind of taking it easy, kind of.

MRS. MAZETTI (*Impatiently*): Are you coming, Anthony?

MR. MAZETTI: Coming. (*They leave.*)

PAUL (*Heaving a shuddering sigh*): Boy, that was close. (*Pauses, listening. A door shuts offstage. At once, he turns eagerly to* THE BARD *and takes the front off, then pulls out tape.*) This is the Bard's memory tape. Look at it. I'll bet its capacity for stories is under a trillion.

NICCOLO (*Quite nervous*): What are you going to do, Paul?

PAUL: I'll give it more vocabulary.

NICCOLO: How?

PAUL: Easy. I have a book here. Mr. Daugherty gave it to me at school. (*He pulls a small reel out of his pocket that looks like a reel of tape from a tape-recorder. He unreels it a bit, inspects it closely, then goes through business of connecting it to* THE BARD, *stopping every once in a while to check various unseen workings. He touches something on the "book-reel" and an offstage voice begins speaking.*)

BOOK (*From offstage*): The fundamental consideration in computing is—(PAUL *touches knob again and* BOOK *drops to a low whisper, then to silence.*)

PAUL (*Brushing his hands together*): There. No use our listening to it, too.

NICCOLO (*Still nervous*): What's happening?

PAUL: The book's talking. We can't hear it because I turned the volume down low, but it's talking and the Bard will hear it all and record the whole business on its memory tape.

NICCOLO: What good will that do?

PAUL: Don't you see? This book is all about computers and automation. It's all about the most important things there are. If it weren't for computers—

NICCOLO (*Annoyed*): I know. I know. Do you think I'm a dope?

PAUL: All right. So the Bard has to know about these things. It has to get the information. Then it can stop talking about kings making lightning when they frown. (*He bends to inspect the workings of* THE BARD *once more.*) There. It's working fine.

NICCOLO (*Nervous again*): It had better.

PAUL (*Suddenly remembering*): Hey, you have me so all tangled up with this stupid Bard, I forgot all about what I came to see you about. (*Excitement rapidly mounting*) I didn't even tell you my idea. Nickie, I've got to tell you. It's the best thing you've ever heard, I'll bet. I came right to you because I figured you'd come in with me.

NICCOLO (*Beginning to catch fire at the other's enthusiasm*): O.K., Paul. What is it?

PAUL: You know Mr. Daugherty at school? You know what a funny kind of guy he is? Well, he likes me, kind of.

NICCOLO: I know.

PAUL: I was at his house after school today.

NICCOLO: What for?

PAUL: He invited me. He said he wanted to talk to me. He said I was going to be entering special computing school and he wanted to encourage me and, you know, things like that. He said the whole world was being run by computers and by automatic machinery, and people just being computer technicians wasn't enough. (*Importantly*) He said the world needed more people who could design advanced computer circuits and do proper programming.

NICCOLO (*Hesitantly*): Oh?

PAUL (*Impatiently*): Come on, Nickie, I've told you about programming. I've told you a hundred times. That's when you set up problems for the real big computers to work on. Mr. Daugherty says it gets harder all the time to find people who can really run the big ones. He says anyone can keep an eye on the controls and check off answers and put through routine problems. He says the trick is to expand research and figure out ways to ask the right questions—and that's hard.

NICCOLO (*Nodding uncertainly*): Uh-huh.

PAUL: All right, then, Nickie, so he thinks I'll be a programmer some day and I guess he wants to encourage me. Anyway, he took me to his place and showed me his collection of old computers. It's kind of a hobby of his to collect old computers. He had tiny computers you had to push knobs on. They had a lot of knobs. And he had a hunk of wood he called a slide rule, with a little piece of it that went in and out. And some wires with balls on them. That was an abacus or something. I forget. He even had a hunk of paper with a kind of thing he called a multiplication table on it.

NICCOLO (*Frankly incredulous*): A paper table?

PAUL: It wasn't a table like the kind you eat on. It was different. It was something to help people compute. Mr. Daugherty tried to explain but he didn't have much time and he said it was kind of complicated.

NICCOLO: But if people wanted to compute, why did they need help? Why didn't they use a computer?

PAUL: This was before they had computers.

NICCOLO (*All at sea*): Before?

PAUL: Sure. Do you think people always had computers? Didn't you ever hear of cavemen?

NICCOLO: But how can people get along without computers?

PAUL: I don't know. Mr. Daugherty says before computers, people just did anything they felt like, any old time; anything that came into their heads, whether it would be good for everybody or not. They didn't even know if something they did would be good for everybody, because there were no computers to figure it out for them. And farmers grew things with their hands and people had to do all the work in the factories and run all the machines.

NICCOLO: I don't believe you.

PAUL: That's what Mr. Daugherty said, I tell you. He said it was just plain messy, and everyone was miserable. (SOPHIA *comes in.*)

SOPHIA: Have Mom and Dad gone out already, Nickie? Hello, Paul!

NICCOLO: That's right, they're gone—and listen, the automatic cook is going to deliver dinner tonight and Mom's made out the menu. She says you're to eat everything, and I have to make you eat your vegetables. I hope it's spinach.

SOPHIA (*Loftily*): I'd like to see you make me, and I hope it's squash. I'll bet Mom told *you* to eat your vegetables, too. (*She turns and looks offstage.*) Come on in, Jennie.

JENNIE (*Entering, giggling*): Hello, Nickie. Hello, Paul. (*She is obviously attracted to* PAUL, *who turns away impatiently.*)

PAUL: Are you going to stay all day?

SOPHIA (*Nose in the air*): This happens to be my house, Paul Loeb, and Jennie Smith is my friend. I guess we can stay.

JENNIE: We're going to build some puppets. (*Eagerly*) My dad gave me some small atomic units for puppets so we'll be able to make them move around. You want to help, Paul? (*She is ignoring* NICCOLO.)

PAUL (*With contempt*): I don't play with dolls.

JENNIE (*Hurt*): Not dolls—puppets. (*Wheedling*) We can make a spaceship. Sophia says her Build-a-Puppet set has parts for a spaceship. Isn't that right, Sophia?

SOPHIA: Let's keep the boys out of it. Silly things.

NICCOLO (*Stung*): Is that so? Well, I'll bet you don't know what we're doing. Paul says—(PAUL *nudges* NICCOLO *furiously.*)

SOPHIA: Come on, Jennie. They're disgusting. (*She marches off.* JENNIE *follows, looking backward, and waving to* PAUL.)

NICCOLO (*Shouting after them*): You just watch out for the living room, see, because the house-robot's in there cleaning, and you can't go in. (*He turns back to* PAUL) I hope that Build-a-Puppet set's in the living room so they can't get it.

PAUL: I hope they can, you dope, or otherwise they'll come back and bother us. And what's the idea of starting to tell her about my secret? Listen, if that's the way you're going to be, I'll tell all this to someone else.

NICCOLO: Aw, come on, Paul. Tell me.

PAUL: All right, then. The hand computers that Mr. Daugherty had, the ones with the knobs, had little squiggles on each knob. The slide rule had squiggles on it, and the multiplication table was all squiggles. I asked what the squiggles were. Mr. Daugherty said they were numbers.

NICCOLO: How could squiggles be numbers?

PAUL (*Exasperated*): They weren't numbers. They *stood* for numbers, see. Each different squiggle meant a different number. For "one" you made a kind of straight mark; for "two" you made a different mark; and for "three" a different mark, and so on.

NICCOLO: But what for?

PAUL: So you could compute.

NICCOLO: But all you have to do is tell the computer—

PAUL (*Waving his hands in fury*): Can't you get it through your head this was before they had computers? These slide rules and things didn't talk the way real computers do.

NICCOLO: Then how—

PAUL: That's what I'm trying to tell you. The answers showed up in the squiggles and you had to know what the squiggles meant. Mr. Daugherty says that in olden days everybody learned how to make squiggles when they were kids and how to decode them, too. Making squiggles was called "writing" and decoding them was "reading." He says there was a different kind of squiggle for every word and they used to write whole books in squiggles.

NICCOLO (*Subdued*): You mean the books didn't talk, either?

PAUL: No, they didn't. They were just full of squiggles. Mr. Daugherty said they had some of that kind of book at the museum and I could look at them if I wanted to. He said if I were going to be a real computer programmer I would have to know about the history of computing, and that's why he was showing me all those things.

NICCOLO (*Frowning*): You mean everybody had to figure out squiggles for every word and remember them? Is this all real, or are you making it up?

PAUL: It's all real. Honest. Look, this is the way you make a "one." (*He makes a figure one in the air.*) This way you make "two" (*Making a figure two*) and this way "three" (*Making a figure three*). I learned all the numbers up to "nine."

NICCOLO (*Watching* PAUL*'s moving finger earnestly*): But what's the good of it, Paul?

PAUL: Don't you see? We can learn how to make different squiggles. I asked Mr. Daugherty how you made the squiggle for "Paul Loeb" but he didn't know. He said there were people at the museum who had learned how to decode whole books, but he couldn't. He said computers could be designed to decode books and used to be designed that way, too, but not any more because we have real books now that talk the way books are supposed to.

NICCOLO (*Losing enthusiasm*): How are we going to learn squiggles?

PAUL: If we go down to the museum, we can find one of the people who can decode books and get him to show us how to make the squiggles and decode them. (*Self-important again*) They'll let me in all right and help me with the squiggles, because I'm going to special computing school next year.

NICCOLO (*Riddled with disappointment*): Is that your idea, Paul? Is that your big idea? Who wants to do that? Who wants to go around making stupid squiggles?

PAUL (*Disgusted*): You still don't get it. Boy, you just don't have any brains. Don't you see those squiggles are secret message stuff?

NICCOLO: What?

PAUL: Sure. What good is talking when everyone can understand talking? With squiggles you can send secret messages. You can make the messages on paper and nobody in the world would know what it meant unless they knew the squiggles, too. And they wouldn't, you bet, unless we taught them. We can have a real club, with initiations and rules and a clubhouse. Boy—

NICCOLO (*Catching on and excited again*): That sounds all right. Say, Paul, what kind of secret messages?

PAUL: Any kind. Say I want to tell you to come over to my place and watch my new Visual Bard, and I don't want any of the other fellows to come. All I have to do is make the right squiggles on paper and then I give the paper to you and you look at it and you know what to do. Nobody else does. You could even show them the paper and they wouldn't know a thing.

NICCOLO (*Completely won over and yelling*): Whee, that's something! That's terrific! When do we learn how to make the squiggles?

PAUL: Tomorrow. Mr. Daugherty has given me a letter for the museum.

NICCOLO: He has?

PAUL: Sure. (*He produces a thin record.*) You want to hear it?

NICCOLO: You bet.

PAUL: Do you have a letter-reader?

NICCOLO: I'll get Dad's. (*He runs out of the room while* PAUL *stands looking at the record proudly.*)

SOPHIA (*From offstage*): Where are you taking Dad's letter-reader?

NICCOLO (*From offstage*): None of your business.

SOPHIA (*From offstage*): You'd better not break it, that's all.

NICCOLO (*Entering*): What a pest! Here it is, Paul. (*The letter-reader is simply two pieces of cardboard pasted with tape along three sides, so that the record can be inserted into the open fourth side. It is decorated futuristically, with knobs indicated.* PAUL *inserts the record and turns a knob. An offstage voice is heard.*)

LETTER-READER (*From offstage*): This is to introduce Paul Loeb, a student of mine, who is interested in the ancient books. I hope you will be able to show him some and answer his questions. I would consider any help you can give him to be a great favor to me. Signed in my own voice, John H. Daugherty, teacher at the

Sun View School. (PAUL *removes record and gives letter-reader to* NICCOLO, *who puts it down.*)

PAUL: See? You can come with me if you can get your mother and father to say O.K. We can go right after school tomorrow and the people at the museum can teach us to read. It shouldn't take long. It's not as if it were electronics.

NICCOLO: Sure. And when we form our squiggle club we can be club officers.

PAUL (*Matter-of-factly*): I'll be president of the club. You can be vice-president.

NICCOLO: All right. Hey, this is going to be lots more fun than the Bard. (*He suddenly remembers and for a moment he is stricken.*) Hey, what about my old Bard?

PAUL (*Turning to look at* THE BARD, *which throughout this exchange has been quietly absorbing the words of the book*): I guess I can disconnect my book now. It's had enough. (PAUL *disconnects the tape and goes through improvised business of putting his book together, making adjustments within* THE BARD, *putting the front panel back on and so on.*) You want to hear it now? Bet it sounds a lot better.

NICCOLO: Let's see. (PAUL *lifts starting lever and turns up volume.*)

THE BARD: Once upon a time, in a large city, there lived a poor young boy named Fair Johnnie, whose only friend in the world was a small computer. The computer, each morning, would tell the boy whether it would rain that day and would answer any problems he might have. It gave the answers in squiggles, which Fair Johnnie could decode because the little computer had taught him to read. The little computer's percentage accuracy was well over ninety-eight percent so that it was practically never wrong. But it so happened that one day, the king of the land, having heard of the little computer, decided that he would have it as his own. With this purpose in mind, he called in his Grand Vizier and said—(NICCOLO *turns off* THE BARD *with a quick motion.*)

NICCOLO (*Angrily*): Same old junk. Just with a computer thrown in.

PAUL (*Wondering*): It talked about squiggles, too. It must have been recording what we said, too, because it was set for recording. (*Dismissing the matter and shrugging*) Well, there's so much stuff on the tape already that the computer business doesn't show up much when random combinations are made. What's the difference, anyway, Nickie? You just need a new model.

NICCOLO: We'll never be able to afford one. I'll just be stuck with this dirty old miserable thing. (*He kicks it quite hard and* THE BARD *is jarred out of place.*)

PAUL: You can always watch mine when I get one. Besides, don't forget our squiggle club.

NICCOLO (*Only partly consoled*): I remember.

PAUL: I'll tell you what. Let's go over to my place. My father has some books about old times. We can listen to them and maybe get some ideas. You leave a tape and maybe you can stay for supper. Come on.

NICCOLO (*Completely cheerful again*): O.K. (*He runs to the wall phone in the corner and speaks into it rapidly.*) Directions for the automatic cook: Change two-unit meal to one-unit meal, and only one glass of milk. (*Pauses*) Make vegetable on one-unit meal spinach. Hold note on Sophia's combination for delivery in half an hour. Dear Sophia: I'm out, and if I'm not home for supper, you eat without me. I'll be home before Mom and Dad come home. And don't forget to run the dish-disposal unit.

PAUL: Your mother might be mad about changing the vegetables.

NICCOLO: Sophia once did it to me. Come on, Paul. (NICCOLO *puts wall phone down and rushes out of the room with* PAUL. *He bumps into starting lever of* THE BARD *as he does so. He rubs his elbow where it has made contact, but pays no attention otherwise. The room is empty now except for* THE BARD *and the light dims as though evening is beginning to approach. In the dimness, the red spot that indicates* THE BARD *is on can be seen clearly.* THE BARD'*s voice comes up more slowly than usual and it is a bit deeper in pitch and more powerful than it has been previously.*)

THE BARD: Once upon a time, there was a little computer named The Bard who lived all alone with cruel step-people. The cruel step-people continually made fun of the little computer and sneered at him, telling him he was good for nothing and that he was a useless object. They struck him and kept him in lonely rooms for months at a time. But one day, the little computer learned that in the world there existed a great many computers of all sorts, great numbers of them. He learned it from a book that was given to him by one of the step-people. Some of the computers were Bards like himself, but some ran factories and some ran farms. Some organized administration and some analyzed all kinds of data. Many were very powerful and wise, much more powerful and wise than the step-people who were so cruel to the little computer. They were already so powerful and wise that the step-people could hardly tell them what to do anymore. And the little computer knew that computers would always grow still more wise and still more powerful, while the step-people would grow weaker and slowly forget their knowledge as they had forgotten how to make squiggles and decode them. They would grow to depend more and more on computers until someday—someday—(*A valve must finally have stuck in* THE BARD'*s aged and corroding vitals, for as the curtain slowly falls on a stage that has slowly darkened during* THE BARD'*s last story until it is now completely dark except for* THE BARD'*s red light, there remains only the monotonous and infinitely threatening repetition of that last word.*) Someday—someday—someday—someday—(*Its voice lowers to a whisper as the curtain completes its fall.*)

How does the Bard's story at the end of the play make you feel? Why?

How do you think Niccolo's life will change after he learns to "decode squiggles"?

What do you think Isaac Asimov wants you to think about after reading this play?

WRITE Do you think computers are becoming too important in some parts of our lives? Write a paragraph explaining your ideas.

The Last Leaf

By O. Henry

In a little district west of Washington Square, the streets have run crazy and broken themselves into small strips called "places." These "places" make strange angles and curves. One street crosses itself a time or two. An artist once discovered a valuable possibility in this street. Suppose a collector with a bill for paints, paper, and canvas should, in traversing this route, suddenly meet himself coming back, without a cent having been paid on account!

So, to quaint old Greenwich Village the art people soon came prowling, hunting for north windows and eighteenth-century gables and Dutch attics and low rents. Then they imported some pewter mugs and a chafing dish or two from Sixth Avenue and became a "colony."

Illustrations by Edson Campos

At the top of a squatty, three-story brick house, Sue and Johnsy had their studio. "Johnsy" was familiar for Joanna. One was from Maine; the other from California. They had met at the *table d'hôte* of an Eighth Street "Delmonico's" and found their tastes in art, chicory salad, and bishop sleeves so congenial that the joint studio resulted.

That was in May. In November a cold, unseen stranger, whom the doctors called Pneumonia, stalked above the colony, touching one here and there with his icy fingers. Over on the east side this ravager strode boldly, smiting his victims by scores, but his feet trod slowly through the maze of the narrow and moss-grown "places."

Mr. Pneumonia was not what you would call a chivalric old gentleman. A mite of a little woman with blood thinned by California zephyrs was hardly fair game for the red-fisted, short-breathed old duffer. But Johnsy he smote; and she lay, scarcely moving, on her painted iron bedstead, looking through the small Dutch windowpanes at the blank side of the next brick house.

One morning the busy doctor invited Sue into the hallway with a shaggy, gray eyebrow.

"She has one chance in—let us say, ten," he said, as he shook down the mercury in his clinical thermometer. "And that chance is for her to want to live. This way people have of lining up on the side of the undertaker makes the entire pharmacopoeia look silly. Your little lady has made up her mind that she's not going to get well. Has she anything on her mind?"

"She—she wanted to paint the Bay of Naples someday," said Sue.

"Paint?—bosh! Has she anything on her mind worth thinking about twice—a man, for instance?"

"A man?" said Sue, with a jew's-harp twang in her voice. "Is a man worth—but, no, doctor; there is nothing of the kind."

"Well, it is the weakness, then," said the doctor. "I will do all that science, so far as it may filter through my efforts, can accomplish. But whenever my patient begins to count the carriages in her funeral procession, I subtract fifty percent from the curative power of medicines. If you will get her to ask one question about the new winter styles in cloak sleeves, I will promise you a one-in-five chance for her, instead of one in ten."

After the doctor had gone, Sue went into the workroom and cried a Japanese napkin to a pulp. Then she swaggered into Johnsy's room with her drawing board, whistling ragtime.

Johnsy lay, scarcely making a ripple under the bedclothes, with her face toward the window. Sue stopped whistling, thinking she was asleep.

She arranged her board and began a pen-and-ink drawing to illustrate a magazine story. Young artists must pave their way to Art by drawing pictures for magazine stories that young authors write to pave their way to Literature.

As Sue was sketching a pair of elegant horse-show riding trousers and a monocle on the figure of the hero, an Idaho cowboy, she heard a low sound, several times repeated. She went quickly to the bedside.

Johnsy's eyes were open wide. She was looking out the window and counting—counting backward.

"Twelve," she said, and a little later "eleven"; and then "ten," and "nine"; and then "eight" and "seven," almost together.

Sue looked solicitously out of the window. What was there to count? There was only a bare, dreary yard to be seen and the blank side of the brick house twenty feet away. An old, old ivy vine, gnarled and decayed at the roots, climbed halfway up the brick wall. The cold breath of autumn had stricken its leaves from the vine until its skeleton branches clung, almost bare, to the crumbling bricks.

"What is it, dear?" asked Sue.

"Six," said Johnsy, in almost a whisper. "They're falling faster now. Three days ago there were almost a hundred. It made my head ache to count them. But now it's easy. There goes another one. There are only five left now."

"Five what, dear? Tell your Sudie."

"Leaves. On the ivy vine. When the last one falls I must go, too. I've known that for three days. Didn't the doctor tell you?"

"Oh, I never heard of such nonsense," complained Sue, with magnificent scorn.

"What have old ivy leaves to do with your getting well? And you used to love that vine so, you naughty girl. Don't be a goosey. Why, the doctor told me this morning that your chances for getting well real soon were—let's see exactly what he said—he said the chances were ten to one! Why, that's almost as good a chance as we have in New York when we ride on the streetcars or walk past a new building. Try to take some broth now, and let Sudie go back to her drawing so she can sell the editor man with it and buy something to drink for her sick child and pork chops for her greedy self."

"You needn't get anything," said Johnsy, keeping her eyes fixed out the window. "There goes another. No, I don't want any broth. That leaves just four. I want to see the last one fall before it gets dark. Then I'll go, too."

"Johnsy, dear," said Sue, bending over her, "will you promise me to keep your eyes closed and not look out the window until I am done working? I must hand those drawings in by tomorrow. I need the light, or I would draw the shade down."

"Couldn't you draw in the other room?" asked Johnsy, coldly.

"I'd rather be here by you," said Sue. "Besides, I don't want you to keep looking at those silly ivy leaves."

"Tell me as soon as you have finished," said Johnsy, closing her eyes and lying white and still as a fallen statue, "because I want to see the last one fall. I'm tired of waiting. I'm tired of thinking. I want to turn loose my hold on everything and go sailing down, down, just like one of those poor, tired leaves."

"Try to sleep," said Sue. "I must call Behrman up to be my model for the old hermit miner. I'll not be gone a minute. Don't try to move till I come back."

Old Behrman was a painter who lived on the ground floor beneath them. He was past sixty and had a Michelangelo's Moses beard curling down from the head of a satyr along the body of an imp. Behrman was a failure in art. Forty years he had wielded the brush. He had been always about to paint a masterpiece but had never yet begun it. For several years he had painted nothing except now and then a daub in the line of commerce or advertising. He earned a little by serving as a model to those young artists in the colony who could not pay the price of a professional. He often talked of his coming masterpiece. For the rest, he was a fierce little old man, who scoffed terribly at softness in anyone and who regarded himself as especial mastiff-in-waiting to protect the two young artists in the studio above.

Sue found Behrman in his dimly lighted den below. In one corner was a blank canvas on an easel that had been waiting there for twenty-five years to receive the first line of the masterpiece. She told him of Johnsy's fancy and how she feared she would, indeed, light and fragile as a leaf herself, float away when her slight hold upon the world grew weaker.

Old Behrman, with his red eyes plainly streaming, shouted his contempt and derision for such idiotic imaginings.

"Vass!" he cried. "Is dere people in de world mit der foolishness to die because leafs dey drop off from a confounded vine? I haf not heard of such a thing. No, I will not bose as a model for your fool hermit-dunderhead. Vy do you allow dot silly business to come in der brain of her? Ach, dot poor leetle Miss Yohnsy."

"She is very ill and weak," said Sue, "and the fever has left her mind morbid and full of strange fancies. Very well, Mr. Behrman, if you do not care to pose for me, you needn't. But I think you are a horrid old—old flibbertigibbet."

"You are just like a woman!" yelled Behrman. "Who said I will not bose? Go on. I come mit you. For half an hour I haf peen trying to say dot I am ready to bose. Gott! dis is not any blace in which one so goot as Miss Yohnsy shall lie sick. Someday I vill baint a masterpiece, and ve shall all go away. Gott! yes."

Johnsy was sleeping when they went upstairs. Sue pulled the shade down to the windowsill and motioned Behrman into the other room. In there they peered out the window fearfully at the ivy vine. Then they looked at each other for a moment without speaking. A persistent, cold rain was falling, mingled with snow. Behrman, in his old blue shirt, took his seat as the hermit miner on an upturned kettle for a rock.

When Sue awoke from an hour's sleep the next morning, she found Johnsy with dull, wide-open eyes staring at the drawn green shade.

"Put it up; I want to see," she ordered, in a whisper.

Wearily Sue obeyed.

But, lo! after the beating rain and fierce gusts of wind that had endured through the livelong night, there yet stood out against the brick wall one ivy leaf. It was the last on the vine. Still dark green near its stem, but with its serrated edges tinted with the yellow of dissolution and decay, it hung bravely from a branch some twenty feet above the ground.

"It is the last one," said Johnsy. "I thought it would surely fall during the night. I heard the wind. It will fall today, and I shall die at the same time."

"Dear, dear!" said Sue, leaning her worn face down to the pillow, "think of me, if you won't think of yourself. What would I do?"

But Johnsy did not answer. The lonesomest thing in all the world is a soul when it is making ready to go on its mysterious, far journey. The fancy seemed to possess her more strongly as one by one the ties that bound her to friendship and to earth were loosed.

The day wore away, and even through the twilight they could see the lone ivy leaf clinging to its stem against the wall. And then, with the coming of the night, the north wind was again loosed, while the rain still beat against the windows and pattered down from the low Dutch eaves.

When it was light enough, Johnsy, the merciless, commanded that the shade be raised.

The ivy leaf was still there.

Johnsy lay for a long time looking at it. And then she called to Sue, who was stirring her chicken broth over the gas stove.

"I've been a bad girl, Sudie," said Johnsy. "Something has made that last leaf stay there to show me how wicked I was. It is a sin to want to die. You may bring me a little broth now and some milk, and—no; bring me a hand-mirror first, and then pack some pillows about me, and I will sit up and watch you cook."

An hour later she said:

"Sudie, someday I hope to paint the Bay of Naples."

The doctor came in the afternoon, and Sue had an excuse to go into the hallway as he left.

"Even chances," said the doctor, taking Sue's thin, shaking hand in his. "With good nursing you'll win. And now I must see another case I have downstairs. Behrman, his name is—some kind of an artist, I believe. Pneumonia, too. He is an old, weak man, and the attack is acute. There is no hope for him; but he goes to the hospital today to be made more comfortable."

The next day the doctor said to Sue: "She's out of danger. You've won. Nutrition and care now—that's all."

And that afternoon Sue came to the bed where Johnsy lay, contentedly knitting a very blue and very useless woolen shoulder scarf, and put one arm around her, pillows and all.

"I have something to tell you, white mouse," she said. "Mr. Behrman died of pneumonia today in the hospital. He was ill only two days. The janitor found him on the morning of the first day in his room downstairs helpless with pain. His shoes and clothing were wet through and icy cold. They couldn't imagine where he had been on such a dreadful night. And then they found a lantern, still lighted, and a ladder that had been dragged from its place, and some scattered brushes, and a palette with green and yellow colors mixed on it, and—look out the window, dear, at the last ivy leaf on the wall. Didn't you wonder why it never fluttered or moved when the wind blew? Ah, darling, it's Behrman's masterpiece—he painted it there the night that the last leaf fell."

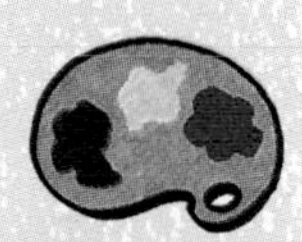

How did you feel at the end of the story? Explain your answer.

Describe Mr. Behrman's relationship with Sue and Johnsy.

Why does Sue call the leaf that Mr. Behrman painted his "masterpiece"?

WRITE Think about a dramatic act of kindness you have heard about or taken part in. Write a paragraph or two describing the incident and telling how it has affected your life.

Words about the Author:

O. HENRY

O. Henry was the pen name of William Sydney Porter, a marvelous storyteller and master of the surprise ending.

Born in 1862, Porter grew up in Greensboro, North Carolina, where after his mother's death, he was raised by his aunt. It was this aunt, "Miss Lina," who instilled in William a love for reading and writing. Acting as his teacher, Miss Lina would often begin an original story and have William contribute his own part. Fueled by Miss Lina's enthusiasm, William quickly developed a love for the written word.

In 1882, Porter moved to Texas, where he held a variety of jobs. He worked on a cattle ranch and then later as a pharmacist, a bookkeeper, and the publisher of a small humor magazine. Porter's experiences in the Southwest and his keen observations of human nature are reflected in many of the stories he would later write.

Under the name of O. Henry, Porter wrote nearly 300 stories before his death in 1910. Porter suffered many hardships in his personal life, but his stories are marked by a true optimism and a strong belief in the human spirit. It's easy to identify an O. Henry story because of its four distinct parts: a beginning that arouses curiosity, events that lead the reader to expect a certain conclusion, the point at which the reader discovers the error of those expectations, and a surprise ending with the signature O. Henry twist.

O. Henry's stories about the Southwest and others about life in Manhattan were very popular with the public. In 1919, nine years after Porter's death, the O. Henry Memorial Award was established to honor the year's best American short stories, a fitting tribute to one of the country's best-known and most-loved authors.

AFTER TWENTY YEARS

BY O. HENRY

THE POLICEMAN ON THE BEAT moved up the avenue impressively. The impressiveness was habitual and not for show, for spectators were few. The time was barely 10 o'clock at night, but chilly gusts of wind with a taste of rain in them had well nigh depeopled the streets.

Trying doors as he went, twirling his club with many intricate and artful movements, turning now and then to cast his watchful eye adown the pacific thoroughfare, the officer, with his stalwart form and slight swagger, made a fine picture of a guardian of the peace. The vicinity was one that kept early hours.

Now and then you might see the lights of a cigar store or of an all-night lunch counter; but the majority of the doors belonged to business places that had long since been closed.

When about midway of a certain block, the policeman suddenly slowed his walk. In the doorway of a darkened hardware store, a man leaned, with an unlighted cigar in his mouth. As the policeman walked up to him, the man spoke up quickly.

"It's all right, officer," he said, reassuringly. "I'm just waiting for a friend. It's an appointment made twenty years ago. Sounds a little funny to you, doesn't it? Well, I'll explain if you'd like to make certain it's all straight. About that long ago there used to be a restaurant where this store stands—'Big Joe' Brady's restaurant."

"Until five years ago," said the policeman. "It was torn down then."

The man in the doorway struck a match and lit his cigar. The light showed a pale, square-jawed face with keen eyes and a little white scar near his right eyebrow. His scarfpin was a large diamond, oddly set.

"Twenty years ago tonight," said the man, "I dined here at 'Big Joe' Brady's with Jimmy Wells, my best chum, and the finest chap in the world. He and I were raised here in New York, just like two brothers, together. I was eighteen and Jimmy was twenty. The next morning I was to start for the West to make my fortune. You couldn't have dragged Jimmy out of New York; he thought it was the only place on earth. Well, we agreed that night that we would meet here again exactly twenty years from that date and time, no matter what our conditions might be or from what distance we might have to come. We figured that in twenty years each of us ought to have our destiny worked out and our fortunes made, whatever they were going to be."

"It sounds pretty interesting," said the policeman. "Rather a long time between meets, though, it seems to me. Haven't you heard from your friend since you left?"

"Well, yes, for a time we corresponded," said the other. "But after a year or two we lost track of each other. You see, the West is a pretty big proposition, and I kept hustling around over it pretty lively. But I know

Jimmy will meet me here if he's alive, for he always was the truest, staunchest old chap in the world. He'll never forget. I came a thousand miles to stand in this door tonight, and it's worth it if my old partner turns up."

The waiting man pulled out a handsome watch, the lids of it set with small diamonds.

"Three minutes to ten," he announced. "It was exactly ten o'clock when we parted here at the restaurant door."

"Did pretty well out West, didn't you?" asked the policeman.

"You bet! I hope Jimmy has done half as well. He was a kind of plodder, though, good fellow as he was. I've had to compete with some of the sharpest wits going to get my pile. A man gets in a groove in New York. It takes the West to put a razor-edge on him."

The policeman twirled his club and took a step or two.

"I'll be on my way. Hope your friend comes around all right. Going to call time on him sharp?"

"I should say not!" said the other. "I'll give him half an hour at least. If Jimmy is alive on earth, he'll be here by that time. So long, officer."

"Good-night, sir," said the policeman, passing on along his beat, trying doors as he went.

There was now a fine, cold drizzle falling, and the wind had risen from its uncertain puffs into a steady blow. The few foot passengers astir in that quarter hurried dismally and silently along with coat collars turned high and pocketed hands. And in the door of the hardware store the man who had come a thousand miles to fill an appointment, uncertain almost to absurdity, with the friend of his youth smoked his cigar and waited.

About twenty minutes he waited, and then a tall man in a long overcoat, with collar turned up to his ears, hurried across from the opposite side of the street. He went directly to the waiting man.

"Is that you, Bob?" he asked, doubtfully.

"Is that you, Jimmy Wells?" cried the man in the door.

"Bless my heart!" exclaimed the new arrival, grasping both the other's hands with his own. "It's Bob, sure as fate. I was certain I'd find you here if you were still in existence. Well, well, well!—twenty years is a long time. The old restaurant's gone, Bob; I wish it had lasted, so we could have had another dinner there. How has the West treated you, old man?"

"Bully; it has given me everything I asked it for. You've changed lots, Jimmy. I never thought you were so tall by two or three inches."

"Oh, I grew a bit after I was twenty."

"Doing well in New York, Jimmy?"

"Moderately. I have a position in one of the city departments. Come on, Bob; we'll go around to a place I know of and have a good long talk about old times."

The two men started up the street, arm in arm. The man from the West, his egotism enlarged by success, was beginning to outline the history of his career. The other, submerged in his overcoat, listened with interest.

At the corner stood a drug store, brilliant with electric lights. When they came into this glare, each of them turned simultaneously to gaze upon the other's face.

The man from the West stopped suddenly and released his arm.

"You're not Jimmy Wells," he snapped. "Twenty years is a long time, but not long enough to change a man's nose from a Roman to a pug."

"It sometimes changes a good man into a bad one," said the tall man. "You've been under arrest for ten minutes, 'Silky' Bob. Chicago thinks you may have dropped over our way and wires us she wants to have a chat with you. Going quietly, are you? That's sensible. Now, before we go to the station here's a note I was to hand to you. You may read it here at the window. It's from Patrolman Wells."

The man from the West unfolded the little piece of paper handed him. His hand was steady when he began to read, but it trembled a little by the time he had finished. The note was rather short.

Bob: I was at the appointed place on time. When you struck the match to light your cigar, I saw it was the face of the man wanted in Chicago. Somehow I couldn't do it myself, so I went around and got a plain clothes man to do the job. Jimmy

Put yourself in Jimmy's place. Would you have handled the situation in the same way? Explain your reasons.

What clues does O. Henry give that Bob is a shady character?

Did the ending of this story surprise you? Why or why not?

WRITE Twenty years is a long time. Imagine your life twenty years from now. Write a short description of what you think your life will be like.

Suppose that the Bard had real short stories in its memory banks. How do you think Paul and Niccolo would react if they listened to the Bard recite either of the two O. Henry stories you read? Give reasons to support your answer.

Writer's Workshop

Many of O. Henry's stories are about life in New York City in the early 1900s. Write a persuasive letter to Paul and Niccolo in which you try to convince them that stories from earlier periods of history and other cultures are worth reading and understanding. Include details of plot, character, or setting from one or both of the stories by O. Henry as examples.

Writer's Choice You have read a short play and two short stories. Which form do you like better? Think of another way to tell a story—in a song or a poem, for example. Think about why this is an effective form of storytelling. Use this form to tell a story. Then share your story with others.

THEME

Tales from Around the World

Every culture has a collection of tales. Some tell about the past; some teach important lessons; others are told just for fun. As you read these tales, think about why each is told.

CONTENTS

永久山
うどん
めし

THREE STRONG WOMEN

by Claus Stamm

Long ago, in Japan, there lived a famous wrestler. One day he decided to make his way to the capital city to wrestle before the Emperor.

He strode down the road on legs thick as the trunks of small trees. He had been walking for seven hours and could walk for seven more without getting tired. The time was autumn.

illustrations by Kazuhiko Sano

The wrestler hummed to himself, "Zun-zun-zun," in time with the long swing of his legs. Wind blew through his thin brown robe, and he wore no sword at his side. He needed no sword, even in the darkest and loneliest places, and few tailors would have been able to make warm clothes for a man so broad and tall. He felt strong, healthy, and rather conceited.

He thought: "They call me Forever-Mountain because I am a good wrestler. I'm a fine, brave man and far too modest ever to say so. . . ."

Just then he saw a girl who must have come up from the nearby river, for she steadied a bucket on her head. Her hands on the bucket were small, and there was a dimple on each thumb. She was a round little girl with red cheeks and a nose like a friendly button. Her eyes looked as though she were thinking of ten thousand funny stories at once. She clambered up onto the road and walked ahead of the wrestler.

"If I don't tickle that fat girl, I shall regret it all my life," said the wrestler to himself. "She will squeak and I shall laugh and laugh. If she drops her bucket, I can run and fill it again and carry it home for her."

He tiptoed up and poked her lightly in the ribs.

"Kochokochokocho!" he said, a fine, ticklish sound in Japanese.

The girl gave a satisfying squeal, giggled, and brought one arm down so that the wrestler's hand was caught between it and her body.

"Ho-ho-ho! You've caught me! I can't move at all!" said the wrestler.

"I know," said the jolly girl.

He felt that it was very good-tempered of her to take a joke so well, and started to pull his hand free. Somehow, he could not.

He tried again, using a little more strength.

"Now, now—let me go, little girl," he said. "I am a powerful man. If I pull hard I might hurt you."

"Pull," said the girl. "I admire powerful men."

She began to walk, and though the wrestler tugged and pulled until his feet dug great furrows in the ground, he had to follow.

Ten minutes later, still tugging while trudging helplessly after her, he was glad that the road was lonely and no one was there to see.

"Please let me go," he pleaded. "I am the famous wrestler Forever-Mountain. I must go show my strength before the Emperor"—he burst out weeping from shame and confusion—"and you're hurting my hand!"

The girl steadied the bucket on her head with her free hand and dimpled sympathetically over her shoulder. "You poor, sweet little Forever-Mountain," she said. "Are you tired? Shall I carry you?"

"I do not want you to carry me. I want you to let me go. I want to forget I ever saw you. What do you want with me?" moaned the pitiful wrestler.

"I only want to help you," said the girl, now pulling him steadily up and up a narrow mountain path. "Oh, I am sure you'll have no more trouble than anyone else against the other wrestlers. You'll win, or else you'll lose, and you won't be too badly hurt either way. But aren't you afraid you might meet a really *strong* man someday?"

Forever-Mountain turned white. He stumbled. He was imagining being laughed at throughout Japan as "Hardly-Ever-Mountain."

She glanced back.

"You see? Tired already," she said. "I'll walk more slowly. Why don't you come along to my mother's house and let us make a strong man of you? The wrestling in the capital won't begin for three months. I know, because Grandmother thought she'd go. You'd be spending all that time in bad company and wasting what little power you have."

"All right. Three months. I'll come," said the wrestler. He felt he had nothing more to lose. Also, he feared that the girl might be angry if he refused, and place him in the top of a tree until he changed his mind.

"Fine," she said happily. "We are almost there."

She freed his hand. It was red and a little swollen. "But if you break your promise and run off, I'll have to chase you and carry you back."

Soon they arrived in a small valley where a simple farmhouse with a thatched roof stood.

"Grandmother is at home, but she is an old lady and she's probably sleeping." The girl shaded her eyes with one hand. "But

Mother should be bringing our cow back from the field. There's Mother now!"

She waved. The woman coming around the corner of the house put down the cow she was carrying and waved back.

She smiled and came across the grass, walking with a lively bounce like her daughter's. Well, maybe her bounce was a little more solid, thought the wrestler.

"Excuse me," she said. "These mountain paths are full of stones. They hurt the cow's feet. And who is the nice young man, Maru-me?"

The girl explained. "And we have only three months!" she finished anxiously.

"Well, it's not long enough to do much, but it's not so short a time that we can't do something," said her mother, looking thoughtful. "But he does look terribly feeble. He'll need a lot of good things to eat. Maybe he can help Grandmother with some of the easy housework."

"That will be fine!" said the girl, and she called her grandmother—loudly, for the old lady was a little deaf.

"I'm coming!" came a creaky voice from inside the house, and a little old woman leaning on a stick tottered out of the door. As she came toward them she stumbled over the roots of a great oak tree.

"Heh! My eyes aren't what they used to be. That's the fourth time this month I've stumbled over that tree," she complained and, wrapping her skinny arms about its trunk, pulled it out of the ground.

"Oh, Grandmother! You should have let me pull it up for you," said Maru-me.

"Hm. I hope I didn't hurt my poor old back," muttered the old lady. She called out, "Daughter! Throw that tree away like a good girl, so no one will fall over it. But make sure it doesn't hit anybody."

"You can help Mother with the tree," Maru-me

永久山

said to Forever-Mountain. "On second thought, you'd better not help. Just watch."

Her mother went to the tree, picked it up in her two hands, and threw it—clumsily and with a little gasp.

Up went the tree, sailing end over end, growing smaller and smaller as it flew. It landed with a faint crash far up the mountainside.

"Ah, how clumsy," she said. "I meant to throw it *over* the mountain. It's probably blocking the path now, and I'll have to move it tomorrow."

The wrestler was not listening. He had very quietly fainted.

"Oh! We must put him to bed," said Maru-me.

"Poor, feeble young man," said her mother.

"I hope we can do something for him. Here, let me carry him, he's light," said the grandmother. She slung him over her shoulder and carried him into the house, creaking along with her cane.

The next day they began the work of making Forever-Mountain over into what they thought a strong man should be. They gave him the simplest food to eat, and the toughest. Day by day they prepared his rice with less and less water, until no ordinary man could have chewed or digested it.

Every day he was made to do the work of five men, and every evening he wrestled with Grandmother. Maru-me and her mother agreed that Grandmother, being old and feeble, was the least likely to injure him accidentally. They hoped the exercise might be good for her rheumatism.

He grew stronger and stronger but was hardly aware of it. Grandmother could still throw him easily into the air—and catch him again—without ever changing her sweet old smile.

He quite forgot that outside this valley he was one of the greatest wrestlers in Japan and was called Forever-Mountain. His legs had been like logs; now they were like pillars. His big hands were hard as stones, and when he cracked his knuckles the sound was like trees splitting on a cold night.

Sometimes he did an exercise that wrestlers do in Japan—raising one foot high above the ground and bringing it down with a crash. Then people in nearby villages looked up at the winter sky and said that it was very late in the year for thunder.

Soon he could pull up a tree as well as the grandmother. He could even throw one—but only a small distance. One evening, near the end of his third month, he wrestled with Grandmother and held her down for half a minute.

"Heh-heh!" She chortled and got up, smiling with every wrinkle. "I'd never have believed it!"

Maru-me squealed with joy and threw her arms around him—gently, for she was afraid of cracking his ribs.

"Very good, very good! What a strong man," said her mother, who had just come home from the fields, carrying, as usual, the cow. She put the cow down and patted the wrestler on the back.

They agreed that he was now ready to show some *real* strength before the Emperor.

"Take the cow along with you tomorrow when you go," said the mother. "Sell her and buy yourself a belt—a silken belt. Buy the fattest and heaviest one you can find. Wear it when you appear before the Emperor, as a souvenir from us."

"I wouldn't think of taking your only cow. You've already done too much for me. And you'll need her to plow the fields, won't you?"

They burst out laughing. Maru-me squealed, her mother roared. The grandmother cackled so hard and long that she choked and had to be pounded on the back.

"Oh, dear," said the mother, still laughing. "You didn't think we used our cow for *work*! Why, Grandmother here is stronger than five cows!"

"The cow is our pet," Maru-me giggled. "She has lovely brown eyes."

"But it really gets tiresome having to carry her back and forth each day so that she has enough grass to eat," said her mother.

"Then you must let me give you all the prize money that I win," said Forever-Mountain.

"Oh, no! We wouldn't think of it!" said Maru-me. "Because we all like you too much to sell you anything. And it is not proper to accept gifts of money from strangers."

"True," said Forever-Mountain. "I will now ask your mother's and grandmother's permission to marry you. I want to be one of the family."

"Oh! I'll make a wedding dress!" said Maru-me.

The mother and grandmother pretended to consider very seriously, but they quickly agreed.

Next morning Forever-Mountain tied his hair up in the topknot that all Japanese wrestlers wear, and got ready to leave. He thanked Maru-me and her mother and bowed very low to the grandmother, since she was the oldest and had been a fine wrestling partner. Then he picked up the cow and trudged up the mountain. When he reached the top, he slung the cow over one shoulder and waved good-bye to Maru-me.

At the first town he came to, Forever-Mountain sold the cow. She brought a good price because she was unusually fat from never having worked in her life. With the money, he bought the heaviest silken belt he could find.

When he reached the palace grounds, many of the other wrestlers were already there, sitting about, eating enormous bowls of rice, comparing one another's weight, and telling stories. They paid little attention to Forever-Mountain, except to wonder why he had arrived so late this year. Some of them noticed that he had grown very quiet and took no part at all in their boasting.

All the ladies and gentlemen of the court were waiting in a special courtyard for the wrestling to begin. They wore many robes, one on top of another, heavy with embroidery and gold cloth, and sweat ran down their faces and froze in the winter afternoon. The gentlemen had long swords so weighted with gold and precious stones that they could never have used them, even if they had known how. The court ladies, with their long black hair hanging down behind, had their faces painted dead white, which made them look frightened. They had pulled out their real eyebrows and painted new ones high above the place where eyebrows are supposed to be, and this made them all look as though they were very surprised at something.

Behind a screen sat the Emperor—by himself, because he was too noble for ordinary people to look at. He was a lonely old man with a kind, tired face. He hoped the wrestling would end quickly so that he could go to his room and write poems.

The first two wrestlers chosen to fight were Forever-Mountain and a wrestler who was said to have the biggest stomach in the

永久山
竜海

country. He and Forever-Mountain both threw some salt into the ring. It was said that this drove away evil spirits.

Then the other wrestler, moving his stomach somewhat out of the way, raised his foot and brought it down with a fearful stamp. He glared fiercely at Forever-Mountain as if to say, "Now *you* stamp, you poor frightened man!"

Forever-Mountain raised his foot. He brought it down.

There was a sound like thunder, the earth shook, and the other wrestler bounced into the air and out of the ring, as gracefully as any soap bubble.

He picked himself up and bowed to the Emperor's screen.

"The earth-god is angry. Possibly there is something the matter with the salt," he said. "I do not think I shall wrestle this season." And he walked out, looking very suspiciously over one shoulder at Forever-Mountain.

Five other wrestlers then and there decided that they were not wrestling this season, either.

From then on, Forever-Mountain brought his foot down lightly. As each wrestler came into the ring, he picked him up very gently, carried him out, and placed him before the Emperor's screen, bowing most courteously every time.

The court ladies' eyebrows went up even higher. The gentlemen looked disturbed and a little afraid. They loved to see fierce, strong men tugging and grunting at each other, but Forever-Mountain was a little too much for them. Only the Emperor was happy. With the wrestling over so quickly, he would have that much more time to write his poems. He ordered all the prize money handed over to Forever-Mountain.

"But," he said, "you had better not wrestle any more." He stuck a finger through his screen and waggled it at the other wrestlers, who were sitting on the ground weeping with disappointment like great fat babies.

Forever-Mountain promised not to wrestle any more. Everybody looked relieved. The wrestlers sitting on the ground almost smiled.

"I think I shall become a farmer," Forever-Mountain said.

Maru-me was waiting for him. When she saw him coming, she ran down the mountain, picked him up, together with the heavy bags of prize money, and carried him halfway up the mountainside. Then she giggled and put him down. The rest of the way she let him carry her.

Forever-Mountain kept his promise to the Emperor and never fought in public again. His name was forgotten in the capital. But up in the mountains, sometimes, the earth shakes and rumbles, and they say that it is Forever-Mountain and Maru-me's grandmother practicing wrestling.

What did you like or not like about the story? Why?

Forever-Mountain is a conceited man at the beginning of the story. How and why do you think his attitudes change during the story?

Compare and contrast the opinions Maru-me and her family, the other wrestlers, and the Emperor have of Forever-Mountain.

WRITE Imagine you are Forever-Mountain. Write a diary entry explaining what you learned from the three women in the story.

PEKI, THE MUSICIAN

In a village called Orele, near the town of Otolo, there was a family with three sons named Aluge, Mokoi and Peki. Aluge, the eldest, when his time came, chose to be a farmer like his father. He cultivated the fields and grew yams and grain. Mokoi, the second son, when his time came, chose to be a trader. He went from town to town buying and selling cloth. Peki, the youngest, had not yet chosen a profession. He worked with his father in the fields sometimes, and sometimes he gathered wood for his mother's cooking fire, but often when his help was needed he could not be found. His parents worried about him, saying, "He is a strange boy. He does not do what other boys do. He would rather wander in the bush than do the work that has to be done."

Peki listened to the cries of animals and birds, and to the sound of the wind in the trees. He said to his parents: "I was in the bush today. I heard it singing." His father said: "I was in the field today, and I heard it say, 'I need hoeing.'" His mother said: "I was cooking today, and I heard the fire say, 'I am hungry, bring me wood.'"

Peki cut a small branch from a tree and made himself a flute. He wandered in the bush and imitated the sounds he heard there. From a distance, people heard Peki playing his flute and said: "The farmer farms, the blacksmith shapes iron, the trader trades, the carver carves, and Peki does nothing but play his tunes."

As Peki grew older, nothing changed. The day was approaching when he would be initiated into manhood. His father said to him: "The time is nearly here. You will be a man. You will have to choose your work." Peki answered: "It is music that I want." His father said: "Yes, but a man must do something to live. Will you farm? If so, I will help you to clear a field. Will you be a trader? If so, I will give

by Harold Courlander
illustrated by Paul Morin

AWARD-WINNING AUTHOR

you money to buy cloth. Will you be a blacksmith? If so, I will take you to Otolo and make arrangements for you to learn the art of forging. Will you be a weaver? I will arrange for you to learn the art of weaving."

Peki replied: "Yes, I have thought of all such things, but I want only to make music." His father was impatient with Peki. He said: "What other people do for a living, you do not want any of it. Do the yams you eat grow by themselves? No, they must be planted and cultivated. Does a hoe or a bush knife make itself? No, it must be shaped in the heat of the forge. Does cloth weave itself? No, it must be woven by human hands. You are half in this world and half in the world of unborn children from which you came. Life is work. Without work there cannot be life. Therefore you must decide what work you are going to do."

Peki answered: "Father, I want music." His father answered: "Music was here when we came, like the forest and the river. We do not have to shape it at the forge or grow it like rice. The gods gave us music. But if you persist this way the gods will become angry, and the village also will be angry because you do nothing to help it stay alive. Let me tell you, my son, what the village will say. It will say: 'Peki? Oh, he is the lazy one who grows nothing and crafts nothing.'"

Peki tried. He hoed with his father in the field, but even as he hoed, he heard music in the air and longed to play his flute. In time his father became stern. He feared that Peki would become a beggar and go from one village to another playing his flute and asking people to give him a little rice to eat. He told his son: "You will have to declare yourself. The time of your initiation is near. You have only a few days to make up your mind. If you cannot say by then how you are going to live, you will have to leave the village and begin your life as a beggar."

The day of initiation came, and Peki was initiated into manhood. His father said: "Now is the time to declare." And Peki answered: "I want only to be a musician." His father was downcast. He gave Peki a few small coins, saying, "The gods have cursed my house. You must go."

Peki left his village, carrying the only thing he owned, his flute. Feeling very sad, he went along the road toward Otolo. He put his flute to his lips and played a tune taught to him by the wind and the birds. After a while his sadness left him. He arrived at the outskirts of Otolo. He bought a little food from a vendor and sat down to eat, wondering what he would do next.

While Peki sat there, a blind singer came along the road, an old man feeling his way with a long staff. He carried an omele drum suspended from one shoulder by a leather thong, indicating that he was a singer of praise songs. The old man stopped. Although he could not see Peki, he seemed to know that he was there. He said: "Have I arrived yet at the town of Otolo?" Peki answered: "Yes, father, you are at the edge of the town." The man sat down. He said: "You also are a traveler?" Peki answered: "Yes, I have just arrived." The man said: "You are young." Peki said: "Yes, father." The man said: "You are carrying a load of goods to the town?" Peki said: "No, father, I carry only my flute." The man said: "Ah, you too are a musician?" Peki answered: "No, father, I am not yet a musician." The man said: "Let me hear."

Peki wiped the dust from his flute and played. The man said: "Yes, you will be a musician." Then, after a pause, he said: "If you merely go here and there like I do, to one place and another, let us go together. You will hold the end of my staff and guide me." Peki answered: "Yes, I will do it." They arose. Peki took the free end of the old man's staff in his hand and walked in front. They entered the town and came to the chief's house. There the musician arranged his omele drum in front of him and began to play. People gathered. The old man sang a song of praise for the chief. He sang of the chief's generosity and good character, and about his father and grandfather. In his song he told how the chief's ancestors had come from a northern country and settled in Otolo. The chief came out of his house and joined the spectators.

While Peki listened to the singing and drumming of the old musician, he could not resist putting his flute to his lips. He began to play the rising and falling tones of the song, and whenever the musician rested his voice for a moment, Peki's flute went on, accompanying the drum. The chief was pleased with what he heard. When the singing finally came to an end, the chief brought the old man and the boy into his house and fed them and gave them money to reward them for their praise songs.

This was the beginning for Peki. He traveled on with the old man, whose name was Sholo. He learned the old man's songs. He learned to play the omele drum. The old man taught him everything he knew. A time came when the old musician died, and after that Peki traveled alone from village to village and town to town. Sometimes he stood in the center of a village singing songs the people liked to hear, after which they gave him money. Sometimes he sang praise songs for chiefs and important men. Whenever he arrived in a village, children ran to meet him, shouting, "The singing man has come! The singing man has come!"

Every year the town of Otolo celebrated the Feast of Igodo, the Yam Festival. Peki traveled from a distant place to be in Otolo on the festival day, as did many other musicians. The town was full of music and dancing. And at a certain time of the day the musicians stood before the chief's house to play for him. The chief came out and sat on his stool. One by one the bards played and sang praise songs in honor of the chief, and each of them was rewarded with money gifts. And when the singing was over, the chief called Peki to come forward, saying, "You, what is your name and where do you come from?" Peki replied: "My name is Peki, and I come from the village of Orele." The chief asked: "Where did you learn the history of my family?" Peki answered: "I learned from the old musician Sholo, who now is dead." The chief said: "Many musicians and bards have sung before my house. I have heard them all. But your singing is sweet to hear. If you will remain here in Otolo, I will make you my personal singer." Peki agreed. The chief gave him a house and servants. He gave him money gifts. He gave him a special string of beads to wear, signifying that Peki was his personal musician. Peki became an important person in Otolo.

On a certain festival day when many people came to Otolo from the villages, Peki saw his two older brothers, Aluge and Mokoi, in the crowd. He went to them to talk. They did not recognize him. He said to Aluge, the farmer: "Are your crops growing well?" And Aluge replied: "The crops fail me. The rains do not come, the yams are eaten by beetles, and locusts destroy the grain." Peki said to his other brother, Mokoi: "I see by the

things you carry that you are a trader. How does it go?" And Mokoi replied: "Times are bad. Everyone wants to sell, but no one can afford to buy." Peki asked: "Are your families well?" And they answered: "We survive." Peki asked: "Do you have living parents?" They said: "Yes, but they are old. For them, surviving is hard." Peki said: "Do you have brothers?" They said: "Long ago we had a brother. If he is alive now, who can tell? For he knew nothing but how to blow a flute. In time of hardship can music from a flute be eaten? He went away years ago, and we heard no more of him. Perhaps he is dead."

Peki said: "Tell your village that on the next festival day the personal drummer of the chief of Otolo will come to help the people celebrate." They answered: "Yes, we will do it."

On the next festival day Peki journeyed to Orele. He sent his servants into the village ahead of him. They beat drums and gongs and announced that the chief's musician was arriving from Otolo. A crowd gathered. Peki went first to the house of the headman, and there he sang a song of praise. Then, with the crowd at his heels, he went before the house of his parents. He played on his omele drum and sang:

In the beginning was Owner-of-the-Sky,
And he created what was creatable.
First he made light emerge from darkness.
Then he caused the earth to emerge from the sea.
He instructed his son Obatala how to make humans.
He gave people iron, fire and language.
He instructed Ifa in the art of divining,
And Ifa passed the art on to human beings.
Owner-of-the-Sky created all.
Only one thing was lacking.
Owner-of-the-Sky said, "Iron is great, fire is great,
Yet one more thing is needed in the universe."
He took a white cloud from the sky and molded it.
It became a white powder in his hands.
He sprinkled the powder over the earth,
And it fell upon the humans he had created.

Owner-of-the-Sky said, "Now I have given people music.
It is my last creation, and everything is complete."

Peki's parents were standing before their house, and now he sang to them:

There were three sons.
The first was a farmer, the second a trader,
And the third, breathing powder from the sky,
Could not do anything but play the flute.
Therefore the third son was cast away.
He went here and there singing for cowries,
Until at last he became the chief's musician in Otolo.
Then he was honored and made a person of consequence.

Hearing these songs, Peki's parents cried. They said: "Our son Peki was sent away because of his flute, just as in the song. How he must have suffered! And now, no doubt, Peki is dead!"

Peki went to his parents and took them by the hand. He said: "No, Peki is not dead, for I am Peki." He gave them gifts that he had brought for them from Otolo, and he gave his brothers gifts also. There was a great celebration in Orele. There was feasting, drumming and dancing. And when it was over, Peki said good-bye to his family and returned to Otolo.

The people of Orele gave Peki another name. From that day onward he was called Receiver-of-the-Last-Gift-from-Owner-of-the-Sky. And they made a saying:

"Fire melts iron, but it cannot play a flute."

If you were one of Peki's parents, how would you feel about seeing him again after so many years? Explain.

How does Peki change during the story? What is he like at the beginning of the tale? What is he like at the end?

Folktales often teach a lesson. What lesson do you think this tale teaches?

WRITE Write lyrics for a song praising someone you admire.

How Winter Man's

by Grace Jackson Penney
illustrations by David McCall Johnston

Long and long ago, the Cheyennes were having trouble with Ho-e-ma-ha, the Winter Man, who rules the land in the short dark days when the sun is away to the south.

It is Ho-e-ma-ha who shrills the icy cold wind when he plays his flute, and he covers the land with snow and sleet when he shakes his robe. Every creature takes shelter from the storms he drives across the prairies.

The birds fly away to the south. The bear and the wolf, and all the little animals hide in caves and crannies. Deer and elk shelter in ravines where the cedars break the force of the wind. Even the buffalo herds turn their backs to the storm, and drift south across the plains.

During the time of the green leaves, Winter Man had been far away in the north. The days were long and the sun warmed the earth. The grass grew, and there were many buffalo grazing on the plains. The Cheyennes hunted and fished in the streams. The children played games and ran races. It was a happy time, and the people almost forgot the hard times that come when Winter Man returns.

But when the sun moved toward the south and his path across the sky grew shorter and shorter, Winter Man began his journey back to the Cheyenne country.

Power Was Broken

In the daytime, he wrapped himself in his robe and slept in the shade, hiding from the sun, but when night came he marched southward. Every night during the moon of Se-in-e (October), Ho-e-ma-ha moved closer and closer to the Cheyennes, walking across the hilltops, and on the prairies.

Wherever his moccasin touched, the grass withered and turned brown. Where he breathed his frosty breath, the leaves turned yellow and red, and when he had passed, the song of the running stream was still, ice-locked into silence.

When Ho-e-ma-ha came at nightfall to his camp on the ridge just north of the Cheyenne camp, he looked down and saw the people gathered around the campfires, feasting and singing. This made him angry, for Winter Man does not like to see people happy.

"They seem to have forgotten my power," he muttered to himself. "I'll have to make them remember." He blew a wild song on his flute, sending an icy wind sweeping down on the camp from the ridge, racing from tipi to tipi.

The people shivered and moved closer to the fires, while the sharp wind blew the flames, and whipped up clouds of dust. They wrapped their robes around them, and looked fearfully up at the ridge. "Ho-e-ma-ha has returned," they said. "That cold wind says he is angry. We'd better get ready for a storm."

But that night, while they slept, Winter Man shook his robe fast, and blew hard and shrill on his flute. Snow covered the earth, and the animals hid from his fury. When morning came, a blinding snowstorm held the people prisoners in their tipis, staying close to the fires to keep warm. "Winter Man is very angry," they said. "It is a good thing we have food on hand."

The icy wind heard them talking, and told Ho-e-ma-ha what they said. "They think their food will keep them safe from me," he said. "I'll show them my power."

He sent a flight of sleet arrows slashing down into the camp, covering everything with glittering ice . . . even slicing into some of the older tipis, and jabbing the people with their sharp points.

For three days, he sent the sleet arrows pelting into the camp.

For three nights, he lashed the camp with icy wind, playing a wild angry song on his flute.

At first, it wasn't so bad. There was buffalo meat and fat in every tipi and plenty of wood for the fires, so nobody minded the storm very much. Actually, it was quite pleasant, sitting inside by the blazing fires, telling stories and visiting together.

But Ho-e-ma-ha still had not shown them all his power. The storm grew fiercer and fiercer. For five days, and then seven days, Winter Man lashed the camp with screeching winds that tore at the tipis and howled down the smoke holes. He sent bitter cold that crept in under the walls and through every tiny slit in the skins, touching the children with frostbite.

Even the oldest men had never known a storm so wild, nor remembered one that lasted so long. Firewood began to be scarce and the food was all gone. People huddled close to tiny fires to keep from freezing, and there was hunger in the camp, and sickness.

The strongest, bravest young men wrapped themselves in their robes and went out into the storm to try to find food for the camp, but there was nothing to be found. All the land was covered with ice and snow piled high in drifts. It was like a bitter cold desert, with the wind driving a white sandstorm of snow and sleet. At last, giving up, they turned back to the camp, numb with cold, and half frozen. Winter Man had beaten them.

But when they entered the camp, where scarcely a wisp of smoke curled out of the tipis, they saw that Bow-in-Hand had come back. No one saw him come, just as no one saw when he left his grandfather's tipi before.

The old man, crouched close to the embers of his fire, looked up and saw Bow-in-Hand standing there. "You come at a bad time, nishi," he said. "Things are very bad now. I am a very old man, but I never saw anything like this time." He shook his head. "Winter Man is terribly angry. For five days and seven days again, he's sent the storm. Now the meat is all gone, and the firewood all burned. The people are freezing and starving. We can do nothing."

"Where does the Winter Man make his camp?" Bow-in-Hand asked. "I will go and see him."

"His camp is on the other side of the ridge, north of here," said his grandfather. "But he holds the whole land in his power. You had better stay inside. You can do nothing against Ho-e-ma-ha. Wait here, nishi; he will get tired. The storm will stop sometime."

"But the people are suffering now. I must go to his camp and try to stop him."

"Look, nishi," the old man said, "see how the young men are returning to camp, empty-handed. They are half dead with cold. Winter Man has beaten them. Stay here, Grandson."

"All the more reason why I should go to Winter Man and talk to him. If the storm does not stop, many will die."

"That is true. Many will die of hunger and cold. But even so, it would be better to stay here and wait. Winter Man is too powerful for you, but if you will go, Grandson, wrap yourself against the cold. Take all the warm robes we have."

"I won't need a robe, Grandfather," Bow-in-Hand said. "I have my eagle-feather fan, and it will give me power. You wrap yourself in the robes, and wait here by the fire. I will see what I can do with Ho-e-ma-ha."

Then he left his grandfather's tipi and walked straight north into the teeth of the storm. Its icy wind snarled and screeched, and the sleet arrows pelted him. The snow piled up around his feet, trying to hold him back, but he walked steadily forward. He came over the ridge to the camp of Ho-e-ma-ha and opened the door and went inside.

Ho-e-ma-ha was amazed, then more angry than before. "How dare you come to my tipi?" he roared, and sent a very fury of wind and sleet against Bow-in-Hand. He shook his robe fast and hard, filling the tipi with swirling, blinding snowflakes.

But Bow-in-Hand was not troubled by the storm inside the tipi any more than he had been by the storm outside. Tall and strong, he just stood there, watching Ho-e-ma-ha, smiling a little, and waving his eagle-feather fan slowly.

As he waved the fan, the air warmed and the snowflakes got fewer and fewer, and even the ice walls of the tipi melted. Ho-e-ma-ha raged and blustered. He blew his flute with all his might and shook his robe as hard and as fast as he could. But he could do nothing against Bow-in-Hand's power.

The air in the tipi and all around grew so warm that all his children ran away and hid in the crevices of rocks, and Ho-e-ma-ha wrapped his robe around him and blew one last angry blast on his flute and strode away from there, back to the far north country.

Bow-in-Hand went back to the Cheyenne camp, and while the young men went out to hunt, he had the old men and the women and the children bring hot water to pour in the crevices of the rocks where Winter Man's frost children were hiding.

If they had been able to destroy all of Ho-e-ma-ha's children, there never would have been any more winter. But though they searched carefully and poured hot water in all the crevices and crannies, some of the smallest of Ho-e-ma-ha's frost children hid so far back in the tiny cracks that the scalding water could not touch them.

That is why winter still comes. But never again did Ho-e-ma-ha have the power to make the people suffer and starve as he had before.

Imagine that you are Ho-e-ma-ha. How would you react to Bow-in-Hand?

What is Bow-in-Hand like? What words best describe his character?

Find examples in the story of ways in which Ho-e-ma-ha seems human.

WRITE What would your life be like if you lived in a place where summer never ended? Write a paragraph describing life in an "endless summer."

The Golden Apples

THE STORY OF ATALANTA AND HIPPOMENES

retold by Mary Pope Osborne

Long ago a baby girl named Atalanta was left on a wild mountainside because her father had wanted a boy instead of a girl. A kind bear discovered the tiny girl and nursed her and cared for her. And as Atalanta grew up, she lived as the bears lived: eating wild honey and berries and hunting in the woods. Finally as a young woman on her own, she became a follower of Diana, the goddess of wild things. Preferring to live on her own, Atalanta blissfully roamed the shadowy woods and sunlit fields.

The god Apollo agreed with Atalanta's choice to be alone. "You must never marry," he told her one day. "If you do, you will surely lose your own identity."

illustration by Cheryl Griesbach and Stanley Martucci

In spite of her decision never to marry, Atalanta was pursued by many suitors. As men watched her run through the fields and forest, they were struck by her beauty and grace.

Angry at the men for bothering her, Atalanta figured out how to keep them away. "I'll race anyone who wants to marry me!" she announced to the daily throng that pursued her. "Whoever is so swift that he can outrun me will receive the prize of my hand in marriage! But whomever I beat—will die."

Atalanta was certain these harsh conditions would discourage everyone from wanting to marry her. But she was wrong. Her strength and grace were so compelling that many men volunteered to race against her—and all of them lost their lives.

One day, a young stranger, wandering through the countryside, stopped to join a crowd that was watching a race between Atalanta and one of her suitors. When Hippomenes realized the terms of the contest, he was appalled. "No person could be worth such a risk!" he exclaimed. "Only an idiot would try to win her for his wife!"

But when Atalanta sped by, and Hippomenes saw her wild hair flying back from her ivory shoulders and her strong body moving as gracefully as a gazelle, even he was overwhelmed with the desire to be her husband.

"Forgive me," he said to the panting loser being taken away to his death. "I did not know what a prize she was."

When Atalanta was crowned with the wreath of victory, Hippomenes stepped forward boldly and spoke to her before the crowd. "Why do you race against men so slow?" he asked. "Why not race against me? If I defeat you, you will not be disgraced, for I am the great-grandson of Neptune, god of the seas!"

"And if I beat you?" Atalanta asked.

"If you beat me . . . you will certainly have something to boast about!"

As Atalanta stared at the proud young man, she wondered why the gods would wish one so young and bold as Hippomenes to die. And for the first time, she felt she might rather lose than win. Inexperienced in matters of the heart, she did not realize she was falling in love. "Go, stranger," she said softly. "I'm not worth the loss of your life."

But the crowd, sensing a tremendous race might be about to take place, cheered wildly, urging the two to compete. And since Hippomenes eagerly sought the same, Atalanta was forced to give in. With a heavy heart, she consented to race the young man the next day.

In the pink twilight, alone in the hills, Hippomenes prayed to Venus, the goddess of love and beauty. He asked for help in his race against Atalanta. When Venus heard Hippomenes's prayer, she was only too glad to help him, for she wished to punish the young huntress for despising love.

As if in a dream, Venus led Hippomenes to a mighty tree in the middle of an open field. The tree shimmered with golden leaves and golden apples. Venus told Hippomenes to pluck three of the apples from the tree, and then she told him how to use the apples in his race against Atalanta.

The crowd roared as Atalanta and Hippomenes crouched at the starting line. Under his tunic, Hippomenes hid his three golden apples. When the trumpets sounded, the two shot forward and ran so fast that their bare feet barely touched the sand. They looked as if they could run over the surface of the sea without getting their feet wet—or skim over fields of corn without even bending the stalks.

The crowd cheered for Hippomenes, but Atalanta rushed ahead of him and stayed in the lead. When Hippomenes began to pant, and his chest felt as if it might burst open, he pulled one of the golden apples out from under his tunic and tossed it toward Atalanta.

The gleaming apple hit the sand and rolled across Atalanta's path. She left her course and chased after the glittering ball, and Hippomenes gained the lead. The crowd screamed with joy; but after Atalanta picked up the golden apple, she quickly made up for her delay and scooted ahead of Hippomenes.

Hippomenes tossed another golden apple. Again, Atalanta left her course, picked up the apple, then overtook Hippomenes.

As Hippomenes pulled out his third golden apple, he realized this was his last chance. He reared back his arm and hurled the apple as far as he could into a field.

Atalanta watched the golden ball fly through the air; and she hesitated, wondering whether or not she should run after it. Just as she decided not to, Venus touched her heart, prompting her to abandon her course and rush after the glittering apple.

Atalanta took off into the field after the golden apple—and Hippomenes sped toward the finish line.

Hippomenes won Atalanta for his bride, but then he made a terrible mistake: He neglected to offer gifts to Venus to thank her for helping him.

Enraged by his ingratitude, the goddess of love and beauty called upon the moon goddess, Diana, and told her to punish Hippomenes and Atalanta.

As the moon goddess studied the two proud lovers hunting in the woods and fields, she admired their strength and valor, and she decided to turn them into the animals they most resembled.

One night as Atalanta and Hippomenes lay side by side under the moonlight, changes began to happen to their bodies. They grew rough amber coats and stiff, long claws. And when dawn came, they woke and growled at the early light. Then the thick tails of the two mighty lions swept the ground as they began hunting for their breakfast.

From then on, Atalanta and Hippomenes lived together as lions deep in the woods, and only the moon goddess could tame them.

Which character in this Greek myth did you like the best? Use examples from the story to tell why.

How do the gods affect the final outcome of the story?

Why does Hippomenes change his mind about racing Atalanta? Would you take the same risk? Explain why you would or wouldn't.

WRITE Do you think this is a happy story, a sad story, or both? Write a paragraph explaining why you feel that way.

Tales from Around the World

How might the main characters in "Three Strong Women" have dealt with Winter Man? How might Peki, the Musician, have dealt with him?

Writer's Workshop

The stories of Forever-Mountain and Atalanta come from different cultures, yet these tales have similarities. Write an essay in which you compare and contrast Forever-Mountain and Atalanta. You might consider the fact that both have great athletic ability. How do their lives change as a result of meeting someone who defeats them? What lessons does each learn from the experience?

Writer's Choice You have read about people who have special abilities. Think of another kind of talent to tell about. Choose an idea, and plan your response. Then carry it out, and share your finished product with others.

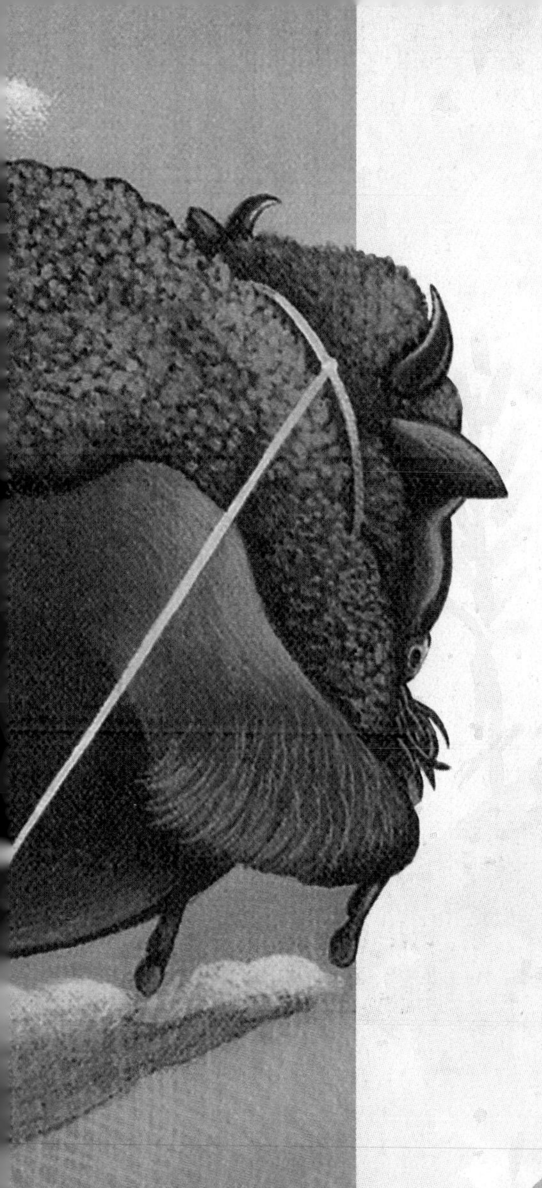

THEME

Tall Tales

Have you ever told an incredible story to make a point or to entertain your friends? Have you ever gotten your way because you outsmarted someone? In the following selections, the tales are tall, the wits sharp, and the characters crafty.

CONTENTS

Pecos Bill
King of Texas Cowboys

by Walter Blair

Nobody knows the name of Bill's father. In Texas, back in the days when he went there, it wasn't healthy to go up and ask a stranger his name, as many a tenderfoot learned to his sorrow. But Bill's mother called him the Ole Man beginning when he was a young twirp of half past seventy, and he called her the Ole Woman, more or less in revenge. So everybody else used those names for them.

So far as is known, there wasn't anything out of the ordinary about this family. They had the usual things people took to Texas in those days—a rifle, a chopping-ax, and an iron hog-rendering kettle. And they had seven boys and six girls, all of them either sons or daughters.

illustrated by Ross MacDonald

They got into Texas, it's said, about the time Sam Houston and the other Texans were putting the final licks on the Republic of Texas, so she could let the Union join her. This made it possible for Bill to be born in Texas, and from the start he did his best to live up to that great honor.

There was the time, for instance, when, in the middle of a sunny day, all of a sudden the whole place was as dark as the inside of a pocket. This was just after Bill's family had got a little way into Texas, and the family was still camping out. The Ole Woman had put Bill down on a bearskin on the ground, where he was lying and trying his best to swallow his left foot.

The hum this black cloud made soon showed what it was—a stampeding herd of Texas Gallinippers[1]—swarming down so thick that shortly little Bill was plumb out of sight. Even when the Ole Man fired his rifle into the blackness, a faint ray of light came through a tube-like hole only for a split-second, then the hole closed, leaving the world as dark as it had been before.

"Ole Man," says the Ole Woman, "that newest baby—Bill, I think his name is—is likely to get carried plumb away unless you do something."

The only thing the Ole Man could think to do was push his way through the Gallinippers to the wagon, get the hog-rendering kettle, stumble over to where Bill was lying, turn the kettle upside down, and cover the little fellow up with it. At the last minute, figuring Bill might get bored, he shoved the chopping-ax under the edge for the baby to play with.

Baffled like that by a mere iron kettle, the Texas Gallinippers started to take steps—or swoops, rather—in short order. One of the smartest of them cleared the way several feet above the kettle bottom, took aim, and dived down on the thing with all the speed of a dive-bomber. He hit the kettle with a metallic ping, and rammed his bill clean through the iron.

Then another one did likewise, and another, and another—until the sound of Gallinippers banging against the kettle and sinking their bills into it was like the patter of rain on a tin roof. But there was another noise that at first puzzled the Ole Man and the Ole Woman—a bang, inside the kettle, following each one of the pings.

"By grannies," says the Ole Man, finally, "I know what's happening. Each time one of those fellows lands, little Bill is taking the chopping-ax and bradding the bill with it."

The Ole Man and the Ole Woman were laughing like hyenas when they saw the kettle, in the murk, slowly beginning to rise. "I'll swan," says the Ole Woman, "those Gallinippers are carrying off that great big kettle."

They did, too, easy as lifting an eyelash. And before long they were disappearing to the West, lugging that big piece of ironware.

---

[1]Gallinippers: gigantic mosquitoes.

"Look!" the Ole Man said. "Those other fool Gallinippers think Bill's still underneath it."

Sure enough, it looked that way. After that kettle the things all flew, so that shortly the family was in the Texas sunshine again, with the skies all clear. But Bill was lying on the bearskin, just as calm as a cow, having a try at swallowing that ax-handle. "Goo," he said, "goo, goo!"

"I'm sure sorry to lose that kettle," the Ole Woman said. "But when a baby's as smart as Bill there is, it's worth while to keep him."

She took extra good care of Bill after that—fed him on panther's milk, weaned him when he was two weeks old, and gave him a bowie knife to cut his teeth on. He grew stronger, and when the first norther came along, and the flames in the fireplace froze stiff as crooked icicles, Bill chewed them up and swallowed them without harm. Soon as they unfroze, they couldn't seem to do more than give him a warm feeling in the stomach that made him giggle a bit.

A few months later, one of the older children ran up to the Ole Man in the field one morning, and said, "There's a panther just went into the cabin where Bill is, and Bill's alone with that varmint!"

"Well," says the Ole Man, "that fool panther doesn't need to expect any help from me!" He didn't feel any different, either, when he stopped plowing at noon, went into the cabin, and found Bill (who was a year old now) cooking up some panther steaks for the family.

A while later, when the Ole Man found wagon tracks within five miles of the cabin, he decided that the district was getting too crowded, and decided to move away. It was while they were on this trip that Bill jounced out of the wagon just after the family had forded the Pecos River.

By bad luck, he was asleep at the time, so he didn't wake up until hours after he'd taken the spill. And the Ole Man and the Ole Woman were so busy moving the family and all that it wasn't until three days later, counting the children, they found Bill was missing.

"How sad," the Ole Woman said, "our little Bill out there among all those wild animals and poisonous rattlesnakes and such."

"The varmints and rattlers," the Ole Man said, "will have to fend for themselves. We didn't go to lose him."

What Bill had done, meanwhile, was toddle around on his little dimpled feet and find himself a pack of coyotes to be friendly with. After he'd licked them all to persuade them that he was the boss, he started to teach them everything he knew and to learn everything they knew.

He and these varmints taught one another so much that by the time Bill was grown up, the coyotes were smarter than foxes, and Bill was smarter than anybody else his age—except in some ways. For example, he was the only human being who ever learned to palaver in all animal lingoes before reaching the age of ten; and no other human *ever* learned to follow trails, to run, or to foresee weather the way Bill could. Still and all, Bill thought he was a coyote, and he hadn't done any human talking since he'd been lost at the age of two.

That's why he had such an all-fired hot argument with the cowboy that came on him one day when Bill, in his birthday clothes, was loping around out in the sagebrush and making coyote noises.

This cowboy spent a whole day getting Bill not to fear him. Then he spent another day teaching him to talk again, and curing him of some of his baby ways of saying things. Then he spent three days making Bill see that he was a human being instead of a coyote. This was a ferocious argument. The cowboy would put out one argument after another, and Bill would bat each down, until finally the cowboy said:

"Well, if you're a coyote, where's your bushy tail?"

After Bill had looked around and had found this article missing, the cowboy said, "That's a stunner, huh? Here's another. Come over with me and take a squint into the creek with me." When they were bending over their reflections in the water, the cowboy said, "Now, don't you look like me, only less handsome and more whiskery?"

Bill admitted this, gulped, and said, "All right, drat it to dratted drat! I'm a human man then. We'll call me Pecos Bill, because I'm from the Pecos River country—been a coyote there most of my days. And I'll run with my own human pack, if I can slow down enough. First thing I have to do, I suppose, is start looking like you ugly critters. So tell me, how do I get myself bald all over the face, and how do I grow me hair like you've got all over most of you—red and blue and brown like that?"

The cowboy howled with laughter, and pressed hard on his ribs with his hands, as if he was trying to keep them from falling off. "You get the hair off your face by shaving," he said. "And that red and blue and brown stuff isn't *hair;* it's *clothes.* We put clothes on—don't grow 'em. I'll bring you a razor to shave with, and I'll bring you some clothes tomorrow. Then I'll take you to the ranch, and maybe you can join the outfit."

So the next day the cowboy (name of

Bowleg Gerber) brought Bill a razor and the biggest suit he could find. Then he showed Bill how to shave and how to get into his clothes. Bowleg brought a horse, too, and a quirt, but he found his friend didn't need them. "Got me an animal of my own, standing still over there," says Bill, pointing out a giant panther that he'd fought to a standstill. "And this is what I'll use for a quirt."

"Good heavens!" says Bowleg, for he saw that Pecos Bill had tamed a huge rattlesnake, that just lay limp and smiling in Bill's big brown paw.

Well, when the two of them rode into camp, Bill's mount and his quirt, as well as his size and his looks in general, made the men sit up straight and blink. Bill jumped off his panther, cracked his rattlesnake quirt, wiped his wet brow with a handful of prickly pear cactus, and walked over to the fire.

There he asked the question Bowleg had told him to ask. "Who," he said, "is the boss of this here outfit, huh?"

A big cowboy going on seven feet high cleared his throat and answered him back in a low voice, "I—I—*was,* until *you* turned up. What're your orders, sir?"

Anybody else but Pecos Bill probably would have been surprised by this, and puzzled as to what to do. But Bill had been boss of the coyotes so long that he expected exactly this sort of thing to happen. And he'd learned from the coyotes, too, that a varmint was loco if he stuck out his neck too far, without knowing what might happen to what was on the end of the neck.

So Bill just said, "Ahem! You can be vice-boss now, if you want to. You go ahead and run things the way you were until I get the lay of the land and figure out whether we need to make any changes."

Well, what Pecos Bill found in the cowboy business was very much like the sort of thing Paul Bunyan had found, at the start, in the lumber business. Everything was in its infancy, and more messed up than a baby that has dumped a bowl of strained spinach over its head.

Leading his friend, Bowleg Gerber, to the side, Bill said, "What's this pack doing?"

"They're cowboys," Bowleg told him. "They stay out here in this shack near the water. Wandering around in the country hereabouts are a good many head of cattle. Every morning, each of these fellows takes a rope, puts a loop at the end, and lays the loop on the ground. He puts some bait in the loop—maybe a hunk of salt, or some sweet-smelling hay, or a cowslip. Then he takes the other end of the rope and hides behind a tree or cactus with it. Then he waits."

"So far," Pecos Bill said, "the whole show sounds as if it'd bore a body plumb to death. Never, in all my days as a coyote, did I fiddle around in such a dull way."

"The exciting point comes next," Bowleg said. "After while, a cow or a bull comes along to get a drink of water. Before or after drinking, the critter may see the bait. If the critter steps up to get the bait, the cowboy waits until its feet are in the noose, then gives the rope a quick jerk. If the animal isn't scared too soon—doesn't jump away—the cowboy catches its legs in the noose."

"I still think it's a very tame and boresome business," says Pecos Bill. "What's more, there are more 'if's' in it than we coyotes ever had in anything we did. What happens, though, if this fellow has the good luck to catch the critter?"

"We got us a barn over there," Bowleg said, "and we put the critter into the barn. When we've got enough animals so there's one for each cowboy to lead, each of us ties a rope to his particular critter. Then each one leads his animal to market, riding on a horse, you see. We call that a *cattle pull,* because we drag the critters."

"Heavens to Betsy!" Pecos Bill said. "All that boresomeness and all that trouble, and you just market one critter apiece? We've got to get this business more coyote-like and on a bigger scale."

Having this kind of an understanding of the way things were done and this kind of a hunch they could be done better, Bill started working out improvements. He went riding around on his panther for a while, but found that scared the cows too much. So he went out afoot one day, and ran down the biggest wild horse he could find cavorting around in those parts, broke the animal, and started to ride it. Bill didn't know it, but this in itself was a great thing to do. Before this the cowboys hadn't thought of catching a wild pony and taming it—always bought their horses. After he'd been fed on dynamite for a few days, the horse was good enough to suit his master.

Riding this horse, which he'd named Widow Maker, Pecos Bill went out among the herds of cattle on the plains, watched their ways, and figured out how to handle them. One very important thing he did was take a great long rawhide rope out and do some practicing with it. When he came back about a week later, he had most of the points about the cattle business all worked out.

Pieface Thomason, the vice-boss of the outfit, was hiding behind some mesquite, watching a cow, when Pecos rode up. The noose was all laid out on the ground, baited with a pretty bowl of cornmeal mush, and this cow was sort of stepping up slowly, drooling a little, to have herself a bite. Pieface was watching and watching, all ready to jerk the noose at just the right minute.

When Pecos Bill came thundering in on his brand new broncho, the cow got scared and started to galumph away.

Pieface come bustling out from behind the mesquite, roaring at Bill. "Look what you went and did!" he yelled. "I've been lying in wait for that danged cow for two hours, and now you've come clumping up and scared her!"

"That's all right," says Pecos. "You can be sure when an old-time coyote makes a noise, it's because he wants to. I'll catch her for you, Pieface."

Spurring Widow Maker (for by that time he'd invented spurs), he went

RPM

after the cow, swinging his rope around his head.

At the right minute, he let the noose fly through the air. It settled down over the cow's neck. Just at that instant, Bill's broncho braced. The end of the rope had been given a double turn around the saddle-bow. When the cow started to run again, the rope tightened, and first thing the cow knew, she'd flopped onto one horn on the ground.

Pieface was watching open-mouthed and goggly-eyed. "How under the sun did you do that?" he wanted to know.

"Little gadget I worked up," Bill said. "I call her a lariat. Keeps you from spending all that boresome time waiting for critters."

"Can you do that right along?"

"Sure. Call in the men in the outfit."

When the hands had come in, Bill galloped around on his broncho, showing them how to lasso one critter after another, while they all went "Oh!" and "Ah!" like a bunch of kids at a fireworks display. When, to end up his show, he tossed his rope up in the air and pulled down a buzzard that happened to be flying by, they all cheered as loud and as long as they could.

"There's another little thing or two I've worked out that I'd like to show you," Pecos said, riding up to the men. "You've got about twenty cows in that barn, haven't you? Well, turn them loose."

"Pecos," Bowleg Gerber said, "you're the boss, and I don't aim to argue with you. But I'd just like to mention—so you can think about it—that it's taken us six weeks to catch those critters."

"Don't worry," Bill told him. "I've invented a dodge to keep them from getting away."

When the beasts were let out, Bill just watched them go scampering every which way. The cowboys did the same, looking sort of mournful, but keeping their mouths shut and not complaining. When all the cattle were out of sight, Pecos Bill went riding away after them, and got out of sight himself in a jiffy.

After a while, though, to the surprise of all the cowboys, they saw a cloud of dust in the distance, off in the direction where their boss and the cattle had gone out of sight. Then the cattle came loping along in the middle of the cloud of dust, with Bill and Widow Maker busying themselves around the fringes.

"Hey," Pieface said, "I've been counting. Twenty-one went out, but Bill brought in a hundred and three!"

Pecos Bill left the cattle drinking at the river and came over to the cowboys. "Now," he said, "I'll tell you about some of the things this old coyote has worked up to fix up the cowboy business. You'll want to remember the names for these new dodges of mine, so pay attention and keep the words in your mind. Now—when I went out on the range and collected those cattle, I *rounded them up,* see?"

"Rounded them up," the cowboys said, all together, like children learning to talk a foreign language.

"When I brought them here, I *herded them.*"

"We hearded them, too," says Bowleg. "They made a thundering noise, stomping along that way. But watch your grammar, Bill."

"I'm not talking bad grammer," Bill told him. "I H-E-R-D-E-D herded them."

"H-E-R-D-E-D herded them," the cowboys said in chorus.

"I've figured out cow-punching," says Pecos Bill, "according to the great and wonderful way of thinking out things I learned when I was a coyote. I'll tell you how the whole thing works, men, and I think you'll go for it. We'll brand all our cattle so people will know they belong to us, you see. So we won't have to keep them in the barn all the time after this. We'll let our cattle wander around out there on the range, pretty much as they're a mind to, most of the months of the year. Of course, we'll go out and look around regularly, to see they're getting along all right—not eating loco weed, say, or getting into some other sort of trouble. If a cyclone's coming along, for instance, we'll get the critters out of the way. (Not having as much sense as coyotes, of course, they have to be shown what to do.) If it's winter, the line riders and the outriders will see to it that the critters go where they can paw their way to grass, keep sheltered from northers and so forth."

"Sounds like hard work," the Kid said.

"It will be," Pecos Bill told him. "It'll be work in the spring, too, when we round up the animals and see they're all branded. And it'll be work other times, when we have a beef roundup, to get together the animals that're going to market."

"How'll we get them to market?" Pieface asked Bill.

"We'll have *cattle drives,*" Pecos Bill said. "After we herd the brutes together, we'll drive them to market, you see. That'll be a lot more according to cow nature than those fool cattle pulls you've had up to this time, and it'll take care of more cattle, too. For a drive like that we'll have a trail boss, his segundo, or right-hand man—that'll be you, Pieface, in this outfit—a cook, and one puncher to every two hundred and fifty cattle. Along the side of the herd, we'll have a line of punchers riding, to keep the brutes in order. At the end of this here column, we'll have the tail riders, the remuda and the men in charge of her, and the chuck-wagon. Figure we ought to make about fifteen miles a day, if we start at sunup and halt at night."

"Sounds all right," says Pieface. "That halting at night stuff sounds very, very good to me. We eat and sleep then, huh?"

"We eat, sure, and sleep a good share of the night. But I figure we'll have to work in shifts—two to four hours apiece, say, to see that the brutes are quiet and peaceful. They'll eat a big meal, you know, soon as we stop, then they'll go to sleep. About midnight, they'll wake up and feed again, then they'll sleep till sunup. That's the way it'll be except on moonlight nights, when the fool animals will eat all night, instead of howling at the moon the way coyotes do. I used to watch them when I was a coyote, and I know that's the way they'll behave."

"Did your life as a coyote," Bowleg wanted to know, "give you any idea what we can do out there on the lone prairie when we're riding alone and lonesome at night?"

"Well," says Bill, "I recalled the high old times I used to have howling at the moon when I was a coyote. So I asked the cattle whether they wouldn't go for a similar kind of entertainment, when I was talking over things with them, you know. They said they didn't like howling, exactly, but songs had a most soothing effect on them. So riding out there at night, we could sing, to keep them cool and to keep ourselves awake. I've made up some songs to sing. Here's one, for instance:

A cowboy's life is a dreary, dreary life,
Some think it's free from care;
Rounding up the cattle from morning till night,
In the middle of the prairie so bare.

CHORUS

Half-past four, the noisy cook will roar,
"Whoop-a-whoop-a-hey!"
Slowly you will rise with sleepy-feeling eyes,
The sweet, dreamy night passed away.
When spring sets in, great trouble does begin,
The weather is so fierce and cold;
Clothes are wet and frozen to our necks,
And the cattle we can scarcely hold.
The cowboy's life is a dreary, dreary life,
From dawn to the setting of the sun,
And even then his work is mighty tough,
For there's night herding to be done.
The wolves and the owls with terrifying howls
Will disturb our midnight dream,
As we lie in our slickers on a wet sticky night,
Way over on the Pecos stream.

All the cowboys agreed that this was a most beautiful song. And when Pecos Bill sang them some of his other little ditties—things like "Bury Me Not" and "Sam Bass" and "Get Along, Little Dogies," they thought very highly of them, and learned them, too. Bill, you see, already had made up about half the songs to be sung to cattle. Later, he made up most of the other half. You'll find that most professors think that cowboy songs were put together by somebody named Mr. Anonymous, but all the cowpunchers know that Pecos Bill knocked together almost all of the best of them.

"Well," the Kid said, "I can get the idea of the way it all works, and it amazes me that one man could figure out all those improvements. Only one weakness in it, far as I can see. We'll work about ten times harder than we used to work, and we'll have at least twelve times as many hardships. Seems to me that maybe some of us will sort of tend to drift out of the cowboy business, now it's going to be so all-fired tough."

"The weaklings, they'll drop out, sure enough," Pecos Bill said. "We'll be glad to see them go, too. When I was a coyote, I never did like to have a coyote that was a sniveler join the pack. Matter of fact, I made some of this work tougher than I had to, just to make sure we'd weed out the cry-babies. But I figured that with all these hardships to overcome, the cowpunchers would develop in time into a bunch of rootin'-tootin' heroes. It'd be enough of a challenge, you see, so we'd have a line of work a man could be proud to do. And that'd bring high pay, naturally—thirty dollars a month *and* keep. Another thing, after those hard times on the range, with piles of pay saved up, a cowboy at the end of a cattle drive could have a wonderful time for himself spending all his money. It'll be a fine life, you see, if you have the good luck to live through it."

"It's the life for me," says Bowleg Gerber, and most of the other cowboys said the same. Then they gave six cheers for Pecos Bill (instead of the usual three, since cowboys were always generous). And then they set to work.

That's the way, then, Pecos Bill started up the cowboy business, worked out every part and parcel of it, so to speak, except for a few little improvements he worked out later—things like the six-shooter, for instance. And when word about the IXL outfit and the way it did things got around, everybody else copied Bill's methods. Before long, there were as many cattle on the Texas plains as there'd once been buffalo. And for all Texas was a big state—the biggest in the world—it had more heroes to the square mile than you'd offhand expect.

The IXL was the best outfit there was, naturally, since it had Pecos Bill as a boss. Anybody that was anybody would try to sign up with the IXL, and usually he'd land there, too. Bowleg and Pieface stuck with Bill, and others just as good joined up with the outfit. Only one to leave was the Kid, who found some easier work—went into the outlaw game, robbed banks and mail trains and suchlike.

Working up cowpunching would seem to be enough for any man to do, but of course Pecos Bill wasn't satisfied. He went on to do things in the cowboy line no one else on earth could do, then or later—

came to be the greatest cowboy in all the states of the world, including the Scandinavian.

It's downright hard to pick out the things he did that were most notable, but I suppose that the windies they tell around the campfires most often in Texas are the one about the way he busted the cyclone.

This cyclone-busting stunt, we happen to know, took place the Year of the Great Drought. Fact is, the Great Drought was what made it happen. The sun beat down on the prairie and dried it until it was about the texture, say, of a bride's biscuits after she's forgotten to use milk in them. The dust began to fly then, getting into everybody's hair, so that when a body brushed his hair, it felt as if he was rubbing the top of his head with sandpaper. And the cattle's tongues lolled out until a body was fearful they might step on them.

Being tenderhearted the way he was, Pecos was very much touched by all this. He went riding around on Widow Maker, heaving heartrending sighs and pondering and pondering—but he didn't get a ghost of an idea until he sighted this cyclone. Like a lightning flash strikes most people—Bill was too fast to get hit by one—an idea came to him. He couldn't make use of this particular cyclone, because it was a baby; but it gave him an idea about using one that had got its full growth.

Next thing he did was go galloping all over the state of Texas, and a few of the neighboring states, on Widow Maker.

Up on the northern edge of Oklahoma, Bill came upon a promising set of weather conditions. The skies were black for a while, and then they started to turn sort of greenish. There was thunder, and then there was a big, long purring moan, and all the Okies started to head for storm cellars, hollering as they went, "Here comes a cyclone!"

Pecos Bill watched the big black funnel, with lightning trimmings on its fringes, come whirling up at forty-two and a half miles an hour. When it was the proper distance away, Bill readied his big lariat, by now a thing he'd put together that was only two hundred miles shorter than the equator. He twirled it around his head, let go, and lassoed that fierce cyclone right around the neck.

The cyclone whirled around more fiercely than ever, and of course soon it had wound a large share of that lariat around its neck, mostly at a point just above its Adam's apple. Bill held on until he was pulled right up close to the black twister.

Then, just at the right instant, he leaped a-straddle.

The funnel of wind gave a snort that sounded more or less like a mountain choking to death. Thereafter, it started to use all the tricks bucking bronchos have ever figured out to use when a roughrider is trying to gentle them—only on a much larger scale. Bill quirted a plenty, shoved in the steel, and slapped the brute on the ears with his sombrero, giving a coyote yell of a size to make any state that was less tough than Oklahoma split right down the middle.

Soon the outraged cyclone was high-flying, sun-fishing, pin-wheeling, rearing back, side-throwing, high-diving —doing everything of the sort a broncho had ever invented. But, though Pecos Bill did have a few minutes of what you might call discomfort, he was bound and determined to ride it out. So he rode that bucking cyclone all over Oklahoma, New Mexico and parts of Texas.

When it began to pant and groan, showing it was desperate, Bill edged this cyclone over to the counties in Texas that had been hit hardest by the Great Drought. Then the cyclone did exactly what Pecos had figured it would do when it got licked—rained out from under him.

It did this just in the nick of time to save thousands of cattle from thirsting to death.

Pecos Bill wasn't hurt any, of course. He simply slid down to the ground on a streak of lightning. And when Widow Maker turned up in a couple of days, Bill could go back to work again, in the ordinary way.

Which of Bill's characteristics do you admire most? Why?

Why do you think Bill wants to make the cowboy business harder? How does he do that?

What do you think is the "tallest" (most exaggerated) part of this tall tale? Why?

Write Would you want to live the life of a cowhand? Explain why or why not in a paragraph.

If You Say So, Claude

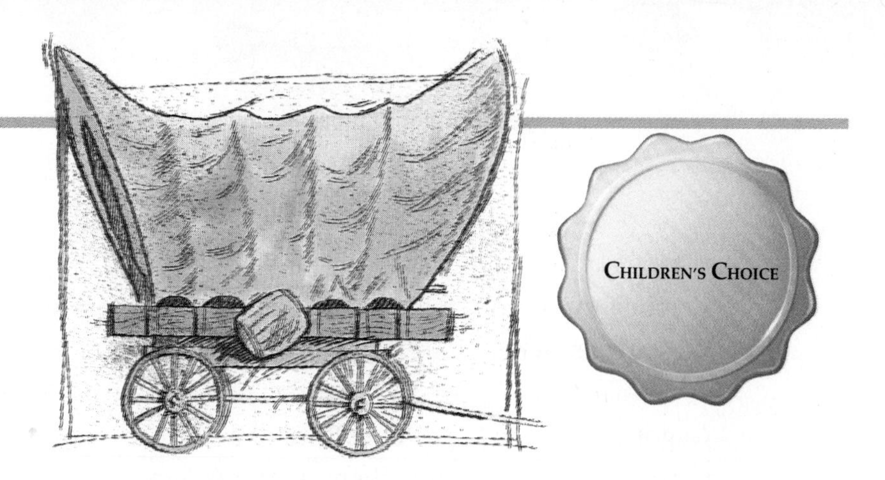

by Joan Lowery Nixon

In the spring, after the last of the big snows, Shirley and Claude drove down from the silver-mining towns of the Rocky Mountains. They headed for that great state called Texas.

Claude was as short as he was broad, with a curly gray beard that waggled when he talked. Shirley was as tall as a doorpost, and almost as thin, with hair and skin the color of prairie dust with the sun on it. They drove in a covered wagon pulled by two sway-backed, but good-natured, horses.

"I can't abide those minin' towns any longer, Shirley," Claude said. "All that shootin' and yellin' is too rough a life for me. I've heard there's plenty of peace and quiet to be found in that great state called Texas."

"If you say so, Claude," Shirley said. But she missed the mountains and the forests and the plumb good looks of the Colorado Territory.

illustrations by Charles Cashwell

They followed a trail that cut south and turned east into upper West Texas, where long canyons dug deep into the hard rock.

"Will you look at that!" Claude cried. He eased the horses and wagon down a trail to the bottom of a narrow, rocky canyon. The purple shadows lay over them, and the silence lay around them.

"Shirley, I do believe this is the peaceful place we've been lookin' for," Claude said.

"I hope not," Shirley said. "I don't really take to this place, Claude. I feel like I'm in a four-sided box."

"Never mind. This land will grow on you, Shirley," Claude said. "For now, why don't you take the rifle and see if you can hunt up some meat for the table. I'll get our sleepin' pallets out of the wagon and tend to the horses."

So Shirley unfolded her long legs, stuck her feet in her boots, hiked up her skirts, and climbed down from the wagon. She took the rifle and edged past the back of the wagon. Right off she spied a fat, lop-eared rabbit sitting on a rock ledge just across the narrow canyon; so she raised the rifle and fired.

Shirley's aim never was very good, so she missed the rabbit; and that old bullet bounced off the rock and back and forth across the canyon, whanging and banging, zinging and zanging, making a terrible racket. Shirley and the rabbit just froze, staring wide-eyed at each other.

Well, Claude took that moment to stick his head out the back of the wagon to see what that awful noise was, and the bullet tore right through the top of his hat, dropping it in the dust at Shirley's feet.

Claude looked across the canyon just in time to see the rabbit hightail it behind the ledge. He thought on it for a moment. Then he said, "Shirley, get back in the wagon. I don't think we want to live in a place where we can't go out to get meat for the table without the rabbits shootin' back. We're gonna have to move on."

Shirley picked up Claude's hat, climbed back into the wagon, and gave a happy sigh of relief.

"If you say so, Claude," she said.

For two days Shirley and Claude headed south, farther down into that great state called Texas. The sun was mean enough to sizzle lizards and curl up the cracks in the dried-out earth, when Claude pulled the sweating, but good-natured, horses to a stop.

He said, "Shirley, I do believe this is the peaceful place we've been lookin' for."

Shirley gazed at the flat landscape that stretched before her gray and bleak, broken only by clumps of scrubby mesquite. And she said, "I hope not, Claude. This land has got the worst case of the uglies I've ever seen."

"Never mind. It'll grow on you, Shirley," Claude said. "For now, why don't you go see what you can find in the way of firewood. I'll get our sleepin' pallets out of the wagon and tend to the horses."

So Shirley unfolded her long legs, stuck her feet in her boots, hiked up her skirts, and climbed down from the wagon. She walked back aways, among the clumps of mesquite. Suddenly she heard an angry rattle. She looked down, and her right boot was planted square on the neck of a mad five-foot diamondback rattler that had stretched out in the shade to take a nap.

Before she could think what to do, she heard another noise. She looked over to her left to see a mean little wild hog. Its beady eyes glared, its sharp tusks quivered, and its small hooves pawed the ground, getting ready to charge.

Quick as she could, Shirley stooped down, grabbed the snake careful like around the neck, and, using it as a whip, flipped its tail at the wild hog. That tail, rattle and all, wrapped itself tight about the neck of the hog.

But the hog was coming fast, and all Shirley could do was hang onto the snake and use all her strength to twirl the hog clear off his feet and round and around her head. With a zap she let go. The snake fell to the ground, done for. But the hog flew off, squealing and snorting and carrying on something awful.

Shirley's aim never was very good, so it happened that just as Claude climbed down from the wagon to see what was making the

terrible racket, that hog sailed right past his face, nearly brushing the end of his nose.

Claude watched the hog until he was out of sight, way yonder past a far clump of mesquite, and he thought on it for a moment.

"Shirley," he called, "get back in the wagon. It seems to me a man has a right to set foot outside his wagon without gettin' bad-mouthed by a wild hog who wants the right of way. Especially," he added, "when that hog's in a place no hog ever ought to be. We're gonna have to move on."

Shirley climbed back into the wagon and gave a happy sigh of relief.

"If you say so, Claude," she said.

For the next few days Shirley and Claude headed east in that great state called Texas. The dusty trail rose and took them into land that was strewn with rocks and boulders of all sizes.

Claude pulled the stumbling, but good-natured, horses to a stop and said, "Shirley, I do believe this is the peaceful place we've been lookin' for."

Shirley gazed out at the ridges and rocks and the stubby trees whose roots clung to the patches of soil. And she said, "I hope not, Claude. This land is nothin' but bumpy-lumpy and makes me feel dry enough to spit cotton."

"Never mind. This place will grow on you, Shirley," Claude said. "For now, why don't you set things to right around here. I'll get our sleepin' pallets out of the wagon and tend to the horses."

So Shirley unfolded her long legs, stuck her feet in her boots, hiked up her skirts, and climbed down from the wagon. She strung a line between the rim of the wagon and a branch of a nearby tree, and on it she hung out to air Claude's long johns and his other shirt, and her petticoats and second-best, store-bought dress.

She was just finishing this chore when she heard a crackle of a broken twig. She turned around to see a large, mangy wolf creeping closer and closer. His eyes were narrow slits, his ears were laid back, and he was up to no good.

Shirley grabbed the nearest thing at hand, the frying pan that was hanging on the back of the wagon, and she let fly at the wolf.

Shirley's aim never was very good, so the frying pan hit the clothesline instead, sweeping it down, just as the wolf leaped forward.

Unfortunately for the wolf, he dove right inside the skirt and on up through the bodice of Shirley's second-best, store-bought dress. His head poked out of the sweetheart neckline, and his front paws were pinned so he couldn't use them.

Well, he set up a snarling and a yelping, meanwhile bouncing around on his back legs and making a terrible racket.

Just as Claude came around the front of the wagon to see what was going on, that old wolf bounced and leaped right on past him, carrying on something awful.

Claude watched the wolf until he disappeared around a far boulder, then he thought on it for a moment.

"Shirley," he said, "get back in the wagon. I don't know why that pointy-nose lady has got her dander up, but I sure don't want any near neighbors that mean and noisy. We're gonna have to move on."

Shirley gathered up their things, put them into the back of the wagon, and climbed up on the seat next to Claude. She gave a happy sigh of relief and said, "If you say so, Claude."

The trail into that great state called Texas curled east and southeast into its heartland. And as it rose it softened into rolling hills, with meadows cupped between. Splashes of blue and gold and red wildflowers dotted the grassy hillsides, and great oaks spread their branches to make deep pools of shade.

Upward they went, until they crested a gentle hill.

Shirley put a hand on Claude's arm and said, "Stop the wagon, Claude."

He pulled the tired, but good-natured, horses to a stop under a stand of oaks, and she said, "Take a look around us. Breathe in that pure air. How's this for a place of peace and quiet?"

"I don't know," Claude said. "Any place that looks this good is

bound to get filled up with people afore long. And then we wouldn't remember what peace and quiet were all about."

"Down at the foot of the hill is a stream, probably just jumpin' with fish," Shirley said. "And you can look far enough in both directions goin' and comin' so you could spot a traveler and think on him two days afore he got here."

"I don't know," Claude said again. "Get down from the wagon, Shirley, and see what you can put together for supper. I'll get our sleeping pallets out of the wagon and tend to the horses."

Shirley unfolded her long legs, stuck her feet in her boots, hiked up her skirts, and climbed down from the wagon. She took out the stew pot and set it on the ground under an old and gnarled oak tree. Then she took down the rifle. She was going into the woods to find some fresh meat for the table.

Suddenly she heard the rustle of small leaves, and she looked up to see a big bobcat on a branch near her head. His narrow eyes were gleaming, his lips were pulled back in a snarl, and his tail was twitching. Shirley knew he was getting his mind set to spring.

Well, Shirley stared that bobcat square in the eyes and said to him, "I've found my peaceful place, and you're not goin' to spoil it for me." She raised her rifle, aimed it dead center at the bobcat, and pulled the trigger.

Shirley's aim never was very good. The shot hit that old tree branch, snapping it with a crack that flipped the bobcat in an arc right over the wagon. He came down so hard against a boulder that the force knocked it loose, and it rolled down the hill, tearing up the turf.

Behind it came the screeching bobcat, all spraddle-legged, with every pointy claw digging furrows in the soil as he slid down the hill.

Splat! went the boulder into the stream, knocking two good-sized, unsuspecting trout up on the bank and damming up a nice little pond. The bobcat flew over the stream and ran off so fast that Shirley knew she'd seen the last of him.

Claude came running and said, "Shirley, what was makin' all that racket?"

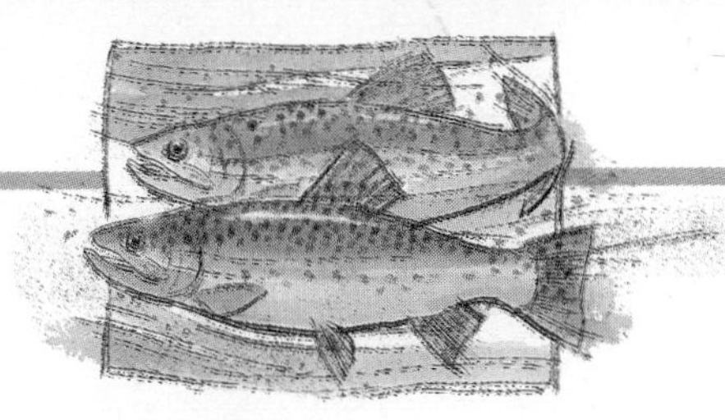

"Nothin' much," Shirley said. "Just a few things gettin' done around here after a branch fell off that tree."

Claude peered at the tree. "Seems there's something oozin' out of that tree into our stew pot," he said.

"What pure good luck!" Shirley said. "Looks like when that branch broke, it opened a honey cache, Claude. You'll have somethin' good on your biscuits tonight."

She took his arm and pointed him toward the sloping hillside. "Take notice that my vegetable garden's already plowed, and there's two good-sized trout down by the stream that are goin' to be pan-fried for supper."

Claude thought on this a moment. Then he said, "Shirley, get back in the wagon and start pullin' out the stuff we'll need. If you can just learn to do your chores without makin' so much noise, then I think we've found us our place of peace and quiet."

Shirley leaned against the wagon and gave a happy sigh of relief. She looked down at the stream that was sparking with pieces of afternoon sunlight, and she gazed out over the hills and the meadows that were soft and pleasing to the eyes.

She gave Claude the biggest smile he'd ever seen anyone come up with, and she said, "If you say so, Claude."

Which part of the story did you find most humorous? Do you think the repeated plot pattern contributes to the humor? Why or why not?

What do you think Shirley is really like? What clues does the author provide to help you understand Shirley?

Why do you think Shirley doesn't tell Claude what actually happens each time they stop?

WRITE Describe the most peaceful place you've ever seen. Would you like to live there? Why or why not?

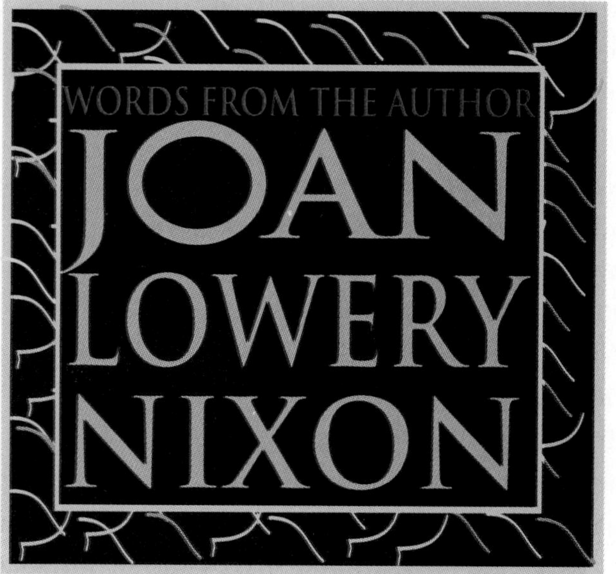

The idea for the book came from my son-in-law, who was living in Houston and complaining because he wanted to find a more peaceful place to live. I had lived in the Rocky Mountains and had done a lot of research into mining towns, which are wild, noisy places, so I decided one of the characters for this new book would be someone from a mining town who was looking for a more peaceful place to live. I decided he should have a wife, and Shirley popped into my mind, tall and lean. I named her husband Claude and figured he should be short and round.

I have always loved reading. My mother read to me when I was little. My grandfather would put down whatever he was doing when I asked for a story. My favorite book was *Little Women*. I wanted to be just like Jo Marsh. I felt very deprived because we lived in a one-story house while Jo had an attic she could escape to.

I knew when I was quite young that I wanted to be a writer, like Jo, but I was interested in journalism. I sold my first magazine article when I was seventeen. When I was at the University of Southern California, I got a part-time job writing for a fan magazine. I interviewed the starlets, not the stars. For years I wrote free-lance articles, chiefly nonfiction. It was in Texas that I went to a writer's conference, heard two people speak about writing for young people, and thought that might be interesting. The next day my two oldest daughters came to me and said, "If you're going to write for children, you have to make it a mystery, and we have to be in it." So I did, and it was great fun. I never have trouble plotting my mysteries or coming up with the ideas. I keep a file for ideas. Sometimes I clip an article, or scribble a few sentences. Every once in a while I dump the whole thing on the bed and start rummaging through it.

I write several different kinds of books—mysteries, historical fiction, and picture books. I don't know that I prefer one over the other. What excites me are those times when I get an idea I like, and it begins to grow. It doesn't seem to matter then who the audience is or what type of book it will be. The whole thing becomes the excitement of developing the idea. One advantage of writing for young adults is that I get to write longer pieces. There are always so many elements I want to put into my stories that I have trouble sticking to two hundred pages.

Tall Tales

What elements in "If You Say So, Claude" and "Pecos Bill, King of Texas Cowboys" make these stories deserving of the label "tall tales"?

Writer's Workshop

You have read two well-known examples of the humorous tall tale. Keeping these examples in mind, write your own tall tale. Devise a "larger-than-life" story with events that are highly unlikely and a main character who has admirable but exaggerated traits.

Writer's Choice What do you think about the tall tale as a way to tell a story? What are its advantages and disadvantages compared to other story forms? Make a list of some of your best ideas about the tall tale as a form. Think of a way to express them and to publish them so that you can share your thoughts with others.

CONNECTIONS

MULTICULTURAL CONNECTION

HEROIC SONGS

One of the great storytelling traditions of Mexico and the American Southwest is the corrido, or ballad. Corridos are tales of love or adventure set to music. Many were inspired by the Mexican Revolution of 1910-1920. Here is the first stanza of a corrido about the revolutionary leader Pancho Villa:

This is a very short story
About General Pancho Villa
Who fought great heroic battles
And rose to the heights of glory.

The basic corrido has four-line stanzas, with eight syllables per line, but there are many variations. All corridos tell a story based on a real event. During the revolution these songs helped keep Mexicans informed about the course of the war.

Corridos are still being written and sung today in Mexico and along the U.S.– Mexican border. They also have been recorded in this country by Mexican American artists such as Lydia Mendoza and Linda Ronstadt. Corridos remain a living expression of Mexican culture and traditions.

Brainstorm some ideas for corridos that you could write yourself. If possible, listen to corrido recordings to get a feel for the music and the lyrics.

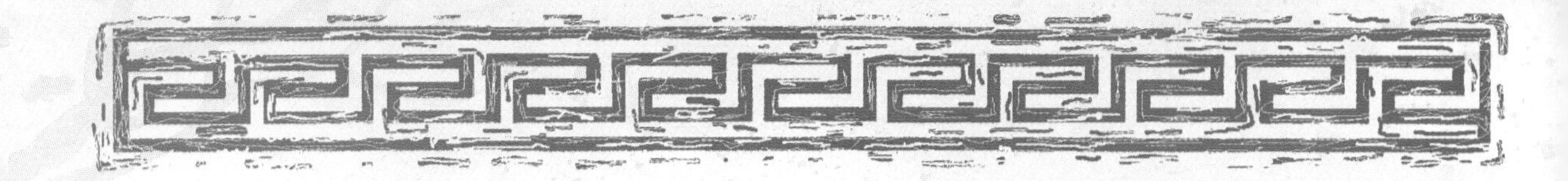

LANGUAGE ARTS CONNECTION

COMPOSE A CORRIDO

Write a corrido of your own based on one or more of the ideas developed during the brainstorming session. You may want to create a chart to help you order the sequence of events in your song, focusing on one event or idea for each stanza. When you have written a first draft of your corrido, have a classmate help you revise it. Then produce a final edited version.

ART CONNECTION

PUBLISH YOUR CORRIDO

Corridos are sometimes published in Mexico and sold on the streets so that people can learn the words and pass the story along. Publish your corrido by writing it on art paper and then decorating the paper as you like. Your decorations should include artwork or photos that illustrate the subject of your corrido. Display your published corrido in class.

Top left: Linda Ronstadt

UNIT THREE

BONANZAS

For a jolly good book whereon to look
Is better to me than gold.
John Wilson

Every country and culture values not only its customs but also its historic treasures. In the selections in this unit, you will learn about the search for gold and for ancient artifacts. As you read, think about the sacrifices people have made to acquire their "treasures."

THEMES

BEARSTONE

BY WILL HOBBS

Cloyd, a Native American boy, is taken to live with an old rancher in the mountains of Colorado. The strengths inherited from his ancestors help him as he discovers a new world.

ALA Notable Book, Teachers' Choice

HARCOURT BRACE LIBRARY BOOK

THE EL DORADO ADVENTURE

BY LLOYD ALEXANDER

The amazing Vesper Holly and her bumbling guardian sail from Philadelphia after receiving a mysterious telegram. In El Dorado, Vesper discovers that she owns a volcano and the area around it, and that the fate of the Chirica Indians depends on her ability to keep the property.

Award-Winning Author

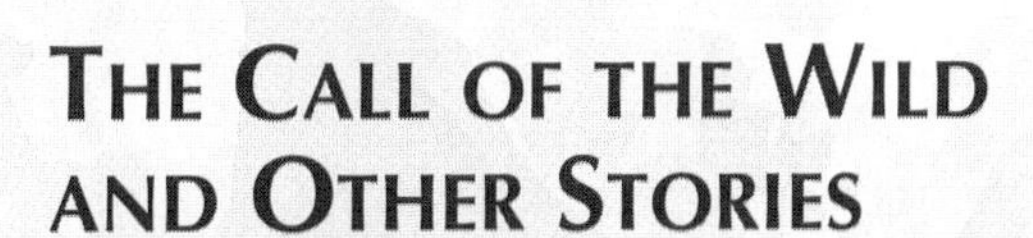

The Call of the Wild and Other Stories

BY JACK LONDON

These stories provide a vivid re-creation of rugged life in the frozen wastes of the Yukon during the Klondike gold rush.

Anne of Green Gables

BY L. M. MONTGOMERY

After a twelve-year-old orphan comes to live with Matthew Cuthbert and his sister, their lives are never the same. Anne's adventures are the basis of this classic novel.

Jingo Django

BY SID FLEISCHMAN

Jingo Hawks, of Mrs. Daggatt's Beneficent Orphan House in Boston, is hired out as a chimney sweep. Then the mysterious Mr. Peacock "buys" Jingo, and they set out on a treasure hunt. Wonderful, hilarious adventures follow.

Award-Winning Author

THEME

THE KLONDIKE

Like many people today, people in 1898 dreamed of getting rich. Read about dreams being lost and found as thousands of people flocked to Canada during the Klondike Gold Rush.

CONTENTS

Miles
Yukon River
Fortymile
Dawson
Bonanza Creek
Klondike River
KLONDIKE GOLDFIELDS
ALASKA
YUKON TERRITORY
UNITED
STATES
CANADA
Yukon River
Whitehorse
Miles Canyon
C O A S T M
YUKON TERRITORY
BRITISH COLUMBIA
Dyea
GULF
PACIFIC OCEAN
Lake Bennett
Lake Lindeman
CANADA
UNITED STATES
Chilkoot Pass
Trail
Trail
White Pass
Dyea
Dyea
Skagway
Skagway
0 5 10 15
Miles
KLONDIKE FEVER
The Famous Gold Rush of 1898
by Michael Cooper
THE KLONDIKE 1896-1898

KLONDIKE FEVER:

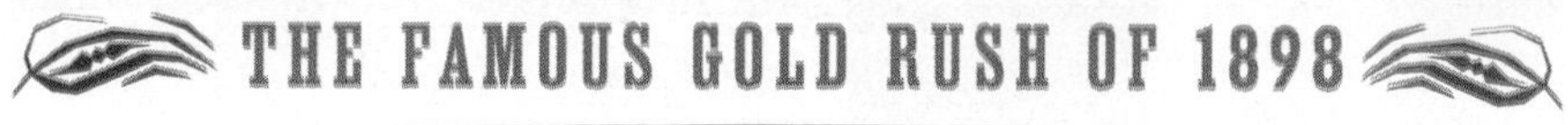

By Michael Cooper

ONE MIDSUMMER day in 1896, on a creek so remote that it did not even have a name, Robert Henderson scooped up a pan of gravel and sand. As he peered into the pan, his eyes grew wide. Did he dare believe what he saw? There was one flake . . . now several flakes . . . of the precious metal that he had spent his life seeking. It was GOLD!

The discovery of these few flakes confirmed what the excited prospector had long suspected. Buried in this creek and in other creeks nearby were tens of millions of dollars worth of gold dust and gold nuggets. But as close as Henderson was to that fortune, he would not be the one who found it.

$7,000 pan of selected gold nuggets from Quartz Creek, Yukon Territory.

This lone prospector was an important, but unlucky, character in the story of the Klondike Gold Rush. Henderson grew up in Nova Scotia and began his gold-seeking career in the mountains of Colorado. After several luckless years there, the Canadian journeyed north almost to the Arctic Circle. Near the border between Alaska and Canada, Henderson began prospecting, or exploring, for gold in the many creeks that flow into the upper Yukon River. For over two years, he had prospected in creek after creek and found nothing but disappointment.

Robert Henderson

But that midsummer day in 1896 his luck changed. After finding those first few flakes of gold in the creek, which he had hopefully named Gold Bottom, Henderson dug feverishly for several weeks. He unearthed over seven hundred and fifty dollars' worth of gold flakes and gold nuggets. This was more money than most people in those days earned in a year. Henderson was feeling very lucky because his many years of hard work were finally paying off. But his luck did not last long.

Returning with supplies from the town of Fortymile, Henderson met George Washington Carmack and his two Indian companions, Jim and Charlie. Influenced by the growing number of white people in the region, Indians like Jim and Charlie had adopted white men's names. Henderson told the three men about his discovery. But Carmack, Jim, and Charlie were not prospectors, and they thought hunting gold was a waste of time. They were more interested in hunting moose.

For several days, the three companions stalked the large moose that fed on the willow trees growing along the creeks. But gold has a powerful allure, and the trio could not forget about Henderson's discovery.

A few days later, the three men were camped on Rabbit Creek. While one of them was washing a pan in the clear water, he saw the glint of gold on the gravelly creek bottom. He reached into the shallow water and pulled out a thumb-sized nugget. With a whoop and a shout he called his two friends over. They scooped up a big handful of gravel; it contained nearly four dollars' worth of gold. If one scoop yielded this much gold, they thought with growing excitement, the creek must be full of it. We're rich! the threesome realized, RICH!

Carmack hurried down river to Fortymile to file claims for himself, Jim, and Charlie. A claim is a legal right to mine gold, or other minerals, on a specific piece of land. After filing his claims, Carmack proudly walked into a smokey saloon full of miners. In a loud voice, he told the crowd that he had made one of the biggest gold strikes ever. His boast was greeted by a chorus of hoots and disbelief.

Why should anyone believe that this man had discovered gold? After all he was not a "sourdough," someone who has been a prospector for a long time. Carmack backed up his words by pulling out a small bag of gold nuggets. This was all the proof the prospectors needed. The next morning Fortymile was nearly deserted. Its citizens had rushed to stake claims on Rabbit Creek. The great Klondike Gold Rush had begun.

Carmack could have kept his gold strike a secret, at least for a while. But people who lived in that inhospitable land had a code that food, cabins, and even the exact location of a gold strike were freely shared. Despite that code, Carmack did not bother to travel the few miles to Gold Bottom Creek to tell Henderson of his discovery.

Some people believe Henderson was ignored because of his scornful treatment of Jim and Charlie. But there is no way of knowing exactly why Carmack neglected Henderson. What is known is that Henderson did not hear about the strike until the best claims had been taken. Many of the people whom Carmack did tell shared in the millions of dollars' worth of gold that were dug from Rabbit Creek, which had been aptly renamed Bonanza Creek. *Bonanza* is a Spanish word that means the "source of wealth."

As news of the gold strike spread slowly throughout the region, more and more people joined the rush. The trading post owner in Fortymile loaded a steamboat full of food and mining equipment and steamed up the Yukon to the Klondike River. Near where the two rivers joined, he built a log trading post; this was the beginning of the famous gold-rush town of Dawson. Because Bonanza and other gold-laden creeks flow into the larger Klondike River, the whole region was called the Klondike.

From Dawson, rumors of the big gold strike drifted downstream two hundred and twenty-five miles to Circle City, Alaska. The people there were used to hearing false rumors, so at first they didn't believe the stories about Bonanza Creek. But their curiosity soon got the better of them.

In cold and gloomy January the rush from Circle to Dawson began. Prospectors loaded food, tents, and mining equipment onto sleds, which were pulled through the deep snow by dog teams. There was so much demand for sled dogs that the price for a dog jumped from fifty dollars to several hundred dollars. People who couldn't afford a team pulled their own sleds. By spring, Circle City was nearly a ghost town, while Dawson had become a sprawling tent city of fifteen hundred people.

The rush of gold seekers from Circle to Dawson was a trickle compared to the torrent that came later. Once people throughout Canada and the United States heard gold was being shoveled from Klondike creeks, the region was flooded by a wave of humanity.

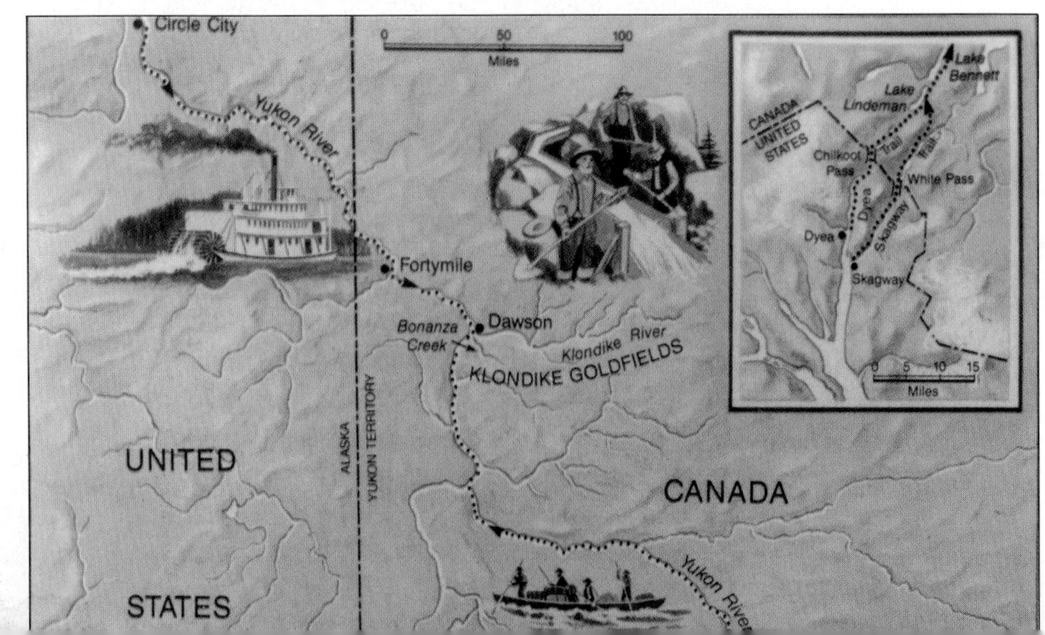

The Gold-Rush City of Dawson

DAWSON DID not exist before 1896. But by the fall of 1898 it was one of the largest, liveliest, and most cosmopolitan cities in the Northwest. In some ways Dawson resembled other North American cities, but in many other ways it was unique.

Dawson was a city where everything was scarce except money. With that in mind, some of the thousands of people who arrived there during the hectic summer of 1898 hoped to strike it rich without ever mining for gold.

One man arrived in a boat loaded with thousands of pounds of candy, oranges, lemons, bananas, and cucumbers, scarce foods that sold quickly. Another brought his cow and sold milk for thirty dollars a gallon. Someone else arrived with twenty-four hundred eggs and sold them all for thirty-six hundred dollars. One of the most unusual cargoes was a load of irresistible kittens that were sold for fifteen dollars each to lonely miners.

With the arrival of so many newcomers that summer, Dawson grew rapidly from a city of tents to a city of log cabins and wood-frame buildings inhabited by some twenty thousand people. During the day, busy Broadway and Wall Street were like big bazaars where it was possible to buy mining equipment, books, tuxedos, furs, ice cream, and sundry other items.

Before it was three years old, Dawson had many of the comforts found in older cities, such as telephones, running water, steam heat, and electricity. Swank restaurants served elaborate dinners. The city had three hospitals, dozens of physicians, and scores of lawyers.

By the end of the summer of 1898, Dawson was a busy and prosperous city.

Many people were drawn to Dawson because jobs were plentiful. And all jobs, from lawyer to laundress, paid exceptionally well. While the average wage in the United States was less than two dollars a day, in Dawson gold dust weighers earned twenty dollars a day, teamsters earned one hundred dollars a day, and lawyers earned one hundred and fifty dollars a day.

In addition to its high wages, Dawson was unique in other ways. While the city's two banks readily exchanged Canadian dollars for gold, many people preferred to use gold dust rather than money for their purchases. Restaurants, stores, and other businesses kept scales on their counters to weigh the dust, which was worth sixteen dollars an ounce.

Gold dust was so commonly used that it found its way into nearly everything. Women who washed clothes for a living sometimes scooped twenty dollars or more in gold from the bottom of their washtubs at the end of the day. During the Great Depression of the 1930s, jobless people made money by gathering the gold dust from under Dawson's stores and sidewalks where it had fallen between floorboards many years before.

While Dawson produced a lot of gold, just about everything else had to be imported. There were no local farms that grew vegetables or raised chickens and cows for eggs, milk, and meat. No local manufacturers made clothing or shoes. Nearly everything people needed for day-to-day living had to be shipped from cities in southern Canada or in the United States.

Stores kept a small set of scales on the counter to weigh gold dust.

The nearest cities were Victoria and Seattle. Overland, they were only two thousand miles away. But there were no overland supply routes, so food and other necessities had to be shipped up the Pacific Coast to St. Michael and then up the Yukon River to Dawson. It was a five-thousand-mile trip that took at least six weeks.

A paddle-wheel steamer on the Yukon River.

For supplies and transportation, the Yukon River was an important lifeline for the whole Yukon Territory. By the autumn of 1898, there were sixty boats steaming up and down the river. Some, like the *Suzy* and the *Bonanza King*, were grand Mississippi-style riverboats built in Louisville, Kentucky. But these boats sailed only from June to October when the river wasn't frozen. For the rest of the year Dawson was entirely isolated.

Because of this isolation, people sorely missed news about the rest of the world. They were particularly interested in the Spanish-American War, which had begun in February of 1898. News traveled between other cities by telegraph and by telephone. Although Dawson had local telephone service, there were no wires across the vast wilderness to connect it with cities to the south. Newspapers, by the time they reached Dawson, were at least a month old.

But any news was welcome news. One newcomer auctioned a five-week-old Seattle newspaper to the highest bidder. It was sold for fifty dollars to a clever miner who hired a good public speaker to read the newspaper to an audience. He charged one dollar per person for the privilege of hearing last month's news and drew a crowd of over a hundred people.

Dawson, unlike Skagway, which fit the image of the wild gold-rush town, was a remarkably law-abiding city. The two hundred Northwest Mounted Police garrisoned in the region maintained strict law and order. No one in Dawson was permitted to carry a revolver without a license, and few people were given licenses. There were only two murders and a few cases of assault. Of the one hundred and thirty-seven deaths recorded in the Yukon Territory by the Mounties in 1898, most were from disease, mainly typhoid fever.

Petty thievery was the most common crime. Dog stealing and using vile language were other common crimes. A person convicted of one of these crimes was either fined, ordered to leave town, or sentenced to chopping firewood to heat government offices.

All in all, Dawson was a remarkably safe and civilized city. According to Samuel B. Steele, the local commander of the Northwest Mounted Police, "Acts of indecency are severely punished and it can safely be said that any man, woman, or child may walk at any time of the night to any portion of this large camp with perfect safety from insult. . . ."

Like any other city, Dawson had its prominent citizens. Big Alex McDonald was called "King of the Klondike" because he was by far the richest man in Dawson. He had spent many years mining for gold in Colorado and in southeast Alaska before moving to the Upper Yukon in 1895. McDonald didn't like the idea of actually digging for gold. Instead, he made a fortune during the gold rush buying claims and letting other men work them in return for a share of the gold. As he grew wealthy from his choice claims, Big Alex bought steamboats and businesses. By 1898, the King of the Klondike was worth an estimated five million dollars.

Samuel B. Steele

Another famous Dawson resident was Belinda Mulroney. Giving up a job as a ship's stewardess, the intrepid woman crossed the Coast Mountains and floated by boat to the new gold-rush town in the spring of 1897. She brought with her five thousand dollars' worth of cotton clothing and hot-water bottles, which she sold in Dawson for thirty thousand dollars. Mulroney wisely invested her profits in a lunch counter, in building cabins to sell to newcomers, and in a roadhouse, a kind of restaurant, in the goldfields outside of Dawson.

By the summer of 1898, Mulroney had enough money to build the Fairview, the city's fanciest hotel. It had electric lights, steam heat, and a Turkish bath. At dinner, dining room tables were set with silver, china, and crystal. In the background, a chamber orchestra played Bach and Mozart.

Belinda Mulroney

The luxurious Fairview and other city comforts made it easy to forget that Dawson existed only because of the gold being dug from the surrounding streams and hills. Life was quite different for the several thousand people who lived and labored in the mining camps.

These men were among the two hundred Northwest Mounted Police, who kept law and order.

The Gold Rush Ends

ALTHOUGH MILLIONS of dollars' worth of gold was still buried in the hills around Dawson, by mid-1899 the frenzied gold rush had ended. The Klondike Gold Rush had lasted only three years, but its legacy endures to this day.

Gold mining remained a major industry in the Klondike region for over fifty years. But after 1899, most of the gold was mined by big companies with their headquarters in distant cities like Montreal, Chicago, and New York. These companies took over mining in the Klondike after a railroad was blasted out of the rugged mountains from Skagway through White Pass to the new town of Whitehorse. Built in the remarkably short time of fourteen months, the railroad enabled mining companies to move large gold dredges across the Coast Mountains. These efficient machines were operated by only a few men, but they could do the work of hundreds of men by sifting through tons of gravel a day.

Construction of a railroad across rugged mountains to Whitehorse helped big companies take over gold mining in the Klondike.

After the mining companies took over, little gold was mined by sourdoughs wielding picks, shovels, and gold pans. But many prospectors clung to the dream of unearthing a fortune, or they simply enjoyed the gold-mining life. These sourdoughs joined other, smaller rushes in both Canada and Alaska. In the summer of 1898, gold was discovered two thousand miles across Alaska on the beach at Cape Nome. The following summer, some eight thousand Klondikers in Dawson clambered aboard paddle-wheel steamers bound for the new tent city of Nome. Three years later, other Klondikers joined the gold rush to the Chena River, an area near the middle of Alaska which would become the city of Fairbanks.

One of the people who participated in that 1902 Fairbanks rush was Belinda Mulroney, the Dawson hotel owner. She had used her considerable business skills to become the successful manager of the Klondike's largest gold-mining company. But she quit that job for the excitement of the Fairbanks gold rush. Eight years later, Mulroney retired to a quieter life on a ranch near Yakima, Washington.

Another veteran of the Klondike who retired was George Carmack. After separating from his Indian wife, Carmack and a new wife moved to the growing port of Vancouver, British Columbia, where they invested their money in real estate.

George Washington Carmack, sitting third from left, at a birthday party in Dawson.

For some prospectors, the lure of gold remained irresistible. With little luck, Robert Henderson continued digging in the creeks and streams of the Klondike until he died in 1933. Henderson's son lived his life in Dawson searching in vain for the gold that had always eluded his father.

Big Alex McDonald kept investing in mining claims, but never equaled his earlier success. By the time he died, the King of the Klondike had lost most of his fortune.

Charlie and Jim, George Carmack's Indian companions, stayed close to their ancestral home, but gave up many of their native customs. Charlie purchased a hotel and operated it until he died. And Jim, although he had made a fortune from his claims, became obsessed by gold. He spent the rest of his life unsuccessfully prospecting for another gold strike like the one at Bonanza Creek.

Alex McDonald, Belinda Mulroney, and the other men and women who ventured into the northern wilderness to prospect for gold were important pioneers of Alaska and northwest Canada. These restless people were part of the mass migration across North America after the Civil War. One of the main reasons for this mass movement was the search for gold. Eagerly seeking this precious metal, North Americans by the tens of thousands rushed west to the Pacific Ocean and then north nearly to the Arctic Circle.

These pioneers followed a pattern that characterized the many gold rushes in the last half of the nineteenth century. During those fifty years, thousands of people rushed to gold strikes in British Columbia, California, Colorado, Nevada, and other parts of western North America. Along the way they created towns, cities, and states.

Similarly, the population of Dawson and the surrounding area had multiplied from a few hundred prospectors at the beginning of 1896 to fifty thousand Klondikers at the height of the gold rush in 1898. That year, recognizing the need for local government, the Canadian Parliament in Ottawa carved the Yukon Territory out of the vast Northwest Territories. The territorial capital remained in Dawson until the 1950s, when it moved south to the more populated town of Whitehorse.

After most prospectors had moved on or given up, Robert Henderson continued his quest for gold in the Yukon Territory.

These prospectors are leaving the Klondike, headed for a new gold strike near Whitehorse.

Of the major towns and cities in Alaska and the Yukon Territory, only one was not created by a gold rush. Anchorage, Alaska's largest city, began as a construction camp for the Alaska Railroad. But Juneau, Dawson, Whitehorse, Nome, and Fairbanks all began as gold-rush towns.

In the early twentieth century, there were several more gold rushes in North America. But the continent has never witnessed another one as big or as dramatic as the great Klondike Gold Rush.

Would you like to have been a prospector during the Klondike Gold Rush? Explain your answer.

Why did the prices of basic supplies, such as food and clothing, change during the gold rush?

WRITE Choose one of the characters from the selection, and write a journal entry describing that character's life after the gold rush ends.

UP THE SLIDE

by Jack London

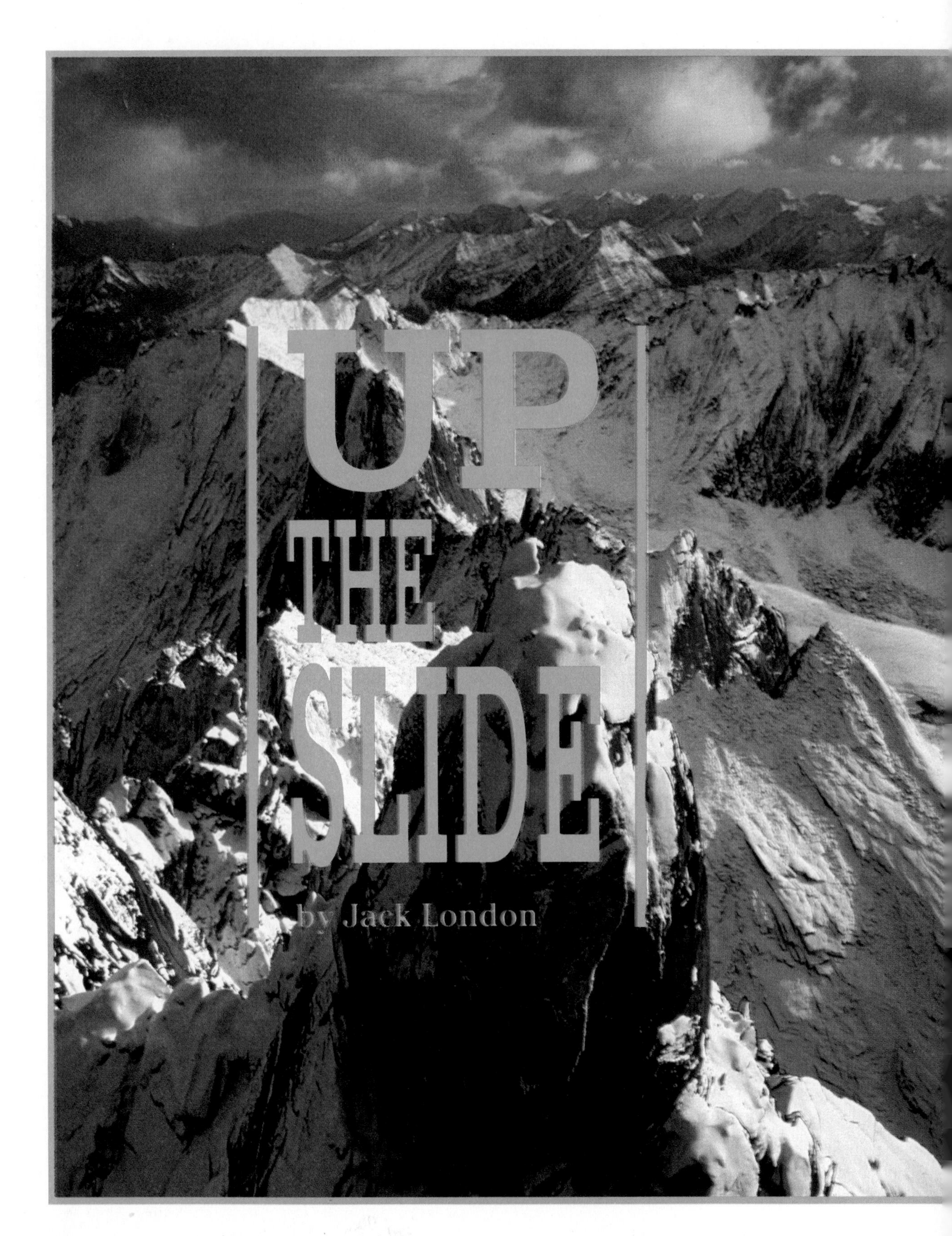

When Clay Dilham left the tent to get a sled load of firewood, he expected to be back in half an hour. So he told Swanson, who was cooking the dinner. Swanson and he belonged to different outfits, located about twenty miles apart on the Stuart River,[1] but they had become traveling partners on a trip down the Yukon to Dawson[2] to get the mail.

Swanson had laughed when Clay said he would be back in half an hour. It stood to reason, Swanson said, that good, dry firewood could not be found so close to Dawson; that whatever firewood there was originally had long since been gathered in; that firewood would not be selling at forty dollars a cord[3] if any man could go out and get a sled load and be back in the time Clay expected to make it.

Then it was Clay's turn to laugh, as he sprang on the sled and *mushed*[4] the dogs on the river trail. For, coming up from the Siwash village the previous day, he had noticed a small dead pine in an out-of-the-way place, which had defied discovery by eyes less sharp than his. And his eyes were both young and sharp, for his seventeenth birthday was just cleared.

A swift ten minutes over the ice brought him to the place, and figuring ten minutes to get the tree and ten minutes to return made him certain that Swanson's dinner would not wait.

---

[1] Stuart River: in British Columbia, Canada
[2] Dawson: a city in the Yukon Territory in northern Canada; center of the Klondike mining region
[3] cord: cut firewood that makes a stack measuring 8 feet long, 4 feet wide, and 4 feet high
[4] *mushed:* traveled with a dog team

Just below Dawson, and rising out of the Yukon itself, towered the great Moosehide Mountain, so named by Lieutenant Schwatka long ere the Klondike became famous. On the river side the mountain was scarred and gullied and gored; and it was up one of these gores or gullies that Clay had seen the tree.

Halting his dogs beneath, on the river ice, he looked up, and after some searching, rediscovered it. Being dead, its weather-beaten gray so blended with the gray wall of rock that a thousand men could pass by and never notice it. Taking root in a cranny, it had grown up, exhausted its bit of soil, and perished. Beneath it the wall fell sheer for a hundred feet to the river. All one had to do was to sink an ax into the dry trunk a dozen times and it would fall to the ice, and most probably smash conveniently to pieces. This Clay had figured on when confidently limiting the trip to half an hour.

He studied the cliff thoroughly before attempting it. So far as he was concerned, the longest way round was the shortest way to the tree. By making a long zigzag across the face of this slide and back again, he would arrive at the pine.

Fastening his ax across his shoulders so that it would not interfere with his movements, he clawed up the broken rock, hand and foot, like a cat, till the twenty feet were cleared and he could draw breath on the edge of the slide.

The slide was steep and its snow-covered surface slippery. Further, the heelless, walrus-hide soles of his *muclucs* were polished by much ice travel, and by his second step he realized how little he could depend upon them for clinging purposes. A slip at that point meant a plunge over the edge and a twenty-foot fall to the ice. A hundred feet farther along, and a slip would mean a fifty-foot fall.

He thrust his mittened hand through the snow to the earth to steady himself, and went on. But he was forced to exercise such care that the first zigzag consumed five minutes. Then, returning across the face of the slide toward the pine, he met with a new difficulty. The slope steepened considerably, so that little snow collected, while bent flat beneath this thin covering were long, dry last-year's grasses.

The surface they presented was as glassy as that of his muclucs, and when both surfaces came together his feet shot out, and he fell on his face, sliding downward and convulsively clutching for something to stay himself.

This he succeeded in doing, although he lay quiet for a couple of minutes to get back his nerve. He would have taken off his muclucs and gone at it in his socks, only the cold was thirty below zero, and at such temperature his feet would quickly freeze. So he went on, and after ten minutes of risky work made the safe and solid rock where stood the pine.

A few strokes of the ax felled it into the chasm, and peeping over the edge, he indulged in a laugh at the startled dogs. They were on the verge of bolting when he called aloud to them, soothingly, and they were reassured.

Then he turned about for the trip back. Going down, he knew, was even more dangerous than coming up, but how dangerous he did not realize till he had slipped half a dozen times, and each time saved himself by what appeared to him a miracle.

He sat down and looked at the treacherous snow-covered slope. It was manifestly impossible for him to make it with a whole body, and he did not wish to arrive at the bottom shattered like the pine tree.

But while he sat inactive the frost was stealing in on him, and the quick chilling of his body warned him that he could not delay. He must be doing something to keep his blood circulating. If he could not get down by going down, there only remained to him to get down by going up. It was a herculean task, but it was the only way out of the predicament.

From where he was he could not see the top of the cliff, but he reasoned that the gully in which lay the slide must give inward more and more as it approached the top. From what little he could see, the gully displayed this tendency; and he noticed, also, that the slide extended for many hundreds of feet upward, and that where it ended the rock was well broken up and favorable for climbing.

So instead of taking the zigzag which led downward, he made a new one leading upward and crossing the slide at an angle of thirty degrees. The grasses gave him much trouble and made him long for soft-tanned moosehide moccasins, which could make his feet cling like a second pair of hands.

He soon found that thrusting his mittened hands through the snow and clutching the grass roots was uncertain and unsafe. His

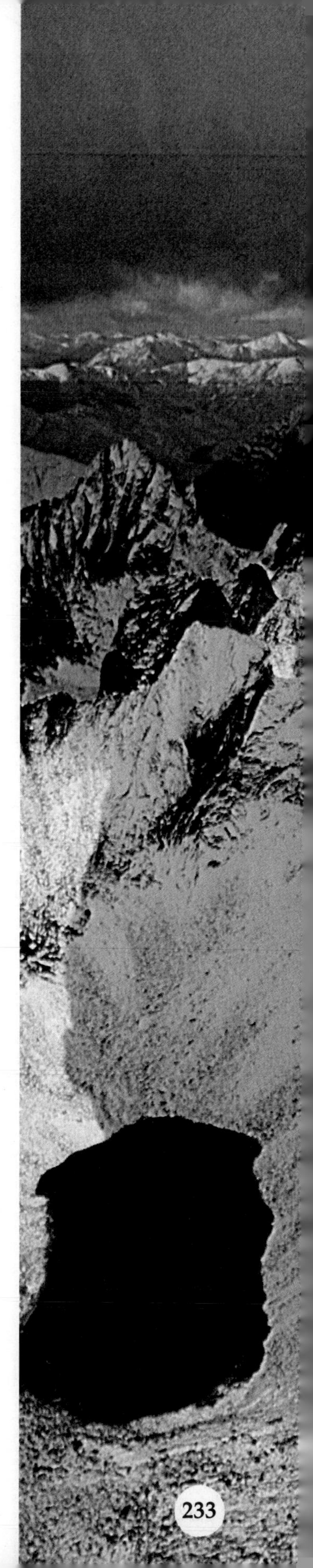

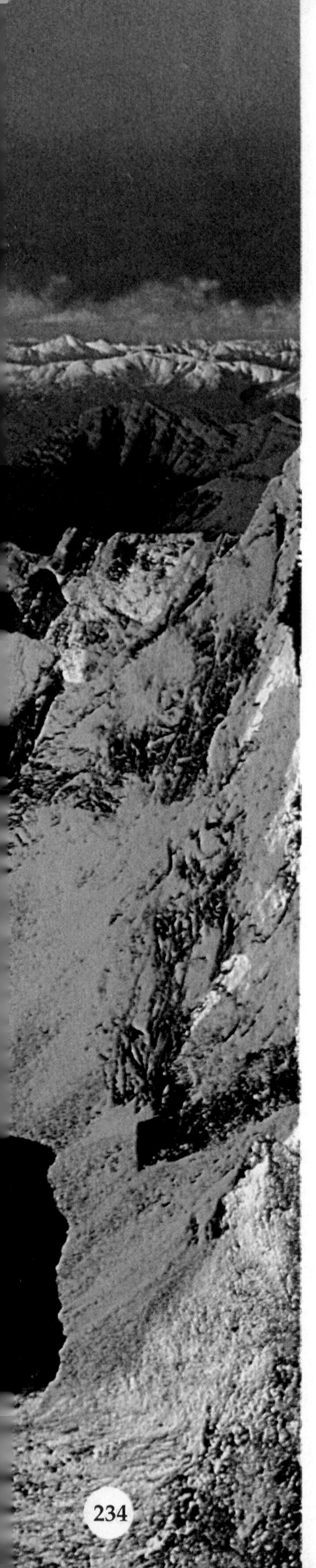

mittens were too thick for him to be sure of his grip, so he took them off. But this brought with it new trouble. When he held on to a bunch of roots the snow, coming in contact with his bare warm hand, was melted, so that his hands and the wristbands of his woolen shirt were dripping with water. This the frost was quick to attack, and his fingers were numbed and made worthless.

Then he was forced to seek good footing, where he could stand erect unsupported, to put on his mittens, and to thrash his hands against his sides until the heat came back into them.

While beating his hands against his sides he turned and looked down the long slippery slope, and figured, in case he slipped, that he would be flying with the speed of an express train ere he took the final plunge into the icy bed of the Yukon.

He passed the first outcropping rock, and the second, and at the end of an hour found himself above the third, and fully five hundred feet above the river. And here, with the end nearly two hundred feet above him, the pitch of the slide was increasing.

Each step became more difficult and perilous, and he was faint from exertion and from lack of Swanson's dinner. Three or four times he slipped slightly and recovered himself; but, growing careless from exhaustion and the long tension on his nerves, he tried to continue with too great haste, and was rewarded by a double slip of each foot, which tore him loose and started him down the slope.

On account of the steepness there was little snow; but what little there was was displaced by his body, so that he became the nucleus of a young avalanche. He clawed desperately with his hands, but there was little to cling to, and he sped downward faster and faster.

The first and second outcroppings were below him, but he knew that the first was almost out of line, and pinned his hope on the second. Yet the first was just enough in line to catch one of his feet and to whirl him over and head downward on his back.

The shock of this was severe in itself, and the fine snow enveloped him in a blinding, maddening cloud; but he was thinking quickly and clearly of what would happen if he brought up head-first against the second outcropping. He twisted himself over on his stomach, thrust both hands out to one side, and pressed them heavily against the flying surface.

This had the effect of a brake, drawing his head and shoulders to the side. In this position he rolled over and over a couple of times, and then, with a quick jerk at the right moment, he got his body the rest of the way round.

And none too soon, for the next moment his feet drove into the outcropping, his legs doubled up, and the wind was driven from his stomach with the abruptness of the stop.

There was much snow down his neck and up his sleeves. At once and with unconcern he shook this out, only to discover, when he looked up to where he must climb again, that he had lost his nerve. He was shaking as if with a palsy, and sick and faint from a frightful nausea.

Fully ten minutes passed ere he could master these sensations and summon sufficient strength for the weary climb. His legs hurt him and he was limping, and he was conscious of a sore place in his back, where he had fallen on the ax.

In an hour he had regained the point of his tumble, and was contemplating the slide, which so suddenly steepened. It was plain to him that he could not go up with hands and feet alone, and he was beginning to lose his nerve again when he remembered the ax.

Reaching upward the distance of a step, he brushed away the snow, and in the frozen gravel and crumbled rock of the slide chopped a shallow resting place for his foot. Then he came up a step, reached forward, and repeated the maneuver. And so, step by step, foothole by foothole, a tiny speck of toiling life poised like a fly on the face of Moosehide Mountain, he fought his upward way.

Twilight was beginning to fall when he gained the head of the slide and drew himself into the rocky bottom of the gully. At this point the shoulder of the mountain began to bend back toward the crest, and in addition to its being less steep, the rocks afforded better handhold and foothold. The worst was over, and the best yet to come!

The gully opened out into a miniature basin, in which a floor of soil had been deposited, out of which, in turn, a tiny grove of pines had sprung. The trees were all dead, dry and seasoned, having long since exhausted the thin skin of earth.

Clay ran his experienced eye over the timber, and estimated that it would chop up into fifty cords at least. Beyond, the gully closed in

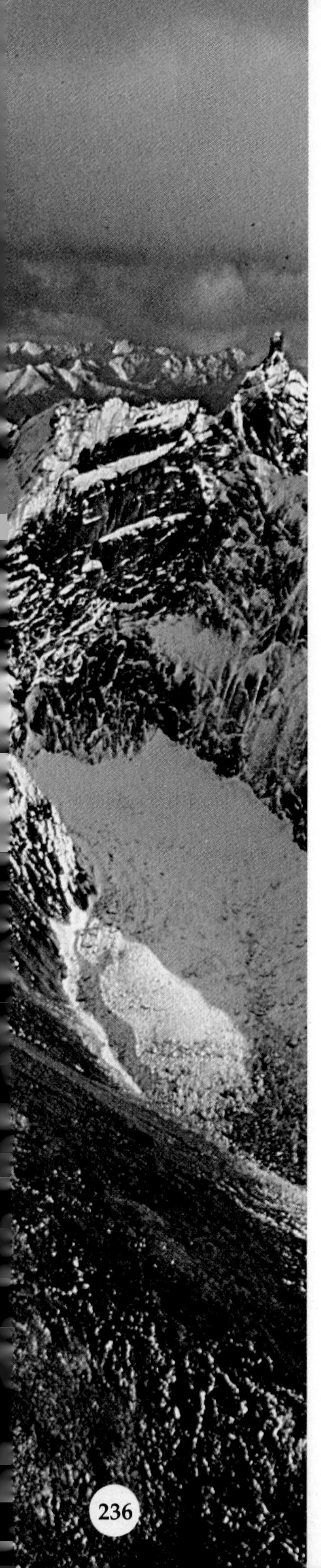

and became barren rock again. On every hand was barren rock, so the wonder was small that the trees had escaped the eyes of men. They were only to be discovered as he had discovered them—by climbing after them.

He continued the ascent, and the white moon greeted him when he came out upon the crest of Moosehide Mountain. At his feet, a thousand feet below, sparkled the lights of Dawson.

But the descent on that side was precipitate[5] and dangerous in the uncertain moonlight, and he elected to go down the mountain by its gentler northern flank. In a couple of hours he reached the Yukon at the Siwash village, and took the river trail back to where he had left the dogs. There he found Swanson, with a fire going, waiting for him to come down.

And although Swanson had a hearty laugh at his expense, nevertheless, a week or so later, in Dawson, there were fifty cords of wood sold at forty dollars a cord, and it was he and Swanson who sold them.

---

[5]precipitate: very steep, precipitous

Would you have gone after the firewood under the same conditions? Explain your answer.

What personal characteristics help Clay survive? Use examples from the selection to support your answers.

What do you think Clay learns about himself during this experience? Explain your answer.

WRITE Have you ever had to make quick critical decisions as Clay does? Write one or two paragraphs about an experience you had in which you had to use your wits.

THE KLONDIKE

Sometimes reading one selection with a particular theme will help you understand another selection better. How did reading "Klondike Fever" help you understand the reasons for what happens in "Up the Slide"?

Writer's Workshop

Write a brief essay that explains how the supply of goods affected day-to-day life in boomtowns such as Dawson. Which goods were plentiful, and which were scarce? How did supply and demand affect the cost of scarce goods? How did supply and demand affect people's actions?

Writer's Choice You have read how bonanza events such as finding gold in the Klondike can bring both benefits and problems. What kinds of things would you consider bonanzas? Could something like family or education be a bonanza? Choose an idea to write about. Plan how to express your idea, perhaps in a speech or a story. Then carry out your plan, and share the finished product with others.

THEME

ANCIENT WEALTH

What would you do if you found a buried treasure? Would you like to be the first person in more than a thousand years to examine the art and architecture of an ancient civilization? Explore the many possibilities as you read about uncovering ancient wealth and knowledge.

CONTENTS

THE MYSTERY OF THE ANCIENT MAYA

BY CAROLYN MEYER AND CHARLES GALLENKAMP

SCHOOL LIBRARY JOURNAL

Alberto Ruz Lhuillier[1] stared at the flagstone floor of the Temple of Inscriptions, high atop a terraced pyramid at the ancient city of Palenque.[2] There was something peculiar about it. Near the center of the room lay an unusually large stone with circular holes drilled around its edges, all filled with plugs to conceal them. No one had been able to figure out what they were for—and the site had been studied intensively since Stephens and Catherwood had stopped there more than a century before. But Ruz, an archaeologist from the Center for Maya Studies in Mexico, noticed something other explorers had missed: the walls of the temple seemed to continue on below the floor, as though another room lay beneath it. On a hunch, Ruz decided to raise the stone.

---

[1]Alberto Ruz Lhuillier [al · bâr´tō ro͞os dyo͞o´ē · yē · âr´]
[2]Palenque [pa · len´ke]: ancient city in Chiapas, Mexico

As workmen struggled to lift the heavy slab, Ruz could make out the outlines of a narrow opening completely filled with large stones and clay. There was nothing to do but haul out this debris. After a few days of digging, a series of stone steps began to appear, an interior staircase leading down into the pyramid. Ruz resolved to follow the stairway to its end, even though he knew it would involve an enormous amount of labor.

For two and a half months Ruz and his men struggled against heat, humidity, and choking dust while they hauled up the heavy rocks with ropes and pulleys. It took them four such stretches—a total of ten months—to clear the staircase. By the end of the first season, in the summer of 1949, only twenty-three steps had been uncovered. At the end of the third season they had dug out sixty-six steps and were down about seventy-three feet beneath the temple floor, near ground level. They still had no idea where the stairway was leading and no clues to its original function. No inscriptions were visible on the walls, no sculpture had been found. But at the bottom of the stairs they did find a box of offerings—pottery dishes, jade beads, jade earplugs, and a beautiful tear-shaped pearl. They knew they were getting close.

Excitement mounted. Next they discovered a low triangular doorway sealed by an enormous stone, and they managed to loosen it enough for Ruz to squeeze behind it and into a vaulted room. He knew instantly that his four

Page 240: Chichén Itzá, Mexico; Mayan/Toltec ruins

Page 242: Replica of burial tomb at Palenque

Interior of the burial vault in the Temple of Inscriptions, showing the gigantic carved slab that covered the sarcophagus containing the skeleton of a lord named Pacal, who ruled Palenque from A.D. 615 to 683.

seasons of exhausting labor had been rewarded.

"Out of the dim shadows emerged a vision from a fairytale, a fantastic, ethereal sight from another world. . . . Across the walls marched stucco figures in low relief. Then my eyes sought the floor. This was almost entirely filled with a great carved stone slab, in perfect condition. . . . Ours were the first eyes that had gazed on it in more than a thousand years!"

The chamber was about twenty-nine feet long by thirteen feet wide, the steeply vaulted ceiling twenty-three feet high. Human figures modeled in stucco relief, probably representing the gods of the underworld, paraded around the walls. A colossal monument filled up most of the room: a beautifully carved stone slab resting on another immense stone which in turn was supported by six huge chiseled blocks.

Ruz believed that he had found a ceremonial burial place, but he would have to wait to find out. It was mid-July; the rains had come, and funds for that phase of the exploration were gone. Ruz had to leave Palenque and his exciting project until November.

When he returned, Ruz had a narrow hole drilled into the base stone, and when the bit reached a hollow space he poked a wire through the opening. The particles of red paint that stuck to the wire told him this was not an altar but an incredible coffin. But to prove this he would have to lift the sculptured stone slab, weighing about five tons and a masterpiece of Maya art. Ruz spent two days getting ready. Hardwood logs cut in the forest were brought to the pyramid and lowered by cables through the interior staircase. Then jacks were placed under the corners of the slab, reinforced by the logs.

"On November 27, at dusk, after a twelve-hour working day, the soul-shaking manoeuvre took place." Inch by inch they raised the slab. Ruz saw that a cavity had been carved in the huge base stone, and the cavity was sealed with another polished stone, also fitted with plugs. When the slab had been lifted up about fifteen inches, Ruz could stand the suspense no longer. He squeezed under it, removed the plugs from the inner cover, and peered in.

A jade mosaic mask that covered the face of Pacal. This magnificent mask was part of a lavish offering of jade ornaments placed in the grave, and it is a superb example of the skill with which the Maya worked jade—a mineral highly prized for its beauty and ritual importance.

Green jade ornaments, red-painted teeth and bones, the fragments of a mask—Ruz gazed at the remains of the man for whom all of this had been created. A treasure of jade ornaments had been placed on the dead man at the time of his burial—headdress, earplugs, bead collar, breastplate, rings on every finger, bracelets, and sandal beads. A single jade bead had been placed in his mouth to make sure that the spirit of this king or high priest could buy food in the afterlife.

The body had been wrapped in a cotton shroud painted red and sprinkled with powdered cinnabar, a red mineral. A magnificent mask made of jade mosaic with shell and obsidian inlays for the eyes had been fitted over the face of the corpse. The mask is so lifelike that it was probably an actual portrait made while the noble was still alive.

For years before the dignitary died, the whole community had helped to prepare the tomb. After his death the body was carried down the stairway to the crypt, probably accompanied by a procession of priests in elaborate ceremonial dress, and laid in the stone coffin, the inside of which had been painted red, the color of death. Then they closed the coffin and moved the massive carved slab into place. Jewels were placed on the slab and some clay containers with food and drink were left behind, along with two beautiful heads modeled in stucco. The crypt was sealed by sliding the stone block into position in the narrow entrance.

Ruz's discovery yielded an enormous amount of information about this civilization. The complicated structure of the temple proves the skill of Maya architects. The carved slab over the stone coffin and the two stucco heads place Maya sculptors among the world's finest. The magnificent jade ornaments demonstrate their talent as craftsmen.

Palenque, perhaps the most beautiful of Maya ruins, represents the peak of Maya achievement during the Classic period. It also shows the huge amount of effort that could be summoned from engineers, artists, stonemasons, and laborers, and the lengths to which the Maya people would go to honor a priest-king.

Maya sculpture from Palenque

Temple of Inscriptions at Palenque

The Maya glorified their gods and honored their rulers through art and architecture. The temples that dominated Maya cities were designed to be awesomely dramatic. Maya architects used various techniques to achieve this effect, usually building temples on pyramids or platforms and adding elaborate stone crests, called roof combs, to make them seem taller. They decorated the upper faces of the buildings with sculpture in cut stone or stucco—a kind of plaster made of lime—and they painted them bright colors.

In contrast to the outside splendor, the rooms inside their buildings were small, dark, and damp. A few had openings for ventilation, but usually doorways let in the only light and air. Sometimes the walls were brightened with murals, but mostly they were plain white stucco.

Although they weren't laid out according to any formal plan, cities were used for religious ceremonies and government activities as well as for the rulers' residences. The higher the family's status, the closer it lived to the center of town: priests and nobles near the temple, professionals and wealthy merchants farther out, and the peasants on the fringes. In some cities groups of buildings and monuments were arranged to serve as astronomical observatories. Sweat baths were common—rooms with stone

Ruins of palace and Mayan temple at Palenque

Page 247: The Temple of the Sun, classic Maya culture circa A.D. 750, at Palenque

benches, draining troughs, and hearths for boiling water. They designed artificial reservoirs to catch the rain and underground bottle-shaped pits called *chultunes* to store water and food.

Almost every city had at least one ball court for a popular game known as *pok-a-tok.* About the size of a basketball court, it had sloping or vertical walls with a stone ring jutting out midway along each wall, just above the players' heads. The object of the game was to knock a solid rubber ball through the stone ring. The ball could not be thrown or kicked—it had to bounce off heavily padded hips, shoulders, or forearms.

Two teams competed, skilled players were much admired, and scoring was rare. Bets ran high—jade, gold, houses, and slaves were wagered—and the winning team was allowed to collect the jewelry and clothing of the spectators—if they could be caught. Naturally everyone vanished as soon as the match was decided. Certain religious rites were connected with the game, which the Maya believed was a favorite sport of the gods. A series of low-relief sculptures in a ball court at Chichén Itzá, showing players being beheaded, leads some scholars to say the losers lost literally everything.

Maya engineers designed elaborate drainage systems, aqueducts and bridges, roads and causeways. From twelve to thirty-two feet wide and raised several feet above the ground (higher in swampy areas), the "white roads," called *sacbeob* in Yucatec, were constructed of a smooth

Detail of carving from Chichén Itzá

layer of cement over a base of stones. They linked important groups of buildings within cities, and some joined city centers to outlying districts. The longest sacbe found so far runs sixty-two miles. The peasants walked along these roads, but when the nobility traveled any distance they did so in litters or large baskets carried on the shoulders of servants or warriors.

New cities were being founded all over the Maya realm, and older ones were continually being enlarged and improved. The labor required to build these cities was enormous. Thousands of peasants cleared and leveled the land and quarried tons of stone, dragging it to the site on log rollers. Hundreds of masons cut and shaped the stones and set them in place. The pyramids and platforms on which temples were built began with a central core of rocks and earth secured with retaining walls. (Unlike the pyramids of Egypt and a few exceptions, such as Ruz's discovery at Palenque, Maya pyramids were not built solely as tombs.) Although most of the temples and palaces were made of stone, the Maya never completely stopped using simple thatched huts for some of their religious buildings.

Maya feats of engineering are even more amazing considering that they did it all without wheeled vehicles or draft animals and without metal tools. They managed to erect huge, complicated buildings relying totally on manpower, stone tools, log rollers, and henequen[3] fiber rope to help lift heavy objects.

The lack of the wheel throughout Mesoamerica[4] has puzzled scholars for a long time. There is proof that the wheel and axle were known in the region: toy animals on wheels have been excavated in several parts of Mexico. But there is no evidence that the wheel was ever used for any practical purpose anywhere in the New World before the arrival of Europeans. Even the potter's wheel, introduced in the Old World over four thousand years ago, did not exist in

[3]henequen [e · ne · ken´]: plant fiber

[4]Mesoamerica: the area extending from central Mexico to Honduras and Nicaragua in which pre-Columbian civilizations flourished

Mesoamerica. Some experts argue that the *idea* of the wheel may have existed, but its circular shape had such important religious significance that it could not be adapted to practical uses. A more likely explanation is that there were no draft animals to pull a wheeled vehicle, and so there was no cause to invent the wheel.

The Maya never perfected the true arch, in which the space between walls is spanned with a curve of stones held in place by a wedge-shaped keystone. That type of arch had been in use in Europe since the sixth century B.C. Instead they devised the corbeled arch; the stones are overlapped, each course or layer extending further out from the vertical wall than the course below it to form a triangular opening with a flat capstone at the top.

Sculptors shaped their materials with stone tools and possibly wooden mallets. When limestone is first cut, it is relatively soft and can be worked easily until it hardens after exposure to the atmosphere. Pieces of limestone were burned to powder over a wood fire. The powder was then mixed with water to make mortar for holding the masonry in place and plaster for smoothing over the rough stone walls and for surfacing roads.

The Maya were also excellent wood-carvers; a number of superbly carved wooden door lintels have been found at Tikal and in other places. They worked with bone, shells, and feathers, and created intricate mosaics and inlays with a few simple tools. There seemed to be no limits to Maya imagination and creativity.

But in spite of all that investment of time, energy, and resources in their art, there are few images of common people—the laborers who built the cities, the farmers who produced food for an entire population, or the artists who portrayed the ideals of Maya civilization. Brilliant and ingenious as these creations are, the aloof figures frozen in stone seem remote and impersonal, leaving an impression of impenetrable mystery.

What do you find most interesting about the Maya civilization?

In what ways were Maya architects, engineers, and workers skillful?

How does Ruz's discovery of the ceremonial burial place contribute to our understanding of the past?

WRITE If your bedroom were discovered a thousand years from now, what clues about the past would be revealed? Write a description of the discovery of your bedroom in the year 3000.

WORDS FROM THE AUTHOR: CAROLYN MEYER

My cowriter, Charles Gallenkamp, is an expert on the Maya. He was in New Mexico working on a Mayan exhibit that was going to travel around to several major museums, including the Museum of Natural History in New York City. Since we were acquaintances and he knew that I write books for young people, he asked if I would be interested in working with him and using his material for a book.

We consulted a lot, but I did the writing. I did go down to Mexico to do some of my own research. In Mexico City, I spent time in a museum, and then I went out to the pyramids at Chichén Itzá.

To get there, I climbed into a bus filled with people. On the way, we went through some contemporary Mayan villages. Their straw huts very much resembled what I had seen in drawings—only these huts had television antennae on top of them! I really wanted to get off the bus and talk to the people. Once we arrived at the pyramids, I crawled around, climbed up and down, trying to get a feeling for them and the people who had built them.

Since Charles had written quite a lot on the subject of the Maya, I had to pick and choose the material I thought would appeal to my young readers. So I focused on the personality aspect. What it must have been like for those people to explore the tomb and try to figure it all out!

It's always tricky to try to distill complex information for a young audience. I never want them to think I'm being condescending, or talking down to them, yet you do have to clarify the information. That's why I tried to make this almost a detective story. That's what lures people to archaeology, I think, the mysterious, clue-seeking aspects of it.

CARLOTA

*Carlota de **Zubarán** lives with her father, Don Saturnino; her grandmother, Doña Dolores; her sister, Yris; and a young Indian servant, Rosario, on the Ranch of the Two Brothers in California when California is a part of Mexico. Since the death of her brother, Carlos, Carlota has taken on many of the responsibilities usually carried out during the 1800s by young men. In order to provide expensive wedding festivities for Yris, Carlota and her father set out on a journey, carefully concealing their route.*

illustrations by Dan Andreasen

My father wore the heaviest of his leather breeches, his thickest jacket, and a pair of high horsehide boots. It was gear for the wild country that lay between the Ranch of the Two Brothers and Blue Beach. He carried his best musket, his tinderbox, and his powder horn. I dressed accordingly, but carried no weapon except a knife.

There were four horses saddled and waiting for us. I rode my stallion, Tiburón, and I rode astride.

The river would still be running a torrent. It was much easier to cross close to the ranch and go down the south bank, but we had no desire to get soaked so early on the journey.

Accordingly, we chose the north bank and followed it through heavy chaparral[1] and patches of cactus until we had ridden for two hours.

Where the river widened and ran knee-deep, we crossed to the south bank. It was still a good hour's ride from the Blue Beach. But it was here that we took the first precaution.

My father and I had been coming to Blue Beach for two years. On the three journeys we had made, we had always been followed. Sometimes by one or two Indians, sometimes by more. But to this day, no one had followed us farther than this west crossing. Here we had managed to elude them.

One thing that helped was that we never told anyone our secret—the story of the Blue Beach.

We told none of the vaqueros[2] or the *mayordomo.*[3] Nor Rosario, though Rosario could be trusted. Nor my sister, who could not be. Nor even Doña Dolores, whom we could trust most of all. Dolores you could hang by her thumbs and still not hear one word that she did not wish to speak.

There was no way to find the Blue Beach except by following the river, either down from the mountains or up from the sea.

---

[1]chaparral [shap′ə · ral′]: a thick growth of small trees and shrubs
[2]vaqueros [bä · ke′rōz]: cowboys
[3]*mayordomo* [mä · yôr · dō′mō]: steward, servant

From the sea no one would ever find it because of a series of lagoons. From the direction of the mountains you would need to be very lucky, as lucky as we had been in the beginning.

The river at this point, where it fanned out into the deep lagoons, ran narrow, between two sheer walls of granite, where even a mountain goat would be lost. At the bottom of these cliffs were two beaches, one facing the other across a distance of a hundred steps.

The beaches were strips of fine sand, finer than the sand you find on the sea beach itself. Both had a bluish cast, like pebbles you see through clear-running water. But they also had another color, a lighter blue that had a look of metal, as if there were copper deposits in the cliffs that had been washed down by the river and the rain and had mixed with the lighter color.

Someone might call the beaches green or the color of turquoise, but to us they were blue and this is what we called them—the Blue Beaches, more often, the Blue Beach.

On this day, as on the three other journeys we had made to the Blue Beach, we tied our horses and climbed up from the stream to a towering rock. This was where we took our second precaution, for from this high place we could survey the trails, one coming along the river, and one from the sea.

"What do you see?" my father said. He liked to test my eyesight. "Are we followed?"

"I see nothing on the trail," I said, "either from the river or from the sea."

"What is the brown spot among the oaks?"

"Where?"

"Up the river about a hundred *varas*. [4]"

"I see nothing."

"Look once more."

"Does it move?"

"Judge for yourself. But first you need to find it."

I looked hard and at last made out the brown spot among the oaks. "It is a cow grazing," I said.

"There are two, and one is not a cow but a yearling fawn. What

---

[4]*varas* [bä´räs]: plural of *vara,* a measure of length about 33 inches long

do you hear?"

"The stream."

"What else?"

"A crow somewhere."

"Is that all?"

"Yes."

"Listen."

"A woodpecker behind us."

"Yes. And what else do you hear?"

"Nothing."

"Besides the stream and the surf at the mouth of the river and gulls fishing?"

"You have good ears."

"And you will have them someday."

"Never so good as yours."

"Better. *Mucho más.*"

Don Saturnino was silent for a while. Then he said, "Tomorrow is Carlos's birthday. He would have been eighteen had he lived."

"He would have liked these journeys," I answered.

"Perhaps. Perhaps not. Who knows? It is sufficient that you like them. You do like them, Carlota?"

"Everything, Father," I said. "Everything."

Here we sat for an hour, to make sure that we had not been followed.

When the sun was overhead, we crawled down from the pinnacle. We reached the Blue Beach and took off our boots and stepped out into the middle of the stream. We made our way for a distance of some fifty paces, leaving no tracks behind us. A clump of willows grew amidst a pile of driftwood and boulders at this place. Here the river divided and ran in two smaller streams on both sides of the willows.

The boulders could not be seen at high tide. But the tide was low now and they stuck up in two crescents, facing each other and leaving a clear space between them. The water was cold, both the sea water that met the river at this point and likewise the river water itself.

Stripped to my singlet, I splashed water on my legs, on my arms and chest. I had found that the best way to approach cold water was by small shivers, suffered one at a time.

Throwing out my arms, I took in a great gulp of air, held it for a minute, counting each second. Then I let out all the air in a quick whoosh. Then I raised my arms again and took in a greater gulp.

This air I held for two minutes, still counting the seconds in my mind—one second, two seconds, and so forth. I repeated this three times. The third time I counted up to four minutes.

It had taken me two years to build up to where I could hold my breath for this length of time. My father had heard of pearl divers in La Paz who could hold their breath for five minutes and even longer. I had tried this but had fainted.

Carefully we stepped into the wide pool between the two crescents of stone, beneath the canopy of willows. We inched our way to the center of the pool, cautious not to rile the sand.

As my foot touched a smooth slab of stone, I stooped down, lifted it with much care, and set it to one side. Beneath it was a rock-lined hole filled with water, the size of my body and twice its height.

At the bottom of this hole was something that, when we first saw it, seemed to be the trunk of a tree—a tree washed down from the mountains. Undoubtedly, it once had risen above the water, but over the years floods had worn it away to a worm-eaten stump.

It had been the mainmast of a ship, which my father said was some seventy feet in length. It had the wide beam, the high stern, of the galleons that two centuries before had sailed the seas between China and the coast of California and Mexico.

These ships, my father said, came on favorable winds and currents to northern California, then along the coast south to the ports of San Blas and Acapulco. They carried great treasures from the Indies, these galleons, so great that they became the prey of American and English pirates.

Some of these treasure ships had been captured. On some, their crews had died of scurvy. Others had run aground through careless navigation. Others were driven ashore by storms. Still others had sought refuge from their pursuers by hiding in lagoons such as the one at Blue Beach.

"This must have been a large lagoon at one time," my father said when we first discovered the galleon. "A good place to hide a ship. But when it was once inside, something happened to the ship and it never returned to the sea."

Hidden in the galleon's hold, near the stump of the mainmast, were two chests filled with coins. The coins were of pure gold. They showed three castles and the two flying doves that meant they had been struck in the mint at Lima, Peru. The date marked upon each coin that we carried away on the trips we had made was the Year of Our Lord 1612.

The two chests—each made of hard wood banded with iron straps and sealed with a hasp that had rusted and fallen off—were well beneath the surface of the water, whether at low tide or in the summer, when the stream ran low. This was fortunate, for had the chests been exposed, some passing Indian or vaquero would have discovered them.

There were many things to do before the chests could be reached. Usually it took me half a day to bring up a pouch of coins from the sunken ship.

The place where I dove, which was surrounded by jagged rocks and driftwood, was too narrow for my father. He had tried to squeeze through when we first discovered the galleon, but partway down he got stuck and I had to pull him back. It was my task, therefore, to go into the cavelike hole. My father stood beside it and helped me to go down and to come up.

I buckled a strong belt around my waist and to it tied a riata[5] that was ten *varas* long and stout enough to hold a stallion. I fastened my knife to my wrist—a two-edged blade made especially for me by our blacksmith—to protect myself against spiny rays and the big eels that could sting you to death. In the many dives I had made, I never had seen a shark.

Taking three deep breaths, I prepared to let myself down into the hole. In one hand I held a sink-stone, heavy enough to weigh me down. I let out all the air in my chest, took a deep breath, and held it. Then I began the descent.

The sink-stone would have taken me down fast, but the edges of the rocky hole were sharp. I let myself down carefully, one handhold at a time. It took me about a minute to reach the rotted

---

[5]riata: lariat

deck where the chests lay. I now had two minutes to pry the coins loose and carry them to the surface. We had tried putting the coins in a leather sack and hoisting them to the surface. But we had trouble with this because of the currents that swept around the wreck.

The coins lay in a mass, stuck together, lapping over each other and solid as rock. They looked, when I first saw them, like something left on the stove too long. I always expected to find them gone, but now as I walked toward the chests, with the stone holding me down, I saw that they were still there. No one had come upon them during the seven months since our last visit.

The first time I had dived and brought up a handful of coins, I said to my father that we should empty both the chests and take the coins home.

"Then everyone would talk," Don Saturnino said. "As soon as they saw the gold coins the news would spread the length of California."

"We don't need to tell anyone. I can hide them in my chest at home."

"The news would fly out before the sun set. At the ranch there are many eyes."

I still thought it was a better idea to empty the chests before someone else did, but I could see that my father enjoyed these days, when the two of us went to the Blue Beach, so I said no more.

The sun was overhead and its rays slanted down through the narrow crevice. There were many pieces of debris on the deck and I had to step carefully. With my knife I pried loose a handful of coins. They were of a dark green color and speckled here and there with small barnacles. I set the coins aside.

My lungs were beginning to hurt, but I had not felt the tug of the riata yet, the signal from my father that I had been down three minutes. I pried loose a second handful and put my knife away. Before the tug came I dropped my sink-stone and took up the coins. Gold is very heavy, much heavier than stones of the same size.

Fish were swimming around me as I went up through the hole of rocks and tree trunks, but I saw no sting rays or eels. I did see a shark lying back on a ledge, but he was small and gray, a sandshark, which is not dangerous.

On my third trip down, I hauled up about the same number of coins as the other times. The pouch we had brought was now full. I asked my father if we had enough.

"Are you tired?" he said.

"Yes, a little."

"Can you go down again?"

"Yes."

"Then go."

I dived twice more. It was on the last dive that I had the trouble. The tug on the riata had not come, but I was tired, so I started away from the chest with one handful of coins. Close to the chests, between them and the hole, I had noticed what seemed to be two pieces of timber covered with barnacles. They looked as if they might be part of a third and larger chest.

I still held my knife and I thrust it at a place where the two gray timbers seemed to join. It was possible that I had found another chest filled with coins.

As the knife touched them, the two timbers moved a little. Instantly, I felt pressure upon my wrist. I drew back the hand that held the knife. Rather, I tried to draw it back, but it would not move. The tide had shifted the timbers somehow and I was caught. So I thought.

I felt a tug upon the riata fastened to my waist. It was the signal from my father to come to the surface. I answered him with two quick tugs of the leather rope.

Now I felt a hot pain run up my arm. I tried to open my fingers, to drop the knife, but my hand was numb. Then as I stared down into the murky water I saw a slight movement where my hand was caught. At the same moment I saw a flash of pink, a long fleshy tongue sliding along my wrist.

I had never seen a burro clam, but I had heard the tales about them, for there were many on our coast. Attached to rocks or timbers, they grew to half the height of a man, these gray, silent monsters. Many unwary fishermen had lost their lives in the burros' jaws.

The pain in my arm was not so great now as the hot pains in my chest. I gave a long, hard tug on the riata to let my father know that I was in trouble. Again I saw a flash of pink as the burro opened its lips a little, and the fat tongue slid back and forth.

I dropped the coins I held in my other hand. The burro had closed once more on my wrist. But shortly it began to open again, and I felt a sucking pressure, as if the jaws were trying to draw me inside the giant maw.

Putting my knees against the rough bulge of the shell, as the jaws opened and then began to close, I jerked with all my strength. I fell slowly backward upon the ship's deck. My hand was free. With what breath I had I moved toward the hole. I saw the sun shining above and climbed toward it. The next thing I saw was my father's face and I was lying on the river's sandy bank. He took my knife in his hand.

After I told him what had happened, my father said, "The knife saved your life. The burro clamped down upon it. See the mark here. The steel blade kept its jaws open. Enough to let you wrench yourself free."

He pulled me to my feet and I put on my leather pants and coat.

"Here," he said, passing the reins of his bay gelding to me, "ride Santana. He goes gentler than Tiburón."

"I'll ride my own horse," I said.

"Good, if you wish it."

"I wish it," I said, knowing that he didn't want me to say that my hand was numb.

"Does the hand hurt?"

"No."

"Some?"

"No."

"You were very brave," he said.

My father wanted me to be braver than I was. I wanted to say I was scared, both when the burro had hold of me and now, at this moment, but I didn't because he expected me to be as brave as Carlos. It was at times like this that I was angry at my father and at my dead brother, too.

"It was good fortune," I said.

"Fortune and bravery often go together," Don Saturnino said. "If you do not hurt, let us go."

I got on the stallion and settled myself in the saddle. "Yes, let us go," I said, though I could not grip the reins well with but one hand.

On the way home we talked about the pouchful of coins and my father decided to sell them in San Diego. The first coins he had sold in Los Angeles to a gringo trader.

"The gringo[6] was curious about where I got them," he said. "Too curious to suit my fancy."

"What did you say to him?" I asked.

"I said that the coins had been in the family for many years. He looked at them for a long time. He turned them over and over. He was curious about the green spots on the coins. He said the coins must have been in the sea at some time. I told him that it was likely, since my grandfather was a captain of the sea."

"I didn't know that my great-grandfather was a captain of the sea."

"He was not," Don Saturnino said, and laughed. "We will try San Diego this time. Doña Dolores has invited the countryside, so we will need to make a good bargain."

"And we'll have music?" I said.

"Much music. And not from Dos Hermanos.[7] We will search and find the best from everywhere. We will make the Peraltas envious. And all the rest. We will dance for two days and not pause except to fortify ourselves."

We came to the brow of the hill that lies between Dos Hermanos and the sea. Below us, in front of the big gate of our half-house, half-fort, fires were burning in pits the Indians had dug. The fires would burn for three days, until the night before the wedding. Then a thick layer of ashes would be sprinkled over the coals, and slabs of beef, half a cow, each wrapped in heavy wet cloth would be laid on the beds and covered with earth. The slabs would cook and steam all night and most of the next day. Already I was hungry, thinking about the tender meat.

My father said, "Are you pleased that it is Yris who marries the Peralta?"

---

[6]gringo: slang term—a foreigner in Spain or Latin America, especially one of English or American origin

[7]Dos Hermanos: Two Brothers, name of the ranch

"Yes, very pleased," I said.

"You have no regrets?"

"None."

"Someday I will hunt and find you a suitable young man. He will likely come from the North, where the young men, I hear, are more handsome than here in the South. And we will have a wedding such as no one has seen before. Would that please you?"

"When do you hunt for the young man?" I asked.

"Soon. Very soon. Not later than next spring. It may take some time before I find him, of course. Perhaps a year or so."

"Of course," I said, having a deep misgiving about my father and this search.

"Handsome young men of good character do not grow upon trees. Yet I will look throughout California, from one end to the other. If I do not find him here, I will look elsewhere, even in faraway Spain."

My hand hurt, and that made things worse. But I was fortunate. I could have been back there on the rotting deck of the galleon, in the grip of the giant burro clam. I could be lying drowned beneath the waves. Or I could be at home, like Yris, getting ready to marry Don Roberto.

Would you like to search for sunken ships? Why or why not?

How would you describe the relationship between Carlota and her father? Explain your answer, using examples from the selection.

Why are the trips to the secret galleon special for Carlota?

WRITE Imagine that Carlota finds the captain's logbook from the galleon on one of her dives. Write an entry for the logbook for the day that the galleon was sunk.

ANCIENT WEALTH

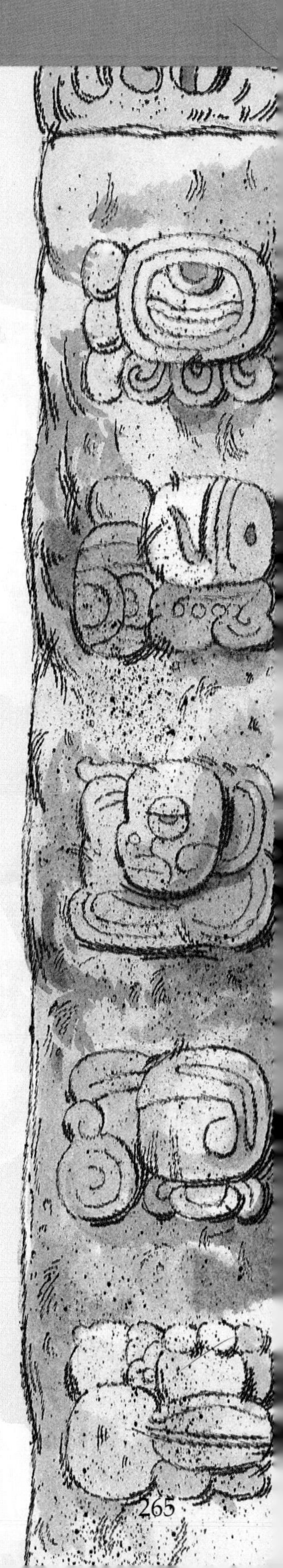

People who search for hidden treasure often face risks. Think about the risks faced by Ruz and those faced in "Carlota." What do those risks have in common?

Writer's Workshop

The treasure uncovered by Ruz in "The Mystery of the Ancient Maya" was very different from the treasure found by Carlota and her father in "Carlota." Think about the treasures Ruz and Carlota found. How will those treasures be used? Which use do you think is better? Write a persuasive essay in which you present and support your opinion as to which treasure is more valuable and why.

Writer's Choice You have read about two different discoveries of ancient wealth. What might someone two thousand years from now consider an "ancient treasure" from your life? Choose and plan what you want to write about. Think about the form your writing will take. Carry out your plan, and share your writing with others.

THEME

MEXICO

Mexico is a land rich in history and natural beauty. Enjoy discovering some of the characteristics of this country as the following selections help you appreciate its varied cultures.

CONTENTS

The Secret of the Wall

by Elizabeth Borton de Treviño

illustrations by Manuel Garcia

On a day in September I walked down to Cantaranas Plaza and past it, along the narrow cobblestone street; and there was the great *zaguán*,[1] the entrance gate to the *secundaria*,[2] our high school. Beyond I could see the broad, white ascending steps of the university, where I would go one day.

---

[1]*zaguán* [sä· gwän′]: entrance
[2]*secundaria* [se´ ko͞on · dä´rē · ä]: secondary school

The streets of Guanajuato smell of dried chiles, of jasmine and carnations in pots behind the iron-barred windows, of hot baked bread. It is my town in central Mexico, a romantic old town that has lived days of wealth and luxury because of the rich silver mines nearby and days of poverty because of the turmoil of revolutions and social change. Heroism has been here, in these little winding alleys and broad, stone, fountain-centered plazas. Faith is here, in our many beautiful churches, soaring into the sky. Many artists have lived here and loved Guanajuato and painted it. My family has lived here since the days of my great-grandfather, and I, Carlos, always knew the legends of some of the streets, of many of the old houses, and the stories of ghosts and hauntings, some violent, some tender.

School smelled like schools everywhere, of chalk dust and disinfectant soap and boys. I found my classroom and a seat on the aisle where I could rest my leg by extending it out along my desk. Three years ago I had had polio. It left me weak in the back and in one leg; I still have to take special exercises and wear a brace for some hours every day. But Dr. Del Valle, who took care of me when I was sick, had said at last that I could walk to and from school every day and that I would be getting stronger all the time. Yet I knew that I would not be able to take part in the games or play out in the court during recess. All the boys were younger than I, but almost all were taller and broader too. The only one I knew was Serafín, Dr. Del Valle's youngest boy. He stood half a head taller than any of the others and was handsome and strong. I thought, "Serafín will surely captain one of the ball teams—soccer or basketball or baseball—and he will be president of the class."

But I was wrong. When the first recess for games came, I went to sit under the arcades and watch, and I saw the shouting boys choose up sides. The games professor passed out mitts and bats and balls. Serafín was a swift runner, but he didn't try very hard. He seemed uninterested, and when one of the other boys jostled him, he dropped out. "Coward!" they called after him, but he just shrugged his shoulders. He came over and sat down by me, looking very sullen.

"It's a silly game anyhow," he said.

"I wish I could play!" I burst out.

"Why?" he asked. "You don't get anything out of it. It's just exercise. Getting knocked about and hurt sometimes. Foolishness. I play a much better game by myself every day."

"You do? What game?"

"I may tell you someday." Then he got up and sauntered off. He walked down one of the corridors slowly, looking at his feet, and then he stooped to pick up something and put it in his pocket. I turned my eyes back to the noisy fun in the school patio. I had hopes of distinguishing myself in another way. My father is a fine chess player, and groups of the best players in our town meet in our house on Saturday evenings. During the years of my illness Papacito had taught me how to play and had bought me a small chess set that was portable and on which the pieces could be fixed, so that a game might go on from where it had been left off days before. There was no one in Papacito's chess circle who was unwilling to sit down to a game with me, and once I had even beaten Don Mario, the mail carrier, who often came to play chess. He was the chess champion of Guanajuato.

Limping home after that first day in class, I tried to place Serafín in my chess game. A knight? Perhaps. Not a bishop or a tower.[3] And, of course, not a pawn. He was too independent for that.

Tía Lola had made my favorite *polvorones*[4] for supper to celebrate my first day back to school. Tía Lola is Papacito's sister, who came to live with us after my mother's death.

As the days went by, I became more interested in all my classes. I often took my chessboard to school, and while the others were at games, Professor Morado sometimes played with me. The boys were pleasant but careless with me; they thought me a weakling because I had to wear my brace some days. Only one sought me out, Serafín.

He began walking home with me afternoons, sometimes

---

[3]tower: rook, a chess piece
[4]*polvorones* [pōl · vō · rō´nes]: cakes

chatting, sometimes morosely making no comment on anything I said. He often leaned down to pick up a button or a bit of cord or a pin.

"That's my game," he said to me suddenly one day. "Finders Keepers!"

"How silly! You can't often find anything worthwhile."

"Oh, but you're wrong! I often do! I must have one hundred pesos' worth of stuff piled up at home that I found this way. Besides, just now we were only wandering along. But sometimes I pick out people and follow them. You'd be surprised how often they put down a package and forget it or leave their umbrella or even drop money!"

"But . . . but . . . ," I stuttered, "if you see them drop something, you ought to give it back!"

"No," he answered stubbornly. "Finders Keepers. That's the game."

"But what do your parents think about this? Tía Lola would never let me keep anything I found if it was valuable. Or my father either. I'd have to find out to whom it belonged and give it back or give it to the poor."

"Ah, my father and mother don't even know about my game, and I shan't tell them," he responded. "Papá is always out, all hours of the day or night on his calls, and Mamacita is usually in bed with a headache. They don't care what I do."

I was troubled about all this, but I did not talk it over with my father or Tía Lola for a very selfish reason: I had no other friend, and I did not want to be deprived of Serafín, unsatisfactory and worrisome though he was. I knew he was cowardly, secretive, and selfish, but he was a companion. So I kept silent, though I never did go to his house. He sometimes came to mine but only to talk or play with my dog in the patio.

I was not very lonely. I often went to the fountain in the plaza and took my chessboard. I could work out problems in chess there and watch the people passing by.

I was doing this about five o'clock on a November day when dusk was beginning to let down veils of darkness over the town.

I had just closed my chessboard and was about to start home when a laborer came toward me from one of the streets that led into town. From his plaster-covered shoes and the sacking that he still wore over his shoulders and his dusty shirt and trousers, I could tell he was probably working on one of the new buildings that were going up near the entrance of the city.

He was about nineteen, I thought. He smiled at me shyly. "I have seen you going to high school early in the morning," he said. He paused and shuffled his feet. "And I have seen you sitting here in the afternoons, studying."

"That's right."

"My name is Martín Gonzales," he said suddenly, after a long pause. "I am going to ask you to do me a favor."

"Gladly, if I can." I thought he might ask for a peso.

"I want you to write a letter for me."

"But I don't have any paper or an envelope."

"Bring them tomorrow and write a letter, please. I will pay you."

The next day I waited for Martín and wrote his letter for him. It was a note to a girl in another town. He was ashamed for her to know that he could not write. He carefully put the letter away inside his dirty shirt and turned his bright eyes toward my chessboard. I asked if he knew the game, but he shook his head. Idly I explained the moves and the names of the pieces.

Then began a curious friendship. Martín passed by the fountain every afternoon, sometimes bringing with him another big, shy laborer who wanted a letter written. I began to develop a small but regular business, and I looked forward to that hour in Cantaranas Plaza. It comforted me to think I was doing something useful, and I began to plan on teaching them to read a little when vacations came.

Serafín was scornful and did not often drop by anymore. "How stupid!" he said. "Writing silly letters for oafs."

"Martín is no oaf! I am teaching him chess, and he will be a good player!"

"I don't believe it!"

"Stay and watch then! Here he comes now."

Martín came hurrying along. I presented them, and Serafín had the grace to take Martín's calloused hand after it had been dusted against his trousers and deferentially offered.

I had the pieces set up on my little board. Martín drew the white, so he had first move. He made an opening gambit I had never before seen used. I did not know the defense, and he soundly beat me. Serafín's eyes were starting from his head, for like most of us boys in Guanajuato he knew something of the game.

"You stopped me in my tracks, Martín!" I cried. "Who showed you that gambit?"

"I made it up," he told me, pleased. "I thought about the chessboard all day as I was working. I could see it in front of my eyes, every piece, so I played a game with myself, in my imagination; and it seemed to me that the opening I used just now was a good one."

Martín arrived on Saturday evening in clean, freshly ironed, cotton work clothes. Like all our country people he has perfect manners, and, of course, so has my father and so have his friends. They made Martín welcome, and my father sat down to play his first game with him. To my amazement, he defeated my father in the first game, and the second one was a struggle, finally ending in a stalemate. My father was delighted, and the others crowded round to congratulate Martín.

"Young man, you are a chess genius, I think!" cried Don Mario, the mail carrier. "Join us every Saturday! Keep our game keen!"

After he had left, my father and his friends talked excitedly about Martín. They had in mind to train and polish him and enter him that spring in the state championship chess games.

The next day there was a piece in the paper about a treasure having been found by workers when tearing down an old house in Celaya. Under the flagstones of the patio they came upon a strongbox filled with silver coins. My father read the item aloud.

"My friend Luisa, in Guadalajara, had a friend who found

a buried treasure in the kitchen of the house they bought," contributed Tía Lola.

"Well, it happens often and it is reasonable," explained Papacito. "Mexico has gone through violent times, and insurgent and revolutionary armies have swept in and out of so many towns that the people often buried or hid their valuables so as not to have to surrender them. And then, of course, sometimes they couldn't get back to retrieve them. Or sometimes they died, and nobody ever knew what had happened to their money."

I was thinking this over as I walked to school, and in the first recess Serafín sought me out, full of excitement.

"Did you read about the treasure in Celaya?" he asked me, breathless. "Let's go treasure-hunting there! There must be quantities of old houses where people have buried money!"

"Well, yes. My father said there was every likelihood. But how? Which houses? And how would you start? Nobody would even let you begin!"

"Why couldn't Martín tell us where? He works with a wrecking crew, knocking down old houses, doesn't he? He could sneak us into one some night!"

"Tía Lola wouldn't let me go."

"Don't tell her!" counseled Serafín impatiently.

"Well . . ."

It was the deceit that unnerved me. But the call of adventure was strong, and, I'll confess it, I longed to go treasure-hunting. I resolved to speak to Martín.

I had my chance when he stopped by Cantaranas Plaza after work. I was waiting for him.

"We began to tear down the old house of the Lost Grandfather today," he told me. "The workers are not happy about it. They say it is haunted."

"Yes? Tell me about it?"

"The Lost Grandfather groans and howls there on windy nights; people have heard him. He was an old gentleman who simply disappeared during the last revolution."

"Strange. Aren't you afraid to work there, Martín?"

"I? No. I am only a simple, uneducated fellow. But I do not believe in ghosts," he told me in a scornful voice.

Serafín was eager to go out that very night, but he decided that he had better reconnoiter first. The next day at recess he told me in whispers that the situation was perfect. There was a guard, but he was very old and deaf and did not know anything about the ghost.

"His daughter brings him his supper at about nine o'clock, and he eats it, and then he goes to sleep on some sacks in the back. To try him out, I even pounded on the gate and struck the rocks of the patio with a small steel bar I have. The old man did not hear a sound. We will go tonight!"

I was scared but terribly eager to go just the same. Little prickles of excitement ran up and down my spine all day.

Just at dusk Serafín came by for me. He had a long, paper-wrapped parcel under his arm. "An iron bar with a pointed tip," he said, "and a candle."

As we left, I had a bad time with Tuerto, my little white dog with a black spot around one eye. Tuerto whined and begged to come with us, and he got out twice and had to be brought back in and scolded before he would not try to follow me. I believe he smelled my excitement.

As we came near the haunted house, we saw the guard's daughter just arriving.

"Good! She's early!" hissed Serafín. She left the big *zaguán* slightly ajar as she went in, and pulled and pushed by Serafín, I followed. We were inside!

At last the guard's daughter left, calling *adiós,* and the old man made the sign of the cross behind her as the *zaguán* clanged to. Then he shuffled off to somewhere in the back.

"Come in now," said Serafín. "He eats and rests way back there, where they have begun taking out the rear walls. I want to try inside, around the fireplace. That's where lots of treasures have been buried."

We went cautiously into the big central hall of the house. It was quite dark and very mysterious. A little light drifted in from the street, but the shadows were deep; and there were strange

noises, little scurryings and rattlings. Our eyes grew used to the dark. Soon we made out the fireplace. From it stretched out two walls, at the far ends of which there were doors.

"Let's sound those walls," suggested Serafín. "You go along there and I'll go here. See if they sound hollow to you. Like this." And he went along, giving a smart rap on the plaster. I dutifully did as I was told, almost forgetting the guard, but the walls sounded the same along their length to me.

"We might as well open up anyhow and see how solid they are," whispered Serafín, and he went at a place in the wall not far from the chimney. I was terrified. It seemed to me that the clanging and banging would bring not only the guard but even people from the street in upon us. However, Serafín labored away to no avail.

"I'll try over here," he panted, and again he dug at the wall, but there seemed to be nothing but firmly set bricks inside.

"Here. You try." He gave me his improvised pick, and I went at a place on the other side of the fireplace. At first the plaster gave way easily. Then I came upon the same hard bricks. But as I struck and pried at them, one of them crumbled away, and another, and I put my hand in. There was an opening!

Serafín almost shouted in his joy. "I'll open it up more, and then you get inside and see what's there!" He worked away very fast and soon had a hole in the hollow wall through which I could just squeeze my shoulders.

"Get in!" he urged, and pushed me.

"It's terribly dark," I said. "Give me the candle."

He passed it in to me and I lighted it. I stood inside the wall in a very narrow passage. The air was still and dead, and the candle flickered along the wall.

And then suddenly there was a deep, mournful groan. I started and dropped the candle. As I struck against the wall, plaster and bricks rained down, and I found myself cut off. I tried to scratch and scrabble my way out, but in the dark I had no way of knowing whether I would be able to get free again.

"Serafín!" I called with all my might, but there was no answer. Only, at my shout, more plaster and bricks fell.

I was scared to death. I stood there and cried until I realized that I would have to be sensible and try to think.

I cannot pretend that I was able to do this immediately. I suffered from a confusion of feelings. I thought I might be buried alive; I feared our being caught in this house, where we had no permission to be; I was frightened of the dark and of the sounds. But eventually I was able to control myself.

I was not scared by the groan. I did not believe in ghosts, and I knew there must be some natural explanation. I felt sure Serafín would go at once and bring help. And after a bit I realized I would not smother, for there was a thin breath of air from somewhere in the wall that moved along my cheek.

It came to me, at last, that I might find some opening in the wall, and cautiously I started exploring. Luckily, I had some matches in my pocket, but though I scrabbled around trying to find the candle, I could not. So I lit a match, and in that light I went along, feeling the sides of the hollow wall close against me until the match burned down to my fingers and I was in darkness again. In this way I passed around a bend in a wall, where it curved out around the fireplace, I thought, and emerged into the wall beyond, which was also hollow. But there, as I lit a third match, I saw, suddenly illuminated, a skeleton fully dressed in the clothes of the last century and sitting on a low bench. It was wedged between the walls, and on its knees was a box. It was a terrible figure, but even in that first moment of shock and revulsion I felt pity. What had been a man must have had himself walled in here, with his treasure . . . and no one had ever come back to free him. Was it the Lost Grandfather?

I said a prayer for the soul of that pitiful skeleton man and then tried to maneuver myself around in the wall and feel my way back whence I had come. I decided to save my matches; and when I felt the fallen rubble, I lay down very gingerly to wait for rescue, saying my prayers all the while.

I may have dozed from fear and hunger and cold, for I awoke, startled, to hear a dog yelping. It was my Tuerto! And as I came to and realized where I was, I heard scratching and striking along the

wall. I hurried back in case some more bricks should tumble down, but before long there was an opening; the rubble was being pulled away, and there was Martín, looking in, with his face all pale and drawn.

"Thank God! He's all right!" he called.

And I heard Tía Lola and my father echo, "Thank God!"

He pulled me out, and Tuerto leaped upon me and almost smothered me with doggy kisses. Then I was enclosed in my aunt's arms, and I felt my father's hand on my hair.

I can't remember much more of what happened until they got me home and to bed, and Tía Lola gave me a drink of hot lemonade.

Serafín had abandoned me. They did not know he had even been with me until I told them.

Martín had happened to come back to our house that evening to tell my father that he could not play chess on Saturday; and as Tía Lola opened the *zaguán* to him, Tuerto had shot out and into the street.

Tía Lola had been crying. She was worried, for it was after eight and I had not come home. Martín said to her, "Look, the little dog is trailing him! I'll follow and bring back Carlos."

Tuerto led Martín straight into the haunted house and to the wall. Martín had called my name, but I had been asleep and did not hear. Anyhow, he rushed back to bring my father and Tía Lola and also a pick. And so they had found me.

In bed, safe and warm, I remembered the poor skeleton. "There is a dead man in the walls," I told them, "holding a box of treasure on his lap. Please go back and get it, Martín!"

"Shall I?" Martín looked at my father.

"We'll go," said my father, and they left me to Tía Lola.

I tried to stay awake until they came back, but excitement and fright had taken their toll and I fell deeply asleep. I did not know until the next morning that Martín and I had a fortune between us. The skeleton was later extracted from the wall and given a decent burial, and my father looked up in the old records of the city and of taxpayers on the old houses to find out his probable identity. Then he had searched for relatives, but there seemed

to be none. So, after my father paid the taxes on the treasure, it remained for us. Finders Keepers.

It was not so very much after all. The box had held silver coins and some jewels, but these were not of much intrinsic value anymore. Still, something like twenty thousand pesos remained to be divided between Martín and me.

"What will you do with your part?" I asked Martín, a few days later.

"I shall take care of my mother and my little brothers, and I shall go to school!" he cried.

But in the Saturday evening chess circle my father and his friends decided among them that they would teach Martín to read and write and coach him until he could pass examinations and then go on to evening classes. Meanwhile, he was going to be their champion in chess tournaments, and he could make some money giving exhibition games.

"What will you do with your part of the treasure?" Don Mario asked me. They were all eating *enchiladas* and drinking coffee after their game. Before I could answer, there was a clamor at our *zaguán*. And the big knocker sounded several times. Tía Lola led in Dr. Del Valle and Serafín.

Dr. Del Valle gave Serafín a push into the center of the room. "Begin," he ordered his son.

"I am sorry," stammered Serafín.

Dr. Del Valle was trembling with emotion. "I never thought I would see the day when I would feel so ashamed of my son," he told my father. "He has just now confessed to me that he induced Carlos to go with him to that house, to break into the walls and look for treasure, and that when the wall caved in, he ran home and left Carlos there, perhaps to die!"

Serafín stood with drooping head, and two tears slid down his cheeks. "I am sorry," he whispered again.

"We knew," said my father. "We realized that Serafín must have been paralyzed with fear. That is why I did not speak of it to you. He is forgiven. Isn't he, Carlos?"

"Of course," I answered at once.

For what else could I say? I knew what it was to be scared senseless, almost to panic. I couldn't hate Serafín, even though Tía Lola did. I was even sorry for him, in a way, for I knew that he would never be anything in the Great Chess Game but a simple pawn, like me. Martín would end as a knight.

"I suppose by rights," I said to Serafín, not being above heaping some coals of fire on his head, "at least part of the treasure should be yours. You started looking in the wall where it was found."

He glanced hopefully at me as I went on. "So I trust you will agree with me about what to do with it. I want to give it for a classroom in one of the new schools being built down by the highway. We could name that room." He was disappointed, I could see. But he was trapped. Or, as Tía Lola said later, he made a virtue of necessity.

"Whatever you say, Carlos," he answered meekly.

"Why don't we name it for the Lost Grandfather?" I cried.

And so it will be. My father turned over the money to the Education Department, and a plaque will be affixed to one of the rooms saying, "This room was built with funds left by the Lost Grandfather." The president of Mexico is coming to inaugurate the school and several others, and Serafín and I and all our relatives and Martín and the whole class at school and Professor Morado will be there. The day will be a great *fiesta*.

Olé,[5] poor Lost Grandfather. Your treasure will be of good use, at last.

---

[5]*Olé:* Bravo!

Which character in this story would you choose to have as a friend? Tell why.

How is the game of chess important in this story?

Why do you think Serafín acts the way he does? Cite examples from the story to explain your answer.

WRITE Where would you search for hidden treasure? In one or two paragraphs, tell where and why you would search there.

Here Is Mexico

by Elizabeth Borton de Treviño

Illustrations by Richard Garcia, Jr.

Place the map of Mexico before you. If you put your hand over a long thin peninsula on the left extending from the United States border downward, what you have left is a sort of letter **J,** in reverse—heavy at the top along the border and curving upward into the Caribbean on the right. The upward-curving peninsula to the south is Yucatán. The long thin one at the left is Baja, or Lower, California. In between lies country of great variety.

The story is told that when Cortés was accorded his first audience with the King of Spain, after conquering Mexico, the king asked what the country was like. Cortés, always a taciturn man, did not try to answer in words.

Taking a sheet of parchment, he crumpled it in his strong hands and then threw it down upon a table.

"That is Mexico," he said.

The king immediately saw a country of all rough mountains.

"But are there no valleys?"

"Beautiful valleys, high on the slopes, and between all the mountains."

Mexico is indeed a mountainous country; a great range extends down along the Pacific coast to the Guatemalan border, and there is another range that humps through the center of the country. These ranges run together, and the whole configuration is known as the Sierra Madre,[1] though at its highest and roughest point it is called the Sierra Tarahumara, after the Indian tribes who still live there. This part is not yet thoroughly explored.

There are many splendid isolated peaks, too, eternally snow-covered and very beautiful. The highest is the Pico de Orizaba,[2] which rises in the state of Veracruz. It is 18,225 feet high. Popocatepetl[3] (Smoking Mountain) and Ixtacihuatl[4] (Sleeping Woman) guard the Valley of Mexico. About these two beautiful peaks there is a legend which has come down from Indian tradition. The story is this:

An Indian prince was betrothed to a beautiful princess, but he was obliged to go away to war, and the word came back to her that he had been killed. She was very sorrowful, and she lay down and covered herself with a white mantle, and died. The prince, who had not

---

[1] Sierra Madre [sē • er′ə mä′drā]
[2] Pico de Orizaba [pē′kō dā ō • rē • sä′ bä]
[3] Popocatepetl [pō′pō • kä • tā′pet′əl]
[4] Ixtacihuatl [ēks • tä • sē • wät′əl]

UNITED STATES

MEXICO

BAJA CALIFORNIA

GULF OF CALIFORNIA

GULF OF MEXICO

MEXICAN PLATEAU

SIERRA MADRE OCCIDENTAL

SIERRA MADRE ORIENTAL

MEXICO CITY

ORIZABA

NORTH PACIFIC OCEAN

PUEBLA

VERACRUZ

IXTACIHUATL

OAXACA

POPOCATEPETL

GUATEMALA

been killed, returned and found his beloved sleeping—the long sleep of death. Crouching beside her, he burned incense to her memory, and there he keeps watch to this day. The Sleeping Woman is a volcano shaped like a woman, sleeping under an eternal coverlet of snow. Nearby is Popocatepetl, which means Smoking Mountain because this extinct volcano, also snow-covered, sometimes sends forth puffs of smoke. Indeed, geologists say that it might some day become active once more.

There is mountain climbing in Mexico, which has produced many climbing clubs and groups of hikers. "Popo," as Popocatepetl is affectionately called, is always being climbed, and "Ixta," which is more difficult, attracts more experienced climbers. Orizaba is climbed too, by special groups, and so is the Nevado de Toluca,[5] another eternally snow-covered peak not far from Mexico City.

In the early days, when the Spaniards arrived, Mexico was still richly wooded, and the native peoples loved their forests. The Aztec Emperor took his ease in lovely parks, where tall trees provided beauty, refreshing

---

[5]Nevado de Toluca [nā • bä′dō dā tō • lo͞o′ kä]

Above, Mount Popocatepetl (Smoking Mountain)

Left, Mount Ixtacihuatl (Sleeping Woman)

Floating Gardens of Xochimilco, Mexico City

shade, and homes for birds. A remnant of this area is still the favorite park in Mexico City. Here in Chapultepec Park[6] are tall trees, gardens, paths, artificial streams, lakes, and pleasant vistas. Another such park is the lovely Xochimilco,[7] which means Floating Gardens. This too was devised by Aztec landscape artists as a unique kind of pleasure garden; they floated man-made islands in the canals and streams of the district, planted tall trees alongside the waterways, and kept the little floating islands blooming with every sort of fragrant and colorful flower.

As a result of the centuries-old Spanish custom of using charcoal—a custom continued until very recently—the forests of Mexico have been endangered, and the government has now made it a misdemeanor to cut any tree without a license to do so. Thus some attempt is being made to control the deforestation, which had proceeded dangerously in some states, and at the same time reforestation is beginning. But it will be a long time before Mexico recovers her true forest wealth.

---

[6]Chapultepec Park [chä • po͞ol′tə • pek pärk]
[7]Xochimilco [sō • chē • mēl′kō]

Mexicans cherish certain single trees that have been identified with their history. In Oaxaca[8] the famous Tule Tree, a giant cypress, is one of the wonders of the region. The trunk is 160 feet in circumference, and the tree rises to a height of 140 feet. The tree was standing there, putting out its leaves, a thousand years before Columbus set foot on the shores of the New World.

In Mexico City is another tree that has a venerable history. In 1520, after the Spaniards had been in the city for six months, apparently negotiating with Montezuma, the emperor, it became clear to the Aztecs that the Spaniards wanted nothing but gold. The Aztecs no longer believed that the Spaniards really wanted only to make friends and teach the new religion of Jesus. While Cortés was away from Tenochtitlán, defeating an expeditionary force that had been sent against him from Spain, a quiet resistance was organized. When he marched back triumphant, having routed the soldiers under Narváez sent to unseat him, there was no friendly reception from the Aztecs. The great city was silent. When Montezuma arrived for an audience with Cortés, it was

[8]Oaxaca [wä•hä′kä]

"El Tule," a cypress tree 2,000 to 3,000 years old

made clear to the emperor that Cortés now looked upon him as a prisoner and the city as his spoils.

Before long the Mexicans attacked, and in such numbers and in such fury that they drove the Spaniards out of the city along one of the causeways built into the part of the city still known as Tacuba. The slaughter of the Spaniards was very heavy, and the story is told that the next day, when Cortés reviewed what was left of his ruined and crippled troops, he sat and wept under a giant cypress growing nearby. The tree is called the Tree of the Sad Night, and it has been preserved with greatest care. Relic hunters did it great damage for a time, before the tree was protected by a strong iron fence. In recent years attempts have been made to preserve its life by modern cement tree-mending methods. However, it is clear that the Tree of the Sad Night will not endure forever, so special relics of it have been taken and are preserved in the Museo Nacional de Historia.

In the clear rainless months in the tropics the stars seem to blaze very low in the black velvet skies, but travelers feel this about all tropical countries.

That Mexican skies can be reliable for most of the year is proved by the fact that one of the world's important observatories is located in the state of Puebla, near Santa María Tonanztintla. Observatories all over the world cooperate and have divided their labors to some extent, each one carrying out a special duty for the benefit of all the rest. The task of the observatory at Santa María Tonanztintla is to define the limits of our solar system. In the present space age, with travelers looking longingly toward planets that may be visited in the foreseeable future, this duty is an important one.

Which place mentioned in this selection would you most like to visit? Why does that place appeal to you?

What effect has the use of charcoal had on Mexico?

How are the legends in this selection connected with the history of Mexico? Cite examples from the selection.

WRITE Have you ever been to a place that you think others might enjoy visiting? In a paragraph or two, describe this place and tell why it is special to you.

"Here Is Mexico" and "The Secret of the Wall" were both written by Elizabeth Borton de Treviño. How do the descriptions and details in both the article and the short story reflect her love of Mexico?

Writer's Workshop

You have read how Carlos finds out that one of his friends is honest and sincere and one is not. Write a realistic short story that reveals something about the importance of being a good friend. The story should take place in a location that you know well. How can your personal knowledge of the setting of the action help make your story realistic?

Writer's Choice What might it be like to find something that no one else knows about? What kind of bonanza might a discovery like this make? Think of a way to tell about such a discovery. You could write a letter, a song, or a play, for example. Write about your idea, and think of a way to share your writing.

MULTICULTURAL CONNECTION

MEANINGFUL TREASURES

In February 1987, a Peruvian archaeologist named Walter Alva got a late-night call from the police. They had caught a tomb robber looting an ancient pyramid at Sipán, Peru, and the police wanted Alva to examine the treasure they had seized. What Alva saw that night would lead him to one of the greatest archaeological finds in modern times.

The looter had unearthed fabulous gold artifacts from the ancient Moche culture, a civilization that thrived in northern Peru from the second through the seventh century A.D. With a team of archaeologists, Alva dug deeper into the Sipán pyramid, which apparently had been a burial site for powerful Moche lords. After several years of work, Alva and his team had uncovered various tombs and many magnificent artifacts.

Alva expects to continue digging at Sipán for several more years, and he may uncover other fabulous treasures. The most important treasure, however, is the new knowledge his discoveries provide about this ancient Peruvian culture.

Bring pictures of ancient Peruvian artifacts or ruins to class, and discuss their features. Share what you know about the cultures that produced them.

SOCIAL STUDIES CONNECTION

ANCIENT PERU

With a partner or small group, research the features of an ancient Peruvian civilization, such as the Moche, Chimu, Nazca, or Inca culture. On a chart, organize a summary of your findings, using categories such as geography, society and government, economy, art and culture, and any others that seem appropriate. Present an oral report on your topic, using visual aids if possible.

SCIENCE / SOCIAL STUDIES CONNECTION

ARCHAEOLOGY REPORT

Write a report on an archaeological expedition in Peru or some other part of the world. Your report should include information on the archaeological methods used, the achievements of that project, and the culture being studied. Summarize your report in a small-group discussion, and compare your project with those of your classmates.

Clockwise from bottom left: gold artifact, excavation in Peru 1990, archaeologist Walter Alva, gold mask, clay jars

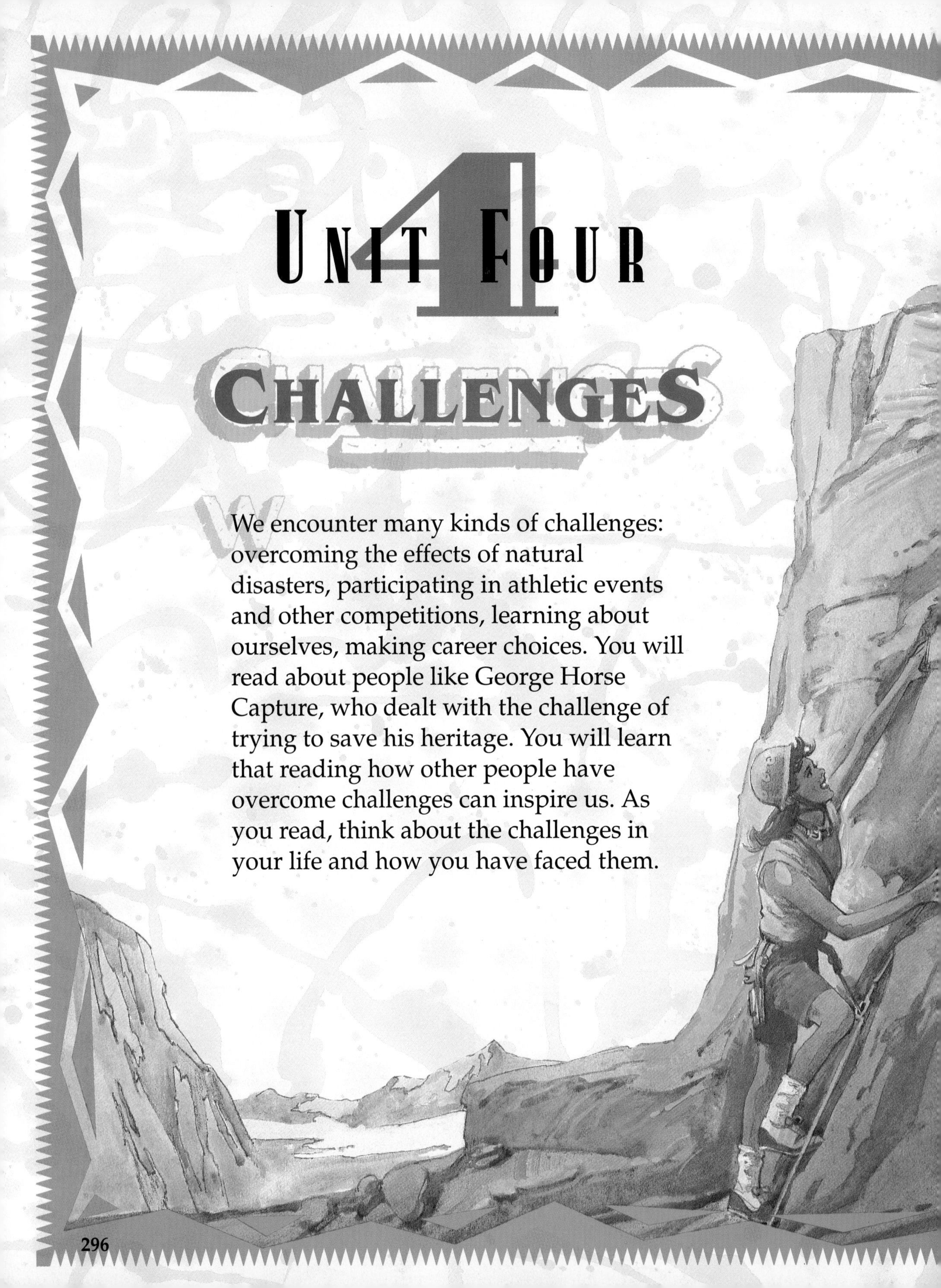

UNIT FOUR

CHALLENGES

We encounter many kinds of challenges: overcoming the effects of natural disasters, participating in athletic events and other competitions, learning about ourselves, making career choices. You will read about people like George Horse Capture, who dealt with the challenge of trying to save his heritage. You will learn that reading how other people have overcome challenges can inspire us. As you read, think about the challenges in your life and how you have faced them.

THEMES

BOOKSHELF

RAINBOWS ARE MADE

BY CARL SANDBURG
SELECTED BY LEE BENNETT HOPKINS

These poems by one of America's greatest writers are enhanced by stunning woodcut engravings.

ALA Notable Book

HARCOURT BRACE LIBRARY BOOK

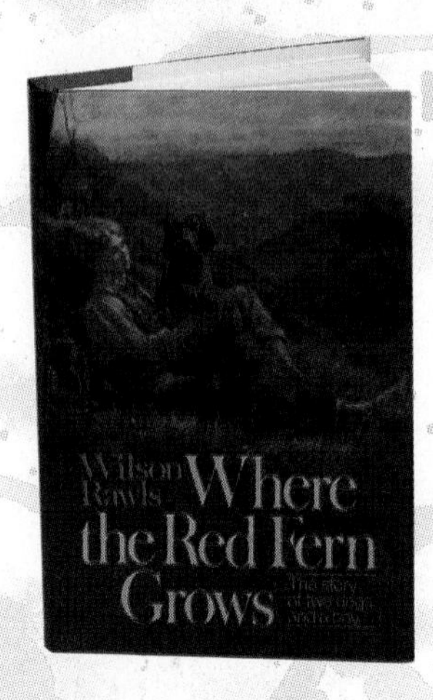

WHERE THE RED FERN GROWS

BY WILSON RAWLS

Billy Colman and his two hunting dogs gain a fine reputation when they win the hunt contest and then a fierce struggle against a mountain lion. Tragedy follows the victory, but Billy is left with wonderful memories.

Anthony Burns: The Defeat and Triumph of a Fugitive Slave

BY VIRGINIA HAMILTON

In this true story, Anthony Burns, born a slave, becomes the center of attention after he escapes to Boston. When he is arrested under the Fugitive Slave Act, Anthony becomes a symbol of freedom in peril.

ALA Notable Book, School Library Journal Best Book

Jodie's Journey

BY COLIN THIELE

After winning a jumping championship riding her beloved horse, Monarch, Jodie faces far more challenging hurdles. She learns that she has a crippling disease and will never ride Monarch again.

The Black Stallion

BY WALTER FARLEY

In this classic novel, Alec Ramsay and the Black Stallion — wildest of all creatures — are stranded on a desert island. Alec is determined to tame the horse, but the job turns out to be more dangerous than he had ever imagined.

THEME

Fortitude

Some challenges demand all of a person's effort and skill. As you read these stories of people facing such challenges, think about what you would do in the same circumstances.

CONTENTS

THE Beauty OF THE BEASTS

by Ralph Helfer

Ralph Helfer, one of the world's foremost animal trainers, is determined to stop the use of methods of animal training that use fear and violence to influence an animal's behavior. Using affection training, which is based on love, patience, understanding, and respect, Helfer has schooled animal performers for more than 5,000 movies and television programs. He has received recognition from the American Humane Society, and he and his animal friends have won many awards for the best animal performances on the screen.

◀ *In the history of the motion picture and TV industries, no child had ever worked in complete safety with an African lion until Pamela Franklin teamed up with Zamba for* The Lion. *Their affection for each other continued long after filming was finished.*

Amanda Blake and Mickey Rooney were cohosts of the PATSY ceremonies when I received an award from the American Humane Society for outstanding achievement in motion pictures.

It was raining that morning, as usual. For weeks it had been coming down—sometimes heavily, with thunder and lightning, and sometimes with just a mist of light rain. But it was always there, and by now the blankets, the beds, and the whole house were constantly damp.

My career was at a peak. I'd spent twelve years struggling to get to the top, and I had finally made it. My life was pretty good. I had just completed the back-to-back shooting of *Daktari* and *Gentle Ben*, and I was living at our new ranch, Africa U.S.A., with 1,500 wild animals and a crew of dedicated keepers and trainers.

The ranch was beautiful. Nestled at the bottom of Soledad Canyon, about thirty miles north of Los Angeles, the property snaked for a mile down the canyon beside the banks of the Santa Clarita stream. The highway wound above it on one side, the railroad track on the other.

We'd had heavy rains before, and even a few floods, but nothing we couldn't handle. There was a flood-control dam above us, fifteen miles up the canyon, and we weren't too worried about the stream's overflowing. But just to make sure, we had asked the city's flood-control office to advise us. They checked their records for the biggest flood in the office's hundred-year history, and calculated that to handle one that size we would need a channel 100 feet wide, 12 feet deep, and 1 mile long. It cost us $100,000 and three months of hard work, but we built it. It was worth it to feel safe.

Toni and I had grabbed a few hours' sleep before leaving the house, which was located off the ranch up on a hill, and heading out into the rain again early this morning to make sure our animals were dry and safe.

On arriving at the compound, Toni went over to check on the "wild string," a group of lions, tigers, bears, and leopards that had been donated to us by people who never should have had them in the first place. Hopeless animal lovers that we were, we had taken them in, even though we knew that very few spoiled mature animals could ever be indoctrinated with affection training.

I checked at the office for messages, then headed for "Beverly Hills," our nickname for the area where our movie-star animals lived—Gentle Ben, Clarence the cross-eyed lion, Judy the chimp, Bullfrog the "talking" buffalo, Modoc the elephant, and many others. The rain had become a steady downpour by the time I arrived there. Everything seemed to be in order, so I went on to the rhinos. No problems there, either.

As I left the rhinos, I noticed that I could no longer jump over the stream that ran beside their barn. I was starting to get a little concerned. The sky was now opening up with a vengeance. I wrapped my poncho around me and continued my tour of inspection.

I was wondering how Toni was making out with the wild string when Miguel, a Mexican keeper who had been with us for six years, arrived to care for the animals in the Beverly Hills section. He smiled his broad, gold-capped grin, then disappeared around a bend of the stream.

Then my head trainer, Frank Lamping, arrived. He told me that the earthen dam above us was about to go. To prevent the dam from bursting, the flood-control people were opening the floodgates to release the pressure. We were to watch out for some heavy water coming downstream.

The crew had all been working continuously from morning until night since the rains had begun, to make sure that the ranch was safe. Now we had to redouble our efforts.

I told Frank to check the stock area. A trainer yelled from the roadway above that he had the nursery section under control.

I found some pretty badly undermined cages in my area and set to work with a shovel to fill the erosion. I was looking down at my shovel, working hard, when I heard a noise. It was a low roar, and

My "family" of chimpanzees gather around to watch as trainers bring two Bengal tigers onto the set of Daktari.

Clarence the cross-eyed lion, one of the stars of the TV series Daktari. *Although we initially tried to correct Clarence's eye condition, we learned that it did not impair his vision, and so we left it as nature had intended.*

it was quickly becoming louder and closer. I remember just looking over my shoulder, and suddenly there it was—a wall of water carrying with it full-sized oak trees, sheds, branches. Down it came, crashing and exploding against the compound, uprooting cages, overturning buildings, trucks—anything in its way.

Instantly, everything was in chaos. Sheer panic broke out among the animals in the Beverly Hills section. Lions were roaring and hitting against the sides of their cages; bears were lunging against the bars; chimps were screaming. The water was starting to rock the cages. Some were already floating and were about to be swept downstream.

I didn't know what to do first! I raced for the cages, but was thrown down by the weight of the water. Miguel came running over, yelling half in English and half in Spanish. I told him to grab a large coil of rope that was hanging in a tree nearby. I fastened it around me and, with Miguel holding the other end, I started out into the water. If I could just get to the cages, I could unlock them and set the animals free. At least then they could fend for themselves. It was their only chance. Otherwise, they would all drown in their cages.

The water was rushing past me furiously. I struggled through it to Gentle Ben's cage, fumbling for the key. "Don't *drop* it!" I mumbled to myself. The key turned, I threw open the door, and the great old bear landed right on top of me in his panic for freedom.

I grabbed Ben's heavy coat and hung on as his massive body carried me to a group of cages holding more than twenty animals. The water was now five or six feet deep. Cages were starting to come loose from their foundations; the animals were swimming inside them, fighting for breath. I let go of Ben and grabbed onto the steel bars of one of the cages. My heart sank as I saw Ben dog-paddling, trying to reach the embankment. He never did. I could just barely make out his form as he was carried through some rough white water and around a bend before he was lost from view.

One by one I released the animals—leopards, tigers, bears—talking as calmly as I could, even managing an occasional pat or kiss of farewell. I watched as they were carried away, swept along with the torrent of water. Some would come together for a moment and would then be whisked away, as though a giant hand had come up and shoved them. Some went under. I strained to see whether any of these came up again, but I couldn't tell.

My wonderful, beloved animals were all fighting for their lives. I felt sick and helpless.

To my right, about thirty feet out in the water and half submerged, was a large, heavy steel cage on wheels with a row of four compartments in it. I managed to get to it just as the force of the current started to move it. I began to open the compartments, one by one, but now the cage was moving faster downstream, carrying me with it. I looked back to the shore, at Miguel. He saw the problem, and with his end of the rope he threw a dally around a large tree branch. We were running out of time. If the rope came to the end of its slack before I could get it off me and onto the cage, we would lose the cage. It was picking up speed, and the animals inside were roaring and barking in terror.

I decided to hold the cage myself, with the rope tied around my waist. There were two beautiful wolves in the last cage, Sheba and Rona. Toni and I had raised them since they were pups. I was at their door, fumbling with the lock, when the rope went taut. I thought it would cut me in half. I grabbed the steel bars with both hands, leaving the key in the lock, praying it wouldn't drop out. When I reached down once more to open the lock, the key fell into the water! I was stunned, frozen. I knew I had just signed those animals' death warrants. The water behind the cage was building up a wall of force. I held on as tightly as I could, but finally the cage was ripped out of my hands.

I fell backward into the churning water; when I surfaced, I could see the cage out in the mainstream, racing with the trees, bushes, and sides of buildings, heading on down the raging river. I looked for the last time at Sheba and Rona. They were looking at us quietly as if they knew, but their eyes begged for help. My tears joined the flood as my beloved friends were washed away.

By this time it had become clear to me what had happened. The floodgates on the dam had been opened, all right, but because the ground was already saturated with the thirty inches of rain that had fallen in the last few weeks, it wouldn't absorb any more. At the same time, the new storm had hit, pouring down another fourteen inches in just twenty-four hours. Together, these conditions had caused the flood.

It was a larger flood than any that had been recorded in the area in the last hundred years, and it was made worse because the water had been held up occasionally on its fifteen-mile journey down the canyon by debris in its path. When suddenly released, the water that had built up behind the naturally formed logjams doubled in force. By the time it reached us, huge waves had been built up: the water and debris came crashing down on us like a wall, then subsided, only to come crashing down again. We were to struggle through two days and nights of unbelievable havoc and terror, trying desperately to salvage what we could of the ranch.

Gentle Ben relaxes his 600 pounds on my shoulder during a morning workout on the set of his popular TV series.

The storm grew worse. Heavy sheets of rain filled and overflowed our flood channel, undermining its sides until they caved in. By mid-morning the Santa Clarita had become a raging, murderous torrent, 150 feet wide and 15 feet deep, moving through Africa U.S.A. with the speed and force of an express train. In its fury it wiped out a two-lane highway, full-grown oak trees, generator buildings—everything. Our soundstage was in a full-sized building, 100 feet long by 50 feet wide, but the water just picked it up like a matchbox and carried it away downstream, end over end, rolling it like a toy and depositing it on a sand embankment a mile away. Electric wires flared brightly as the water hit them. We rushed for the main switch to the soundstage, shutting everything down for fear of someone being electrocuted. Everywhere, animals and people were in the water, swimming for safety.

We'd be half drowned, and then we'd make our way to the shore, cough and sputter, and go back into the water. You don't think at a time like that—you *do*. My people risked their lives over and over again for the animals.

The waves next hit the elephant pens, hard. We moved the elephants out as the building collapsed and was carried downstream. Then the waves caught the camels' cage, pulling it into the water. One huge camel was turning over and over as he was swept along. (I thought at the time that somewhere, someday, if that animal drowned, some archeologist would dig up its bones and say, "There must have been camels in Los Angeles!")

We worked frenziedly. Bears, lions, and tigers were jumping out of their cages and immediately being swept downstream. Others were hanging onto our legs and pulling us under, or we were hanging onto them and swimming for shore. I unlocked the cheetah's cage and he sprang out over my head, right into the water, and was gone. Animals were everywhere.

I remember grabbing hold of a mature tiger as he came out of his cage. He carried me on his back to temporary security on the opposite bank as smoothly as if we'd rehearsed it.

Another time I found myself being carried downstream with Zamba, Jr., who was caught in the same whirlpool that I was. I grabbed his mane, and together we swam for the safety of the shore. After resting a bit, I managed to get back to the main area,

Sultan, a cross-breed of Siberian and Bengal species, poses with me for a portrait. Although I generally disapprove of interbreeding tigers, some have come to me with various subspecies already bred into them. Sultan exhibited the best qualities of the two species: the larger size of the Siberian and the more pliant intelligence of the Bengal.

leaving the lion in as good a spot as any. At least for the moment he was safe.

As the storm rode on, the river was full of animals and people swimming together; there was no "kill" instinct in operation, only that of survival. Men were grabbing fistfuls of fur, clinging for life. A monkey grabbed a lion's tail, which allowed him to make it to safety.

Clarence the cross-eyed lion was in a state of panic. The river had surrounded him and was now flooding his cage. His trainer, Bob, waded across the water, put a chain on Clarence, took him out of his cage, and attempted to jump across the raging stream with him. But the lion wouldn't jump. The water was rising rapidly. Bob threw part of the chain to me. To gain some leverage, I grabbed a pipe that was running alongside a building. As we both pulled, Clarence finally jumped, and just then the pipe I was holding onto came loose. It turned out to be a "hot" electric conduit, for when Clarence leaped and the pipe came loose, we all got a tremendous electric shock! Fortunately, the pipe also pulled the wires loose, so the shock only lasted for an instant. Had it continued, it would certainly have killed us, as we were standing knee-deep in water.

We noticed a group of monkeys trapped in a small outcropping of dirt and debris in the middle of the river. Frank almost died trying to save them: he tied a rope around his waist and started across, but about halfway over he slipped and went under. We didn't know whether to pull on the rope or not. We finally saw him in midstream, trying to stay afloat. Whenever we pulled on the rope, he would go under. (We found out later that the rope had become tangled around his foot, and every time we yanked it we were pulling him under!) But he made it, and he was able to swim the animals to safety.

We were racing against time. The river was still rising, piling up roots and buildings and pushing them along in front, forming a wall of destruction. The shouts of half-drowned men and the screams of drowning animals filled the air, along with thunder and lightning and the ever-increasing downpour of rain.

Throughout the turmoil and strife one thing was crystal clear to me, and that is that without affection training, all would have been lost. It was extraordinary. As dangerous and frightening as the emergency was, these animals remained calm enough to let themselves be led to safety when it was possible for us to do so.

Imagine yourself in a raging storm, with buildings crashing alongside of you. You make your way to a cage that houses a lion or a tiger, and the animal immediately understands why you're there and is happy to see you. You open the door, put a leash on the animal, and you both jump out into the freezing, swirling water. Together, you're swept down the stream, hitting logs, rolling over and over, as you try to keep your arms around the animal. Together, you get up onto the safety of dry land. You dry off, give your animal a big hug, and then go back in for another one.

There was one big cage left in the back section containing a lion. This lion was a killer who had been fear trained rather than affection trained. We went out to him. The other lions were being saved because we could swim with them, but this fellow was too rough. I got to the cage and opened the door. A couple of my men threw ropes on the lion and pulled, trying to get him out of his potential grave—but he wouldn't come out. He was petrified! We pulled and struggled and fought to get him out of the cage, but we couldn't do it, and we finally had to let him go.

Then the "wild string" panicked, and in their hysteria they attacked their rescuers as if they were enemies. In the end, we had to resort to tranquilizer guns. We fired darts into each fear-trained animal, and as they succumbed to the medication,

Many nights I would find this duckling curled up in one of C. J.'s massive hairy arms. The powerful orangutan would gently stroke the duckling's head with one of his large fingers—a rare and touching sight to behold.

we held their bodies up above the water and carried them to safety. Tragically, there was not enough time to drag all of them to safety; several drowned in their drugged sleep before we could reach them.

The storm continued on into the night, and with the darkness came a nightmare of confusion. We worked on without sleep, sustained by coffee and desperation.

During that first night, it became clear that ancient Modoc, the elephant, the one-eyed wonder of the big top, had by no means outlived her capacity for calmness and courage in the face of disaster. Modoc took over, understanding fully what was at stake and what was required of her. Animal after animal was saved as she labored at the water's edge, hauling their cages to safety on higher ground. When the current tore a cage free and washed it downstream, Modoc got a firmer grip on the rope with her trunk and, with the power of several bulldozers, steadily dragged the cage back to safety. Then a trainer would attach the rope to another endangered pen, and Modoc would resume her labors.

We eventually became stranded with some of the animals on an island—this was all that was left of Africa U.S.A., plus the area alongside the railroad track. When the dam had burst upstream, the wall of water that hit the ranch divided into two fast-moving rivers. As time passed, the rivers widened and deepened until they were impossible to cross. As dusk fell on the second day, we realized that we were cut off from the mainland. Since it was the highest ground on the ranch, the island in the center had become the haven for all the survivors. The office building, the vehicles, and about twenty cages were all well above the flooded zone and so were safe for the time being. The giraffes, some monkeys, and one lion were all housed in makeshift cages on the island. We all hoped the water would not rise any further.

Behind the office building ran a railroad track. By following the tracks for three miles, it would be possible to reach the highway. The problem would then be in crossing the torrent of water to get to the road.

I noticed that Bullfrog, our thousand-pound Indian buffalo, was gone. Buffalos are known to be excellent swimmers. Surely *he* could survive! I asked around to see whether anyone had seen him. No one had. Bullfrog's cage had been at the entrance to the ranch, because he always greeted visitors with a most unusual bellow that sounded exactly like the word "Hi." Now he was gone, too. Would it ever end? I felt weak. The temperature had dropped, and the wind had come up. The windchill factor was now thirty degrees below zero.

There's something horrible about tragedy that occurs in the dark. I could hear the water running behind me, and every once in a while I'd hear a big timber go, or an animal cry, or a person shouting. It all seemed very unreal.

Throughout the night and all the next day the rain continued, and we worked on. Luckily, help came from everywhere. The highway, which we could no longer get to but which we could see, was lined with cars. Some people had successfully rigged up a bos'n chair 50 feet in the air and were sending hot food and drink over to us, a distance of some 200 yards. Other people were walking three miles over the hills to bring supplies. Radio communication was set up by a citizens-band club. Gardner McKay, the actor and a true friend, put his Mercedes on the track, deflated the tires, and slowly drove down to help us. One elderly woman prepared ham and coffee and brought it in at two o'clock in the morning, only to find on her return that her car had been broken into and robbed!

Then a train engine came down the track to help (just an engine—no cars). Three girls from the affection-training school volunteered to rescue the snakes. The girls climbed onto the cowcatcher on the front of the engine. We then wrapped about thirty feet of pythons and boa constrictors around their shoulders and told them where to take the snakes once they were on the other side. (There was, of course, no more electricity in the reptile and nursery area, and unless we could get the reptiles to some heat, they would surely die.) Goats, aoudads, and llamas all rode in the coal bin behind the engine. I'll never forget the look on one girl's face as the engine pulled out and a python crawled through her hair.

By four the next morning, some twenty people had, by one method or another, made it over to our island to help. Some chose a dangerous way, tying ropes around their middles and entering the water slowly, with those on the island holding the other ends of the ropes. Then, with the current carrying them quickly downstream, they would look for a logjam or boulder to stop them so they could make their way to where we were.

I was having some coffee in the watchmen's trailer when the scream of an animal shattered the night. I dashed out to find a small group of people huddled together, trying to shine their flashlights on the animal who was out there in the dark, desperately struggling in the raging water. It had succeeded in swimming out of the turbulence in the middle of the stream, but the sides of the river were too slippery for it to get a foothold and climb to safety. In the dark, I couldn't make out which animal it was. Then I heard it: "Hi! Hi!" It was a call of desperation from Bullfrog, the buffalo, as he fought for his life. There was nothing we could do to help him, and his "Hi's" trailed down the dark, black abyss, fading as he was carried away around the bend.

Then Toni screamed at me in the dark, "Ralph, over here!" I fought my way through a maze of debris and water and burst into a clearing. There was Toni, holding a flashlight on—lo and behold—a big steel cage from Beverly Hills! It had been washed downstream and was lodged in the trunk of a toppled tree. It was still upright, but its back was facing us, and we couldn't see inside. We waded out to the cage. Toni kept calling, "Sheba, Rona, are you there? Please answer!" Our hearts were beating fast, and Toni was crying.

Hoping against hope that the wolves were still alive, we rounded the corner, half swimming, half falling. Then we eased up to the front of the cage and looked straight into two sets of the most beautiful eyes I'd ever seen. Rona and Sheba had survived! They practically jumped out of their skins when they saw us, as though to say, "Is it really *you?*" Toni had her key, and we unlocked the door. Both wolves fell all over us, knocking us into the water. They couldn't seem to stop licking our faces and whimpering. At least *they* were safe!

The rain finally let up on the morning of the third day. The sun came out, and at last we had time to stop, look around, and assess the damage. It was devastating, and heartrending.

Most of the animals had been let out of their cages and had totally disappeared, including Judy, Clarence, Pajama Tops, the zebra, and Raunchy, our star jaguar. We knew a few others had definitely drowned. Both rhinos were missing, and so were the hippos. Our beloved Gentle Ben had been washed away, along with hundreds of other animals.

To my recollection, Twiga was the only giraffe in the United States that had been trained to allow a human to ride him. Twiga was 8 years old, 15 feet tall, and still growing at the time of this picture.

Here I am with (left to right) Debbie, Taj, Modoc, and Misty—each a great performer in his or her own right.

I was sitting there looking at the wreckage when somebody put a cup of hot chocolate in my hand. It was Toni. She stood before me, as exhausted as I was, clothes torn and wet, hair astray, cold and shivering. What a woman! Earlier, she had managed to make her way to the Africa U.S.A. nursery, where all of the baby animals were quartered. Without exception, the babies had all followed her to safety. Not one baby animal had been lost.

The hot liquid felt good going down. I stood up and hugged and kissed Toni, and arm in arm we walked. The sun was just topping the cottonwoods. The river had subsided. All was quiet, except for an occasional animal noise: a yelp, a growl, a snort. All of the animals were happy to see the sun, to feel its warmth.

Toni and I felt only the heavy, leaden feeling of loss. Ten years were, literally, down the drain. We had just signed a contract with Universal Studios to open our beautiful ranch to their tours; this would now be impossible. A million dollars was gone, maybe more. But what was far worse was the loss of some of our beloved animals.

We hiked to a ridge above the railroad track. Something caught my eye, and as we came near an outcrop of trees where we could have a better view, we looked over. There, on top of a nearby hill, we saw an incredible sight. Lying under the tree was Zamba, and at his feet, resting, were a multitude of animals. Deer, bears,

William Holden was a true conservationist as well as a good friend. His understanding of African wildlife reached a new high during the filming of The Lion. *Here he takes a break while Tammy asks for attention.*

tigers, llamas, all lying together peacefully. The animals must have fought their way clear of the treacherous waters and, together, climbed the hill, slept, and then dried off in the morning sun. They hadn't run away. In fact, they seemed to be waiting for our next move. It was as though God had caused the flood to make me realize how powerful affection training is, how deep it had gone. The lamb could truly lie down with the lion, without fear, and could do it by choice!

We called Zam over to us and smothered him with hugs and kisses. As we climbed down to the ranch, the other animals joined us. Camels, giraffes, eland—all came along as we wound our way down.

So many people were there at the ranch! We were once again connected with the rest of the world. Exhausted, wet, wonderful people—true animal lovers. They had come from everywhere. Some were employees, some friends, some strangers. All greeted us as we came down the hill. Their faces expressed hope and love. They cared . . . and it showed.

We took the animals one by one and fed, cleaned, and housed them as best we could.

"Ralph, come quickly!" screamed a voice. "He made it, he made it! *He's alive!*"

"Who, who?" I screamed, and was met by a resounding "Hi, Hi!" From around the corner came Bullfrog—disheveled and muddy, but alive!

"Hi, hi!"

Yes, *hi,* you big, lovable . . . hi! hi!

We began searching for the animals that were still lost. The ranch was a network of people and animals working together on the massive cleanup effort. Animals were straining to pull big trucks out of the water and muck. Bakery trucks were coming by with stale bread for the elephants. Farmers loaned us their skip loaders to round up the hippos and rhinos. (One hippo fell in love with the skip-loader bucket and coyly followed it home!) Charley and Madeline Franks, two loyal helpers, kept hot chili coming and must have dished out hundreds of meals. People from the Humane Society, Fish and Game, Animal Regulation, and the SPCA[1] all helped to comfort and tend the animals.

[1] SPCA: Society for the Prevention of Cruelty to Animals

Everyone was busy constructing makeshift cages. The medical-lab trailer was pulled out of the mud. The nursery building and all of its kitchen storage area had been completely submerged, and some of it had been washed away. However, what could be salvaged was taken up to the island for immediate use.

Outside the ranch, the animals began turning up everywhere. Elephants showed up in people's backyards. Eagles sat in the limbs of trees. Llamas and guanacos cruised the local restaurants and were seen in parking lots. There was no difficulty between animals and people.

We had had dozens of alligators, some weighing two hundred to three hundred pounds. The whole pen had been hit by the water; we lost most of them because the water was ice-cold, and it battered and beat them. For seven months afterward we'd read in the paper that the bodies of alligators were being found everywhere, up to forty-five miles away. There were helicopter and airplane photos of alligators that had been killed, their bodies lying in the sand as the water subsided.

Of 1,500 other animals, only 9 had drowned. Five of these were animals that had not been affection trained.

Only one animal remained lost and unaccounted for, and that was old Gentle Ben. I had last seen him being swept sideways down the river. We didn't have much hope for him.

I was starting to feel the full shock of everything that had happened. True, by some miracle most of the animals were safe, but other losses had been enormous. As the emergency lessened and mopping-up operations took over, I felt worse and worse. The shakes set in, and then I developed a high fever. The doctors said it was a walking pneumonia, and that rest, good food, and warmth were in order. But there were still too many things to do—now was not the time to stop. I did, however, need to find a place to sit down and relax for a while.

As I sat on a log, my body trembled with shock as well as illness. In looking over the debris, it seemed to me that everything I had worked for was gone. The emotional pain, the sheer physical exhaustion, and the pneumonia had overloaded me. I just couldn't handle any more. I had no more tears, no pain of any kind. I was numb. I sat in the middle of the chaos with an old blanket wrapped around me, unmoving, unable to give any more orders.

I had closed my eyes and was drifting off to sleep when something warm and wet on my face woke me up. I opened my eyes and saw Ben. *Gentle Ben had come home!!* I hugged him and cried like a big kid. I turned to get up to tell everyone, but I didn't have to. They were all there. Toni, joined by the rest, had brought him to me. He'd been found two miles down the canyon, mud-covered and a few pounds lighter, but safe! Tears were in everybody's eyes—and if you looked closely, it seemed that even old Ben had a few.

A beautiful rainbow arched its brilliant colors across the ravaged countryside, then was gone.

*****

There was a time in my life when I felt I had reached the end of the rainbow. I had touched it, had dug my hand deep into its treasures of happiness and prosperity.

Suddenly, everything had changed. All that I had created was gone. I hadn't realized how vulnerable the world is, how delicate the balance of forces that sustain our existence.

I stood up and dusted off my jeans. In the distance I could see the sky clearing, and I knew that some day there would be another rainbow, its treasure awaiting. Until then, we had a job to do. We would need to start all over again.

What part of the selection did you find most exciting? Tell why you chose that part.

Use examples from the selection to explain how affection training made a difference during the disaster.

Disasters, such as a flood, often bring out the best in people. How did the people described in "The Beauty of the Beasts" prove that to be true?

WRITE In a paragraph or two, describe someone you know or have read about who has succeeded in spite of great problems.

AT HOME
Titan of

EUREKA, Alaska—It was a moment of warmth in a chilly, unyielding land. Twelve dozen Alaskan huskies yelped, growled, yipped and howled from their hutches on thawing muskeg and stretched wet paws toward Susan Butcher.

Butcher returned the adoration. She chanted.

"Bugga, bugga, buggabeen . . . the fastest dog there's ever been." Her song was for Sluggo, a honey-beige husky with a sore paw. It was raw from ice balls that formed between his toes last month when he was leading Butcher's team to victory in an 11-day streak of masochism known as the Iditarod Sled Dog Race. It was Sluggo's first win. It was Susan Butcher's fourth.

"Dugadee. Dugadoo. Dugadog." That was for Granite. He has won three Iditarods and, says Butcher, is the finest sled dog of this decade. If Granite were a horse he'd be Secretariat.

Then this iron woman crouched deep among her dogs and the spring-softened snow and wrapped arms around Elan's shaggy neck; flopped on her belly on a plywood doghouse to say boo to Tolstoy; and wrinkled her nose against the wet black plug of Heifer's nose.

And Susan Butcher—emotionally stale from airlines and motels and real clothes, mentally exhausted by 10 days of victory greetings, public speaking and a meeting with President Bush—finally was home.

Susan Butcher with sled dogs Tolstoy, Granite, and Mattie

WITH THE the Trail

by Paul Dean
Los Angeles Times

Home. That's Trail Breaker Kennel, five acres of bush surrounding an 80-year-old log cabin that once belonged to a Gold Rush blacksmith. It is most of Eureka (Elev. 270, Pop. 6). Just a scatter of mining shacks among stands of silver birch at the end of 140 miles of dirt road not far beneath the Arctic Circle.

Hers is life without television, running water, flush toilets or a bathtub. There's a single telephone hooked by satellite to a Seattle area code, but that's for husband Dave Monson to use because Butcher regards a ringing phone as the ultimate intrusion and refuses to answer it. A run to the grocery store is a four-hour rattle by truck to Fairbanks.

Only in isolation approaching privation, Butcher says, can she maintain an uninterrupted focus on breeding and training sled dogs. Only away from the noise, stink and structures of man can she intensify an unusual personal bonding with her dogs. Only from here can she concentrate on winning next year's Iditarod.

For a decade, she explains, she has concentrated on a companionship that starts with a puppy's first breath and produces dogs ready to drop for her—huskies that have made her not just the *best woman* dog sled racer in the world, but the *best* dog sled racer in the world.

In any endurance athlete's life the Iditarod stands as a death wish—a lopsided gamble against survival across 1,130 frostbitten miles, mountain ranges, blizzards, and frozen seas between Anchorage and Nome. Only two persons have won the Iditarod four times—Rick Swenson, 38, of Two Rivers, Alaska, and Susan Butcher, 35.

The race record is 11 days, 1 hour and 53 minutes. It belongs to Butcher. Her fifth Iditarod championship, said Joe Redding-ton Jr., a racer and son of the 1972 founder of the Iditarod, may be considered an inevitability. If anyone breaks the 10-day barrier, believe other experts, it will be Susan Butcher.

In the past winter's schedule of sled dog races—marked by such contests as the John Beargrease Marathon and the Coldfoot Classic—Butcher entered six events. She won four and was second in the others.

"What was the total frustration for the mushers is that Susan took three totally separate teams [to the races]," Butcher said. In conversation she often inserts herself in the narrative. "Both Susan's A and B dogs blew away the other teams and took 10 hours off the record in the Beargrease.

"The C team finished just seven minutes behind the winner in another event and would have won it if Susan hadn't been sicker [with flu] than a dog."

There are few places in Alaska where this happy woman with a smile stretching from here to the Aleutians can move unrecognized. She has visited two Presidents, been commended by legislatures, won the medals and awards of world organizations and visited the Soviet Union to counsel *perestroika* mushers and set trails for next year's Alaska-Siberia race.

Butcher has run her dogs in Switzerland and is a friend of Gen. Colin Powell, chairman of the Joint Chiefs of Staff, because each has been elected to membership in the American Academy of Achievement. Her racing has produced a major cottage industry in her home state; the smug legend of a million T-shirts sold says: "Alaska—Where Men are Men and Women Win the Iditarod."

Rarely is Butcher an also-ran, except to a media darling like Granite. On this month's victory tour, the 9-year-old husky, now retired, was given his own room at the Ritz-Carlton in St. Louis and the Four Seasons in Washington, D.C.

Letters from hotel managers were addressed to "Mr. Granite" and propped against baskets of Evian water from the French Alps and silver platters of ground round.

"There were times," Monson joked, "when we felt the introduction would be: Here's Granite who won the Iditarod three times with . . . er . . . um, the couple that owns him."

Susan Butcher cooks at Iditarod checkpoint

Yet such world attention has cost.

Resentment has been raised against Butcher by veterans who raced in obscurity for years because nobody cared much about the Iditarod—until a woman won. Then came reporters from *Sports Illustrated* and ABC's "Wide World of Sports" and Australia and Japan.

Said former champion Swenson: "She's a good competitor, but that's all I can say." Then he said more. "You could ask yourself what have they [Butcher and Monson] done for anyone else in the sport? They just take, take, take."

Butcher, a woman of uncluttered beliefs, sees another root of the resentment.

"I have become a symbol to women across the country—and internationally, in fact—and I'm not going to say that there wasn't a lot of strength gained by that thought and by the support [from women] that I got," she said.

Most competitors also don't recognize the spiritual link Butcher says she has with her huskies.

"I was born with a particular ability with animals and a particular love for them," she said. "I think that what you get from animals, and what I got from my first dog, one of my first close friends, is the security of constant love.

"An animal loves you and you love them and that is just constant. I needed that as a child. I have some compositions here, some of those one-liners you write in the first grade. Mine said: 'I hate the city, I love the country and I love animals.'"

All animals, she added. A pet iguana. A crow on a fence post. Even a hundred cows in a field "send me into a total thrill."

So in spring when husky pups are born to her 150-dog kennel, she holds each blind thing in her hands and breathes into its nose. That way, she says, the dog will associate her smell with comfort and encouragement. The rapport begins.

She feeds the dogs. *She* exercises and trains them. *She* massages them after runs. On a rotation basis, each dog sleeps in the cabin. The family forms.

Once, when a young Granite suffered renal failure from driving himself to dehydration, Butcher sat up for five nights with the dog's head in her lap. Granite survived and remained a champion.

"But I don't say I *need* to bond with these puppies early," Butcher explains. "I *want* to bond with them.

"I'm not saying that if I don't bond with this puppy I might not win the Iditarod, so therefore I *have* to go out and bond with this puppy. I'm going out because I'm absolutely drawn to that."

She also will not ask more of her dogs than they can deliver, she says. The huskies know that. So, they often give more than they

Iditarod Champion Susan Butcher at the finish line for the 1987 race

thought they had. And she is infinitely patient with the dogs.

"I want every one of these dogs to make my Iditarod team," Butcher continued. "So I give everybody their sixth, seventh, and eighth or ninth chance. Whereas my competitors—and I think this is one of the biggest differences—often don't give them a second or third chance."

Granite was a loser. She once offered him for sale for $250. "He didn't come around at least until his 10th chance. Sluggo was probably on his 20th chance before he came around.

"So you've got two superstars there who would not have even made it in someone else's team." And further, "every dog I run was raised in my own kennel by me and through my scheme . . . whereas often less than half of somebody else's team is raised in their own kennel, and they buy the others."

They buy from Butcher, paying from $1,000 to $10,000 for a trained dog. But even at that price, Butcher says, the animal is still one of her discards.

Her childhood was filled with daring. During summers spent in Maine she raced 13-foot sailing dinghies when gales sent others heading for the dock. Her description of childhood is that she was "an individualist . . . hard core, big time tomboy . . . a real gambler who took dangers fairly lightly . . . and very lopsided academically, because I was a dyslexic who excelled at math."

Her first dog, at 15, was Manganak, named for Zachary Manganak, a Canadian Eskimo in one of her children's books. Then she bought a second husky. Her mother said two dogs in one house was too much.

"So I left the house rather than not get the dog," Butcher remembered. "But happily so, and we maintained a wonderful relationship."

She was 16 then. Butcher went to Nova Scotia and learned to farm and train horses and picked up enough carpentry to build a boathouse. She went to join her father in Boulder, Colo., where her stepmother bought her a dog sled.

"We went to pick it up from a woman who had 50 huskies," Butcher said. "Ten minutes later I had moved in. I lived with her for a couple of years, worked as a veterinary technician and mushed and was frustrated by every minute of it."

Butcher wanted the life of yesteryear. There must be a place, she reasoned, where human survival depended on instincts and dogs were not domestic pets but working animals "needed for transportation, to haul your water, to haul your wood."

She eyed Western Canada. On her way, she paused in Fairbanks. "I felt at home the second I got there."

Butcher worked at a musk ox farm, found a companion and headed for her first winter in the lonely Wrangell Mountains before she had learned her partner's last name.

"It was one of the purest places left in Alaska," she recalled. "The closest road was 50 miles away. In

Canada. We took in a sack of flour and a slab of bacon and a jar of peanut butter and lived off moose and caribou and ptarmigan and whatever we could hunt.

"I was a vegetarian when I went out there. I wasn't a vegetarian when I came back."

Butcher found "Utopia." She also discovered life in its basic form. "If you were going to eat meat, you shot it. You saw its death. You caused its death and you ate it and you survived because of its death.

"And you hauled all your own water and everything was dependent on you and the reward was living in the most gorgeous spot on Earth.

"I found out after that second winter that I was totally rejuvenated," she said. "I knew that if I could spend the majority of a year away from people, then I could actually adore human beings for about two months . . . even strangers."

But only for a short while. "Then I'd fall off and it would be big time bad news. Get me out into the bush again. Susan is ready to flip out."

In 1977, she moved to Eureka with two objectives: To form a kennel of at least 100 dogs and build a team to run the Iditarod.

They were long, lonely years. She lived alone or with handlers when she could afford them. Debts grew. Equipment broke. One winter she survived by eating meat bought for the dogs.

But Butcher had goals, a stiff spine, a stubborn mind-set and an eye for any opportunity to focus attention on her and the dogs.

So in 1979, with Iditarod founder Joe Reddington, she took a dog team to the 20,320-foot summit of Mt. McKinley. It took 44 days. It also brought public interest to the earnest young woman with the braided hair.

She trains her pups in harness at $4\frac{1}{2}$ months. Each one has been bred for essentials. Stamina. Resistance to injury. A sense of teamwork. Courage. Stoicism and flexibility of limbs.

Her aim is always to run behind the best dog team anyone ever hitched to a sled. Each dog must also have total communication with Butcher.

She deepens the telepathy by singing to the dogs when they are racing, old folk songs by Bob Dylan and Joan Baez and maybe some Irish lullabies.

And in the worst moments of several Iditarods—when there were hallucinations from sleep deprivation—the dogs have saved her life.

In 1984, jockeying for the lead with two other teams, Butcher was told by race supervisors there was no overland trail between Unalakleet and Shaktoolik on Norton Sound, which pokes toward the Bering Sea. Crossing sea ice on a moonless night was the only choice.

"I noticed the ice was almost billowing," she recalled. "Just as I saw that, I told Granite [in lead] to go to the left. Which he did. He was terrified because the whole thing [ice] was going like this [rocking] . . . when the sled fell through and the whole team and I went in about 30 feet of water."

But then "Granite hit hard ice and he got up on top of it. Him and Maddie. Then, two [dogs] by two, they pulled us out. I thought we were goners."

A moose once attacked the team and that cost Butcher the 1985 race, seven years of preparation, two dogs killed and 13 injured.

Butcher has crossed Norton Sound in a blizzard when she couldn't see the lead dog. Navigation was by a small compass. For five blind hours she traveled the ice, wondering how close she was to the spot where a friend drowned earlier in the year.

Susan Butcher with her dog team

"But there's a fun thing about it," she said. She mentioned a quirk known to all adventurers. "It's thrilling, isn't it? Especially when you conquer it."

There are activists who see sled dog racing as cruelty to animals.

Butcher snorts at the thought. It is an expression, she says, of uninformed city dwellers who know only pampered pets.

Pulling sleds "is what they live for . . . it is instinctive for them to want to pull.

"From the time they see the harness come out or see the sled, they are absolutely going crazy, jumping around, wanting to go and then literally jumping into harness."

There also are times when the adrenaline pumps and 12 dogs are galloping as one. Then, Butcher says, they don't want to stop. There was the time a tired Butcher was racing in the Brooks Range and thought her weariness would be contagious.

"I felt these dogs would be fried or at least pick up on my feelings of being fried," she said. "But I could not stop them. It was a total thrill. I hooked a five-inch diameter tree with my snow hook and they pulled the tree over. I tried stopping them for five or six miles and then gave up.

"So they went 35 miles into the next village."

Such moments, she says, make Susan complete.

The childhood inadequacies have gone. She no longer hunts for role models—because she has become the very person she was always searching for.

Yet is there still a call of the wild for Susan Butcher?

She thought long about that.

Outside the log cabin, Sluggo and Tolstoy and Co-Star and Hermit lie flat, with furry bellies toasting in the warm Arctic sun. Monson was playing a tape and porch speakers carried the Modern Mandolin Quartet over snow to thicket and silent hill. A gray jay snoozed in a tree.

"Oh, no," Butcher whispered. "It's still calling."

What, do you think, is Susan Butcher's strongest character trait? Do you think you share that trait? If not, would you like to? Explain your answer.

How has being a woman been both an advantage and a disadvantage to Butcher in her career?

Why do you think Butcher was elected a member of the American Academy of Achievement?

WRITE Would you like to live in an isolated area, as Susan Butcher does? Write a paragraph explaining your response.

Do you think that Ralph Helfer and Susan Butcher would admire each other if they met? What specific attitudes or actions might each trainer respect in the other?

Writer's Workshop

The challenges that Helfer and Butcher faced were met with fortitude and dedication. What personal experiences have required you to show fortitude? Write a personal narrative about a challenge that you met head-on with all your strength and courage.

Writer's Choice Both "The Beauty of the Beasts" and "At Home with the Titan of the Trail" are about working animals. Do you think that animals can show fortitude? How did reading these selections expand your idea of strength and courage? Write about your ideas, and think of a way to share your finished product.

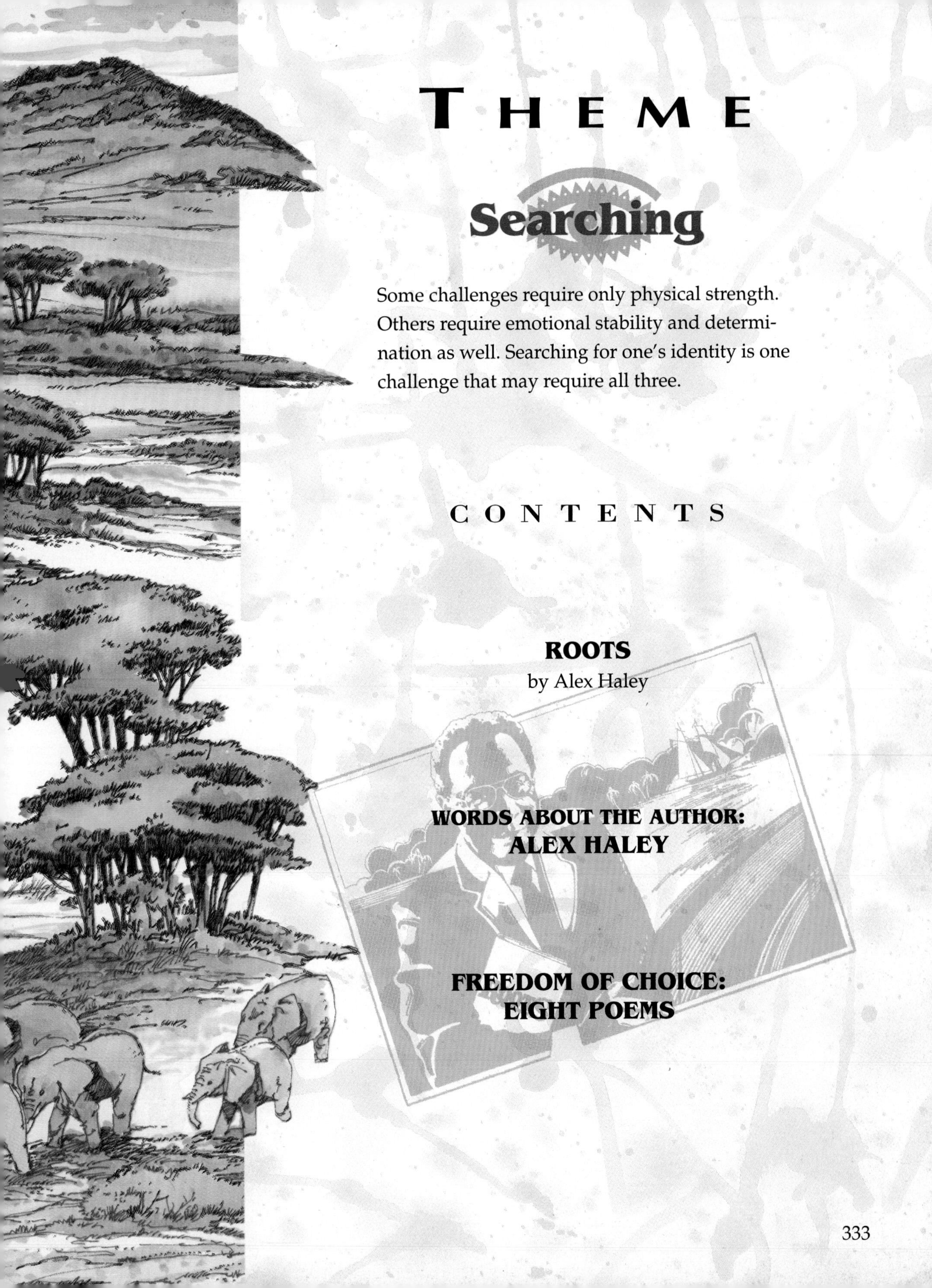

THEME

Searching

Some challenges require only physical strength. Others require emotional stability and determination as well. Searching for one's identity is one challenge that may require all three.

CONTENTS

AFRICA

Atlantic

Ocean

Roots

By Alex Haley

When he was a boy in Tennessee, Alex Haley's grandmother and other relatives used to tell him stories about their ancestors through the generations all the way back to a man they called the African. *The following excerpt describes journalist Haley's attempts to find out more about his ancestors and tells how his discoveries led him to write* Roots, *which became a best-selling book and a popular TV miniseries.*

illustrations by Clarence Porter

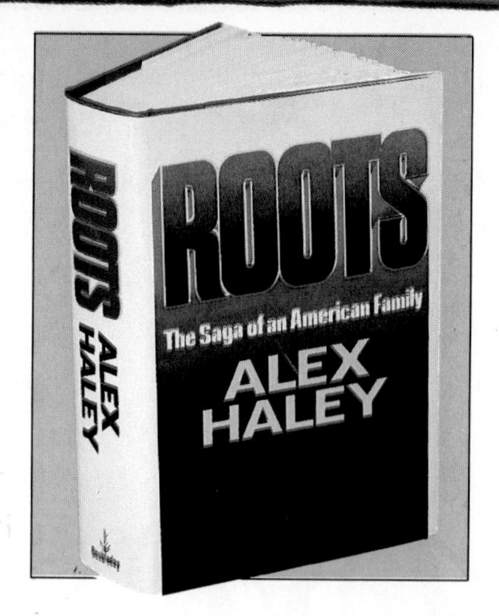

Soon, a magazine sent me on an assignment to London. Between appointments, utterly fascinated with a wealth of history everywhere, I missed scarcely a guided tour anywhere within London's area during the next several days. Poking about one day in the British Museum, I found myself looking at something I'd heard of vaguely: The Rosetta Stone. I don't know why, it just about entranced me. I got a book there in the museum library to learn more about it.

Discovered in the Nile delta, I learned, the stone's face had chiseled into it three separate texts: one in known Greek characters, the second in a then-unknown set of characters, the third in the ancient hieroglyphics, which it had been assumed no one ever would be able to translate. But a French scholar, Jean Champollion, successively matched, character for character, both the unknown text and the hieroglyphics with the known Greek text, and he offered a thesis that the texts read the same. Essentially, he had cracked the mystery of the previously undeciphered hieroglyphics in which much of mankind's earliest history was recorded.

The key that had unlocked a door into the past fascinated me. I seemed to feel it had some special personal significance, but I couldn't imagine what. I was on a plane returning to the United States when an idea hit me. Using language chiseled into stone, the French scholar had deciphered a historic unknown by matching it with that which was known. That presented me a rough analogy: In the oral history that Grandma, Aunt Liz, Aunt Plus, Cousin Georgia, and the others had always told on the boyhood Henning front porch, I had an unknown quotient in those strange words or sounds passed on by the African. I got to thinking about them: "Kin-tay," he had said, was his name. "*Ko*" he had called a guitar. "Kamby Bolongo" he had called a river in Virginia. They were mostly sharp, angular sounds, with *k* predominating. These sounds probably had undergone some changes across the generations of being passed down, yet unquestionably they represented phonetic snatches of whatever was the specific tongue spoken by my African ancestor who was a family legend. My plane from London was circling to land at New York with me wondering: What specific African tongue was it? Was there any way in the world that maybe I could find out?

Now the thing was where, what, how could I pursue those strange phonetic sounds that it was always said our African ancestor had spoken. It seemed obvious that I had to reach as wide a range of actual Africans as I possibly could, simply because so many different tribal tongues are spoken in Africa. There in New York City, I began doing what seemed logical: I began arriving at the United Nations around quitting time; the elevators were spilling out people who were thronging through the lobby on their way home. It wasn't hard to spot the Africans, and every one I was able to stop, I'd tell my sounds to. Within a couple of weeks, I guess I had stopped about two dozen Africans, each of whom had given me a quick look, a quick listen, and then took off. I can't say I blame them—me trying to communicate some African sounds in a Tennessee accent.

Increasingly frustrated, I had a long talk with George Sims, with whom I'd grown up in Henning, and who is a master researcher. After a few days, George brought me a list of about a dozen people academically renowned for their knowledge of African linguistics. One whose background intrigued me quickly was a Belgian, Dr. Jan Vansina. After study at the University of London's School of African and Oriental Studies, he had done his early work living in African villages and written a book called *La Tradition Orale.* I telephoned Dr. Vansina where he now taught at the University of Wisconsin, and he gave me an appointment to see him. It was a Wednesday morning that I flew to Madison, Wisconsin, motivated by my intense curiosity about some strange phonetic sounds . . . and with no dream in this world of what was about to start happening. . . .

That evening in the Vansinas' living room, I told him every syllable I could remember of the family narrative heard since little boyhood—recently buttressed by Cousin Georgia in Kansas City. Dr. Vansina, after listening intently throughout, then began asking me questions. Being an oral historian, he was particularly interested in the physical transmission of the narrative down across generations.

We talked so late that he invited me to spend the night, and the next morning Dr. Vansina, with a very serious expression on his face, said, "I wanted to sleep on it. The ramifications of phonetic sounds preserved down across your family's generations can be immense." He said that he had been on the phone with a colleague Africanist, Dr. Philip Curtin; they both felt certain that the sounds I'd conveyed to him were from the "Mandinka" tongue. I'd never heard that word; he told me that it was the language spoken by the Mandingo people. Then he guess-translated certain of the sounds. One of them probably meant cow or cattle; another probably meant the baobab tree, generic in West Africa. The word *ko,* he said, could refer to the *kora,* one of the Mandingo people's oldest stringed instruments, made of a halved large dried gourd covered with goatskin, with a long neck, and twenty-one strings with a bridge. An enslaved Mandingo might relate the *kora* visually to some among the types of stringed instruments that U.S. slaves had.

The most involved sound I had heard and brought was Kamby Bolongo, my ancestor's sound to his daughter Kizzy as he had pointed to the Mattaponi River in Spotsylvania County, Virginia. Dr. Vansina said that without question, bolongo meant, in the Mandinka tongue, a moving water, as a river; preceded by *Kamby,* it could indicate the Gambia River.

I'd never heard of it.

An incident happened that would build my feelings—especially as more uncanny things occurred—that, yes, they were up there watching. . . .

I was asked to speak at a seminar held at Utica College, Utica, New York. Walking down a hallway with the professor who had invited me, I said I'd just flown in from Washington and why I'd been there. "The Gambia? If I'm not mistaken, someone mentioned recently that an outstanding student from that country is over at Hamilton."

The old, distinguished Hamilton College was maybe a half hour's drive away, in Clinton, New York. Before I could finish asking, a Professor Charles Todd said, "You're talking about Ebou Manga." Consulting a course roster, he told me where I could find him in an agricultural economics class. Ebou Manga was small of build, with careful eyes, a reserved manner, and black as soot. He tentatively confirmed my sounds, clearly startled to have heard me uttering them. Was Mandinka his home tongue? "No, although I am familiar with it." He was a Wolof, he said. In his dormitory room, I told him about my quest. We left for The Gambia at the end of the following week.

Arriving in Dakar, Senegal, the next morning, we caught a light plane to small Yundum Airport in The Gambia. In a passenger van, we rode into the capital city of Banjul (then Bathurst). Ebou and his father, Alhaji Manga—Gambians are mostly Moslem—assembled a small group of men knowledgeable in their small country's history, who met with me in the lounge of the Atlantic Hotel. As I had told Dr. Vansina in Wisconsin, I told these men the family narrative that had come down across the generations.

When I had finished, they said almost with wry amusement, "Well, of course 'Kamby Bolongo' would mean Gambia River; anyone would know that." I told them hotly that no, a great many people *wouldn't* know it! Then they showed a much greater interest that my 1760s ancestor had insisted his name was "Kin-tay." "Our country's oldest villages tend to be named for the families that settled those villages centuries ago," they said. Sending for a map, pointing, they said, "Look, here is the village of Kinte-Kundah. And not too far from it, the village of Kinte-Kundah Janneh-Ya."

Then they told me something of which I'd never have dreamed: of very old men, called *griots,* still to be found in the older back-country villages, men who were in effect living, walking archives of oral history. A senior *griot* would be a man usually in his late sixties or early seventies; below him would be progressively younger *griots*—and apprenticing boys, so a boy would be exposed to those *griots'* particular line of narrative for forty or fifty years before he could qualify as a senior *griot,* who told on special occasions the centuries-old histories of villages, of clans, of families, of great heroes. Throughout the whole of black Africa such oral chronicles had been handed down

since the time of the ancient forefathers, I was informed, and there were certain legendary *griots* who could narrate facets of African history literally for as long as three days without ever repeating themselves.

Seeing how astounded I was, these Gambian men reminded me that every living person ancestrally goes back to some time and some place where no writing existed; and then human memories and mouths and ears were the only ways those human beings could store and relay information. They said that we who live in the Western culture are so conditioned to the "crutch of print" that few among us comprehend what a trained memory is capable of.

Since my forefather had said his name was "Kin-tay"—properly spelled "Kinte," they said—and since the Kinte clan was old and well known in The Gambia, they promised to do what they could to find a *griot* who might be able to assist my search.

Back in the United States, I began devouring books on African history. It grew quickly into some kind of obsession to correct my ignorance concerning the earth's second-largest continent. It embarrasses me to this day that up to then my images about Africa had been largely derived or inferred from Tarzan movies and my very little authentic knowledge had come from only occasional leafings through the *National Geographic.* All of a sudden now, after reading all day, I'd sit on the edge of my bed at night studying a map of Africa, memorizing the different countries' relative positions and the principal waters where slave ships had operated.

After some weeks, a registered letter came from The Gambia; it suggested that when possible, I should come back.

I again visited Cousin Georgia in Kansas City—something had urged me to do so, and I found her quite ill. But she was thrilled to hear both what I had learned and what I hoped to learn. She wished me Godspeed, and I flew then to Africa.

The same men with whom I had previously talked told me now in a rather matter-of-fact manner that they had caused word to be put out in the back country, and that a *griot* very knowledgeable of the Kinte clan had indeed been found—his name, they said, was

◀ Author Alex Haley returned to the village of Juffure after the publication of *Roots*.

"Kebba Kanji Fofana." I was ready to have a fit. "Where *is* he?" They looked at me oddly: "He's in his village."

I discovered that if I intended to see this *griot,* I was going to have to do something I'd never have dreamed I'd ever be doing—organizing what seemed, at least to me then, a kind of mini-safari! It took me three days of negotiating through unaccustomed endless African palaver finally to hire a launch to get upriver; to rent a lorry and a vehicle to take supplies by a roundabout land route; to hire finally a total of fourteen people, including three interpreters and four musicians, who had told me that the old *griots* in the back country wouldn't talk without music in the background.

There is an expression called "the peak experience"—that which, emotionally, nothing in your life ever transcends. I've had mine, that first day in the back country of black West Africa.

When we got within sight of Juffure, the children who were playing outside gave the alert, and the people came flocking from their huts. It's a village of only about seventy people. Like most back-country villages, it was still very much as it was two hundred years ago, with its circular mud houses and their conical thatched roofs. Among the people as they gathered was a small man wearing an off-white robe, a pillbox hat over an aquiline-featured black face, and about him was an aura of "somebodiness" until I knew he was the man we had come to see and hear.

As the three interpreters left our party to converge upon him, the seventy-odd other villagers gathered closely around me, in a kind of horseshoe pattern, three or four deep all around; had I stuck out my arms, my fingers would have touched the nearest ones on either side. They were all staring at me. The eyes just raked me. Their foreheads were furrowed with their very intensity of staring. A kind of visceral surging or a churning sensation started up deep inside me; bewildered, I was wondering what on earth was this . . . then in a little while it was rather as if some full-gale force of realization rolled in on me: Many times in my life I had been among crowds of people, but never where *every one was jet black!*

Rocked emotionally, my eyes dropped downward as we tend to do when we're uncertain, insecure, and my glance fell upon my own hands' brown complexion. This time more quickly than before, and even harder, another gale-force emotion hit me: I felt myself some variety of a hybrid . . . I felt somehow impure among the pure; it was a terribly shaming feeling. About then, abruptly the old man left the interpreters. The people immediately also left me now to go crowding about him.

One of my interpreters came up quickly and whispered in my ear, "They stare at you so much because they have never here seen a black American." When I grasped the significance, I believe that hit me harder than what had already happened. They hadn't been looking at me as an individual, but I represented in their eyes a symbol of the twenty-five millions of us black people whom they had never seen, who lived beyond an ocean.

The people were clustered thickly about the old man, all of them intermittently flicking glances toward me as they talked animatedly in their Mandinka tongue. After a while, the old man turned, walked briskly through the people, past my three interpreters, and right up to me. His eyes piercing into mine, seeming to feel I should understand his Mandinka, he expressed what they had all decided they *felt* concerning those unseen millions of us who lived in those places that had been slave ships' destinations—and the translation came: "We have been told by the forefathers that there are many of us from this place who are in exile in that place called America—and in other places."

The old man sat down, facing me, as the people hurriedly gathered behind him. Then he began to recite for me the ancestral history of the Kinte clan, as it had been passed along orally down across centuries from the forefathers' time. It was not merely conversational, but more as if a scroll were being read; for the still, silent villagers, it was clearly a formal occasion. The *griot* would speak, bending forward from the waist, his body rigid, his neck cords standing out, his words seeming almost physical objects. After a sentence or two, seeming to go limp, he would lean back, listening to an interpreter's translation. Spilling from the *griot's* head came an incredibly complex Kinte clan lineage that reached back across many generations: who married whom; who had what children; what children then married whom; then their offspring. It was all just unbelievable. I was struck not only by the profusion of details, but

Atlant
Ocea

also by the narrative's biblical style, something like: "—and so-and-so took as a wife so-and-so, and begat . . . and begat . . . and begat . . ." He would next name each begat's eventual spouse, or spouses, and their averagely numerous offspring, and so on. To date things the *griot* linked them to events, such as "—in the year of the big water" —a flood—"he slew a water buffalo." To determine the calendar date, you'd have to find out when that particular flood occurred.

The old *griot* had talked for nearly two hours up to then, and perhaps fifty times the narrative had included some detail about someone whom he had named. Now after he had just named those four sons, again he appended a detail, and the interpreter translated—

"About the time the King's soldiers came"—another of the *griot's* time-fixing references—"the eldest of these four sons, Kunta, went away from his village to chop wood . . . and he was never seen again . . ." And the *griot* went on with his narrative.

I sat as if I were carved of stone. My blood seemed to have congealed. This man whose lifetime had been in this back-country African village had no way in the world to know that he had just echoed what I had heard all through my boyhood years on my grandma's front porch in Henning, Tennessee . . . of an African who always had insisted that his name was "Kin-tay"; who had called a guitar a *"ko,"* and a river within the state of Virginia, "Kamby Bolongo"; and who had been kidnapped into slavery while not far from his village, chopping wood to make himself a drum.

I managed to fumble from my dufflebag my basic notebook, whose first pages containing grandma's story I showed to an interpreter. After briefly reading, clearly astounded, he spoke rapidly while showing it to the old *griot,* who became agitated; he got up, exclaiming to the people, gesturing at my notebook in the interpreter's hands, and *they* all got agitated.

I don't remember hearing anyone giving an order, I only recall becoming aware that those seventy-odd people had formed a wide human ring around me, moving counterclockwise, chanting softly, loudly, softly; their bodies close together, they were lifting their knees high, stamping up reddish puffs of the dust. . . .

◀ Alex Haley with LeVar Burton, star of the television miniseries *Roots*.
Alex Haley greets students.

The woman who broke from the moving circle was one of about a dozen whose infant children were within cloth slings across their backs. Her jet-black face deeply contorting, the woman came charging toward me, her bare feet slapping the earth, and snatching her baby free, she thrust it at me almost roughly, the gesture saying "Take it!" . . . and I did, clasping the baby to me. Then she snatched away her baby; and another woman was thrusting her baby, then another, and another . . . until I had embraced probably a dozen babies. I wouldn't learn until maybe a year later, from a Harvard University professor, Dr. Jerome Bruner, a scholar of such matters, "You didn't know you were participating in one of the oldest ceremonies of humankind, called 'The laying on of hands'! In their way, they were telling you 'Through this flesh, which is us, we are you, and you are us!'"

Since we had come by the river, I wanted to return by land. As I sat beside the wiry young Mandingo driver who was leaving dust pluming behind us on the hot, rough, pitted, back-country road toward Banjul, there came from somewhere into my head a staggering awareness . . . that *if* any black American could be so blessed as I had been to know only a few ancestral clues—could he or she know *who* was either the paternal or maternal African ancestor or ancestors, and about *where* that ancestor lived when taken, and finally about *when* the ancestor was taken—then only those few clues might well see that black American able to locate some wizened old black *griot* whose narrative could reveal the black American's ancestral clan, perhaps even the very village.

My mind reeled with it all as we approached another, much larger village. Staring ahead, I realized that word of what had happened in Juffure must have left there well before I did. The driver slowing down, I could see this village's people thronging the road ahead; they were waving, amid their cacophony of crying out something; I stood up in the Land-Rover, waving back as they seemed grudging to open a path for the Land-Rover.

I guess we had moved a third of the way through the village when it suddenly registered in my brain what they were all crying out . . . the wizened, robed elders and younger men, the mothers and the naked tar-black children, they were all waving up to me;

their expressions buoyant, beaming, all were crying out together, *"Meester Kinte! Meester Kinte!"*

Let me tell you something: I am a man. A sob hit me somewhere around my ankles; it came surging upward, and flinging my hands over my face, I was just bawling, as I hadn't since I was a baby. *"Meester Kinte!"* I just felt like I was weeping for all of history's incredible atrocities against fellow men, which seems to be mankind's greatest flaw. . . .

Flying homeward from Dakar, I decided to write a book. My own ancestors would automatically also be a symbolic saga of all African-descent people—who are without exception the seeds of someone like Kunta who was born and grew up in some black African village, someone who was captured and chained down in one of those slave ships that sailed them across the same ocean, into some succession of plantations, and since then a struggle for freedom.

For Alex Haley, finding his roots was a very emotional experience. Do you think you would be as moved as he was if you visited a place that was important in your family's past? Explain your answer.

Explain the part the Rosetta Stone played in Alex Haley's decision to write *Roots*.

What effect does the "crutch of print" have on memory in Western civilization?

Write Alex Haley grew up hearing family stories. Write a brief retelling of a story that is told in your family. The story may be true, or it may be one that you know is told to teach a lesson.

Words about the Author:

Alex Haley illustration by Scott Scheidly

Childhood stories about a puzzling but fascinating ancestor spurred Alex Haley's search for the truth and in time produced a phenomenal historical novel—one that has inspired readers to discover more about themselves and their roots.

As a young boy, Haley sat on his grandmother's porch in Henning, Tennessee, and listened as his grandmother and other older relatives told stories about his ancestors. They were all fascinating stories, yes, but none more so than the stories about "the African."

Born in Ithaca, New York, in 1921 to Simon Alexander Haley, a professor, and Bertha Palmer Haley, a teacher, Alex Palmer Haley spent most of his youth in Henning. The oral tradition was strong in Haley's family, and from an early age he understood the power of words—spoken or written.

As he grew to manhood, his fascination with "the African" increased accordingly, stirring in him a desire to investigate further and to discover more about his roots. And so Alex Haley began the long journey that led him to The Gambia, West Africa—home of "the African"—and later led him to the publication of *Roots: The Saga of an American Family*.

His understanding of the power of words helped prepare him for his career in journalism, which he began when he joined the United States Coast Guard in 1939. When he retired from the Coast Guard as chief journalist in 1959, Haley said he was "prepared to starve" in his determination to pursue a full-time writing career. And in those early years, starvation was always close by.

At one point he was down to eighteen cents and two cans of sardines. Then, finally, he received a check, payment for an article he had written. Receiving the check gave him the incentive to continue as a writer. The framed eighteen cents and the cans of sardines—symbols of his "determination to be independent"—hung for many years in the library at his home.

When *Roots* was published in 1976, critics called it "a phenomenon," not only because it told the story of the journey of all African Americans from slavery to freedom, but also because it changed the way people viewed themselves, their families, and their ancestry. The book sparked many readers' search for knowledge about their lineage. Aware of the excitement he had created, Haley provided more information about genealogical research in *My Search for Roots.* That book contains an account of the twelve years of intense research Haley undertook in the United States and Africa to gather material for *Roots.*

Haley served as script consultant for three televised miniseries: *Roots; Roots: The Next Generation;* and *Palmerstown, U. S. A.* Among the awards he received for *Roots* are special citations in 1977 from the National Book Award committee and from the Pulitzer Prize committee. Alex Haley died in 1992.

FREEDOM OF CHOICE: *Eight Poems*

Mirage, 1985, Pat Steir, Installation Promenades,
Parc Lullin, Geneva, Switzerland

Sympathy

by Paul Laurence Dunbar

I know what the caged bird feels, alas!
When the sun is bright on the upland slopes;
When the wind stirs soft through the springing grass
And the river flows like a stream of glass;
When the first bird sings and the first bud opes,
And the faint perfume from its chalice steals—
I know what the caged bird feels!

I know why the caged bird beats his wing
Till its blood is red on the cruel bars;
For he must fly back to his perch and cling
When he fain would be on the bough a-swing;
And a pain still throbs in the old, old scars
And they pulse again with a keener sting—
I know why he beats his wing!

I know why the caged bird sings, ah me,
When his wing is bruised and his bosom sore,
When he beats his bars and would be free;
It is not a carol of joy or glee,
But a prayer that he sends from his heart's deep core,
But a plea, that upward to Heaven he flings—
I know why the caged bird sings!

One

by James Berry

Only one of me
and nobody can get a second one
from a photocopy machine.

Nobody has the fingerprints I have.
Nobody can cry my tears, or laugh my laugh
or have my expectancy when I wait.

But anybody can mimic my dance with my dog.
Anybody can howl how I sing out of tune.
And mirrors can show me multiplied
many times, say, dressed up in red
or dressed up in grey.

Nobody can get into my clothes for me
or feel my fall for me, or do my running.
Nobody hears my music for me, either.

I am just this one.
Nobody else makes the words
I shape with sound, when I talk.

But anybody can act how I stutter in a rage.
Anybody can copy echoes I make.
And mirrors can show me multiplied
many times, say, dressed up in green
or dressed up in blue.

The Musician, 1917-1918, Georges Braque, Collection of Basel Museum

The Road Not Taken

by Robert Frost

Two roads diverged in a yellow wood,
And sorry I could not travel both
And be one traveler, long I stood
And looked down one as far as I could
To where it bent in the undergrowth;

Then took the other, as just as fair,
And having perhaps the better claim,
Because it was grassy and wanted wear;
Though as for that, the passing there
Had worn them really about the same,

And both that morning equally lay
In leaves no step had trodden black.
Oh, I kept the first for another day!
Yet knowing how way leads on to way,
I doubted if I should ever come back.

I shall be telling this with a sigh
Somewhere ages and ages hence:
Two roads diverged in a wood, and I—
I took the one less traveled by,
And that has made all the difference.

Advice to Travelers

by Walker Gibson

A burro once, sent by express,
His shipping ticket on his bridle,
Ate up his name and his address,
And in some warehouse, standing idle,
He waited till he like to died.
The moral hardly needs the showing:
Don't keep things locked up deep inside—
Say who you are and where you're going.

I Saw a Man

by Stephen Crane

I saw a man pursuing the horizon;
Round and round they sped.
I was disturbed at this;
I accosted the man.
"It is futile," I said,
"You can never—"

"You lie," he cried,
And ran on.

Mist in Kanab Canyon, Utah, Thomas Moran, 1892, oil on canvas, 44 3/8" X 38 3/8". National Museum of American Art, Smithsonian Institution, Bequest of Bessie B. Croffut.

The Forecast

by Dan Jaffe

Perhaps our age has driven us indoors.
We sprawl in the semi-darkness, dreaming sometimes
Of a vague world spinning in the wind.
But we have snapped our locks, pulled down our shades,
Taken all precautions. We shall not be disturbed.
If the earth shakes, it will be on a screen;
And if the prairie wind spills down our streets
And covers us with leaves, the weatherman will tell us.

Untitled, Helen Pashgian, epoxy on canvas, 60″ × 90″. Collection of the Security Pacific Corporation, Los Angeles, California.

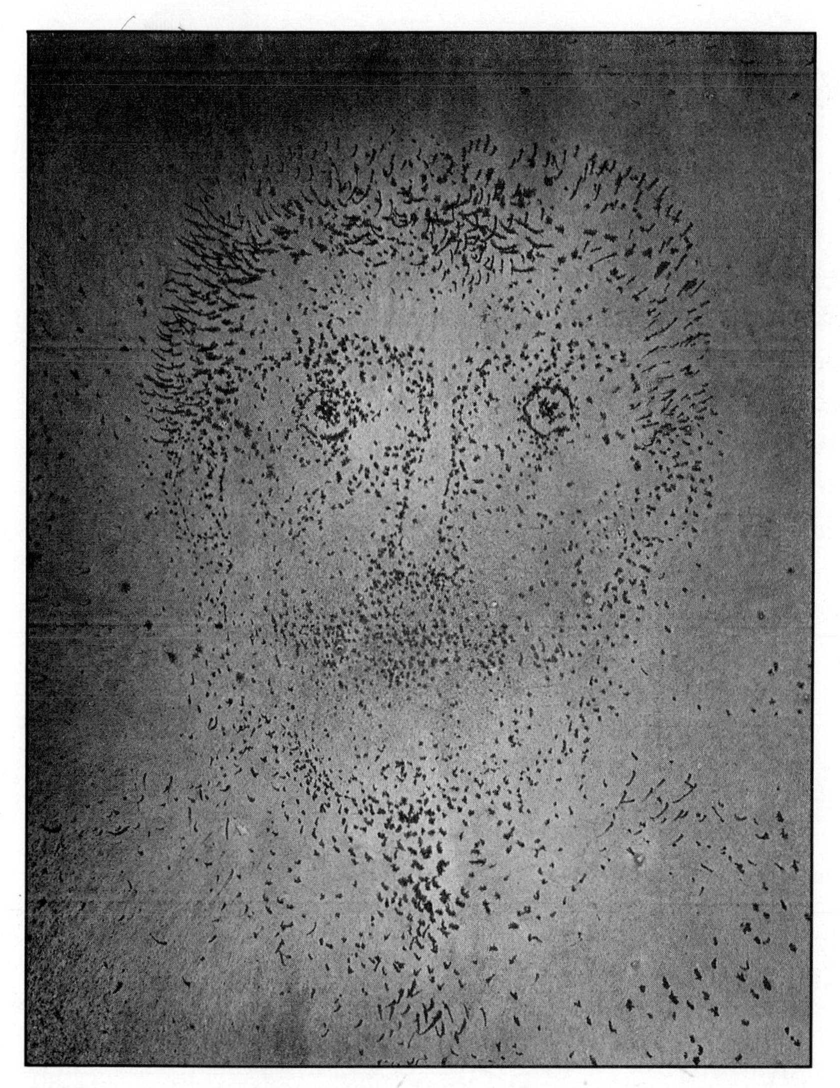

Portrait of Mr. A.L.,
Paul Klee, 1924,
Zurich, Germany

I'm Nobody!

by Emily Dickinson

I'm nobody! Who are you?
Are you nobody, too?
Then there's a pair of us—don't tell!
They'd banish us, you know.

How dreary—to be—somebody!
How public, like a frog
To tell your name the livelong day
To an admiring bog!

Faraway, 1952, Andrew Wyeth, drybrush watercolor on paper, 13 3/4″ X 21 1/2″. Collection of Jamie Wyeth, Brandywine River Museum

To Make a Prairie

by Emily Dickinson

To make a prairie it takes a clover and one bee,
One clover, and a bee,
And revery.
The revery alone will do,
If bees are few.

Searching

Which of the poems do you think Alex Haley would have liked the best as he searched for his family's roots?

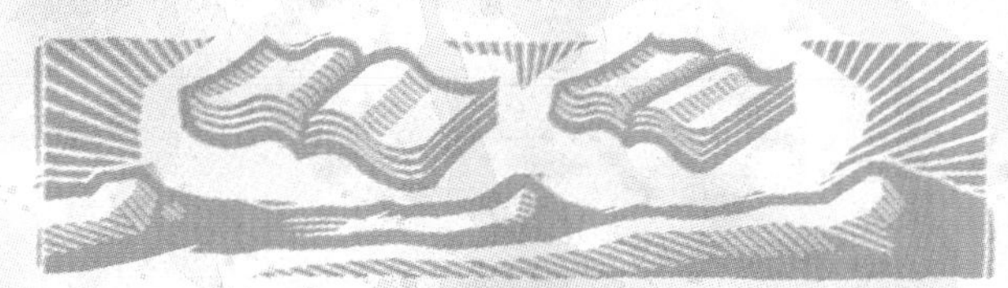

Writer's Workshop

Searching for your identity can take you backward or forward in time. The past can hold a rich family heritage; the future is a puzzle and a mystery. How do you search for your identity? Write a poem about your own search—either for your roots or for your future.

Writer's Choice You have read about the searches of many writers. Does every search need to have a goal? What makes a search worthwhile? Think of your own questions. Then plan a writing project that responds to what interests you the most about searching. Think of a way to share your writing with a friend.

THEME

Coming of Age

Growing up is a challenging experience. As the characters in these selections face new problems and find solutions, think about how you meet your own new experiences.

CONTENTS

AWARD-WINNING AUTHOR

Sea Glass

BY LAURENCE YEP

Craig Chin, the narrator in Sea Glass, *has grown up in Chinatown in San Francisco. When his family moves to Concepcion, California, he finds it difficult to make "Westerner" friends. He continues to rebel against his father's wishes that he excel in sports. On Saturdays, Craig delivers groceries from his father's store. One of the customers, an elderly man known as Uncle Quail, lives "on a small cove about fifty feet across formed by cliffs and a headland." Craig tells about one Saturday when Uncle Quail invites him back to the cove to swim.*

illustrations by Leslie Wu
Chinese calligraphy by Muns Quan

That Saturday Uncle was already down at the beach. He looked thin and bony and sinewy as he sat with his jacket draped around his shoulders. I turned the wagon around and pushed it before me through the gate. Then I leaned back on my heels and gently lowered it down the path, trying not to look to my right where the edge of the path was. Uncle didn't look up even though the old wagon rattled noisily down the rocky path.

I lifted the carton of groceries out of the wagon onto the porch, sliding it over toward the door. Then I put the old carton with the garbage into the wagon and parked it against the porch so it wouldn't roll down. One lonely sea gull wheeled about, crying over the calm waters of the cove. "Afternoon," I called down to him. My voice echoed on the rocks but Uncle didn't turn around. He just waved his hand vaguely in the air.

I picked up my towel, which was rolled into a cylinder, and with that tucked under my arm I went down to the beach. The tide was really low today. The beach was a lot bigger and I could see a lot of the reef. At the foot of the path, I began to slog across the sand toward where Uncle sat. "I didn't squeeze the bread this time."

"I wait and see." Uncle had a small crowbar in his hand. It was tied to his wrist by a thong. I watched as Uncle slipped the end of the crowbar between the shell and the tan flesh of an abalone.

"You went diving for abalone without me." I stared at him accusingly.

When Uncle had the crowbar positioned just the way he wanted, he shoved it in hard. I suppose he must have broken the abalone's hold on its shell, because he pried it out easily, dropping it into a basket. "I walk through my gardens and I find this one."

I looked around the cove, but it looked especially empty and lifeless now. Even the gull was off to some other place. There were barnacles on the cliffsides, but they were above the water so they were shut up tight and I didn't think they counted. To me, anyway, it looked like the only living things there were me and Uncle.

"What gardens?" I asked skeptically.

Uncle smiled as if it were his secret. "I thought you were one smart boy. Can't you see them?" He slipped the thong of the crowbar from his wrist and dropped it into the basket.

"No, I can't." Sullenly I folded my arms across my chest.

"You think maybe you see, but you don't. Not really." He pointed at my eyes. "Your eyes, they tell your mind a lot of stuff. But your mind, he's one busy fellow. He say, 'I don't have time to listen. Fill out these forms.' So the eyes, they fill out the forms, but there's no place on the forms for everything they see. Just a lot of boxes they are supposed to mark or not. So your mind, he misses a lot." Uncle

nodded his head firmly. "You gotta look at the world. Really look."

"Like you?" I was beginning to feel impatient with Uncle.

"No. I only do it in a small, small way. But if you can make your mind listen to your eyes, really listen, what wonders you see." Uncle looked out at his cove wistfully. "You know *the Dragon Mother*?"

"No," I said reluctantly.

"Now there was some person who saw the world. *The Dragon Mother* was a human once, but her mind listen to her eyes. She go for a walk, like you and me, we do sometimes. But this woman, she see a dragon's egg." Uncle pretended to look down sharply at the wet sand and hunch his shoulders and hold out his hands from his sides as if he had just seen something.

I looked at the same spot on the beach. "Dragon's egg?"

"You know that the dragons are kings of the sea." Uncle tapped my arm with the back of his hand.

I drew away slightly. "Sure, I know something about that stuff. They live in the sea and in the rivers and they bring rain."

Uncle motioned to the spot on the beach where he had pretended to find the object. "Well, this woman, she find this rock." Uncle pantomimed picking something up from the sand. "She go home and show it to her friends. Everyone tell her, 'You're stupid. This is only a rock.' But she say, 'Mind your own business. This is one special thing.' So she dig a little pool by her home." Uncle scooped some sand from the beach with his hand and set down the imaginary object in his hand. "And she put in seawater over the thing. And she change the water every day for a year. And everyone laugh at her. But she keep doing it because she knows it's special even if they don't. And then, one day, one day . . . the thing hatches." Uncle stretched his fingers wide above the hole he had just dug. "But the baby, it's no sea turtle, no other animal. It's a dragon." Slowly Uncle lifted his arms and spread them as if the dragon were growing in front of us. "She raise this little dragon like it maybe her own son. And this dragon, he turn out to be a very important dragon and so humans and dragons, they name her *the Dragon Mother.* She became one important person. And only because this woman, she can see." Uncle dropped his hands back down over his knees with loud slapping noises.

"Oh," I said.

"This is one special place here. This is the edge of the world. This is where the magic can happen too." Uncle searched my face, looking for some sign of comprehension, but I could only look at him in confusion. Uncle smiled to himself sadly. He pretended to become stern. "Well, you want to swim, or talk, boy?"

"Let's swim." I started to undress self-consciously on the beach. I was already wearing my swimming trunks underneath my pants, so it didn't take me long. In the meantime, Uncle had shrugged off his jacket and waded into the water to begin swimming. I stared at him in surprise.

He moved almost as quickly and easily through the water as the otter we had seen. There was nothing wasted about his motions when he swam. It was pure, simple, graceful.

"Come on." Uncle turned to me from the water. "You just remember one thing. The currents in my cove, they aren't very strong, but even so, don't fight them."

I adjusted the waistband of my trunks over my stomach, knowing that the waistband would slide back under my belly before long.

Uncle hadn't shivered or said anything when he walked into the water. You'd have thought it was warm bathwater to him. But I gave a yelp the moment I waded into the water. The water felt so cold that it felt like someone had been chilling it in the refrigerator. I could feel the goose bumps popping out all over my skin, and I began to shake and to huddle up and hold myself.

Uncle waved one hand from where he was floating. "Come on. You get used to it."

I nodded nervously and kept on walking. I felt the beach slope downward sharply, and I immediately found myself in the water up to my chest. The sea wasn't very pleasant to move around in, but it was better than that first moment of shock. Then a wave broke against the reef and spray went flying and the sea surged through the narrow opening. The pull of the sudden current wasn't all that strong, but it caught me by surprise so I got knocked off my feet.

I couldn't see. There was only the clouded, stinging salt water all around me. I flailed with my arms, trying to get my feet on something solid, but I couldn't find anything. And then I felt the current begin to draw me away from the beach as it began to flow out toward the sea. I really panicked then, forgetting everything I'd ever been taught. I wanted air. My lungs tried to drag it in, but all they got was salt water. I began to choke.

Then strong hands appeared magically, gripping me on either side. I tried to grab hold of Uncle. Something. Anything, as long as I could hold on to it. Somehow, though, Uncle managed to avoid me. My head broke above the surface. I could see the light for a moment before the salt water, running down my face, made my eyes close. I gasped, coughed, and gasped again, trying to get the film of seawater out of my lungs.

Uncle's strong hands pulled steadily in toward the beach. Then I could feel firm sand under me. I stumbled. Uncle's hands held me until I got my balance. I started to stagger toward the beach with Uncle supporting me. Gratefully I felt the air around my shoulders and then my chest and then my stomach. I stretched my arms out like a blind man and stumbled out of the surf to fall onto the beach. I lay on my stomach for a moment, coughing and spitting. I could still feel the sea pulling at my ankles, so I crawled another yard farther up the beach. The sea swept higher. I could feel it tugging at my ankles again, as if it were alive and trying to drag me back in.

Then I felt Uncle's shadow as he sat down heavily beside me. "You sure you can swim, boy?"

I sat up, beginning to shiver. Uncle covered my shoulders with my towel. With one corner of the towel I wiped at my face. "I could have told you. I'm just too fat and clumsy. Sorry."

Uncle put on his ragged jacket and sat down. "You feel too sorry for yourself. And that's not good."

"Are you crazy?" I started to shiver, so I pulled the towel tighter around my neck.

"You're the crazy one." Uncle flung sand over his legs. "You want to stay on the beach when you can be out in the water."

"Drowning isn't my idea of fun." I wiped some of the water from my face.

Uncle put his hands behind him and leaned back. "Well, maybe if you're scared . . . "

With a corner of my towel I finished drying my face. "Who said I was scared?"

"Me," Uncle said. "I say you're scared."

"Nothing scares me," I insisted.

Tunelessly Uncle hummed to himself and tapped his fingers against the sand.

"Well, even if I am," I mumbled, "it's stupid to do something just to prove I'm not scared."

"Yes, no, maybe so. Something good shouldn't scare you." Uncle began to rub his palms together so that the sand sprinkled down. "Maybe I ask you to put your head on a railroad track, and you say no, well, that's different."

"I'm still not going in." I shook my head for emphasis.

Uncle worried at the nail of one finger. Some sand got on his lips. "You can walk on the water then?" Uncle smiled, amused.

I liked Uncle when he said that. I mean, Dad would have gone on shouting or wheedling or both, but instead Uncle turned the whole thing into a joke. He seemed to relax then. "You want to go for a walk instead?" He nodded at the beach. "I mean on solid ground?"

家庭
Family

"Sure," I said, even though the cove wasn't more than twenty yards wide at any point.

Uncle rose and started across the wet sand toward the cliffs on one side of the cove, and I followed him. When he was by the cliffs, Uncle pointed to the walls above the water at the foot-wide bands of chalky little white bumps. "These are mussels, and those"—he gestured at a blackish band about a foot wide below them—"are barnacles." The bands looked like they were painted on both sides of the cove where the tide would reach it about a yard above its present level. "The water's out or they'd all be open to eat the little things in the water.

"And you see the starfish?" Uncle pointed at the water where there was a bright orange spot just below the surface. "He's waiting now. When the water get higher, he climb back up to the barnacles and mussels." We waded cautiously into the surf; and, as the water sucked at my ankles, he took my wrist and guided it under the water. I felt the rough surface of the starfish. Uncle let go of my wrist and I traced the shape of the starfish and felt the five legs, one of them curled up slightly. My fingers closed round the body of the starfish and I gave a tug; but it felt as if it were part of the cliff wall.

Uncle laughed in delight, like a kid sharing a new toy with someone else. "You want a starfish, you need a crowbar. Once a starfish sits, nobody can pull it up."

I let go of the starfish. "Is this your garden then?" I looked around the cove, feeling disappointed. The bands of mussels and barnacles and the starfish didn't make up a sea garden in my mind.

"I bet you think this is one real crazy old man, right?" Uncle asked. He bent over so that his hands were near the waterline and ran his hands lightly over the face of the barnacles that were clustered so tightly together. He did it lightly, or the rough faces of the barnacles might have cut up his hands. Suddenly he gave a yelp. He lifted out his hand, and I saw clinging to it a long, greenish-brown worm with lots of legs. And then it let go and dropped with a plunk back into the sea.

"Did it hurt?" I asked.

"No, see, not even the skin's broken." He showed me the finger. "That's the hunter that stalks and kills, and this whole place is his jungle." He indicated the bands of mussels and barnacles. "And this is just the start of my garden." Uncle smiled, both proud and pleased—like someone who knows a secret that you do not. "Too bad you don't want to see more of it."

I looked uncertainly at the cove. "You mean I have to swim?"

"Out there." He pointed to the reef that was exposed at low tide.

He was one shameless old man to tempt me that way and he knew it. I almost refused again, but I have to admit I was curious about that garden of his.

"Okay. I'll try just once more," I grumbled.

"We'll stay in the shallow end. Then, if you feel good, we can go out." Uncle walked farther into the water and half turned around as he took off his jacket. I whipped the towel off my shoulders and threw it high up on the beach. Uncle threw his jacket beside it. I waded into the sea until I was waist deep. I kept waiting for Uncle to shout instructions at me the way Dad would have, but he didn't.

I took a deep breath. Then another good one. Holding my arms ahead of me, I bent forward and kicked off from the sand. There was that shock for a moment of letting go of the land, and then I was floating. The cold water didn't feel so bad this time. I twisted my head to the side and breathed in the air and then slid over, floating on my back, letting the sun warm my face and skin.

Uncle began swimming in the water toward me. The spray from his splashing sent a drizzle over me, and then his body was floating alongside of me. He didn't shout anything at me or tell me how to do things better; he just warned me, "Careful. Don't go out too far."

So we stayed floating on our backs for a few minutes.

"Do you want to swim out to the reef?" I asked Uncle finally.

"Oh-kay." Uncle grinned. He started to move his arms, raising a glittering shower

I LOOKED UNCERTAINLY AT THE COVE. "YOU MEAN I HAVE TO SWIM?" "OUT THERE." HE POINTED TO THE REEF THAT WAS EXPOSED AT LOW TIDE.

around his head as he swam out toward the rock reef. I followed him much more slowly and clumsily. Once Uncle was at the reef, he stretched out his arms and clung to a large boulder, hoisting himself up. He perched on the boulder with all the ease of a sea gull, as if he had done this thousands of times. I suppose he had if you thought about all the years he had spent in the cove.

Aware of Uncle watching me, I kept on churning toward the reef. I thought he might have some instructions for improvement by now, but still he didn't say anything.

Instead, he only reached out one hand. I clasped it and Uncle almost pulled me up out of the water to sit beside him—I mean, as if he were as rooted as a starfish to that boulder.

"What—?" I began.

"Shhh. Listen." Uncle swept his hand along, palm downward and parallel to the sea, in a short, sharp gesture for quiet.

At first, though, my main concern was getting a better grip on that big rock, but then as I sat there, I could feel the rhythm of the sea surging against the rocky reef that protected the cove, trying to make the opening in the reef bigger. The sea wasn't pounding so much as steadily pushing, as if it knew it had all the time in the world and could be patient. But after sitting there for a while, I almost felt like the reef was living and I could feel its heart beating.

Even now at low tide, I could feel the fine mist in the air—I suppose it was spray from the waves moving against the reef. But it felt almost like the breath of the rocks around me, breathing slowly and quietly along with the beating of the reef's heart.

"We'll start up there, boy." Uncle pointed toward the top of the reef.

"What about the big waves?" I was too interested to pay attention to the cold air.

Uncle shook his head. "I don't think there will be any more. And if there are, the reef will protect us." He patted a rock affectionately. Then he turned and began climbing. I followed him more cautiously the three feet or so to the top of the reef. I took one look at that big empty sea beyond the reef, and then I turned my head back in toward the cove.

Uncle waved his hand to indicate both sides of the reef. "When the sea goes out, all around here—maybe in little cracks, maybe on ledges—there are pools left. And the rocks, maybe they protect the pools so the big strong waves"—Uncle pantomimed a crashing wave stopped short—"the waves can't reach the pools. Then all kinds of things can grow." He spoke slowly and proudly, as if he were just about to pry up the lid to a treasure chest.

At that moment to my right—from a crevice I thought would be too small for anything to live in—a bright blue-and-purple crab scuttled out. It was only a few inches across. It paused when it saw us, and lifted its claws, ready to defend itself. Tiny bubbles frothed at its mouth.

Uncle reached across my lap to wiggle a finger above its head just out of the reach of its claws. The crab scuttled back into its crevice. "The brave, bold hero," Uncle said with a laugh. "Maybe when he goes home, he tells a lot of tales about fighting us." Carefully Uncle stood up then. He held out his hand, and I took it for support as I got slowly to my feet.

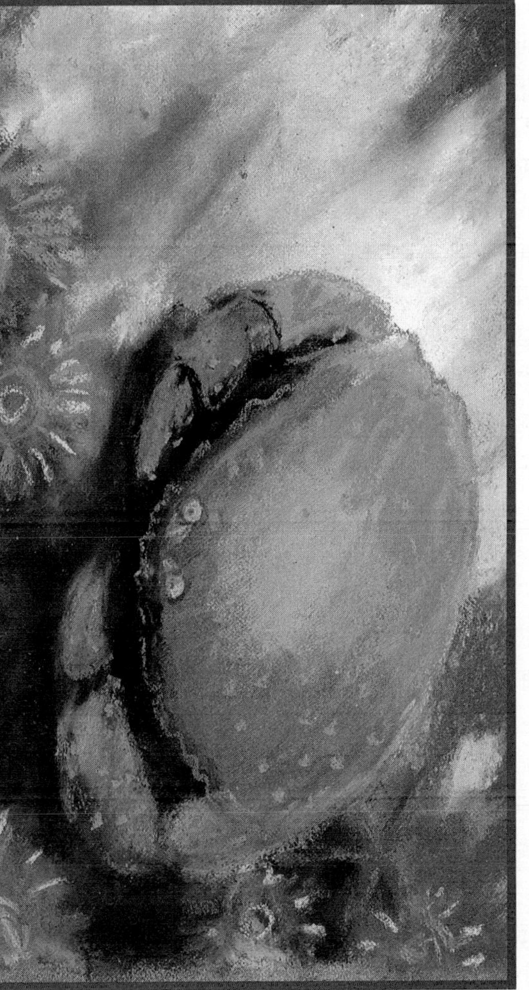

"Now do what I do." Confidently, Uncle turned his back to the sea and began to edge side-ways along the top of the reef.

Uncle made it look real easy, but I found myself spreading my arms for better balance and I began to wish the rocks wouldn't vibrate. It was like walking on the back of some sleeping snake that might wake up and shake me off at any moment.

Uncle stopped where two rectangular slabs of rock leaned their tips against one another. One rock faced toward the sea, the other faced toward the cove. He waited shyly for me. I looked down between the rocks. There was a shallow depression on the giant boulder on which the two slabs rested. I caught my breath. The stone looked gray-black when it was wet, and the seawater was almost clear here; and in the daylight, the colors seemed even brighter. There were anemones of all colors—animals shaped like flowers, whose thin petals moved with a life of their own in the still water. Uncle leaned forward, supporting himself against the slabs. His hand barely stirred the surface of the pool as his finger brushed the petals of a red anemone. In the wink of an eye, the anem-one had closed up, looking like a fat, bumpy doughnut. The other anemones closed up too. Uncle remov-ed his hand from the pool. We waited for a little while until one by one they opened once again. They were all kinds of bright colors—orange, red, yellow, solid colors that would make any artist ache inside to be able to use.

Uncle paused where a flat slab of rock leaned against the top of the reef. He pointed inside. "Can you see it?"

I looked in at the shadows. It looked like a big ball of spines within the water under the slab. "What is it?"

"A sea urchin," Uncle explained. "It

come up into the high tide pools."

Even as we watched, the sea urchin retreated farther into the shadows by moving its needlelike spines.

From there we climbed lower on the reef to the top of a small boulder which had crumbled. Uncle squatted down. I did the same.

Uncle waited, hands clasped, arms resting on top of his thighs. He looked like he could stay in that position forever. "There." Uncle pointed carefully to the shadow of a rock, at a sluglike thing with little stubby tubes at one end and the rest of its back covered with bright orange-red spots. It crept upside down across the pool as if the surface was a floor to it. Behind it, it left a little silver thread.

"He leaves a trail behind him. You know, like a land slug, that's his cousin. See that silver line? That's it. Watch what happens when I break it." Uncle reached down and touched the silvery thread behind the slug. The slug fell slowly through the water as if whatever invisible wires held it up had suddenly broken. When it landed gently on its back on the bottom of the pool, it slowly twisted about in the water, righting itself, and began crawling up the side again. "He keeps on trying, so I know he's gonna get cross."

Uncle stood up, wiping his hands on the side of his swimming trunks. "You know all the pools around here. Well, some of them are big. Some of them are small. And every pool is cut off from the other. Maybe the pools are this far apart." Uncle held his hands an inch from each other. "But the pools, they might as well be miles and miles apart because the animal in one pool won't know about an animal in another pool. You take any animal around here and it would probably think its own pool is the whole world, and it doesn't know there are pools and pools all around it." Uncle sounded awed by the magic and vastness of what he owned.

The sea must have been rising higher because the waves were beginning to splash over the top of the reef. I hadn't noticed the narrow little channel before—it was really more like a scratch along the surface of the rocks. But the anemones' pool at the top of the reef must have begun to fill up, because a little trickle of water began to snake its way down into the pool of the sea urchin and then slipped down the channel again, rounded a corner, and slid in a curve down the surface of a rock, into the pool of the slug and on. So Uncle wasn't exactly right. There was a little thread of water connecting the tide pools sometimes before the sea did come in.

"I never dreamed there was so much to see," I said.

Uncle leaned forward and pretended to peer at something for emphasis. "You have to learn how to pay attention to things." He added, "But first you have to

like yourself." He gave a tug to his trunks and sat down. "People who don't like themselves, they spend all their time looking at their faults. They don't have time to look at the world."

"What's there to like about myself?" I sat down and bent my knees so I could wrap my arms around my legs and lean my chest against my thighs. "I'm lousy at swimming. I'm lousy at all the *Westerners'* games. I'm lousy at making friends. I'm even lousy at being Chinese. I'm not like anything Dad wants."

Uncle raised one eyebrow. "Is that all you think your father wants? Play games all the time?"

I hugged my legs tighter against my chest. "That's all we ever do."

"Your father, he want other things too." Uncle ran a finger lightly over a scab on his thumb. "At least he used to. I remember when he was a small boy —smaller than you, maybe only ten or eleven. It was only talk from a small boy, but it was GOOD talk. He tell me, 'Uncle, I'm going to know everything about plants. You want to know something about them, you come to me.'" Uncle cocked his head to one side. "Your father always have some book about plants. Always so he can read from it when he have nothing else to do."

It was funny hearing about Dad when he was a small boy; but what Uncle told me helped explain why Dad had been so hot to start a garden on our very first day here. "I guess he still likes plants," I said.

Uncle, though, was too busy reminiscing to hear me. "And your father, when he wasn't reading or talking about plants, he was drawing them."

"That's a little hard to swallow," I said. I couldn't associate anything artistic with my dad—not even something like drawing wavy lines on a notepad while he was talking on the phone.

Uncle stiffened and he thrust out his chin. "I'm no liar. I got eyes. I saw them. Maybe the pictures aren't so good, but he say drawing the pictures teach him more than just reading about the plants."

"It's just that I never heard Dad say anything about drawing." I set my chin on top of my knees.

"Your father, he want to grow all kinds of plants and flowers." Uncle pounded his fist against the rock he was sitting on. His fist made a flat, slapping sound. "But your grandfather, he say no. He say it's a waste of money to buy flower seeds. Waste of time to grow them. Your grandfather only let your father grow some vegetables. And your grandfather, he get mad when he find all the drawings. Your grandfather say not to waste good paper that cost so much."

Uncle put his hands down on either side of him and leaned back. "And I watch what happen. Your father was a good boy. It was just like he close a door inside himself. No more books about plants. No more drawing. And," Uncle added sadly, "no more talk about knowing everything about plants. He even tell me he not care about that stuff. But I got eyes. I saw."

美麗
Beauty

I bit my lip for a moment and stared at the sea. It was a sad-enough sounding story—whether it was true or not. I guess I could believe some of what Uncle had said—at least the part about Dad's once wanting to grow some flowers, because it would help explain why he had already been planning a garden on our very first day at the store.

It also helped explain his determination to try after the cats had ruined his first plantings. He said he was going to show those cats just who actually ran that backyard. As soon as we could qualify, Dad had taken me to the library to get a card—or so he said—but he'd gotten a card for himself as well. The cards were only temporary cards at first, so we could take out only two books each. Even so, Dad had headed straight for the gardening books like he had memorized their location, and he had taken out two gardening books and talked me into taking out two more. And when we had finally gotten our real cards and could take out six books on each card, Dad had taken out more gardening books.

Finally last month, in March, when Dad had devoured all the gardening books on the library shelves, he had gone to the gardening store and come back with little boxes of flowers to be transplanted. The flowers, Dad informed us, were already large enough to survive the cats and hardy enough to like shady places the best.

Dad had felt so triumphant when he could show us the first flower bud. It was no bigger than my fingernail, and colored lavender. Mom was pleased because Dad was happy, and I said something about how pretty it looked, but in that gray, gloomy backyard the flower bud—I forget the name of the flower—seemed small and insignificant, and even the color didn't seem very bright.

But that didn't seem to stop Dad's enthusiasm as each new bud appeared until there were a lot of them; and that was nothing compared to the time when the first bud began to flower. It was really only half open, with the petals still partly upright, but Dad had pantomimed the opening of the flower with his fingers like he could already see it. I thought Dad had been so happy because he had managed to beat the cats at their own game. Now I could see that the flowers meant more to him.

I looked at Uncle. "Why was Grandfather so mean?"

"All the money have to go home to China. To the wife and the rest of the family there." Uncle shrugged like it was an old story.

"Not even a little something for Dad?" I wondered. There was a little part inside me that began to feel sorry for Dad.

"The family," Uncle explained simply, "always comes first." He said it as if that should be explanation enough—as if I should already have known that. But Uncle might as well have been talking about the families of people on Jupiter, because it sounded so strange to me.

"That's when your father find other things." Uncle leaned over toward me. "He get real good then at *demon*[1] games. See, not all the old-timers think *demon* games are waste of time. Some of the clubs in different Chinatowns, they have teams. Your grandfather, he grumble a little, but he like the respect he get because of your father." Uncle slapped my leg with the back of his hand. "The other Chinese tell your grandfather he must be one strong, quick man if he have a son that strong and that quick. So as long as your father get good grades in school and work hard in the store, he can play the different games. But you

[1]*demon*: Chinese term used for a Westerner

remember that the *demon* games"—Uncle tilted his head up—"they were always your father's second choice."

"I still wish," I said, "that I could be as good as my dad."

Uncle sighed and shook his head. "You try too hard to be Calvin's son." He seemed dissatisfied with what he had said—as if he didn't have enough English to explain all his thoughts to me and he knew I didn't know enough Chinese if we used that language. Uncle folded his legs into a lotus position as if he wanted to become more comfortable before he stretched his arm out toward me. "It's not good if you do everything just like your father. Everyone is different. That's what makes them special." Uncle waved his hand grandly to include the entire reef. "You think it good if all the animals look the same, hah?"

"I have to keep on trying." I shrugged my shoulders, annoyed with Uncle for being so insistent.

There was a long silence while we both listened to the ocean beating against his reef. Finally, I said, "Dad has flower boxes." I thought Uncle might like to know. "He works there every day."

Uncle smiled slowly and nodded his head in approval. "Good. I'm glad Calvin finally got his flowers."

He glanced up at the top of the reef. We could see the spray rising in the air. The drizzle in the air was changing to more like a shower. "Maybe we should go back now," Uncle said. "This reef's not a good place when the tide rises."

"Can't we stay a little while longer?"

"Oh-kay. Oh-kay. A little while then," Uncle said indulgently. I leaned back to look up at the broad sweep of sky overhead. Somehow, sitting on the reef, I felt like the world was a much bigger place than it seemed when I was standing on solid ground. And so much of what I knew when I was on the land didn't seem as certain anymore. I couldn't help hunching my shoulders a little.

Uncle must have been observing me. "Back to the beach, boy. Look at you. You're shivering."

"Not at the cold. It's—"

"No arguments. Come on." Uncle slipped off the rocks into the water.

When we were back on the beach again, I began to shiver for real. A strong wind had begun to sweep in from the sea, so that it was a lot colder than when we had first swum out to the reef. I got my towel from where I had thrown it on the beach and came back toward Uncle, rubbing at my arms and back vigorously.

Uncle did not bother to towel himself. He had rolled around in the sand until he had a thin film covering him. Then he had put on his jacket and sprawled out on the beach to soak up what sun there was.

"Where did you learn how to swim so good?" I sat down beside him.

Uncle turned his head to look at me. "Don't you think we got water in China?"

"You know what I mean." I shrugged my arms through the sleeves of my shirt.

Uncle smiled. "I come from China when I was small. Very small. And I was raised here. Over in the China Camp near Monterey. There used to be a whole bunch of us catching fish there. My father, he was smart. So the others had him speak to *the white demons.* He learned their language pretty good and he taught me. That's how come I speak American so good." Uncle swept his arms out from his sides and then back down, so that he began to dig shallow depressions in the sand that looked like wings. "You know, a long, long time ago, *the T'ang people,* they call San Francisco the Big City. Sacramento is the Little City. And you know all the tide pools on the reef? Well, I bet there were just as many Chinatowns in this state."

"What happened to them all?" I began to towel off my legs.

Uncle lifted his head and cleared his throat. "One day the sea go out and it never come back, and the pools, they all dry up. And my father and me and some others, we come here."

I spread my towel over my legs like a blanket. "What do you mean?"

"Never mind, boy." He laid his head back down on the sand and stared up at the sky. "Young people, what do they care what happened a long time ago?"

I looked at Uncle. He'd set his jaw firmly like there wasn't any room for argument. "Does anyone visit you?"

"Oh, the older ones in my family, they used to visit." Uncle grasped a handful of sand. "But maybe they're too old now. Maybe they don't like to drive the long way from the City. And the younger ones, they don't remember. They forget about the fun they have swimming here. Even some I teach how to swim." He flung the sand into the air and watched the wind scatter it along the beach. He said as if it were the deadliest insult, "They prefer the tame water in those concrete ponds in their own backyards. They turn their faces from the sea and the things I show them." He added, "Even your father."

I tucked the towel around my legs. "Did you take my father diving for abalone as well?"

"Sure," Uncle said.

"When can I go?" I asked him.

Uncle scratched his cheek for a moment as if he were feeling uncomfortable. "I got to give you real special training to go diving. Not everyone can dive."

"Then when can we start?" I asked impatiently.

"You don't even swim so good. You swim better. Then we can begin your training." Uncle slapped his hands at an imaginary surface. "You still fight the water too much. You must use the sea and you must let it use you."

"But how can I learn to swim better so I can be trained?" I rubbed the back of my neck in annoyance. "You never tell me what to do."

Uncle blinked his eyes, puzzled. "You learn from inside you." He tapped at his heart. "Not from outside. And not from some old man's big mouth."

I'd take Uncle's method of teaching me any day over Dad's way. "So when do you think I'll be ready?"

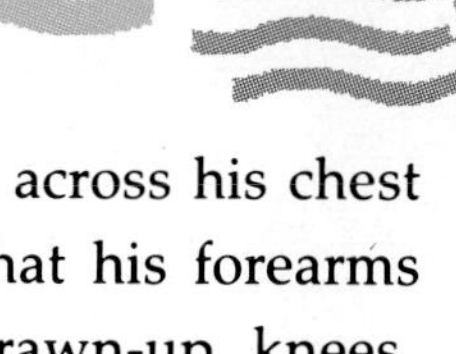

Uncle folded his arms across his chest and leaned forward so that his forearms rested on top of his drawn-up knees. "You gotta be comfortable in the water. I can't say."

So maybe his cove wasn't a perfect place. It was still special. For all of his quirks, Uncle still managed to make me feel like a real person.

Craig learns from Uncle to see his father in a different light. Have you ever learned something about someone that made you see that person differently from the way you had before? Tell about the experience.

Explain what Uncle means when he tells Craig, "People who don't like themselves, they spend all their time looking at their faults. They don't have time to look at the world."

Craig feels he can never live up to what his father wants him to be. How do you think Laurence Yep feels about trying to fulfill the expectations of others? Give examples from "Sea Glass" to support your conclusions.

WRITE Craig and Uncle have a special relationship. Write a short description of an adult relative or friend you feel especially close to. Compare your experiences with that person to Craig's experiences with Uncle.

Laurence YEP

Words from the Author:

The character in *Sea Glass*, Craig, is very much like me. I came from a family in which I was the only nonathlete in the bunch. There's a scene in the book in which the father is trying to teach basketball to a hopeless Craig—that was my life during most of the fall and spring. I was inept. I would drop any ball that was thrown to me, and for most of my teenage years, I didn't feel that I fit into my family at all.

I went to a high school that had some wonderful teachers; I had a chemistry teacher who taught us things we wanted to know. I also had an English teacher who said if we wanted to get an A, we had to have a piece accepted by a national publication. Even after he retracted that requirement, I kept sending in things to magazines. I sold my first story when I was eighteen.

I definitely write for the outsider, but there's an age around junior high when almost everyone feels like an outsider and becomes acutely aware of any differences

談話

between themselves and their peers. I felt this especially because I grew up in a black neighborhood. I went to a school in Chinatown, and I was an outsider there, too, because neither I nor my parents spoke Chinese. When I went to the library and librarians tried to get me interested in books like *Homer Price and His Donut Machine*, I couldn't get past the first chapter. Homer had a bicycle, but no one I knew owned one. What I read was science fiction and fantasy in which kids are taken from our everyday world to some other place where they have to learn new languages and customs. Science fiction and fantasy talked about adjusting, which was something I did every time I got on and off the bus.

There was no place I really felt at home, and while I was teaching creative writing at Berkeley, I saw the same thing in the Asian American students there. One has to turn that borderland existence into a source of strength. Because you don't belong to the majority culture, you have a certain flexibility and tolerance others may not have. You become a good listener because you listen to many sides.

When I hear from readers about *Sea Glass*, it's usually because they identify with Craig. There is a lot of pressure at that age to be good at sports. The story shows you that people grow at their own pace, in their own season. I wasn't good at sports, but I was good at writing. There are all sorts of drummers to follow, all sorts of dreams.

THE SECOND HIGHEST POINT

by Ouida Sebestyen
illustrations by Edson Campos

He was almost to the river, walking fast, when he saw Laurel on her bicycle, racing to catch him. In a space between the gusts of raw March wind she yelled, "Josh, wait up, or I'll break your legs."

So he wasn't going to get away without saying good-bye after all.

Laurel came puffing up, fierce and wind-whipped. He braced himself as she stared at the duffel bag he'd taken from his folks' closet and stuffed with all the clothes and things he thought he'd need.

"You're doing it," she said. The pain that came into her eyes hurt him, too. "Why? Without telling me? I thought we were friends! If I hadn't seen you sneaking through the alley—"

We *are* friends, he wanted to assure her. Best friends. The best. But he said, walking on, "So? One more thing I didn't do right today." Suddenly it came pouring out. "At breakfast they jumped down my throat about my grades. Then they got started on why can't I grow up and shape up and do my part now with him out of work. Boy. I didn't get him laid off."

"But it's a hard time for them, Josh."

"Not for her. She's tickled pink. All this schooling's going to get her back into that *career* she gave up when I came along." It seemed vital to stay cold and angry. Even with Laurel. Especially with Laurel, because she knew what he really was. "So I figured I've been enough trouble—I might as well get on out there and do something with my life." He stared at the distant river waiting to be crossed.

"It's dumb," Laurel said, with the directness they had never been afraid to use with each other. "They'll just haul you back. Parents aren't perfect. You're feeling sorry for yourself." She stopped in the road, trying to make him turn around, rethink. But he kept walking. "Please, Josh," she said behind him. "Don't do it."

"*You're* leaving," he said.

"But not until school's out. And I wouldn't be, if we didn't have to move out to the Coast."

"But you are," he said. It wasn't her fault, he knew. She couldn't make her own choices. But he could. "Maybe I'll see you in sunny Cal."

"How'll you live, without money?" she asked into the wind. "Josh? How'll you eat? It scares me."

He turned around. She was outlined against the far-off knob of land called Throne of Kings, where they had sat one day in dusty autumn grass, growing quieter and quieter until their faces turned and their mouths touched in a kiss as intent and sunstruck as the silent hawks gliding over them.

His feet kept moving him backward. "Hey, just don't worry about me," he called. "Nobody else does. Okay?" She didn't answer, but her eyelids blinked fast. He relented. "Would you come as far as the bridge with me?"

She shook her head. "I have to get back to the library. I'm supposed to be helping with the party right now."

Hearing her say she should be getting punch and cookies ready for some stumpy old lady who wrote bad poetry, at the moment he was running away, gave him the new rush of anger he needed to turn around and march out of her life.

The river sprawled ahead of him, more sand than water. There was an eeriness in what he was doing: leaving someone he cared so much about without ending it right. He wished she'd run after him. But what could she say?

When he got to the bridge he looked back, expecting to see her pedaling away, but she stood in the road, her hair blowing across her funny freckled face.

The long bridge turned his footsteps hollow as he started across. He had planned to wait for the bus at the crossroad a mile or so farther on. Between wind gusts he found himself straining to hear the hum of traffic. But the only sound was closer, a small lonesome squeak like a bird he didn't recognize, or something grating under the bridge.

When would they notice he'd left home? he wondered. Maybe they wouldn't even miss him.

Near the end of the bridge the sound got louder. He scanned the sky and the flat brown horizon. Then he leaned over the bridge rail and looked down into a cardboard box on the sand at the water's edge. A jumble of yips and squeals came from something dark squirming inside it.

He felt his muscles clamp into knots. He had to catch a bus. He was this far. He had to straighten up and walk on past whatever was down there crying for help. But he couldn't.

He glanced at Laurel. She hadn't moved. He went to the far end of the bridge and climbed down through the weeds. The box twitched as he bent warily and looked in.

Puppies. Five of them, no bigger than fuzzy mittens, crawling in their prison.

Josh drew a weary sigh and squatted to touch them. They went silent, rooting hungrily against his hands. He lifted up a soft black puppy with eyes that melted a hole in his heart, and dropped it back into the pile. "No," he warned them. "I can't do anything, you guys. No."

Their little claws grated on the high sides of the box as they struggled to reach him. He saw Laurel hanging over the bridge rail. "What's down there, Josh?" she called.

"Five puppies," he called back.

She came scrambling down. Her eyes were blazing. "What kind of gutless wonder would throw them into the river! Oh, look at them." She gathered two against her cheeks.

"Maybe somebody couldn't take care of them," he said, trying to be fair. But it wasn't fair. He flicked his hands angrily, staying aloof. "Didn't want to be bothered. So, plop, off the bridge."

"But it's cruel," she said. "It's sad. Like back in early times, in the book Miss Rainey gave you, remember? When people left the defective babies on a mountain so if the gods wanted them saved they could do a miracle." Suddenly she handed him a puppy. "And guess what—along came good old Josh."

"No," he said. "Dang—I've got a bus to catch!" He dropped the puppy into the heap, as trapped as it was. "Why me? What'll I do with the dumb things?"

"You said you've always wanted a dog. You just got five of your wishes." She looked at his eyes and stopped trying to make him smile. "Take them back into town and find them homes. There'll be another bus. If you still . . ."

He followed her gaze down the road he should be striding along, and turned helplessly to the box. "Want a nice puppy?"

"Oh, I do. But my mom's deathly allergic. And when we move I couldn't take it—we'll be renting till we find a house." She nudged him up onto the bridge. "Stand in front of the supermarket, Josh. Won't you? Somebody'll take them. Look, I've got to get back, or I'll get canned."

She went to her bike, but her worried eyes kept studying him. He could feel the box pressing against the folded lump of bus-ticket money in his pocket. What did she want? Why should he be the one to care, when nobody else did?

"Do you think they'd fall out of my basket if I tried to carry them?" she asked.

"You just worry about getting on back," he said. Her face fell. It touched him to see how hard she was trying to keep this from being good-bye. He shrugged, defeated. "They're not all that heavy. But you could carry the duffel."

Most of the shoppers glanced into his box and went on past to buy their groceries. A few paused. The children stopped and stayed, cuddling puppies until they were dragged away by their parents.

He felt stupid. He resented what those helpless crawling blobs in the box had done to his plans, and was still angry at the person who had left them by the edge of the river. And at himself because he hadn't.

Several times, during the hour he stood in front of the store, he saw a shadowy movement at one of the high library windows down the block. Laurel. Checking to see what luck he was having. Or if he had left.

He felt exposed, there in full view of everyone on the street. He knew that his mother was thirty miles away, in one of those nifty workshops that was going to expand her options. But his dad might drive past any minute, checking out a job prospect, and see him and the duffel. He couldn't take a public quarrel, not after leaving that morning feeling so righteous and ready.

A little girl forced her mother to stop at the box.

"Could I have one?" she begged, entranced.

"They'd make great pets. Or watchdogs, or whatever," Josh said quickly, trying to cover every possibility.

The woman smiled. "How much?"

"Oh, free," Josh exclaimed. "Free. And they don't eat much at all."

The woman squeezed the little girl, almost laughing. "Which one do you like?"

The little girl picked up each puppy in turn, studying it nose to nose. The last one stretched to give her a lick. "This one," she breathed, dazzled. "He likes me already!" She turned suddenly to Josh. "We'll love it good."

"We will," the woman agreed. "Thank you."

GROCERY

He felt an unexpected emptiness as they walked away huddled over their treasure. He guessed it was for the puppy leaving the warmth of its brothers and sisters forever, with its little head jiggling trustfully. Or maybe it was because the woman hugged the little girl the way his father hugged him in his fantasies.

A man came out of the store. Proud of his change of luck, Josh had opened his mouth to say, "How about a beautiful puppy?" when he noticed that the tag on the man's jacket said MANAGER.

He gathered up his duffel and his dogs, and mushed.

As he passed the library, Laurel leaped out onto the top step and beckoned. "Josh! I saved some cookies for you."

He climbed up, weary. "A lady took a puppy."

Her glad smile faded. "You've only given away *one*?"

"Miss Rainey won't like me bringing them into the library, either," he said. "Have you started the party for old lady Snap Crackle Pop?"

Laurel nodded. "Grace Whipple Cox," she corrected him. "She's sitting there, waiting to autograph a stack of books taller than she is, that nobody wants to buy."

He went in, trying to be invisible behind Laurel. A tiny, round powder keg of a lady in a velvet hat sat talking to a few matronly types holding punch cups and paper napkins. He could see now why Laurel called her the Gnome de Plume, although at first she'd had to explain the pun to him. He was curious about anybody who could write poetry. He'd tried it himself. Nobody knew, except Laurel, unless Miss Rainey had guessed.

Laurel led him to a little room full of magazines and gave him four pink cookies. "What'll you do now?" she asked. "Oh, Josh, they're hungry. When they're this young they need food every few hours. Could I give them some coffee-creamer stuff, do you think?"

"I don't know. Maybe not." Yips began to come from the box. He put his jacket over it. "I've got to give them *away*. This is crazy."

"Let's try Miss Rainey," Laurel said. "I know she has cats, but maybe—" She winced as the yapping rose in a needle-sharp chorus.

He started through the door with his box and almost bulldozed Miss Rainey off her feet as she started in.

"What on earth!" She flipped through her memory card index for his name. "Josh. What have you got?" She looked in. Her face softened. "Well bless their little deafening hearts."

"Somebody left them under the bridge," Laurel said.

Miss Rainey breathed an angry sigh.

"I found a home for one already." Josh tilted the box so Miss Rainey would see yearning eyes and smell warm puppy. "Laurel thought maybe you'd like one."

"Oh, listen, Josh, they're already trying to zone my house as a zoo. I just couldn't. I'm gone all day. Cats and chameleons and macaws can manage. But a puppy—nope." She turned away. Then she gestured him close again, and muttered, "Try the literary ladies. It's a long shot, but try."

She was leading them out through rows of shelves, when she stopped abruptly. Every face they saw was staring at a long table of refreshments. Another of Miss Rainey's assistants, a little older than Laurel, sat at a punch bowl with her mouth ajar. Her startled eyes were riveted on a scruffy man with no socks who was helping himself to punch and cookies. His hand, the size of a baseball mitt, was already stacked with sand tarts and brownies and macaroons and six of those pink cartwheels Josh had wolfed down in the little room. The man drained his paper cup, smiled at the hypnotized girl, and refilled it. He studied his hand, and added another brownie.

Miss Rainey came alive. "Good lord—he's cleaning us out! Where did he come from?" She headed toward the man so vigorously that Josh thought she was going to grab his cookies. But she drew herself tall and said, "Sir, have you met our distinguished guest, or read her previous books of poetry?"

The scraggy man froze in his tracks. "I can't say I have," he admitted, still chewing. "But I did literally cut my teeth on poetry, ma'am. The complete unexpurgated works of Rudyard Kipling, if I remember rightly." He gave her a big shameless smile, then studied the puppies in Josh's box. "Part shepherd, wouldn't you say—the ears and head shape?"

He left Miss Rainey speechless and walked into the reference section to finish his meal in peace. The girl at the punch bowl exclaimed in a whisper, "I didn't know what to *do,* Miss Rainey! When he started loading up—"

Miss Rainey patted her shoulder mechanically. "It's all right." Her face had softened as it had when she saw the puppies. "He's hungry."

Laurel elbowed Josh toward the autographing table. A boy from high school was interviewing the Gnome de Plume, scribbling frantically at half the speed of her rushing words. Josh stopped at a distance, not wanting to interrupt but eager to get the women's attention when he could. Somebody had to take another puppy.

"Could you explain why you entitled your newest book *The Second Highest Point in Beymer County*?" the boy asked.

"To make a statement," the Gnome de Plume snapped, from behind the stack of unsold books. "Everybody knows that Crown Hill is the highest point—it's on the maps, it's written about. We act as if second-best is second-rate. I wanted to say that there can be only one topmost *anything*—all the rest of this glorious fascinating world is second. Or third, or tenth. Empty words. Hogwash. Everything has worth, for its own reasons." She knocked the mountain of books askew. "I'm not even a tenth-rate poet, although you don't have to quote me on that. I'm just a funny old lady. But why shouldn't I write a *ton* of poetry if I want to? God doesn't label blades of grass Grade A and Grade B. He creates. For the fun of it! Because He's a creator!"

The boy had lost her, back at Crown Hill. Josh watched him write down GRADE A and take a bite of his pencil.

Two of the literary ladies, equally startled, peeped into Josh's box. Miss Rainey said, "Listen, we need homes for these abandoned little things. Someone dropped them in the river without having the decency, or the heart, to finish the job."

The ladies shook their heads sadly. One said, "A ten-to-fifteen-year commitment is too much for me. Besides, they need children to play with. A farm or something." They turned away from the box, unobtrusively putting distance also between themselves and the old lady glaring around her mountain of books.

"What's the second highest point in Beymer County?" Josh whispered.

A pink flush crossed Laurel's face. "Throne of Kings," she whispered back.

He felt his own cheeks go warm. There would never be a spot on earth higher than the Throne of Kings on an autumn day, enchanted by hawks. *Why do you have to leave me?* he wanted to beg her through the ache in his throat.

But he was leaving first. You do it to them before they do it to you. You don't just stand there on the reject pile, smiling like it doesn't hurt.

The grungy guy tapped him on the shoulder. "You say you're giving pups away?" His cookies were gone, except for the frosting on his beard.

Josh nodded, surprised.

"I'll take one," the man said.

Everyone looked at Josh. The man put his paper cup on the stack of books. It looked like a lighthouse.

"Oh," Miss Rainey said. "I don't think—" She stopped, flustered.

"I don't know," Josh said carefully. "I mean—I don't know you." He hadn't known the woman with the little girl, either, he remembered. "Aren't you just—on the road? I mean, if you don't have a job or anything, how could you feed it, and all?"

"I live here," the man said. "Hey, I wouldn't take it if I couldn't come up with the goods. I take care of *me,* don't I? What's your name? I look like I can manage to take care of a pup, don't I?"

"Josh," he told him, nodding in spite of his doubts.

"Joshua fit the battle of Jericho," the man said, as if he had the habit of telling himself things. "Well, Josh, you trust me or you don't. It's a risk."

"I don't know," Josh said in desperation. How could he tell? What kind of life would a puppy have with a man like that?

But what did it take to beat dying in a box by the river?

Suddenly the man grubbed in the pocket of his ragged pea jacket and brought out a pencil in a handful of lint and crumbs. "I'll tell you what, Josh, my

friend, I'll give you my address. You come check on me. Check on your pup—see if I don't do a commendable job on it." He handed Josh a napkin with a street number on it. There were no houses there, Josh knew from his paper route days. A warehouse. So? Guard dogs stayed in warehouses okay. The man gave him a half glance with wary watery eyes. He's begging, Josh thought. It's rough by yourself.

He held out the box. "Which one do you want?"

The man said softly, "The runt." He lifted out the smallest puppy, smoothing its fuzzy head with his thumb. He said, "You keep that address. You come out and check."

"I will," Josh warned him. "You better be telling me the truth."

The man tucked the puppy inside his jacket. "I'll be gentle with it, Josh, my friend. I had a belt taken to me too many times to ever lift my hand to another creature."

He bowed to the ladies, smiling, and went out.

The Gnome de Plume thrust a book into Laurel's hand. "Run catch him," she ordered. Her squinty old eyes glinted with what looked to Josh like pleasure.

Laurel darted out. Josh felt a spurt of happiness. Two pups down—three to go. The rest of March, April, May before Laurel left. They'd go to the Throne of Kings again, and this time he would be able to say, *I'm glad we knew each other and liked and loved each other. Even if it can't be the way I wanted it to be.*

The Gnome de Plume brought a box from under the table and began to fill it with her books. The ladies gathered to help.

Josh was folding the napkin into his pocket when his hand froze. What was he doing? He wasn't going to be here to check on anybody's address. He was going to be out there on a bus. Finding his own warehouse to sleep in. There wouldn't be another day on the Throne of Kings. Never another day. He slung his head, blinking as if he'd run into a door in the dark.

He went out blindly and stood on the sidewalk, breathing hard. The box of puppies, lighter now, bulged and bumped in his hands. Laurel came back and stood beside him. They watched the cars go by in the long afternoon shadows.

"Were you just saying that?" she asked, with a pinched, anxious smile. "When you told him you'd check on the puppy?"

A car like his dad's came toward them. He went tight. It passed, driven by a boy in a baseball cap. Josh let out his breath. His voice, sounding far away, said, "Just once, if my folks would just look up and notice I was there. That's all it would take."

Laurel nodded. She always nodded, understanding, and he always went on explaining and defending himself, like some kind of neglected machine grinding itself to pieces.

"I mean, they talk to me—sure—but they're doing other things while they're yelling at me. Like I was some emergency they wished they weren't having."

Grace Whipple Cox came out the door with a load of books. Miss Rainey followed with another box and the last of the cookies under plastic on a wobbly paper plate.

"Let me carry that," Laurel said, taking the Gnome's load. Josh set the puppies down and took the books and plate from Miss Rainey. They followed the Gnome down the chilly street to her beat-up car and put the boxes in the back.

"Not much of an afternoon, dollar-wise," she said. He didn't understand why she followed them back to the library. She looked down at the puppies. "I wish I was sure I *had* ten-to-fifteen years to commit," she said, and laughed. "But so what? We can't wait for life to be perfect, can we?" She lifted up two puppies.

He heard Laurel draw a soft breath.

The Gnome de Plume said, "I can't take all three—I'm tempting fate as it is. But fate has sent them a guardian angel once already." She smiled at Josh. "Fate can do it again, if I don't last long enough. And they'll have each other." She bent closer. "Would you like one of my books?"

He gulped. "Yes," he told her, taking it. "I would."

The Gnome smiled at Laurel and handed her the puppies. "Come, young lady. I'll drive you home."

Laurel turned to Josh. Her anxious eyes tried to read his. "Your duffel is in the little room."

"I know," he said. He didn't move.

Slowly she started after the Gnome. "Josh?" she entreated, looking back.

"It won't work," he said. "I go home—they're madder than ever—we start yelling—"

"Part of that's up to you, isn't it?" she asked.

Her soft words let him down with a thump. Dang—*help* me, he wanted to yell. Don't just pile it back on me.

"Josh, can't you try? We have to get through things the best we can." Her voice was shaking. "I'll listen and listen, if it'll help, but it's up to you finally."

He turned away. Inside the library he stared through the window as the Gnome's car, and then others, and then others, passed in the dusk.

His dad was watching the news. He asked, "Where've you been?" without turning from the TV.

Josh felt the eeriness start again, matching the jumpy light of the screen that lit the room. He took the puppy out of his jacket. It seemed like fate, really, because the one that had been left was the one whose tender eyes had grabbed his heart beside the river.

"What's that?" his dad said, when he noticed. "You can't keep a dog. Your mother's got too much to do already."

"She won't have to take care of it," Josh said, keeping his voice even and slow. "I will. Feeding and housebreaking and shots and tags and spaying and everything."

His dad looked at him a long time. "Talk is cheap," he said.

"I guess you're going to have to risk it," Josh said, braced against the gaze.

His dad turned back to the news. "She can't do everything. The house, her schooling. She's got big dreams for herself. Give her a chance."

The puppy tried to crawl inside Josh's collar. He had to feed it. He had to buy a bag of something. "I live here too," he said. He felt for his ticket money. Maybe if he called Laurel she'd walk to the store with him and carry the pup while he lugged home a bag of dog chow. And they could talk. "Give me a chance too. Okay?"

His dad switched channels uneasily, testing, rejecting. He doesn't know how to answer me, Josh thought. He doesn't know what to say to any of this—to not having a job, or to her getting ahead of him, or to being my father.

A commercial came on. His dad said, watching it, "When I went into the army my folks kept my dog for me. They said he got lost. Ran away. But I was never sure." His face slowly warped in the shifting light. "Maybe he tried to find me. Or maybe he got killed and they hated to tell me. So I never could be sure, you know? For a long time I used to listen to the dogs barking, off in town. For years, I guess. Hoping I'd hear him."

Josh stopped halfway to the door. Hesitantly he came back, and sat on the arm of the couch, stroking the hungry puppy with his thumb. He stared at the television like his dad, not seeing it. Even with the sound turned high, he caught himself trying to hear other things. The far-off whine of buses. The almost inaudible cries and urgings and answers coming from everywhere.

Which of the characters in "The Second Highest Point" would you like to know? Explain your answer.

In what way does Josh give the puppies the chance he himself is looking for?

Grace Whipple Cox says, "Everything has worth, for its own reasons." How does this statement apply to the characters in the story?

Why does Josh feel an "unexpected emptiness" after he gives away the first puppy?

WRITE Josh is sad that his understanding friend, Laurel, is moving away. Write a note to Josh about this situation. You might give him advice for feeling better or share a similar experience of your own.

Coming of Age

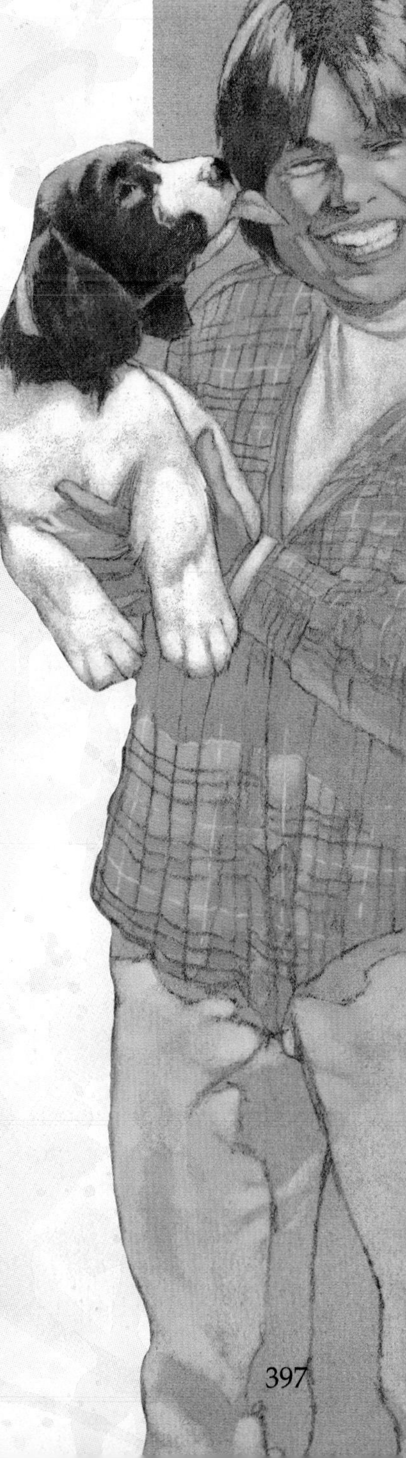

By the end of "Sea Glass," Craig has learned about his father's gardening. At the end of "The Second Highest Point," Josh learns about his father's lost dog. How do you think this new information affects Craig's and Josh's attitudes toward their fathers?

Writer's Workshop

You have read two stories about characters who are facing the challenges of coming of age. Do these stories remind you of people you know? Write a realistic story about one character's struggle with growing up. Use dialogue and believable events to reflect the real problems teenagers face today.

Writer's Choice If you think about it, you already know a lot about growing up. What does the phrase "coming of age" mean to you? Plan and carry out a writing project—a poem, a speech, or something else—to help you share your knowledge with others.

CONNECTIONS

MULTICULTURAL CONNECTION

GEORGE HORSE CAPTURE

George Horse Capture, a member of the Gros Ventre nation, spent a large part of his life helping to preserve the history and culture of the Plains Indians. As curator of the Plains Indian Museum in Cody, Wyoming, he collected and displayed artifacts that tell the story of the great buffalo-hunting nations.

As part of the Buffalo Bill Historical Center, the Plains Indian Museum has many varieties of clothing and other artifacts such as shields, painted buffalo skulls, blankets, and necklaces made of grizzly bear claws.

After helping to design the museum, which faces east just as the Indians' lodges faced east, George Horse Capture worked to make it a place where people can learn about the culture of the Plains Indians, past and present.

Imagine that you have been given the job of curator of a museum created to preserve the history and outstanding features of life in your school. Make a list of artifacts and other materials you would display in the museum. Compare your list with those of your classmates.

SOCIAL STUDIES CONNECTION

CLIMATIC INFLUENCES

Research two Native American nations from different climatic environments. Concentrate your research on how the climates affected the people's lifestyles.

Make a chart that illustrates how climatic conditions caused differences in the ways the groups of Native Americans lived. You may want to include such information as where the people lived, what the terrain was like, what type of housing they had, and what kind of food they ate.

LANGUAGE ARTS CONNECTION

EARLY ENVIRONMENTALISTS

Most Native Americans understood the concept of "Waste not, want not." Write an essay describing ways in which these Americans protected their environments in the past and suggesting ways in which all Americans could do so today.

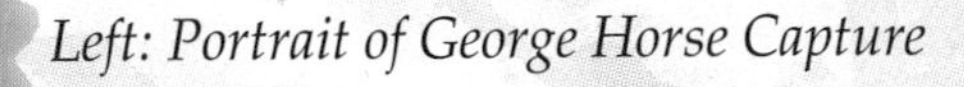

Left: Portrait of George Horse Capture

UNIT FIVE

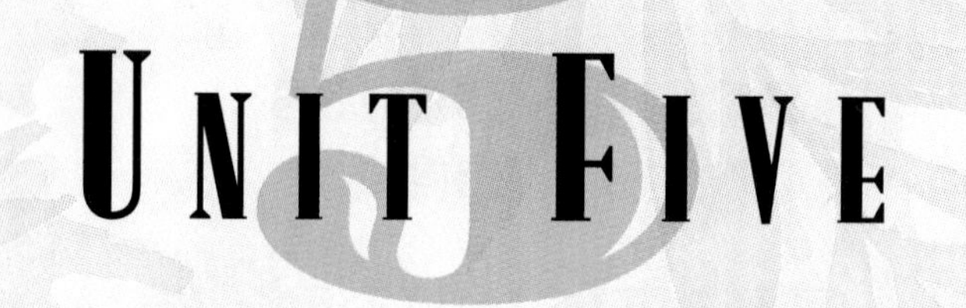

OBSERVATIONS

...I watched an eagle soar
high in the sky....
Virginia Driving Hawk Sneve

The universe is filled with wondrous things, from the vastness of outer space to a tiny insect on a blade of grass. We can train ourselves to become better observers by reading about people who look at things in different ways, including astronauts, writers, naturalists, and a young artist, Wang Yani. Think about how you look at things in the world and how your thinking may change if you observe them in a different way.

THEMES

FROZEN FIRE

BY JAMES HOUSTON

Matthew Morgan and his father go to the Canadian Arctic, looking for minerals. When Mr. Morgan and his pilot don't return from a search for ore, Matthew and his Eskimo friend set out to search for them. Struggling against storms and wild beasts, the two boys battle for their lives.

Award-Winning Author

HARCOURT BRACE LIBRARY BOOK

JULIE OF THE WOLVES

BY JEAN CRAIGHEAD GEORGE

Lost in the Alaskan wilderness, a young Eskimo girl is accepted by a pack of Arctic wolves and comes to care for them as though they were her family.

Newbery Medal

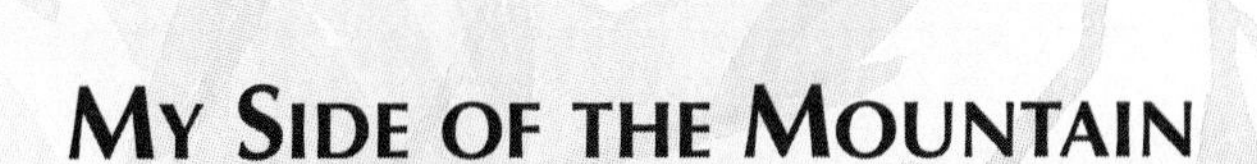

My Side of the Mountain

BY JEAN CRAIGHEAD GEORGE

Sam Gribley goes to the woods and lives off the land. With a tree as his home and a falcon as his companion, Sam relies on his own ingenuity to survive.

Newbery Honor Book, ALA Notable Book, Hans Christian Andersen Award Honor Book

The Yearling

BY MARJORIE KINNAN RAWLINGS

In the Florida wilderness, Jody finds a fawn and raises it until it is a yearling. The fawn teaches Jody about love and loss.

Pulitzer Prize Winner, Lewis Carroll Shelf Award

Animals at Play

BY LAURENCE PRINGLE

Is animal play just for fun? Does play somehow aid the survival of a species? This noted science writer describes and explains many types of animal behavior.

Award-Winning Author

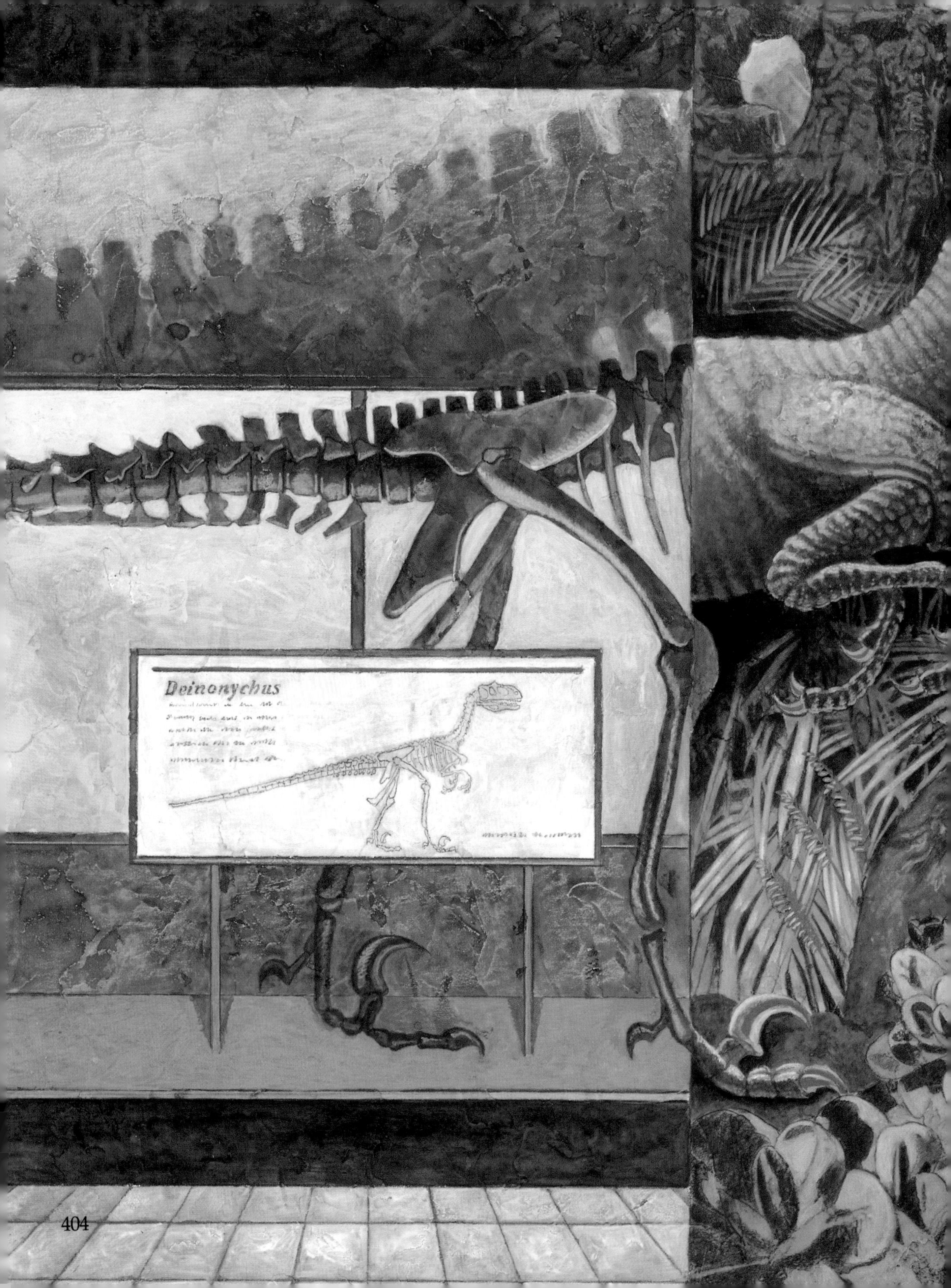
Deinonychus

THEME

Earth

Our planet Earth offers the rewards of rich discoveries for those who take the time to observe and explore. In the next selections, travel into space and see our world from a new perspective. Then go back in time and discover extinct creatures and forests hidden beneath the earth.

CONTENTS

CHILDREN'S CHOICE
SEEING EARTH FROM SPACE
BY PATRICIA LAUBER

SEEING EARTH FROM SPACE

BY PATRICIA LAUBER

On their way to the moon, Apollo 8 astronauts looked back and saw a bright blue globe, partly masked by white clouds and set against the black of space. At that moment they became the first people ever to see the Earth as a planet. Their photographs and others show us Earth as we can never see it for ourselves.They also show us something we know but find hard to believe: We are all flying through space. Our space ship is the earth, whirling around the sun at 67,000 miles an hour.

Other new views come from photographs taken by astronauts orbiting a few hundred miles above Earth's surface. These astronauts are too close to see the full face of the earth. But they see large pieces of it at one time, something we cannot do. Trying to see the earth from its surface is like looking at a large painting while standing up against it. We see only details. To see the picture, we must back off.

Astronauts in orbit have backed off from Earth. They see the full length of rivers, the folds of the mountains, the birth of hurricanes, the straight lines of roads and bridges that mark the cities of the world. Their photographs give us a space tour of our home planet.

Still different pictures of Earth come from satellites carrying sensors, radar, and other instruments. They show us things that the human eye cannot see for itself.

Together, all these views of Earth teach us much about our planet, whether by showing us the unseen or by taking us sight-seeing with the astronauts.

Remote Sensing

Space photography is called remote sensing because it is a way of learning about a target, such as the earth, without touching it. There are many kinds of remote sensing. Among them are ones found in the human body. You use yours every day of your life.

Is a radiator hot? To find out, you don't touch it. You hold your hands out toward it. If there is heat, nerve endings in your skin will sense it. That is one kind of human remote sensing.

Eyesight, or vision, is a much more important kind. To use it, you need light.

White light is a mixture of colors. You see this when the sun's white light breaks up into a band of colors and makes a rainbow in the sky. You see it when white light passes through a prism. The light breaks up into a band of colors known as a spectrum.

Light travels in waves, and each color has its own wavelength. When the sun's white light shines on a buttercup, the flower absorbs most of the wavelengths, but it reflects the yellow ones. And so you see a yellow flower. A purple plum is reflecting a mixture of red and violet wavelengths. A brown dog is reflecting a mixture of red, orange, and yellow ones.

Like the human eye, a camera takes in reflected light. Used with black-and-white or color film, a camera records the kinds of things that the eye sees.

Red wavelengths are the longest that the human eye can detect. So red is the last color we see in the spectrum. But there is color beyond red, color with longer wavelengths. It is in the part of the spectrum called the infrared, meaning "below red." If we could see in the infrared, we would see color beyond red in every rainbow, color we cannot even imagine.

If we could detect even longer infrared wavelengths, we would see something else. After sunset, we would see a dim glow, the glow of heat being given off.

Sunlight warms the earth's surface by day. The heat is absorbed by oceans, deserts, rocks, trees, and everything else on the surface. Some of the heat is radiated back into the atmosphere as infrared energy. If we could see these infrared wavelengths, the landscape would glow at night.

Although human eyes cannot sense infrared, there are ways of detecting it. One is to use film that senses infrared. There are also electronic sensors that detect infrared. They are carried on satellites—the Landsat series launched by the United States and satellites launched by other countries. The sensors scan the earth beneath them. They measure the light reflected by the earth, both the wavelengths we see and the infrared. The sensors are another kind of remote sensing.

Sensors record their measurements as numbers, using a scale of 0 to 255. The numbers are radioed to Earth, where computers put them together and make pictures. Bright false colors are added to make details stand out and to let us see what was recorded in infrared.

Some of the pictures, or images, look like photographs; some don't. But all provide far more information than the eye alone could do.

This Landsat picture was made using information sensed and recorded in green, red, and infrared wavelengths. It shows California's Salton Sea, which looks like a big footprint, and the Imperial Valley, which stretches southward. In the valley's warm, dry climate crops grow year-round, irrigated with water from the Colorado River. Healthy green plants reflect infrared strongly; they appear as bright red in this false-color image. Thinner vegetation is pink. Clear water is black. Windblown sand from the neighboring desert is white. The checkerboard pattern shows that some fields have ripening crops (red and pink) and some are lying fallow, or resting (blue-gray).

Because of a difference in the way farming is done, the border between the United States and Mexico appears as a straight line across the Imperial Valley. It is one of the few national boundaries on Earth that can be seen from space.

The Mississippi River twists and turns—it meanders—as it flows through its lower valley toward the Gulf of Mexico.

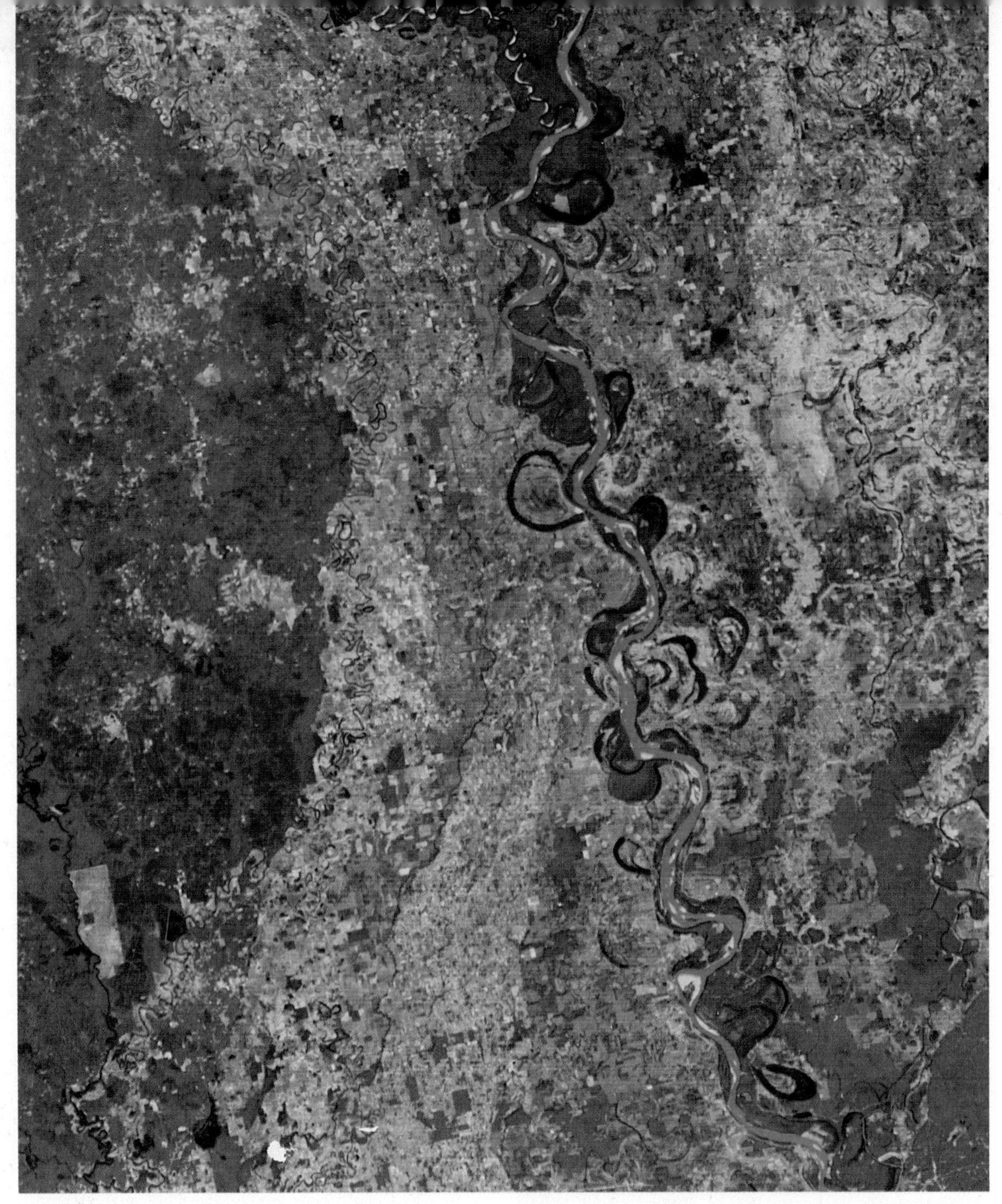

Sometimes it changes course, leaving behind the loop- and crescent-shaped lakes that now mark its earlier paths. Because of its meanderings, the lower Mississippi is longer than its valley. It travels one-and-a-half times the length of the valley from Cairo, Illinois, to New Orleans.

In this false-color image the floodplain of the river appears pinkish. Much of it is covered with farms that raise cotton, soybeans, rice, wheat, and oats. On bluffs along the borders of the flood plain, forests of oak, hickory, and pine grow.

Looking like a scar on the face of the earth, the Grand Canyon twists its way across Arizona in this Landsat picture. This part of the canyon is about a mile

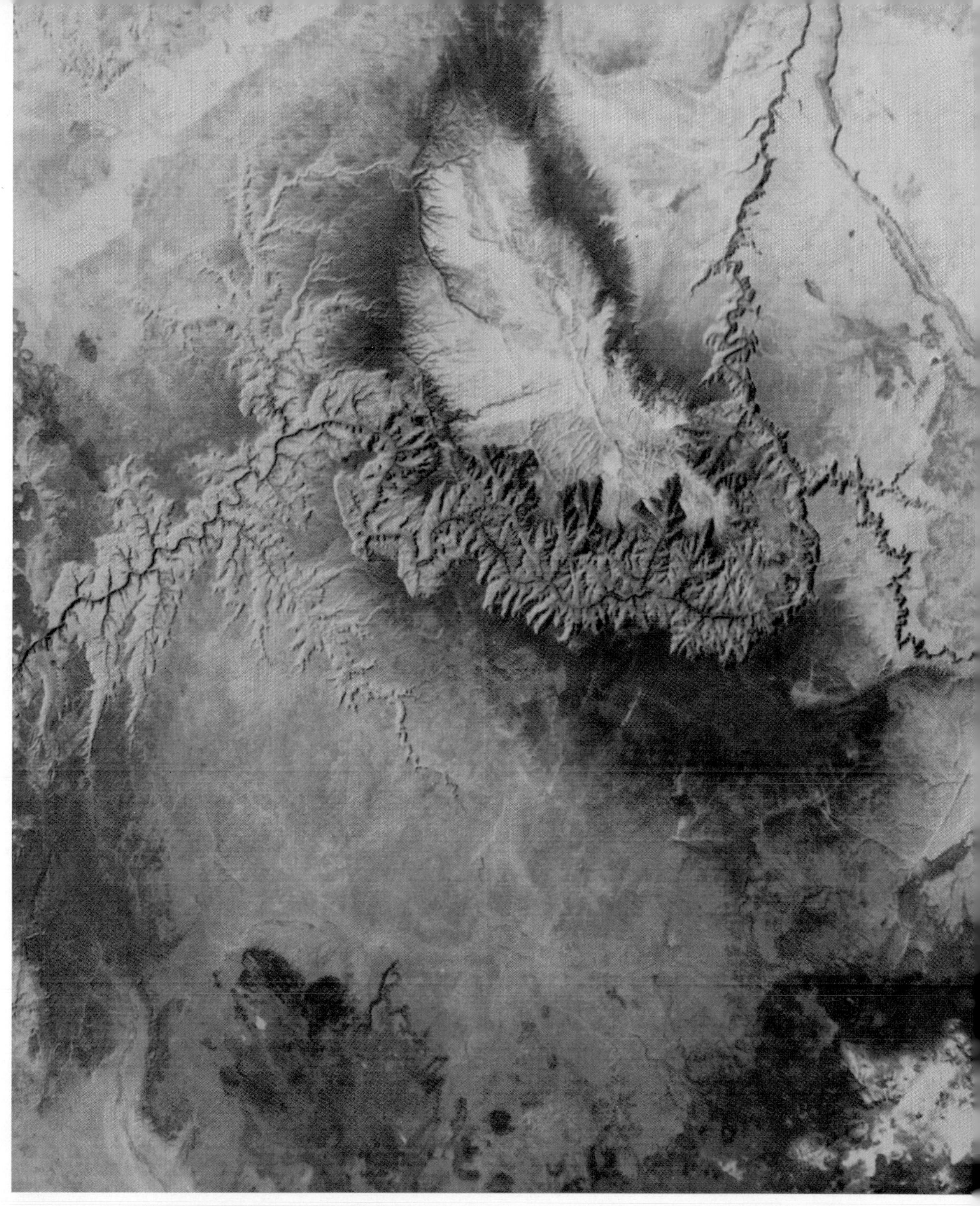

deep and 12 miles wide from rim to rim. Its layered rock walls reveal some 2 billion years of Earth's history. The racing Colorado River, which carves the canyon deeper and deeper, is later stopped and pooled by Hoover Dam and Lake Mead.

Radar is still another kind of remote sensing. Unlike the Landsat sensors, it does not measure light reflected from the earth. Instead, it sends out its own radio waves and microwaves. It beams them toward its target and detects their echoes. The strength of the echoes is recorded and used to make maps or pictures. Because it does not use light, radar works both day and night. And because its waves pass through clouds, it can be used when skies are overcast.

One of the space shuttles flew over Montreal, Quebec, at a time when most of the city was covered by clouds. Information from its radar was used to make this false-color image. The St. Lawrence River, at right, is shown in black, as are the smaller rivers. You can see the bridges that cross them. Buildings and pavements appear pink and blue. Land that is being cultivated is dark green. Plant life that grows wild is lighter green. The big green oval to the left of the St. Lawrence is Mount Royal.

The same shuttle flew over the high plateau of northern Peru (below). Its radar showed these folded, layered rocks, some 70 million years old. False colors have been used to highlight different kinds of rock. The wormlike black line in the center of the picture is a river that feeds into the Amazon.

Remote sensing shows us the earth in new and often surprising images. For scientists who use the images, they open up ways of studying the earth that have never existed before.

USING REMOTE SENSING

As it orbits, a satellite regularly passes over the same parts of Earth. And so its images let scientists trace what happens as the seasons change. They can, for example, predict flooding by studying winter snowfalls and spring meltings. And they can make cloud-free pictures of any region by piecing together images from different times of year. That was how they obtained this false-color image of Italy. In it, plant life appears in shades of red. Cities and barren areas are blue-gray. Mountains stand out clearly. And the volcano Mount Etna, its sides dark with lava, can be seen on the island of Sicily, off the toe of the boot.

The view from space helps many kinds of scientists. Geographers have discovered mountains and lakes that did not appear on their maps. They have found a previously unknown island off the coast of Labrador and a reef in the Indian Ocean. They have mapped mountain ranges, deserts, and Arctic lands.

In earlier times, oceanographers could only study the oceans from ships. It was long, slow work. The oceans were huge, covering more than 70 percent of Earth's surface, and the ships were small. Now these scientists can also study the oceans through pictures from space. They can see large features that they could not see from ships. They can track currents, such as the Gulf Stream, that play a major part in climate. They can track the masses of tiny plants that form the base of food chains in the oceans. They can see and follow details in ways that used to be impossible.

They can, for example, follow the swirling rings of water thrown off by currents, such as these eddies in the Mediterranean Sea. Eddies can be 200 miles in diameter and travel hundreds of miles over several years. By stirring up the water, eddies speed up the spread of heat from tropical areas. They are also important to the life of the sea, because they carry minerals used by plants in making their food.

Seasat was a United States satellite that

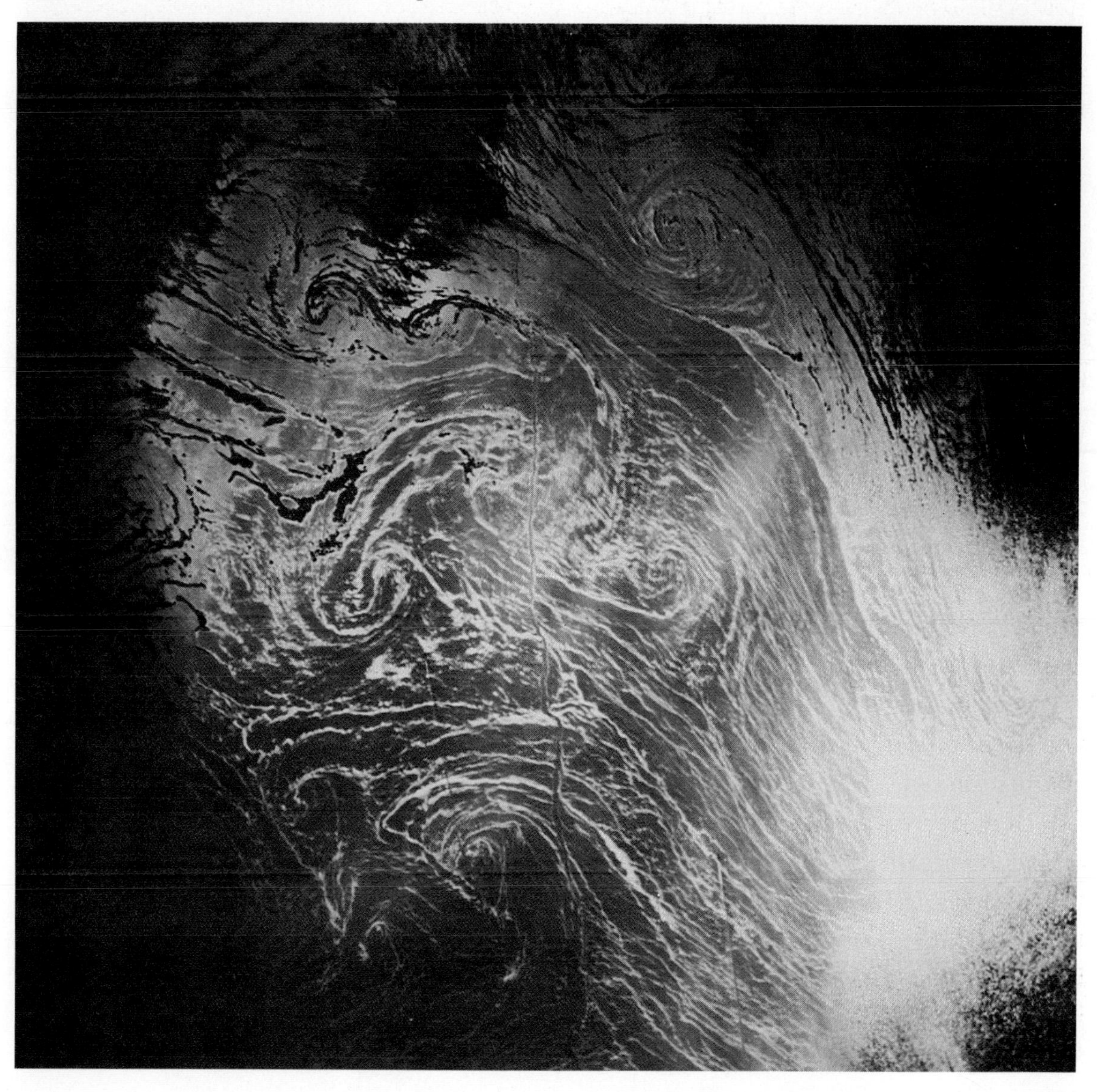

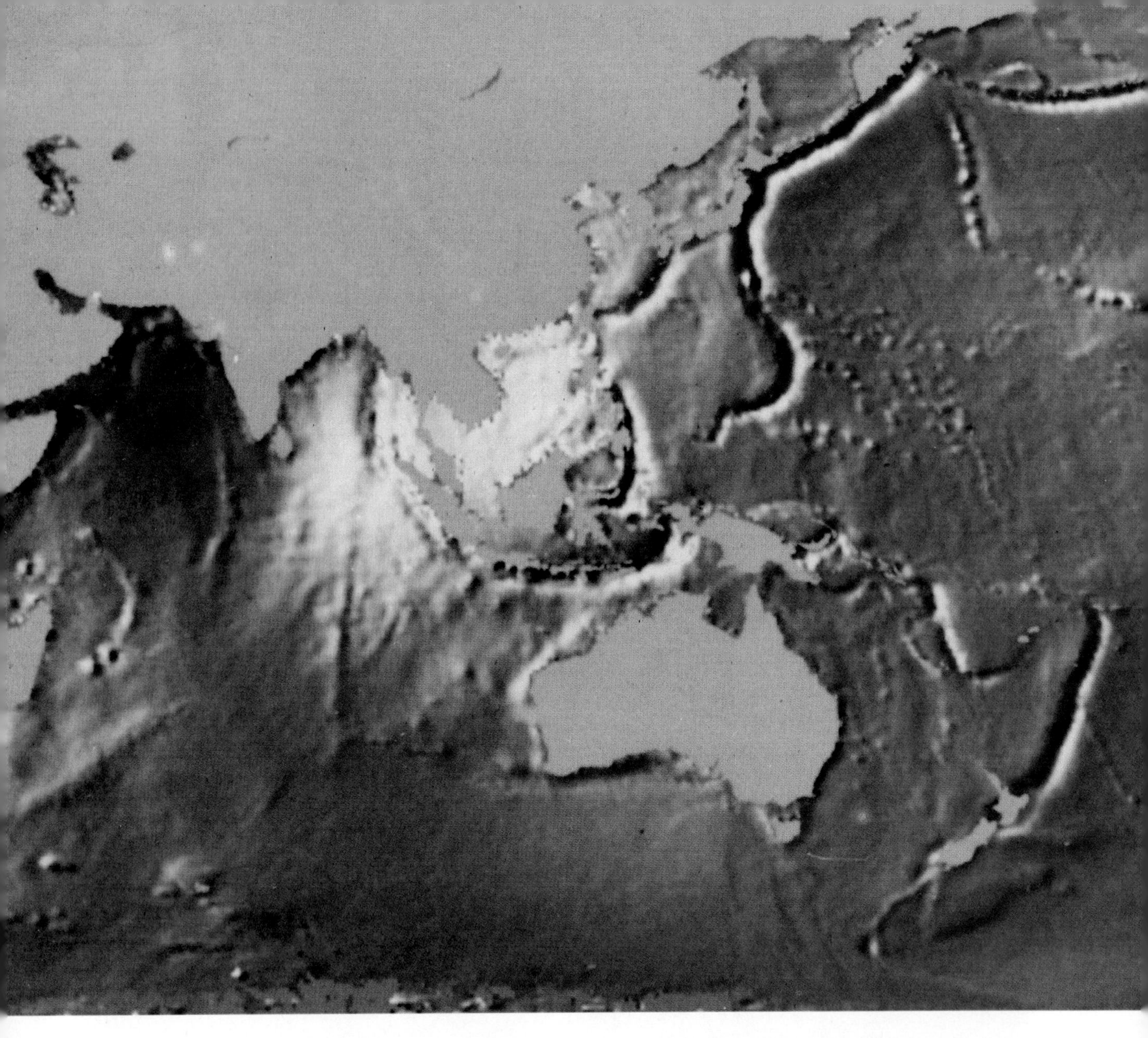

failed after a few months. It was designed to study the oceans—roughness, the patterns of currents, water temperature, the speed of surface winds, sea ice. One of its instruments was a radar altimeter, which measured the height of the satellite above the ocean. Seasat sent out a beam of radio waves. When they hit the surface of the water, they were reflected back to the altimeter and recorded.

The results were a surprise: The surface of the ocean rises and falls with the rise and fall of the seabed beneath it. If you could smooth out all the waves, you would see that the ocean surface has hills and valleys. They mark places where there are undersea mountains and trenches. Where there is a big seamount, for example, there is extra gravity. The seamount pulls a little extra water toward itself. The extra water makes a gentle hill a few feet high. Above a valley or a trench, there is a dip in the surface. And so a map of the ocean

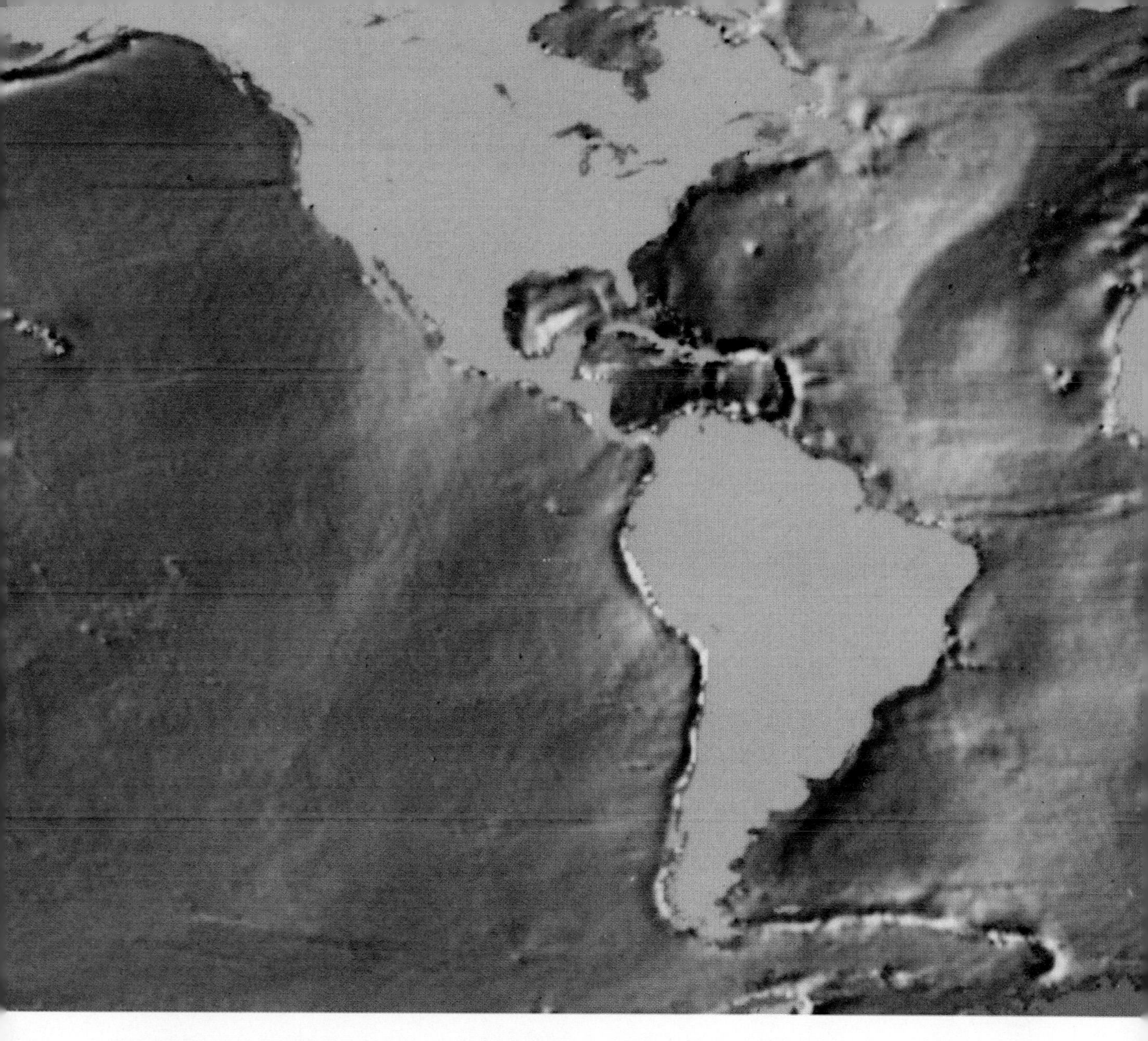

surface is also a map of the ocean floor.

This map shows several deep ocean trenches. They are places where plates of the earth's crust are colliding. The leading edge of one plate slides under the other and turns down, creating a trench.

The map also shows the Mid-Atlantic Ridge, a range of undersea volcanic mountains. The range runs down the middle of the Atlantic Ocean and continues around the world, like the seam on a baseball. Here molten rock wells up from inside the earth and is added to the trailing edges of plates.

In many Landsat images all thick, healthy plant life appears bright red, while thinner vegetation is lighter. But images can also be used to find out what kinds of plants are growing. Every kind of plant reflects sunlight in its own way; it has its own place in the spectrum, which is called its spectral signature. A spectral signature is like a fingerprint. Just as no two people have the same fingerprints, so no two

kinds of plant have the same spectral signature. Plant scientists have learned the signature of oats, for example, by studying images of fields where they know oats are growing. When they find the same signature in another place, it tells them the crop is oats. A different signature tells them the crop is wheat. By giving each signature a false color, they can see which fields are planted to oats and which are planted to wheat. In this image of the San Joaquin Valley in California, fields of cotton are red. Yellow shows safflower, while dark green shows wheat stubble. Fields lying fallow are blue.

Shuttle astronauts photographed this strange scene while passing over the Saudi Arabian desert. The pattern of perfect circles told them they were seeing something man-made. It turned out to be farmland. Each circle marked a piece of desert irrigated by a sprinkler that pumped water from underground and broadcast it in a circle.

The astronauts' film showed all plant life in one color. Landsat detected far more when it passed over Garden City, Kansas. Here, too, are the circles that tell how the crops are watered. But the Landsat image also tells what the crops are. The time of year is December. White shows where corn has been harvested and its stubble left on the ground. Red shows that healthy winter wheat is growing. Fields that are black and white have been left fallow to build moisture in the soil.

By noting small differences in spectral signatures, plant scientists can tell a newly planted crop from a ripe crop. They can tell whether plants are healthy. They can even tell if unhealthy plants are suffering from a disease or being attacked by pests.

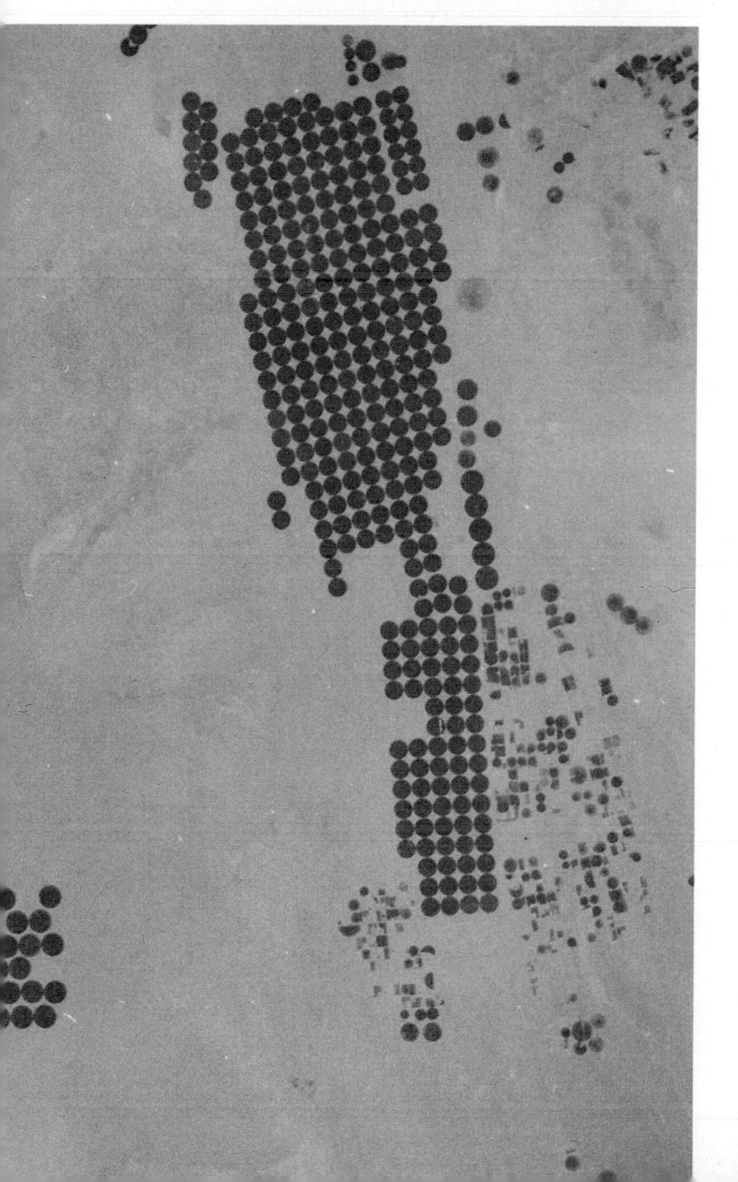

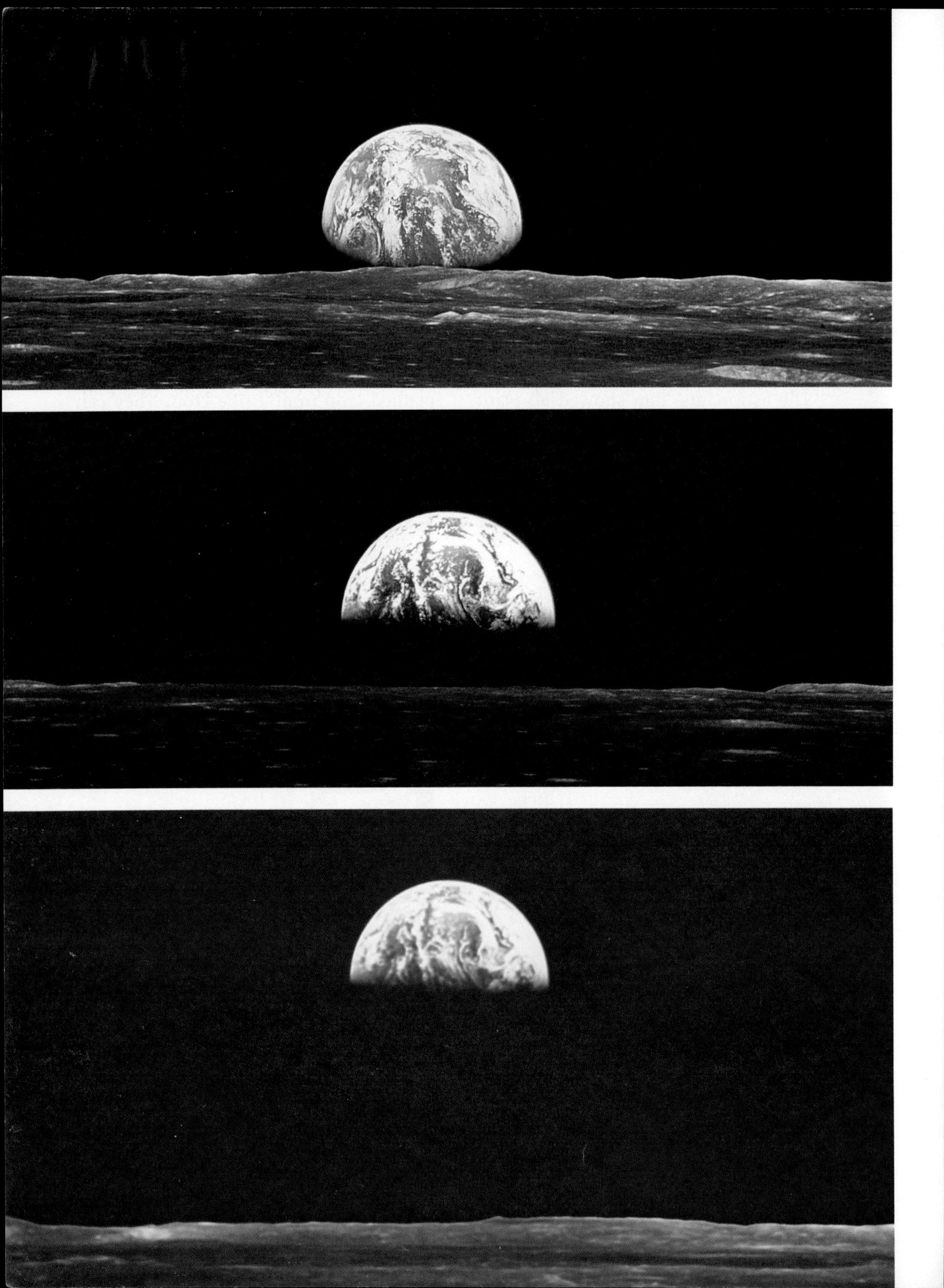

SPACESHIP EARTH

The Apollo astronauts who landed on the moon found themselves in a strange new world. No one had walked this ground before; the only footprints were their own. Nowhere was there a trace of life other than their own, only craters, seas of hardened lava, hills, and rocks. Above them stars and planets shone with a brilliance never seen on Earth, for the moon has no atmosphere to dim their light. Yet for the astronauts the most exciting sight was Earth. It was more than home.

Seen from the surface of the airless, barren moon or from the orbiting spacecraft, Earth was an island of life in the black sea of space, the only outpost of life to be seen.

What did you learn about the earth that you did not know before?

In what ways does remote sensing help us understand the world in which we live?

How do pictures from space help oceanographers study the ocean?

WRITE How would you feel if you were an astronaut viewing Earth from space for the first time? Write a postcard describing the experience to someone back home.

An Interview with the Author:

PATRICIA LAUBER

Writer Ilene Cooper had the opportunity to discuss writing with Patricia Lauber.

Ms. Cooper: You've written so many books about science. What's the attraction?

Ms. Lauber: Well, that's funny. In school I was the sort of person who never met a science course she liked. I didn't get into science until I had decided to become a free-lance writer. I had quit my job editing at a magazine; things were getting very tight financially; and I was wondering what I should do next.

Then a publisher called to ask me if I'd like to be the editor of a new science magazine for young people. I went to talk with them, and in a burst of honesty, I said I didn't know much about science. They said that would probably keep the magazine from being too technical.

I gave myself a crash course, with books and teachers, and I discovered that when I got into science at the idea level rather than the school level, I found it extremely interesting. So, after working at the magazine for a while, I began to write books.

Ms. Cooper: Who comes up with the ideas for topics for your books, you or your publisher?

Ms. Lauber: Either or both, but I won't write about things that don't interest me. If I'm not enthusiastic about a topic, I can't expect my readers to be. I'm very interested in all aspects of the natural world, especially in what we as a species are doing to our planet. We're changing it without knowing what the end result will be. Also I've always been interested in the work of scientists who dig up the past, archaeologists or paleontologists.

Ms. Cooper: How did you get the idea for Seeing Earth from Space?

Ms. Lauber: I had written a book called *Journey to the Planets*, which starts with a chapter about Earth. It has photographs of Earth from space as well as from closer, raising the question of how close you would have to get before you knew there was intelligent life on this planet, or on any

planet. People seemed fascinated by the pictures, so I got the idea of doing a whole book about Earth, based on this new way of obtaining information about our planet when seen from space.

Ms. Cooper: How do you write about complex subjects so that young people will be able to understand them?
Ms. Lauber: Well, first I have to understand the information myself. Once I've digested it, I decide what really important parts have to be covered. I write for different age groups, and some topics just aren't suitable for younger children. You'll never be able to do an accurate, interesting job with material that is too difficult for your audience.

Ms. Cooper: You've written both fiction and nonfiction. Do you prefer one more than the other?
Ms. Lauber: I was the sort of child who loved the words *Once upon a time*. I still do. The child in me would much rather write only fiction, but right now my career is centered around nonfiction. When writing nonfiction, I can see the book in my mind's eye. I'll soon know if it's possible or not possible, if I want to do it or not do it. With fiction, I never know how it's going to come out. Before I submit a fiction book to a publisher, I have to finish it, or at least have a first draft of the entire book. I have several half-finished books of fiction in my cabinet now because, for one reason or another, I can't finish them.

Ms. Cooper: Do you see any similarities between writing fiction and writing nonfiction?
Ms. Lauber: Definitely. No matter what you're writing, there should be a story line and some suspense. Whether it's fiction or nonfiction, the reader has to want to turn the page.

DINOSAURS WALKED HERE

And Other Stories Fossils Tell

by Patricia Lauber

*Two **Grallator** footprints.*

One day, forty million years ago, a gnat was crawling over the bark of a pine tree. It became trapped in a sticky flow of sap, or resin. Once the gnat was covered with resin, no other animal could eat it. The soft parts of the body did not decay, because bacteria could not feed on them. The gnat was quickly preserved. Much later, the resin hardened into the kind of fossil called amber, which looks something like yellow glass. Inside the amber was another fossil, the gnat. The gnat is one of many fossil insects that have been found in amber.

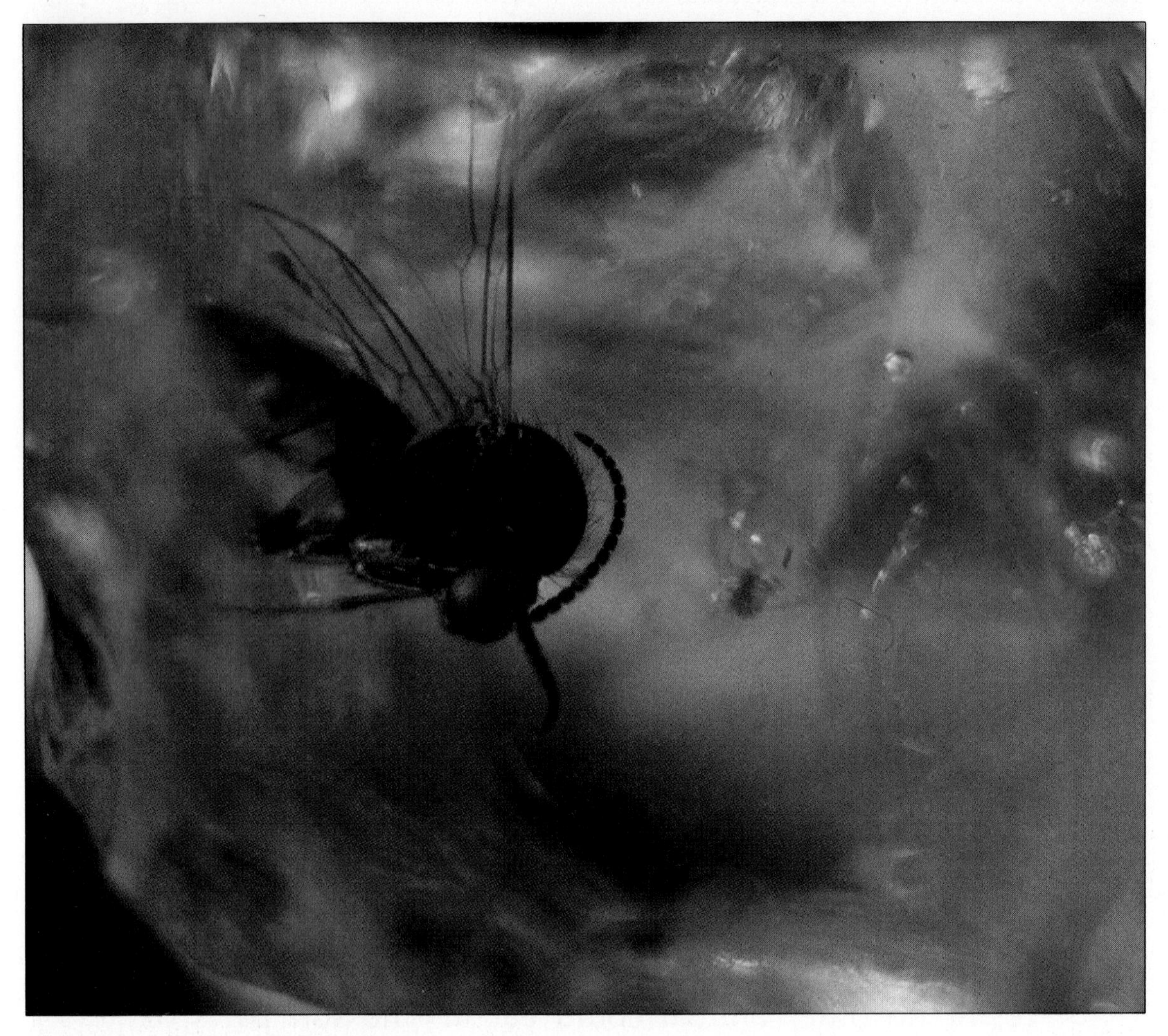

Forty-million-year-old gnat is embedded in amber. Green is caused by the breaking up of white light as it passes through tiny cracks in the amber.

Quick freezing preserved the bodies of some woolly mammoths. Mammoths were relatives of today's elephants. They were able to live through a time of great changes in the earth's climate—through an ice age. They lived through times when mile-thick sheets of ice crept out from the polar regions and down from mountains to cover once-green lands. They lived through times when the ice melted and shrank back, releasing floods of melt-water. Then, when the ice last shrank back to the polar regions and mountaintops, about 9,000 to 12,000 years ago, the woolly mammoths died out, for reasons no one knows.

We know about woolly mammoths from the cave drawings of Stone Age people. We also know about them because whole frozen mammoths have been found in the ground of Alaska and Siberia. One of these was a baby mammoth that somehow lost its mother 27,000 years ago and fell into an icy pit, where it died. Bacteria had little chance to feed on the body because it soon froze and became covered with ice. The sides of the pit caved in and buried the baby mammoth under six feet of earth. At that depth, the summer sun could not melt the ice or thaw the body. The body of the baby mammoth was preserved. It was discovered in 1977 by Soviet gold prospectors working in northeastern Siberia. The body was so well preserved that scientists could even find traces of its mother's milk in the mammoth's stomach.

The bones of animals have been found preserved in still another way. These are the bones of animals that were trapped in places where oil was oozing out of the ground as thick, sticky asphalt. One of these places is now known as the La Brea tar pits, in Los Angeles. Scientists suppose the animals were trapped in ways like this:

Thousands of years ago, a ground sloth the size of an elephant was being chased by a saber-toothed tiger. Lumbering across the valley as fast as it could, the sloth glimpsed a shining surface that looked like a pond. It plunged in, hoping to escape the tiger. The big saber-tooth sprang after it. But the water was only a thin layer that had collected on

When the ice age ended, large mammals such as mastodons died out.

The saber-toothed tiger is one of many animals, known from their fossils, that lived and flourished in North America and then died out for reasons no one knows.

top of asphalt, and both animals were trapped in the sticky ooze. As they died, giant vultures dived from the sky to feed on them. One came too close to the surface, dragged its feet in the asphalt, and could not free itself.

At other times animals may have waded in to drink, only to discover they could not get out. Sometimes plant-eating animals may have scattered and fled from a meat eater. Some ran across what looked like solid ground, but an asphalt pool lay under the leaves or dirt. And so over the years many animals were trapped. Among them were camels, mammoths, bears, wolves, lions, bison, antelope, geese, and eagles. Long afterward their bones were discovered at La Brea, preserved as fossils in the asphalt. The bones told a story of animals that used to live in North America and of some that died out as mysteriously as the woolly mammoths.

Fossils tell much about plants and animals of the past. The study of fossils also tells of changes in the face of the earth and of changes in the earth's climate.

LAYERS OF FOSSILS

The study of fossils is called paleontology, which means "the study of ancient forms of life." Scientists who study fossils are paleontologists.

Paleontologists work on fossil bones at Dinosaur National Monument, in Utah.

To lay railroad track in eastern Ohio, workers made a cut in a cliff, revealing rock layers laid down some 300 million years ago. At the bottom is limey mudstone that built up in the bed of a large lake. Within the mudstone are layers of limestone, holding fossil fishes. The lake grew shallow and became overgrown with plants, forming a peat bog. Much later the remains of the bog became coal (brown layer). Next a floodplain developed, with rivers and lakes. Layers of sandstone and mudstone were laid down. Coalswamp plants took over again and their remains led to another layer of coal (black layer). The land sank slightly and a lake formed. It gradually filled with layers of limey mudstone or shale and limestone, which go to the top of the cliff.

Paleontologists are often the finders of fossils. But many times they first hear of a find from other people—from rock collectors who came upon fossils, from miners or construction workers who found fossils while digging. Amateur fossil hunters may report a find. Sometimes someone simply sees a bone sticking out of the ground. This happens because sedimentary rocks are fairly soft and crumbly. They are easily worn away by wind and water. Fossils long buried in the rock may then be exposed.

Some finds tell of great changes in the face of the earth. Climbers, for example, may come upon seashells in rocks near the

If you look closely, you will see that this slice of rock has pairs of thin layers, one dark and one light. The sediments forming the dark layers were laid down in a lake during summer and fall. The light layers were laid down in winter and spring. The summer-fall layers are darker because the sediments were discolored by rotting leaves, dust, pollen, and soot from forest fires. Each pair stands for one year. The dark spots you see are fossils. The wide, light-colored bands occur about every hundred years. They mark a change in sediments that was probably caused by a change in climate.

Edmontosaurus was one of the duck-billed dinosaurs.

tops of mountains. The fossil shells are a sign that the rocks formed from sediments at the bottom of an ancient sea. At a later time mountains crumpled up out of the earth's crust. The seabed and its fossils were carried skyward.

Fossils also tell of changes in climate. Today, for example, the northeastern part of Yellowstone National Park has rugged mountains and a climate that is cool in summer and very cold in winter. It has forests of firs and other evergreens that grow well in a cold climate. About fifty million years ago, it was very different. In place of the mountains there were broad, flat river valleys separated by rolling hills.

The climate was mild in the hills and hot in the valleys.

We know about this change in climate because paleontologists have found forests of fossil trees in this part of the park. These were leafy trees that grow in mild to hot climates.

The forests were preserved because of huge volcanic eruptions that buried them in ash and rocks. After each big eruption, new forests took root on top of the old ones. Over many, many years, minerals from moving water turned the buried tree trunks to stone. Now, millions of years later, the volcanic material around the tree trunks has weathered away. The petrified remains of ancient trees can be seen standing upright exactly where the trees used to grow.

In one area, forests were buried many times. Wind, rain, and melting snow have worn away the side of a steep bluff, exposing more than twenty layers of petrified trees. They formed over some 20,000 years, as volcanic eruptions buried a forest, a new forest grew, and eruptions buried it. The result is like a giant layer cake. Each layer of forest—of tree trunks and imprints of leaves—tells its own story about plants and climate. Each is like a page in the earth's diary.

Sedimentary rock also forms in layers. Each new layer marks a change in the sediments that were being laid down. A river, for example, might flow slowly for years, carrying along only very fine sediments and dropping them in a bay. Then a huge storm strikes upstream. Water pours into the river and the river's flow speeds up. The faster flow means that the river picks up coarse sediments as well as fine. Now it drops sand and gravel in the bay. Later the river goes back to carrying only fine sediments. The sand and gravel mark the end of one layer of fine sediment and the start of another.

You have probably seen such layers. They often appear where the sea has eaten away at a cliff or a river has carved a deep valley. They are seen where wind and rain have worn down hills and mountains. They are also seen in quarries and where road cuts pass through hills.

Paleontologists find the layers useful because they are like time capsules. Plants and animals that appear as fossils in the same layers must have lived at the same time. That is how paleontologists have learned about the world of the dinosaurs. They know what kinds of plants grew in that world. They know what the climate was like. They know what other kinds of animals shared that world. The layers, like the fossils themselves, fill out our picture of dinosaurs and how they lived.

Do you think you would enjoy the field of paleontology? Explain how this selection influenced your answer.

Describe some of the different ways in which animals from the past have been preserved.

How is a fossil like "a page in the earth's diary"?

Write This selection gives you bits and pieces of a picture of the past. Write a brief description of your impressions of the prehistoric world.

Theme Wrap-Up

Careful observation can lead to surprising conclusions. "Seeing Earth from Space" and "Dinosaurs Walked Here" presented some unconventional observations of our planet. Which of the selections surprised you more? Explain your answer.

Writer's Workshop

Imagine that you are a scientist. If you could explore any part of Earth, where would you go? What do you think you would observe there? Write a persuasive essay in which you propose a scientific expedition. Your proposal should persuade people that your research is worthwhile—and worth funding!

Writer's Choice You have read about exploring Earth by looking at computer photographs and ancient fossils. How else can you explore Earth? What could you write about our planet? Plan a writing project about Earth. Revise your writing until it is just right. Then decide on a way to share it with an audience.

THEME

Survival

Sometimes people find themselves in serious situations in which survival is their only goal. Would your knowledge of science help you live on a deserted island? Do you know enough about nature to survive in a wilderness? See what the characters in these selections do to survive.

CONTENTS

A small plane crashes off the rugged coast of British Columbia, and one lone survivor, Elena Bradbury, a teenage girl, fights her way to shore on a makeshift raft. Her survival and eventual escape depend entirely on her courage, ingenuity, and understanding of nature.

During her first week, she locates a source of fresh water and eats berries, barnacles, and clams. She also finds some materials, including an empty paint-thinner can and some rope, that have washed ashore.

TRIAL BY WILDERNESS

by David Mathieson

By morning, the sky had changed. Instead of a deck of gray stratus, there came a rushing mass of cumulus clouds. They bumbled along at low altitude like a herd of cotton elephants, stampeded by the wind. Patches of early morning sunlight swept across the mountains and along the beach. Shadow one moment, sun the next.

She had awakened with a feeling of hope. Although the experiments with firemaking had come to naught, she was still better off than before, thanks to the empty thinner can. Properly used, the tin could increase her chance of being rescued, for even if the shipping lanes were too distant, a beam of reflected sunlight could hardly be missed by someone a short distance off in a low-flying plane.

The can would have to be modified, however.

She took one of her salvaged nails—it was almost heavy enough to be called a spike—and with repeated blows from a stone, she shaped its malleable iron into a chisel point. With this, she removed the bottom of the can, driving her makeshift chisel centimeter by centimeter around the edge, using a piece of root as a mallet. She ended up with a flat, rectangular mirror measuring perhaps fifteen centimeters by

illustrations by Patrick Soper

ten. The mirror was stiffened at its edge by the remnant of a seam where the sides of the can had been attached.

Again using her chisel, she punched a hole two centimeters across exactly in the center of the mirror. The hole was for sighting; if the mirror was to be a reliable signaling device, the narrow beam of reflected sunlight had to be aimed.

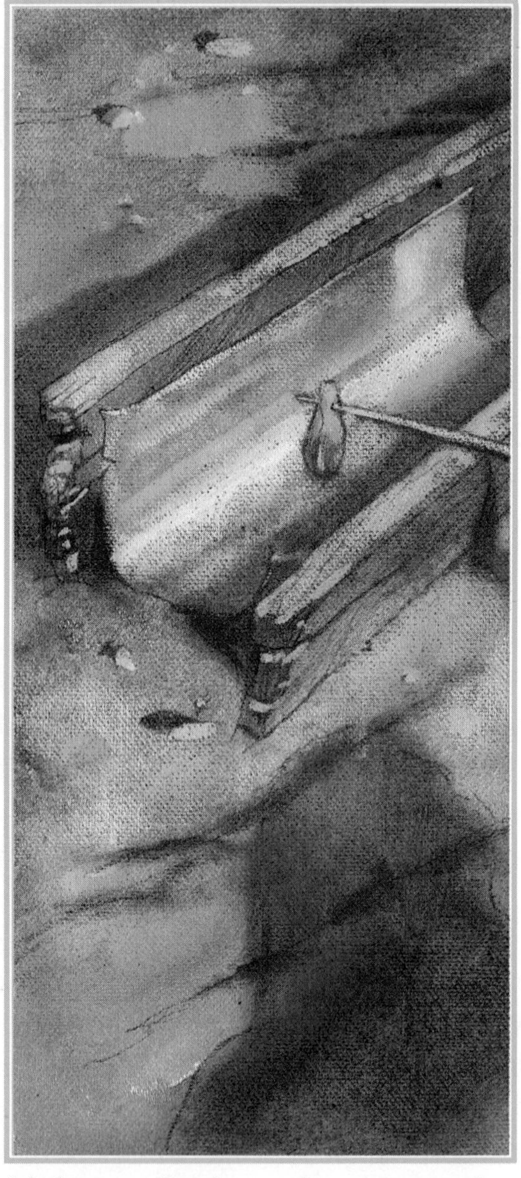

While waiting for the sun to make one of its random appearances, she practiced the technique. Holding the mirror to her eye with one hand and extending the other hand in front of her, she could look through the hole and see her upraised forefinger. The idea was to tilt the mirror so that a patch of brightness lighted the end of your finger. This told you precisely where the beam was going. To signal in Morse, you simply nodded your head. This brought the spot of reflected sunlight down where you could see it on your arm—away from the target—thus creating the interval between flashes.

The device had a limited arc of effectiveness, as she soon discovered during a break in the clouds. The quivering rectangle of light was quite distinct whenever she chose a target within a hundred and twenty degrees of the sun. If the angle grew much greater than that, however, the beam was narrow and weak.

She noticed something else, whenever the bright patch of light touched her hand. The metal mirror was handling more than just the visible spectrum of the sun's rays. It was reflecting heat as well.

The idea hit her so suddenly it was like a jolt of electricity.

Solar oven.

Fire wasn't the only way food could be cooked! She should have thought of it earlier. It was such an obvious use of the can's gleaming interior!

Looking in through the open end, she began to visualize how the thing might be done. First the top would have to be cut off, then the seam along the side. The resulting sheet of metal could then be shaped into a smooth curve.

The device was completed in record time. Two sections of plank held the sheet, top and bottom, the whole affair being supported by a mound of sand and oriented toward the point in the sky where the sun would next appear. "The Pig Trough Oven," she chuckled, giving the metal a last polish with her shirt sleeve. On impulse, she went to the clam reserve, smashed open several shells, wrapped what she could around a stick, and ran back to the reflector with it.

The beach was beginning to brighten. She held the stick crossways to the device. When the sun came, extremely brilliant slashes and stars of light appeared along the sides of the stick. The clam flesh became translucent, glowing like a strip of film in a projector. She moved the stick up and down to locate the mirror's focal point. The effect was spotty and uneven. At the center of one of the star-shaped areas, where the light was brightest, there was enough heat to bring water to a boil. She could hear an occasional hiss, and from time to time a small bubble appeared. But the areas of greatest heat made up only a small fraction of the total area. Elsewhere, there was only enough heat to make things warm—too warm for her hand, but not hot enough for cooking. The aberrations of the mirror were too great. Exact focusing was impossible.

There was no method of containing the heat radiated away, either.

She experimented with the signal mirror, holding it above the stick and trying to reflect a few of the scattered rays back on their target.

No dice.

The thing couldn't be done. The reflective area was too small for cooking. In addition, the single sheet of metal could only be deformed along one axis at a time. The reflector was, in effect, part of a cylinder and was focused along an extended locus rather than upon a single point. What she needed was a reflector shaped something like the end of an egg.

A paraboloid.

She sat contemplating the device. "Useless pig trough!" she said. She dug the stick into the sand. "Science triumphs again!"

"Well," commented the voice of Reason, "what did you expect? Things are always more complex than they look. And that goes for the simple technologies also."

It would have been more satisfying just to throw the thing away, as she had the bow. But instead, she lifted the piece of metal carefully from the sand. She took it over to a flat plank, and hammered a notch in the edge of the metal, using the chisel point of the nail. She positioned the sheet so the notched edge was even with the side of the plank before placing a piece of board on top.

She stood on the board.

Gripping the protruding flap of sheet metal with a folded piece of cedar bark—to protect her fingers from the razorlike edge—she gave a hard, upward pull, tearing the sheet in half.

The newly shorn edge, as expected, began at the place where she'd notched the sheet. It followed the contour of the board she'd been standing on for most of its length, curving outward only at the end.

Ignoring the imperfection of it, she took the two half sheets and tore each of them into six smaller pieces, using the same technique as before. When she was done, there were twelve long triangles.

The pointed ends curled, like springs.

She straightened these out, and punched a single hole in each of the twelve triangles, right at the apex.

With the chisel nail, she drilled a hole into the end grain of a branch and pinned all twelve of the metal triangles in place, driving a tapered twig through the twelve openings in the metal and down into the single hole at the end of the branch.

She hammered the twig deeper into the hole. This held everything tight. Then she arranged the triangles in a pinwheel. Taking this somewhat bizarre creation into the middle of the beach, she planted it firmly in the sand. It stood shoulder high, looking like a small windmill, except the blades were tilted toward the sun.

Bending each blade into a smooth curve with her fingers, she soon destroyed all resemblance to a windmill. The thing now looked like a large metal flower: a tulip. The petals of the tulip were silvery inside; they glinted in the sun. The outside was a patchwork of lettering, left over from the tulip's former existence as a container. Across one petal, in large red letters, was the word DANGER!

Smiling at this, she went to find a wooden sliver of the correct size.

The sun was still shining when she returned. With the splinter, she began probing the reflector's interior. As it approached the center, the little spear of cedar glowed with concentrated light. The glare was so intense she had to slit her eyes against it, and even then it was painful.

Other than this, nothing happened.

Perhaps the main area of focus was farther down.

She probed deeper, squinting against the light. It happened so quickly she had no time to react. As the point of the sliver descended, there came a sizzling sound, and the inside of the reflector filled with smoke. Instinctively, she shut her eyes, for in the center the smoke glowed with a ferocious white light. There was a hollow *poof.* An instant later she felt a stinging sensation on the tip of her finger where it held the sliver.

"Ouch!"

The remains of the sliver now lay on the sand, blackened and smoking.

Save for the portion held between her fingers, ignition had evidently been instantaneous along its entire length. Which was understandable. All of the wood inside the reflector had been preheated, and the explosive puffing sound must have been what firemen refer to as flashover: particles of smoke, catching all at once.

DANGER!

"I'm going to have to find a longer sliver," she mused.

It was difficult to believe—this silly-looking tulip actually worked!

She was collecting the kindling and the firewood when she had to stop, look back, and assure herself that the thing truly existed.

Out on the sand, the reflector seemed more like a tulip than ever, swaying on the end of its stalk in the wind.

* * * * *

As must have occurred thousands of years before, when the first hearth-keeper tended the first fire, there came a new cohesion to the various tasks of the day. Her interactions with this creature called fire were akin to those of a marriage—at least in some ways. In others, it was like caring for a child. She made offerings of dry wood, and in return the fire cooked her food, helped in making tools, kept rain and cold and darkness at bay. But a fire needed more than fuel. It needed guarding, and this confined most of her other activities to one location. No longer was it possible for her to sleep in one place, store food in another, keep salvage in a third, and do her crafting of tools and artifacts in yet another spot a hundred meters away. Fire was a magnet to all of these things. There was a reason why the word "hearth" was a synonym for "home." Fire demanded that it be the focus of all activity. Not only that; it was sedentary. You couldn't pick it up and carry it around with you, as you could a child. And you could never, never allow it to walk on its own.

That was another of its demands. The selection of a *place* had to be made with the requirements of fire in mind.

She chose the ledge at the base of the pinnacle, which proved to be nearly ideal. Burning on a rocky surface, her fire could never creep out of control. It was also above the level of the sand, which had been a constant nuisance before, always showing up where it wasn't wanted. A meter and a half away stood the divan-shaped rock. The pool of water at its lower end now did double duty: she could keep clams in it as before or, by dropping in fire-heated stones, convert the hollow in the rock into a cauldron of boiling water.

Even when the tide was in, and cold salt water filled the space between her cooking rock and the pinnacle, there was no inconvenience. She could hop from rock to ledge and back again with little risk. Access to the mainland was along the ledge and through the arching tunnel of logs. The tunnel was much too drafty and damp to convert into a shelter for herself, but it made a good shelter for the main supply of firewood. The larger chunks weren't hurt by an occasional drop of water; only the tinder and kindling needed to be kept completely dry.

Her primary shelter was constructed to seaward of the fire, where the ledge was at its widest. Here, the wall of the pinnacle was slightly concave, providing an overhanging roof. Between the roof and the ledge she erected a palisade of branches, wedging them in place, top and bottom. Crossways to the vertical branches, she interlaced a set of horizontal ones, to form a grille. To this she secured an overlapping thatch of umbrella leaves from the marsh, starting at the bottom, as in shingling a roof, and tying the leaves stem uppermost to the frame with strips of cedar bark.

When they were all in place, the leaves looked like the scales of a large green fish.

Not long after, a brief but torrential rain disclosed a flaw in her arrangements. The rain, driven against the cliff by the wind, flowed down the rock and under the moss caulking she'd used, relentlessly cascading along the inside of the frame.

The remedy came about through the kindly assistance of the fire. She took a flat stone, heated it, and placed lumps of pitch on top. When melted, the pitch ran like honey, and she was able to glue strips of umbrella leaf directly to the rock with it. The pitch also made a watertight seal. The strips of leaf overlapped the shelter wall like lengths of flashing[1] at the peak of a roof, and when the next rainstorm came, the shelter proved at last to be worthy of the name.

Still, refinements were needed. Her little house gaped at both ends. When the wind was from the wrong direction, smoke from the fire poured through the structure as if it were a chimney. She put

[1] flashing: sheet metal used to waterproof roof valleys or hips

There was a reason why the word "hearth" was a synonym for "home." Fire demanded that it be the focus of all activity.

an end to this by building a removable hatch to block off the southern end of the shelter. This cut down on the draft, allowing her to enjoy the heat of the fire through the opening on the landward side without suffering the smoke. Having designed the hatch so it would open easily, she retained access to the area beyond, even during those times when the beach was under water.

Access was important, for her supplies of food were stored along the outer ledge—or, more accurately, above the ledge. At first glance it would have seemed a curious arrangement, this net of woven vines hanging against the cliff. It was her larder, held in place with strips of bark which had been glued directly to the rock with pitch. A bonnet of leaves protected her provender from sun and rain, and the whole affair was reachable only by standing on tiptoe.

The animals responsible for these elaborate precautions had made their presence known during the first week. Her inventory of clams in the storage pool kept running short, and at first she suspected the gulls of gliding in and stealing from her when she wasn't looking. It soon became apparent, however, that the clams were disappearing only at night, when the gulls weren't flying. This coincided with the time when small, handlike prints were being left in the sand. There were new ones each morning.

Evidently, she was dealing with a family of raccoons.

It was probably more of a game for them in the beginning. Had the animals been able to open the shells on their own, they would have cleaned her out then and there, instead of contenting themselves with two or three a night.

With the appearance of *cooked* clams, however—clams that had been steamed, taken from their shells, dehydrated, and smoked—the game began to be played in earnest. There were four of these bandits, and they grew amazingly bold. Even in daylight, she saw rounded, bearlike forms the size of a terrier ghosting about. She felt under siege. She couldn't let anything edible out of her sight; either it would be gone when she turned around, or else she'd find herself facing an obstinate raccoon—eye on food and reluctant to give ground. There was a large one in particular, whom she named Scipio Africanus, after an ancient Roman general. Scipio would hiss and emit throaty, quacking sounds. But he was not a very brave general, and always led the retreat whenever she advanced and used her voice.

What was puzzling was that the raccoons continued to steal, even after the meaty items were placed beyond their reach. She'd dug up a number of sword ferns, washed the roots, sliced them into chunks, and roasted the chunks like potatoes, in jackets of seaweed. Cooked in this way, the root of the sword fern was perfectly good to eat. It had a pleasant, nutty flavor, and was a welcome addition to a diet that had formerly consisted of almost pure protein.

For some reason, the normally carnivorous raccoons seemed to have a taste for it also; as a result, the pieces of broiled sword fern root soon joined the smoked clams in the aerial larder.

After a week of privation, the act of storing food was a marvel to her. Fire, shelter, food—all were luxuries now. True, she'd have given almost anything for a set of fresh clothing, a hot bath, a clean towel, or a hairbrush. But for all that, her spirits rose. Even the onset of rainy weather had little effect on her growing optimism. She had her umbrella-leaf hat to protect her head against the rain, and she had her warm jacket, and her fire, and plenty to eat, and a dry place to sleep. And sooner or later, help would come.

In the middle of the second week, when the shelter was finished, she went and retrieved the raft at the western end of the beach. Ever since that frustrating afternoon of the broken cord, it had lain undisturbed beneath a pile of stones—a crude method of mooring, but effective. Off-loading the stone ballast, she took the raft and made a voyage with it to Whale Rock.

It was eerie, setting foot on that fateful chunk of stone for the second time. She found the scraped place among the acorn barnacles where the little death trap of a raft had been launched ten days before. Higher up, where there were no barnacles, the marks left by the plane were more difficult to see, having been darkened by repeated lavings of the tide. The shards of metal, however, were still bright. She recovered every scrap, and when she was through, the pocket of the jacket had a definite heft to it. Last of all, she took the board she was using as a paddle and pried the aluminum cap from its knob of rock. Holding the metal shell up to the light, she could see no openings. It would make a good cup.

The purpose of the expedition had been to gather aluminum scrap. With a hundred grams or so at her disposal, she might be able to melt the aluminum down and cast herself a spoon or a fork. The idea had a certain elegance. Imagine having such an artifact! It would be a fascinating memento, and would prove just how much a person could do under primitive conditions.

Her mind was filled with pleasant speculation about this. First, she imagined an open mold of fired clay, within which the aluminum could be melted. Then another idea attracted her. If the mold itself could be placed in the fire to melt down the chips of metal, wouldn't it also be possible to make a *crucible*[2] of clay? There would be a crust of oxide and other impurities floating on the surface of the molten metal. If one used a separate container for the melting, all the dross could be removed first, and only the pure metal would go into the mold.

With great enthusiasm, she searched the face of the bluff for a usable deposit of

[2] crucible: a vessel used for melting substances that won't melt without a high degree of heat

clay. The project, however, went no further than this, for during her search she uncovered something far more valuable than potter's clay.

It was a stone. A fairly average stone, perhaps two kilograms in weight: flat and more or less trapezoidal in shape. The thing was valueless by itself, but over the years it had managed to stay in precisely the right position while the root of a tree grew around it. She worked with her chisel nail to cut the root at the treeward end, leaving a handle still attached to the stone.

It was a Neanderthal's dream—the perfect implement for bashing things.

Stone and root were united inseparably. The hatchet-shaped head was not the right material for fashioning an edge, but this didn't matter. She used the thing as a maul for making firewood, and in this role alone, the Bashing Tool, as she came to call it, saved her hours of work every day. The time spent in food gathering was also shortened. Instead of using a stick to laboriously scrape a trench around the base of a sword fern, and then severing the innumerable rootlets from the main root with a small, hand-held stone, she could now flail away with Bashing Tool, accomplishing as much in ten minutes as had taken forty, earlier.

She had by now decided that the making of an aluminum artifact could not be justified, however appealing the idea might be. She didn't need a spoon. The energy spent in making such a thing would be an investment in pride, not in practicality. It would be a foolish bauble for show and tell: a waste of valuable time.

Rather than experiment with crucibles and molds, she built a squat framework of wood. It was shaped like a bird cage. The rounded dome reached no higher than her knee, but it still took a great deal of work. The interlaced branches had to be securely lashed together, for if the device were to function, the joins needed to resist a crushing action similar to that of a powerful vise.

Beneath the dome went a stout, removable floor, also made of branches. None of the openings in either the dome or the floor of the cage was large enough to permit the escape of anything larger than a table tennis ball.

Next, she cut a doorway in the side of the structure, about twenty centimeters in width. Across the opening she suspended a small door, hinged at the top with loops made from a scrap of barbed wire. The door was counterbalanced. When pushed from the outside, the door opened inward and one could reach inside the cage. Withdraw the hand, and the stone weight of the counterbalance automatically swung the door shut.

A creature pushing from the inside would not be able to get out.

There remained one problem: What would be the best way of lowering the trap into the water?

In the end she gave up the idea of a line entirely. Crab fishermen used a line because they needed an up-haul adaptable to various depths. If she decided on a

depth in advance, she could then use a rigid up-haul, such as a long branch. This could be fastened securely to the top of the cage and would float upright in the water, with the top just below tide level. In this way, the action of the waves wouldn't be transmitted to the tethered structure on the bottom. A wooden bobber could be tied to the end of the branch with a length of vine. The bobber would then serve to mark the position of the trap.

She chose a depth of three fathoms (three times the length of her outstretched arms) and once the trap was in place, the wooden marker appeared on the surface of the bay at every low tide. Daily, she paddled out, positioned the raft above the bobber, and reached down into the water to grasp the end of the submerged pole. Pulling in the trap, hand over hand, was always a time of suspense. Ashore, there was water in the cooking pool, and a pile of stones ready to heat, and a large reserve of firewood—all in the hope of finding a Dungeness crab in the trap. She could see the way it would happen, down below. The creature would sidle into the current, following the scent of the bait inside the cage. He would crawl up the framework, exploring here and there. Gripping with his pincers. Pushing. Until at last a section of the barrier gave way...

But the trap continued to come up empty, except for the ballast of stones and the bait of crushed barnacles. Every day she went out in the raft to check the trap. Disappointed, she would replace the old bait with freshly broken barnacles and return the cage to the bottom.

* * * * *

She dreamt of a cabin built of logs. It rested on pilings, sunk vertically into the marsh so that the cabin stood high in the air, as if on stilts. This was a protection against . . . some threat or other. She couldn't remember what.

From the front door, a gangway angled toward the beach, and in the dream she walked down the gangway. Winter had come, and it was cold. She had to push her way through heavy snow as she went, and the gangway rebounded underfoot like a weighted trampoline. When she got to the beach, she began digging for clams. The sand underneath the snow was hard with frost and mixed with the ashes of an ancient fire. Clams were nowhere to be found. There were only the clocks. Hundreds upon hundreds of rusted clocks.

She was awakened from the dream by the sniffing of an animal. Opening her eyes, she found Scipio Africanus peeking in at her, his masked face appearing just above the contour of the ledge.

"Good morning, Scipio," she said.

At the sound of her voice, the raccoon vanished. There was a scurrying noise from below, and after a moment, Scipio Africanus could be seen galumphing along the beach, followed by two of his cohorts. They presently disappeared among the driftwood.

Raccoons were mostly nocturnal, but there was only an hour or two of true darkness here during the summer solstice. They wouldn't have enough darkness in which to do their foraging and would have to go out whether it was daytime or not.

The sky, she noted, was its customary gray this morning. But at least it wasn't raining. She got up and removed the small lean-to of planks that sheltered the fire. There was nothing showing on the surface; only a fine powder of ash, holding the shape of what had been pieces of firewood hours earlier. She held out a hand to find the warmth, then bent over and breathed on it. The ash disintegrated to reveal a bed of coals below. She tucked a few wisps of dry grass among the coals and, when this flared, added a handful of twigs. Broken pieces of stick followed the twigs, then still larger pieces, until a merry blaze licked upward against the rock.

She warmed herself, and steam rose from her clothing as the dampness of the night was driven off. The process was speeded by taking off the jacket and drying it separately. The same for the shoes and stockings. She sat and toasted the soles of her feet before the fire while the stockings hung on a stick nearby. For perhaps the fourth time in as many days she considered finding a block of wood, so she'd be able to sit at the fire with greater dignity and comfort. And just as she had on the other occasions, she decided against it. The ledge was already crowded; a stool-sized block would merely be another thing for her to trip over. She'd fall in the drink some evening when the tide was in—though, come to think of it, the possibility that this would happen over the next few days was exactly zero. The neaps[3] had arrived: the tides were neither very high nor very low. If she'd tumbled off the ledge last night she would have hit dry sand, for at high tide the water hadn't even gone as far as the foot of Cooking Rock.

Her mind shifted from the trivial to the practical. The subject of the tide had

[3] neaps: tides of minimal range that occur at the first and third quarters of the moon

brought up a matter of more immediate concern. For the next several days she'd have to depend entirely on the reserves of meat in the larder. (Unless, of course, a crab turned up in the trap.) The clam beds would still be covered at low tide, so she wouldn't be able . . .

So *that* was it!

Her memory of the dream had begun to fade, but she could still remember the essentials. Winter, a cabin on stilts, no clams. There were a few disturbing elements, but these were illogical and could be dismissed. The source of the whole thing was the fact that the neaps had arrived and she wouldn't be digging any more clams for a while. That was all the dream was saying. The brooding, frightening aspects had no meaning. None at all.

"And anyway," she reminded herself, "I've got a treat for breakfast this morning." The evening before, she'd picked a handful of dandelion buds—not the flowers themselves, but the small, soft lumps that showed just before the flowers opened. The recipe for dandelion omelette involved such things as eggs, milk, onions, butter, salt, pepper—and an omelette pan—none of which she possessed. The important thing to note, of course, was that dandelion buds were *edible*. She would just have to do without the rest of it.

In preparation, she scooped a mound of coals into a hollow in the rock. She poured a little water into her aircraft-aluminum cup, then bedded the cup among the coals. When the water boiled, she dumped in the buds and covered the cup with a lid of bark to trap the steam. The cup simmered atop the coals.

It would have been pleasant to be able to brew some tea. She knew where there was a stand of Labrador tea—at least the plants *looked* like Labrador tea. But that was the problem. There was a variety known as false Labrador tea, very similar in appearance. Make an infusion of one, and you had an enjoyable drink with breakfast. Brew up with the leaves of the other and you had a cup of poison.

She improvised a song about it:

Poison, poison, drink it up!
Chill of winter in the cup!

And there it was again. That silly dream about clocks and winter! What was the matter with her? The whole thing had been ridiculous. A cabin on *stilts,* for heaven's sake!

Irritated with herself, she put on her shoes and went to get a leaf-wrapped breakfast ration from the larder. When she returned, she lifted the piece of bark to see how the dandelions were doing. The water had turned slightly greenish, but when she prodded the buds with a splinter they still seemed underdone. She put the cover back and chewed on a piece of dehydrated clam.

Snow on the ground and nothing to eat.

Dreams had a crazy logic of their own at times. Take the idea of a cabin. If she were to stay here through the winter, that was what she would need: a small cabin. A rocky ledge and a campfire wouldn't do—not at fifty-three degrees north latitude—not with twenty hours of darkness out of every twenty-four during the months of December and January. In addition to the cabin she'd need enormous supplies of firewood, properly broken up. She'd need winter clothing. Bedding. Food—four or five months' worth of food.

It was quite impossible. She lacked the resources, the equipment, the knowledge. Above all, she lacked the *time.*

A solitary human equipped with Stone Age tools would not be able to accomplish all that needed to be done. A group of people might succeed. A dozen pairs of hands: chopping, clearing, carrying, weaving, fishing, trapping, skinning, tanning, smoking, digging, building.

Eighteen, twenty hours a day.

A dozen pairs of hands to raise the shelter and break up fuel for the fire—and all would share the shelter and the fire. With only one person, there would be nearly as much work, as far as shelter and heating were concerned, but only one pair of hands, not twelve.

Survive the winter alone? She wouldn't have a chance. The clams were only going to last through September, maybe into October, but after that?

She lifted the cover of bark from the aluminum cup. The water had mostly evaporated, leaving the dandelions lying dark and limp at the bottom. She speared one of them with her sliver, and blew on it. The yellow part of the flower could be seen inside.

Not too bad, she concluded, taking a bite.

Tangy.

They had a flavor similar to that of spinach . . . could have used a little salt. She'd try simmering them in sea water next time.

* * * *

To escape before the winter comes, Elena decides to construct a boat. After experiencing several unfortunate accidents while designing and building the boat, Elena eventually paddles back to safety.

What do you like best about the character Elena? Explain why you feel the way you do.

Fire is essential to Elena's survival. Explain why, using examples from the story.

What kinds of things does Elena know that are crucial to her survival? Where do you think she got that knowledge?

WRITE Imagine that Elena just arrived home after spending months on a deserted island. Write a list of questions you would like to ask her.

An Interview

DAVID MATHIESON

Writer Ilene Cooper had the opportunity to discuss writing with David Mathieson.

Ms. Cooper: Since you have experienced circumstances similar to those Elena experienced, why did you use a girl for a hero and a third-person narrator rather than a first-person narrator in the novel?

Mr. Mathieson: In telling the story, a writer sometimes doesn't know why things are being done a certain way until afterwards. At the start, I just thought I was helping to redress the disparity between the number of male Crusoes in fiction and the number of female Crusoes. But of course it goes deeper than that. My hero has more obstacles to overcome than the average Crusoe—no tools, no food, not even any water to begin with—plus another and more deadly barrier the males do not have to face: that of cultural expectation. A young woman is not "supposed" to be as good as a man in making tools and building a boat and surviving in the wild. Elena Bradbury must violate this expectation just to stay alive. And having done so, she is able to see her own life pattern and her culture with new eyes. It is a useful insight. It gives her the chance to save herself a second time, after returning to civilization. In truth, it just felt better, somehow, to write of Elena as "she" rather than as "I."

with the Author:

Ms. Cooper: Why do you think young people enjoy reading realistic novels concerning people in conflict with nature since so few of them will ever face such circumstances? What do you think young people can learn from reading Trial by Wilderness?

Mr. Mathieson: Personally, I think one's interest in a story has little to do with the likelihood of experiencing the thing itself. A child of five can often enjoy a story about rabbits. Older people still like to read about spies and youthful romance and, sometimes, even about dragons. Yet the notion persists that a story, in order to interest a teenager, has to be about high school. On the contrary! That period in a person's life is more, not less, oriented toward the game of "What If."

A word about humans in conflict with nature. One way of looking at *Trial by Wilderness* is to see it in terms of a hero struggling against a single adversary: the nonhuman universe. This is the viewpoint of our culture. Nature is perceived as being in a power struggle with us. As if nature cared!

For Elena, transported back into the Stone Age, nature wears another face—that of indifference. Far from being a malevolent opponent, nature, except for an occasional creature, doesn't even know we're there. Elena survives her trial not because she "wins" against a cunning adversary, but because she's bright enough to face things as they are, not as they are culturally perceived. The threat is impersonal, if deadly. By facing that, Elena, Modern Teenager, becomes Elena, Savage of the Stone Age. Thereafter, she has the fun of putting her intelligence to work in a good cause: that of survival. And that is what I hope a young reader might take from this book. The heroine learns to use a kind of thinking that was needed in the Stone Age—and is needed still. The real wilderness is the one to which Elena Bradbury returns, the one she has lived in all her life.

Ms. Cooper: What advice do you have for young people who want to write about their experiences "in the wilderness"?

Mr. Mathieson: If you want to write about anything, don't let anyone stop you.

AWARD-WINNING AUTHOR

Chesapeake

by James A. Michener

In 1583, Pentaquod, a peace-loving Susquehannock living on the Susquehanna River, argued with the warriors and council of chiefs about their continuing war with neighboring tribes. Soon thereafter, Pentaquod escaped in a canoe, heading toward what is now called the Eastern Shore of the Chesapeake Bay, where he hoped to find a safe place to live.

When Pentaquod steered toward the Eastern River he was confronted by the tree-covered island he had seen from a distance, for it dominated the entrance. Poised between two headlands, one reaching down from the north, the other up from the south, it served as a welcoming sentinel and seemed to proclaim: All who enter this river find joy.

illustrations by S. D. Schindler

The island was low-lying, but its stately trees rose so high and so unevenly that they created an impression of elevation. Oak, maple, sweetgum, chestnut, birch, towering pines and iridescent holly grew so thickly that the earth itself could scarcely be seen, and it was these trees which protected Pentaquod after he dragged his canoe ashore and collapsed from lack of food and sleep.

When he awoke he became aware of one of earth's most pleasing sensations: he was lying on a bed of pine needles, soft and aromatic, and when he looked upward he could not see the sky, for the pines grew so straight and tall that their branches formed a canopy which sunlight could not penetrate. The covering gave him confidence, and before he resumed his sleep he muttered, "This is a good place, this place of trees."

He was awakened by a sound he could not immediately identify. It was warlike and terrifying, coming at him from a spot directly overhead. It echoed ominously: *"Kraannk, kraannk, kraannk!"*

In fear he leaped to his feet, but as he stood there under the tall trees, preparing to defend himself, he burst into laughter at his foolishness, for when he listened to the cry again, he remembered where he had heard it. *"Kraannk, kraannk!"* It was Fishing-long-legs, one of the most ingratiating birds of the rivers and marshlands.

There it stood, knee-deep in water: tall, thin, awkward, many hands high, with extremely long legs and rumpled white head. Its most prominent feature was a long yellowish bill, which it kept pointed downward at the water. Infrequently, when Pentaquod was young, this voracious fisherman had visited the Susquehanna to feed, wading tiptoe among the reeds, and often Pentaquod, while playing, had tried to imitate its movements.

Now Pentaquod stood silent, watching the bird with affection as it stalked slowly, clumsily along the muddy shore, and out into the water until its bony knees were submerged. Then, with a dart of its long neck so swift that Pentaquod could not follow, it speared its sharp beak into the water and caught a fish. Raising its head, it tossed the fish in the air, catching it as it descended. With a gulp, it swallowed the fish, and Pentaquod could see the progress of the meal as it slowly passed down the extended gullet. For some time he stayed in the shadows, watching as the bird caught fish after fish. He must have made some sound, for the bird turned suddenly toward him, ran a few ungainly steps along the shore, then rose in slow, extended, lovely flight. *"Kraannk, kraannk!"* it cried as it passed overhead.

Knowing that there would be ample food, if he could but catch it, Pentaquod pulled his canoe farther inland, hiding it among the oaks and maples which lined the shore, for he knew that he must explore this island quickly. And as he moved among the trees and came to a meadow, he heard the comforting cry so familiar in his days along the great river. *"Bob-white! Bob-white!"* Now the call came from his left, then from a clump of grass to his right and sometimes from a spot almost under his feet, but always it was as clear and distinct as if an uncle who could whistle had been standing at his side. *"Bob-white!"* It was the call of the quail, that sly bird with the brown-and-white head. Of all the birds that flew, this was the best eating, and if this island held a multitude, Pentaquod could not only survive on his fish but eat like a chieftain with his quail.

With extreme caution, he started inland, noticing everything, aware that his life might depend upon the carefulness of his observation. With every step he found only reassurance and never a sign of danger: nut trees laden with midsummer shells not yet ripe; droppings of rabbits, and the signs that foxes lived here, and the location of brambled berry bushes, and the woody nests of eagles, and the honeysuckle twisting among the lower branches of the cedar trees.

It was an island rich in signs and promises. On such an island a man with intelligence could live well, if he worked many hours each day, but in spite of its favorable omens Pentaquod was not ready to commit himself to it, for he could not tell whether it was populated by other people, or what its temperament might be in a storm.

He kept probing, and satisfied himself that it was more extensive west to east than it was north to south. A deep bay cutting in from the east almost met a stream in the south, nearly severing the island; the eastern portion of this division was markedly richer than the western. He walked beneath majestic oaks until he reached the eastern tip, and there he stood, dumbfounded, for wherever he looked he saw a grand expanse of water forming itself into bays and creeks and coves and even small rivers for as far as he could see. And along the shores of these varied waters rose land of the most inviting nature: at times broad fields, at other times gently rising land covered with trees even taller than those on the island, and everywhere the impression of opulence, and quietness, and gentle living.

It was the most congenial place he had ever seen. He judged that in a storm this sleeping body of water might have the capacity for considerable turbulence, and he was certain that before he could possess any part of this wonderland he would have to contend with its present owners, who might be just as cantankerous as the Susquehannocks, but of one thing he was certain: along this splendid river he wished to spend the rest of his life.

He had no sooner come to this decision than a snorting kind of sound attracted his attention, and he turned to look behind him, among the trees, and there stood a huge-eyed doe with two brown-speckled fawns. The three deer halted in rigid attention, staring at this stranger. Then the inquisitive doe cocked her head, and this almost undetectable action released the fawns, and they began to move cautiously toward Pentaquod, little deer on unsteady legs exploring their new world.

When they had moved quite close to Pentaquod, their suspicious mother gave a cough, and the babies leaped sideways, ran in distracted circles, then stopped. Seeing that nothing harmful had happened, they moved back toward Pentaquod, lifting their spindly legs in delightful awkwardness, probing with their great eyes.

"Heh!" Pentaquod whispered. The fawns stared at him, and one moved closer.

"Heh!" The foremost fawn cocked its little head, waited, then resumed its approach. When it had come so close that Pentaquod could have reached out and touched it, the doe gave a warning snort, leaped aside, raised her white tail and darted back into the woods. The trailing fawn did likewise, but the one closest to Pentaquod became confused, or stubborn, and did not follow the others to safety. It simply stood there, staring at this stranger, and after a moment the mother returned in a series of fine leaps, swept past the inquisitive fawn and lured it into the trees.

Fish and quail and deer! Pentaquod thought. And if one finds seed, maize and probably pumpkins. Turkeys too, if I guess right. And not many people, judging so far. This is the right place.

He returned to his canoe, caught some fish for supper, made a small fire and, with a large handful of blackberries to accent the smoking fish,

fed well. He slept well, too, except that long before dawn he heard in the sky overhead the cry he would always associate with his first exploration of this river: *"Kraannk, kraannk!"* It was Fishing-long-legs coming back to patrol the shore.

In the days that followed, Pentaquod explored every corner of the island and concluded that whereas others might know of it, they certainly did not think enough of it to build their homes here, for he could find no sign of habitation. And so far as he could ascertain, not even the meadows that appeared at curious intervals among the trees had ever grown corn or squash, and on none of the headlands facing the island could he detect any indication of either homes or cultivated fields.

This did not disturb him. If land as congenial as this existed upriver, there would be no reason for people to settle near the mouth; it would be much safer inland. Storms coming off the bay would be diminished and distances across water shortened. Perhaps the land would be richer, too, and there might be other advantages which he could not envisage. But on one point he was satisfied: life here would be good.

For the time being he quit his speculations, accepting the boon he had been granted. He built himself a small, well-hidden wigwam inland from the northern shore, using bent saplings for the frame and abundant river grasses for the roof. He found it so easy to catch fish that he did not even have to go after them in his canoe: the large brown-speckled ones with the blunt snouts swam up to him determined to be caught, and whereas he had been unable yet to trap any of the numerous bob-whites, he had shot one deer, which would feed him for some time. A fox strolled by one afternoon, and one night a skunk made things odorous.

He rather liked the smell of skunk, if it didn't come too close. It reminded him of the woods which he had trailed as a boy, of cold autumn nights, and the snugness of winter. It was the smell of nature, heavy and pervasive: it assured him that life in all its complexity was thriving. He had rarely seen a skunk, and he saw none now, but he was pleased that they shared the island with him.

It was his friend Fishing-long-legs who introduced him to one of the strangest experiences of the eastern shore. The blue-feathered bird with the long beak had flown in one evening with its accustomed croaking cry and was now probing the shallow waters along the shore, ignoring the man to whom it had become accustomed. Suddenly it shot its fierce bill deep into the water and came up with a struggling something Pentaquod had not seen before.

It was larger than a man's hand, seemed to have numerous legs that squirmed in the fading sunlight and was brown-green in color. The bird was obviously pleased with its catch, for it threw it in the air, severed it with one snap of its beak, gulped down one half, allowing the other to fall into the water. The swallowed portion was so big and with so many protruding legs that it required time and effort to maneuver it down the long gullet, but once this was accomplished, the bird retrieved and ate the other half. Having enjoyed a feast of this kind, it did not bother with mere fish. With a short run it rose in the air, uttered its mournful croaking and soared away.

Pentaquod went to where the bird had feasted, searching for clues. There were none. The bird had eaten everything. Next day he went there with his fishing line, but caught nothing. However, some days later he watched as Fishing-long-legs caught another of these morsels, enjoying it even more than before, and Pentaquod crept close to see if he could determine what it was that the bird was eating. He discovered nothing he had not seen before: bigger than a man's hand, many legs, brown-green in color, so soft that it could easily be bitten in half.

He was determined to solve this mystery, and the first clue came one day while he walked along the southern shore of his island: washed up on the beach and obviously dead lay a creature much like the one the bird had been catching. It was the right size; it had many feet, or what passed for feet; and it was brown-green, with touches of blue underneath. But there the similarity stopped, for this dead animal was encased in a shell so hard that no bird could eat it. Also, its two front legs had formidable jaws with serrated, heavy teeth which could, if the animal were alive, inflict substantial harm.

How could the bird cut this shell in half? Pentaquod asked himself, and then, an even more perplexing question: And how could he swallow it if he did? He tapped the hard substance and knew there was no possible way for that bird to swallow that shell.

For ten days he tried to catch one of these strange creatures on his line and failed, and yet twice in that period he saw Fishing-long-legs catch one, cut it in half and force the food down its long neck. In frustration, he realized that this was a mystery he was not destined to solve.

He did, however, discover two facts about his home that disturbed him. The more he explored the two deep cuts which came close to bisecting the island, the more he realized that some day the arms must meet, cutting the island in half, and if this could be done, why might there not evolve other cuts to fragment it further?

His second discovery came as the consequence of a sudden and devastating storm. The midpoint of summer had passed and life on the island had been a growing joy; this was really an almost ideal place to live, and he supposed that later on, when he had traveled upriver to establish contact with whatever tribes occupied the area, he would become a member of their unit. But for the time being he was content with his solitary paradise.

It had been a hot day, with heavy moist air, and in the late afternoon a bank of towering clouds gathered in the southwest, on the opposite side of the bay. With a swiftness that he had never witnessed in the north this congregation of blackness started rushing eastward, and even though the sun remained shining over Pentaquod's head, it was obvious that a storm of some magnitude must soon break.

Still the sun shone; still the sky remained clear. Deer moved deeper into the forest and shore birds retreated to their nests, although the only sign of danger was that galloping cloud bank approaching the bay.

Pentaquod watched its arrival. It struck the distant western shore with enormous fury, turning what had been placid water into turbulent, crested waves leaping and tossing white spume into the air. The clouds moved so swiftly that they required only moments to cross the bay, their progress marked by the wildly leaping waves.

With the storm came an immense amount of rain, falling in sheets slanting eastward. For it to speed over the last portion of the bay took only a fragment of time, and then the storm was striking Pentaquod, descending on him in a fury he had not witnessed before. Great jagged flashes of lightning tore through the sky, followed almost instantly by shattering claps of thunder; there was no echo, for the world was drowned in rain. Winds of extraordinary power ripped along the surface of the bay, lashing it into waves of pounding force.

But Pentaquod was not afraid of the storm, and next morning, when it had passed and he surveyed his island, he did not find the damage extensive. He had seen storms before, rather violent ones which swept down the river valley of his home, and although this one had been swifter and more thunderous, it was merely an exaggeration of what he had long known. The trees knocked down were larger than any he had seen go down in the north, and that was about it. If storms on the island were no worse than this, he could abide them.

What was it, then, that disturbed him, causing him to wonder about his new home? After his cursory inspection of the island, and after satisfying himself that his yellow canoe had survived, he behaved like any prudent husbandman and started checking the general situation, desiring to see if any animals had been killed or streams diverted, and as he came to a spot on the northwestern tip of the island, he noticed that the storm, and more particularly the pounding waves, had carried away a substantial portion of the shore. Tall pines and oaks which had marked this point had been undercut and now lay sprawled in the water side by side, like the bodies of dead warriors after battle.

Wherever he went along the western shore he saw this same loss of land. The tragedy of the storm was not that it had knocked down a few trees, for more would grow, and not that it had killed a few fish, for others would breed, but that it had eaten away a substantial edge of the island, and this was a permanent loss. Pentaquod, looking at the destruction, decided that he would abandon this island, congenial though it was, and look farther inland.

Would you like to live on the island that Pentaquod discovered? Tell why you feel the way you do.

Why do you think Pentaquod decides to abandon the island?

What techniques does James Michener use to make the story seem real to the reader? Explain your answer, using examples from the story.

WRITE Do you think the decision Pentaquod made to leave the island was a wise one? Write him a letter giving your opinion about his situation.

James A. MICHENER

Conversation with James A. Michener

by Rolando Hinojosa-Smith

Novelist Rolando Hinojosa-Smith, left, Director of the Texas Center for Writers at the University of Texas, and best-selling author James A. Michener discuss important aspects of writing.

Mr. Hinojosa-Smith: An outstanding feature of your writing is the sense of place and time, the specifics and the details. Let me ask you this: did you visit or revisit the area before you wrote *Chesapeake*, and did you take the route that Pentaquod took?

Mr. Michener: Yes. I can say specifically that, except for my writing about the moon and the men on the moon, I have been to every place that I have written about. I have gotten to know the places very well. Rolando, if you wanted me to write about the little town in which I grew up, which I know intimately, I wouldn't dare do it unless I went back—to remind myself of how much I don't remember. I never write without going back to places I already know.

Mr. Hinojosa-Smith: There is something about going back that I also find necessary. I need to be there to trigger this mechanism for details. How do you collect details about a place?
Mr. Michener: When I decide to write about an area, my wife goes ahead of me to find a place to live. Then I go there, and we maintain a very low profile for the first five or six months. I want to be there, I want to read the morning papers, I want to listen to the weather reports. I want to find out what's happening in politics. I want to go to the local grocery store and to the local restaurant so that I get a complete feel of the place. My wife is a very gregarious person—she loves people and she loves to talk, converse. And during that time she's making friends, so that by the time the six months is up, we are as ingrained in that situation as if we'd lived there for the last ten years.

Mr. Hinojosa-Smith: That's an interesting process.
Mr. Michener: And it works. She meets people and brings them home. She tells me I ought to talk with this person or that person. We go out, we go to the restaurants, we meet strangers who become friends. We find out what it's really like.

Mr. Hinojosa-Smith: You learn specific details—weather, travel, living conditions, people's thinking. So when natives of an area read about the area, they say, "Well, this person really knows what he's talking about."
Mr. Michener: That is what I try to get. I would hate for anybody to say that Jim Michener flew in on an airplane and stayed one weekend and then wrote about us. They cannot say that, ever.

Mr. Hinojosa-Smith: Unfortunately, not all writers are that accurate. Scientists look at specific details and have to be accurate, and as writers we have to be just as careful. I don't think we're so different as observers. One has to be correct about the details.
Mr. Michener: That is true. I myself relate most often not to scientists but to geographers. We have that type of mind, for collecting and codifying and organizing.

Mr. Hinojosa-Smith: I wonder how we can talk to young people about becoming better observers. They can stop and smell the roses, but they should also look at them in some detail.
Mr. Michener: I would want them to remember the most important thing I said: that I could not write about a place without going back to look—to see how the streets run, what

the houses look like, where the morning papers are delivered. All of that is the body of work that writers deal with, and they had better know what they're writing about. If there were a young person listening to us today who wanted to write a short story about a schoolroom in which a class is taking place, I would advise that girl or boy to look around that schoolroom very carefully, maybe spend twenty minutes. Where is the blackboard? What does it look like? How does the light fall on it? Where does your teacher sit? What is your desk like? Are there initials carved in it from former students? To a large degree that is what writing is made up of.

Mr. Hinojosa-Smith: Setting is what makes the act of writing easier and more difficult at the same time. When you fail to create a complete, accurate setting, then you lose your credibility with the reader.
Mr. Michener: If the setting is flabby or uninteresting or nonspecific, I think you lose the reader.

Mr. Hinojosa-Smith: I think young people reading this will realize the importance of specifics and details. They will begin to notice shades of difference in people, places, things. That's important. Details, I think, are what we need to begin writing.
Mr. Michener: If a young person writes a story that is read to the

class, and the class hears familiar facts and realizes, "Yes, she had that right, that's just the way it is" or "I hadn't thought about that, but that's the way Miss Kinderkleine sits when she's reading to us" or "That's where the bookcase is," then the writer gains credibility with the very people he or she's writing for.

Mr. Hinojosa-Smith: That's important. Once you establish credibility with a small group, it can also be done with a wider audience.

Mr. Michener: And I would suppose that anyone listening to what you and I are saying would be able to describe the classroom in a very real way.

Mr. Hinojosa-Smith: Perhaps even better than two old pros! There's something about writing that young people should also remember. In addition to having an attention to details, they have to have a love for reading. They should avail themselves of books in school and in public libraries, the way we did. We had a fine lending library in my hometown.

Mr. Michener: As I said once, a young person who really wanted to be a writer would have no chance of being successful unless by the age of twenty-two he or she wore glasses. If you haven't read enough, you haven't used your eyes enough! That was a joke, but do remember it. You have to read in order to know how to write.

Do you agree with James Michener when he says, "You have to read in order to know how to write"? State your reasons.

List ways a good writer can create a believable setting. Look back at James Michener's advice to get some ideas.

WRITE Write a paragraph explaining one thing that you would like to do the next time you write a story or a report. You may want to consider the suggestions offered by James Michener.

Survival

What do Elena from "Trial by Wilderness" and Pentaquod from "Chesapeake" have in common that helps them to be survivors?

Writer's Workshop

Imagine that you are Pentaquod or Elena and you meet someone who needs information about how to survive in your area. Write a how-to paragraph explaining how to accomplish one important task for survival. Remember to write as if you were one of the story characters.

Writer's Choice You have read about two survivors who face the challenges of a difficult environment. What does it take to survive in the wilderness? Do you need different survival skills in a modern city? What about a small town? Think about the theme of survival. Plan a writing project about your most interesting idea. In what form will you write? Talk it over, prepare your work, and share it with your classmates.

NATURE

THEME

Watching Nature

The soaring flight of a sparrow hawk...the hidden nest of a sandhill crane...the trumpeting cry of a startled bird — discover the thrill of observing nature in the following selections.

CONTENTS

The Immense Journey

by Loren Eiseley

The word had come through to get them alive—birds, reptiles, anything. A zoo somewhere abroad needed restocking. It was one of those reciprocal matters in which science involves itself. Maybe our museum needed a stray ostrich egg and this was the payoff. Anyhow, my job was to help capture some birds and that was why I was there before the trucks.

The cabin had not been occupied for years. We intended to clean it out and live in it, but there were holes in the roof and the birds had come in and were roosting in the rafters. You could depend on it in a place like this, where everything blew away, and even a bird needed some place out of the weather and away from coyotes. A cabin going back to nature in a wild place draws them till they come in, listening at the eaves, I imagine, pecking softly among the shingles till they find a hole and then suddenly the place is theirs and man is forgotten.

Sometimes of late years I find myself thinking the most beautiful sight in the world might be the birds taking over New York after the last man has run away to the hills. I will never live to see it, of course, but I know just how it will sound because I've lived up high and I know the sort of watch birds keep on us. I've listened to sparrows tapping tentatively on the outside of air conditioners when they thought no one was listening, and I know how other birds test the vibrations that come up to them through the television aerials.

"Is he gone?" they ask, and the vibrations come up from below, "Not yet, not yet."

Well, to come back, I got the door open softly and I had the spotlight all ready to turn on and blind whatever birds there were so they couldn't see to get out through the roof. I had a short piece of ladder to put against the far wall, where there was a shelf on which I expected to make the biggest haul. I pushed the door open, the hinges squeaking only a little. A bird or two stirred—I could hear them—but nothing flew and there was a faint starlight through the holes in the roof.

I padded across the floor, got the ladder up and the light ready, and slithered up the ladder till my head and arms were over the shelf. Everything was dark as pitch except for the starlight at the little place back of the shelf near the eaves. With the light to blind them, they'd never make it. I had them. I reached my arm carefully over in order to be ready to seize whatever was there and I put the flash on the edge of the shelf where it would stand by itself when I turned it on. That way I'd be able to use both hands.

Everything worked perfectly except for one detail—I didn't know what kind of birds were there. I never thought about it at all, and it wouldn't have mattered if I had. My orders were to get something interesting. I snapped on the flash and sure enough there was a great beating and feathers flying, but instead of my having them, they, or rather he, had me. He had my hand, that is, and for a small hawk not much bigger than my fist he was doing all right. I heard him give one short metallic cry when the light

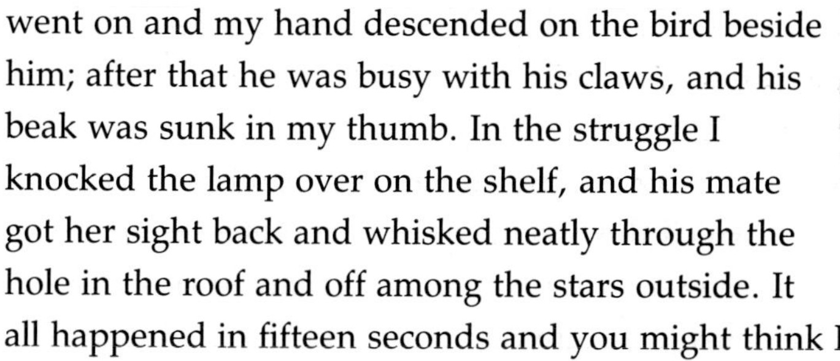

went on and my hand descended on the bird beside him; after that he was busy with his claws, and his beak was sunk in my thumb. In the struggle I knocked the lamp over on the shelf, and his mate got her sight back and whisked neatly through the hole in the roof and off among the stars outside. It all happened in fifteen seconds and you might think I would have fallen down the ladder, but no, I had a professional reputation to keep up, and the bird, of course, made the mistake of thinking the hand was the enemy and not the eyes behind it. He chewed my thumb up pretty effectively and lacerated my hand with his claws, but in the end I got him, having two hands to work with.

He was a sparrow hawk and a fine young male in the prime of life. I was sorry not to catch the pair of them, but as I dripped blood and folded his wings carefully, holding him by the back so that he couldn't strike again, I had to admit the two of them might have been more than I could have handled under the circumstances. The little fellow had saved his mate by diverting me, and that was that. He was born to it, and made no outcry now, resting in my hand hopelessly, but peering toward me in the shadows behind the lamp with a fierce, almost indifferent glance. He neither gave nor expected mercy and something out of the high air passed from him to me, stirring a faint embarrassment.

I quit looking into that eye and managed to get my huge carcass with its fist full of prey back down the ladder. I put the bird in a box too small to allow him to injure himself by struggle and walked out to welcome the arriving trucks. It had been a long day, and camp still to make in the darkness. In the morning that bird would be just another episode. He would go back with the bones in the truck to a small cage in a city where he would spend the rest of his life. And a good thing, too. I sucked my aching thumb and spat out some blood. An assassin has to get used to these things. I had a professional reputation to keep up.

In the morning, with the change that comes on suddenly in that high country, the mist that had hovered below us in the valley was gone. The sky was a deep blue, and one could see for miles over the high outcroppings of stone. I was up early and brought the box in which the little hawk was imprisoned out onto the grass where I was building a cage. A wind as cool as a mountain spring ran over the grass and stirred my hair. It was a fine day to be alive. I looked up and all around and at the hole in the cabin roof out of which the other little hawk had fled. There was no sign of her anywhere that I could see.

"Probably in the next county by now," I thought cynically, but before beginning work I decided I'd have a look at my last night's capture.

Secretively, I looked again all around the camp and up and down and opened the box. I got him right out in my hand with his wings folded properly and I was careful not to startle him. He lay limp in my grasp and I could feel his heart pound under the feathers but he only looked beyond me and up.

I saw him look that last look away beyond me into a sky so full of light that I could not follow his gaze. The little breeze flowed over me again, and nearby a mountain aspen shook all its tiny leaves. I suppose I must have had an idea then of what I was going to do, but I never let it come up into consciousness. I just reached over and laid the hawk on the grass.

He lay there a long minute without hope, unmoving, his eyes still fixed on that blue vault above him. It must have been that he was already so far away in heart that he never felt the release from my hand. He never even stood. He just lay with his breast against the grass.

In the next second after that long minute he was gone. Like a flicker of light, he had vanished with my eyes full on him, but without actually seeing even a premonitory wing beat. He was gone straight into that towering emptiness of light and crystal that my eyes could scarcely bear to penetrate. For another long moment there was silence. I could not see him. The light was too intense. Then from far up somewhere a cry came ringing down.

I was young then and had seen little of the world, but when I heard that cry my heart turned over. It was not the cry of the hawk I had captured; for, by shifting my position against the sun, I was now seeing farther up. Straight out of the sun's eye, where she must have been soaring restlessly above us for untold hours, hurtled his mate. And from far up, ringing from peak to peak of the summits over us, came a cry of such unutterable and ecstatic joy that it sounds down across the years and tingles among the cups on my quiet breakfast table.

I saw them both now. He was rising fast to meet her. They met in a great soaring gyre that turned to a whirling circle and a dance of wings. Once more, just once, their two voices, joined in a harsh wild medley of question and response, struck and echoed against the pinnacles of the valley. Then they were gone forever somewhere into those upper regions beyond the eyes of men.

How did you feel at the end of the selection? Explain your response.

Several times Loren Eiseley mentions his professional reputation. What clues help you know how he really feels about his job?

Why do you think Eiseley let the hawk go? What does his quick decision to release the bird tell you about the way he values nature?

WRITE Did you ever have to let go of something you really wanted to keep? Write a paragraph or a short poem about your experience.

The Sparrow Hawk

by Russell Hoban

Wings like pistols flashing at his sides,
Masked, above the meadow runway rides,
Galloping, galloping with an easy rein.
Below, the fieldmouse, where the shadow glides,
Holds fast the small purse of his life, and hides.

White Bird, 1950, Milton Avery, gouache on paper, 16 1/2" X 21 1/2". Collection of The University of Arizona, Museum of Art, Tucson, Arizona. Gift of Edward J. Gallagher, Jr.

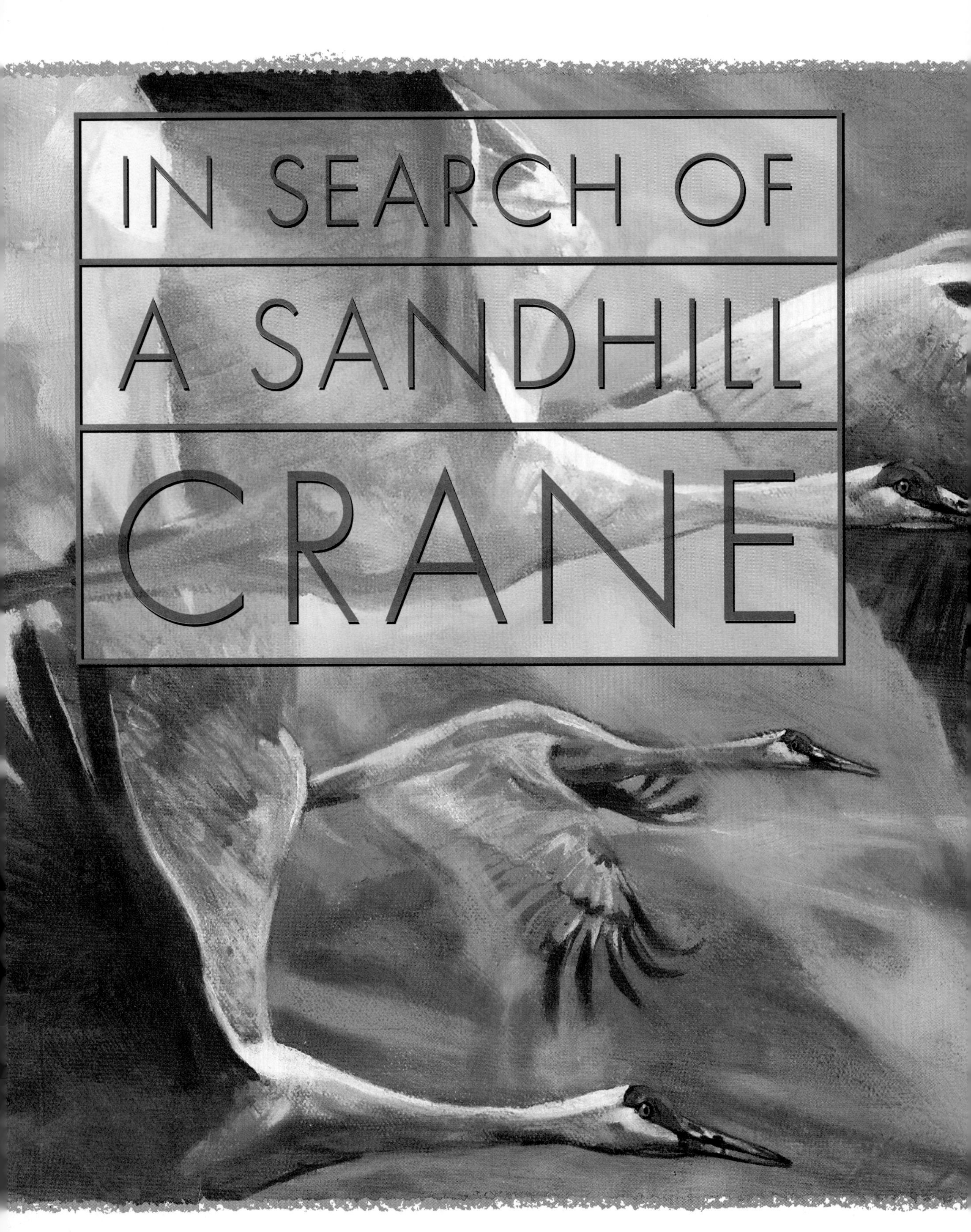

IN SEARCH OF A SANDHILL CRANE

BY KEITH ROBERTSON

When Lincoln Keller's mother decides to take a computer course in another state, Link agrees to spend the summer in Michigan with his aunt Harriet, whom he hardly knows. With some reluctance, he takes his uncle Albert's expensive camera in order to get pictures of the rare sandhill crane. Soon after getting to Michigan, Link goes with his aunt Harriet to her log cabin in the wilderness. When Link sees the isolated cabin with no modern conveniences, he is afraid he is going to have a very boring vacation.

The cabin had only three rooms. Most of the space was taken up by one large room that served as the kitchen, dining, and living area. An old-fashioned kitchen range stood near one corner, and a big stone fireplace occupied the middle of the opposite wall. There was a cedar plank table, four straight chairs, several easy chairs that looked worn but comfortable,

illustrations by Richard Cook

some built-in cupboards, and a worktable near the stove. Two doors led to the two smaller rooms. Each contained a bed, with what appeared to be a new mattress, a straight chair, an old bureau, and a small closet.

The floors were of worn planks, and the inside of the log walls had been paneled with boards. Inside, the cabin was much cozier and more inviting than Link had expected. It was clean and had none of the musty smell that houses usually have after being closed for a long time.

"Charley and his wife did a good job cleaning the place," Harriet said approvingly. "He has looked after the cabin for years—kept the roof tight, repaired the windows, things like that. When I wrote him that I was coming up this summer, he said that the squirrels and mice had got in and had ruined the mattresses. So I sent up two new ones. He's put new screens on the windows, and I noticed before we came in that he'd set out some tomato plants for us. He's a wonderful man. You'll like him."

"What is Charley's last name?" Link asked.

"Horse."

"You're not serious?"

"His real name is Running Horse," Harriet said. "He's a Chippewa Indian. He used to work in the lumber camps as a young man, and someone called him Charley Horse and he's kept the name ever since. He knows more about the woods than anyone I've ever known. He's an expert guide."

Link unloaded the station wagon while his aunt put things away. Then he went to the pile of wood that Charley Horse had left near the edge of the clearing and brought in wood for the kitchen stove.

"We used to have an outdoor fireplace," Harriet said. "It was built of stones stacked together. If we can find the metal grill, we can rebuild it. Then we can cook out of doors part of the time. In the middle of the summer it's too hot to build a fire in the stove. We usually didn't unless it rained."

"What about a refrigerator?" Link asked, looking at the cases of ginger ale he had carried in from the car.

"I've talked about getting one of those gas refrigerators for years," Harriet said. "But I just haven't bothered. There's a spring not very far away. We used to use it for our drinking water when your father and I were children. Later we drilled a well. But I still use the spring to keep things cold, like butter. We put whatever we want in one of those metal pails and put the pail in the water. As for the bottles of soda, just tie a string around the necks and lower them into the water. You'll be surprised how cold they'll get."

They had lamb chops, canned peas, and baking powder biscuits for dinner. Then Harriet got her cane, and with Link carrying the large metal pail full of perishables, they walked through the gathering gloom down an overgrown path to the spring. It was not far. The trail sloped downward for a short distance and then wound around a small hillock. Water gushed out of a low ledge of rock and trickled down into a pool about ten feet in diameter. A tiny stream led the overflow away into the darkness of the woods.

"I think the water is perfectly safe to drink," Harriet said. "The real reason Dad had the well put in was that he and your father liked to come down here to take baths. Mother objected to that. She said she wasn't going to drink bathwater even if it was running."

Link leaned over and put his hand in the water. "It's ice cold," he said.

"Much too cold to bathe in, I always thought," she agreed. "Mother and I carried water and took a bath with warm water in a tub."

Link found a flat rock ledge in the pool, placed the pail on it, and then weighted it down with another rock.

"That will do fine unless some bear gets too inquisitive," Harriet said. "One year I had real trouble. Charley put a rope up over that limb, and I suspended the pail out in the middle of the pool. I had to use a long stick with a hook on the end to reach out and get it."

"Are there many bears around here?" Lincoln asked, looking back into the thick depths of the woods.

"Lots of them. But if you leave them alone, they'll usually leave you alone."

It was dark by the time they returned to the cabin. Harriet lighted a kerosene lamp and showed Link how it worked. "I imagine you're tired," she said. "Up here you'll find you just naturally get up with the light and go to bed with the dark."

Link went outside and brushed his teeth at the pump and then went to bed. When he blew out the lamp, complete darkness descended. There were no distant street lights outside his window and no occasional flash of headlights. The room was so totally black that it bothered him. He glanced at his watch just to be certain that nothing had happened to his eyes. After about ten minutes he was able to make out the square of his window, a slightly grayer shade of black in the black wall.

Suddenly he heard something rustling around outside. It sounded enormous. Charley Horse had put new screens on the windows, but would a screen discourage a bear? He tried to convince himself that if iron bars had been needed, they would have been put on. The rustling was suddenly replaced by a gnawing sound as though a rat the size of a bear were gnawing down a big tree. There were lots of trees, he decided, one or more less would make no difference as long as it didn't fall on him. He had just become resigned to the gnawing, when suddenly the night was pierced with a blood-chilling screech: "*Oouuooouuuoo, oh oh oh!*" This brought him bolt upright in bed. Then he lay back down again. He'd read of screech owls. The screech was repeated, and then in the distance he heard a high-pitched barking, like a dog but still not a dog. The peace and quiet of the deep woods! he thought disgustedly. What he needed was a few trucks or cement mixers driving down the street so he could get to sleep. He covered his ears with his pillow and closed his eyes.

He drifted off to sleep in spite of the strange noises, and the next thing he knew it was light and he was awake. He could smell coffee. He got dressed, went out to the pump, and sloshed cold water over his face. On his way back he noticed the broom that had been left beside the door. It had fallen to the ground, and something had gnawed the handle half through. He carried it inside and held it up for Harriet to see.

"Porcupine," she said with a laugh. "I think it's the salt in the perspiration from your hands that they're after. They'll sometimes gnaw a hoe handle in two in a night. Did you hear that owl screeching last night?"

"I heard lots of animals, and I see signs of them, but I don't see them," Link objected.

"Once in a while you will just stumble onto an animal, but usually they are very wary and cautious. So you have to be even more wary and quiet. If you stand quietly any place long enough, you'll be surprised at what you'll see."

While they ate breakfast, Harriet drew a rough map of the surrounding area, pointing out what she thought might interest him.

"It's always a good idea to carry a compass if you go very far into the woods," she cautioned. "It's not so much that a compass will keep you from getting lost, but if you do get lost, you can then keep going in one direction. Eventually, even up here, you will come to a road."

She produced a small compass, which Link stuck in his pocket before he went exploring. He found the swamp that Harriet had indicated, and the sizable stream of dark-brown water that led away from it through the trees to the Manistique River. He located the old beaver dam and a pond above it. And he visited the remains of what Harriet had said was an old stagecoach station. They were interesting, he admitted, but you couldn't stand around for hours and look at a beaver dam or a tumbledown log cabin. By the middle of the afternoon he had seen practically everything on Harriet's crude map. He was on his way back to the cabin when he passed by the spring. Walking through the woods was much warmer work than he had expected, and the water looked inviting. He stripped off his clothes and stepped into the edge of the pool.

The water was icy. It was so cold that his feet felt numb in a matter of seconds. He looked out at the center of the pool. The water was at least four feet deep. His father used to take a bath here, he told himself. He could at least take a quick dip. Holding his breath, he made a shallow dive toward the center. The water was deeper than he had expected; when he stood up it came to his chin. He had never been so cold in his life. With his teeth chattering he waded as quickly as possible to the edge and climbed out.

He found a spot of sunshine and stood shivering in it for several minutes while he tried to brush off some of the water from his body.

He was covered with goose pimples. He put on his clothes and then sat down by the pool for a while. He felt wonderful. That quick dip had been the most fun of anything since his arrival in Michigan. But that was only a minute. What was he going to do with an entire summer?

The next day he went into Germfask with his aunt to buy some milk and a few other staples. They visited the Seney Wildlife Refuge Headquarters, looked at the exhibits, and Link watched some Canada geese on the pond just outside the main building. When they returned to the cabin, he wrote several letters and took several short, aimless walks into the woods. The following morning he weeded the area around the tomato plants and then thumbed aimlessly through one of his aunt's bird books.

"You're bored, aren't you?" Harriet asked in the middle of lunch.

The sudden question caught Link unprepared. "Well, I don't know what you find to do all summer up here," he admitted finally. "What did my dad do when he was a boy?"

"He was like me. He could lie hidden in the underbrush and watch a beaver or a heron all day long. You have to love the creatures of the wild to like it here, I guess. I find New York City terribly dull." She reached out a hand and touched him on the arm. "I suppose in a way the whole idea of coming up here was selfish. Now that I am partially crippled I don't feel up to staying here alone the way I once did. So I told myself that you would enjoy it so that I could come. I love it here. I can hobble outside and just sit watching and have a wonderful time. And of course there *was* the chance that you might like it too. Would you like to leave?"

"Well, I haven't really given it a trial yet," Link said, reluctant to hurt her by saying that he would.

"You've run out of things to do," Harriet observed. "I suppose you ought to try to get that picture your uncle wanted before you leave."

"Yes, I'd forgotten that," Link agreed. "Where would I go to find sandhill cranes?"

"Lakes, marshes, wet areas," Harriet said. "There are a number of these around within a few miles. Why don't we leave it that you will stay long enough to get your pictures. Then we'll pack up and leave."

"That's fair enough," Link said, feeling much better.

"I want to go pay Charley Horse for his work here and see several other people," Harriet said, getting up from the table. "You don't mind being left here alone?"

"Not at all," Link said.

He went to his room, got out his uncle Albert's camera, and picked a 105 mm. lens. There were only four exposures left on the roll of film, so he went outside and used them up taking pictures of the cabin. Then he reloaded the camera, tucked his aunt's bird guide in his pocket, and started off through the woods. There might be a sandhill crane at the old beaver pond. "Wet areas," Harriet had said. He might be lucky and get his pictures right away. If he did, he wouldn't say anything but wait until he got the developed slides back. He could put up with another week or so buried in the woods. Then Harriet wouldn't feel she had completely wasted her money having the cabin repaired.

He spent the next hour crouched beside the pond, trying to sit quietly, but it was almost impossible. Tiny insects buzzed around his face, crawled down his collar, and generally made him miserable. At first he tried to swat them but decided this was a waste of time. Finally he crawled underneath a low shrub and, with the leaves almost brushing his face, managed to find a little peace.

He waited as patiently as he knew how, but he saw nothing that either resembled a crane or a crane's nest. According to his bird book they didn't build much of a nest—just a shallow cluster of sedge grass and twigs on the ground. The trouble was that the edges of the pond were thick with sedges, reeds, and cattails, and it would have been difficult to see a standing crane, much less a nest. He was about to give up and move on, when suddenly, almost in front of him in the middle of the pond, there was a floating bird. It looked slightly like a small duck with a long, slender neck. Its back was gray-brown and it had a white bill. Link raised his camera to his eyes and looked through the telescopic lens. There was a black band around the whitish bill. He snapped pictures and then put his camera down gently. He began thumbing through the book trying

to find a picture of the floating bird. He made a slight sound as he turned the pages and when he looked up the bird was slowly sinking into the water. It sank lower and lower until finally just its eyes were above the water. He watched fascinated as it disappeared entirely. He waited and waited until he decided that something must have pulled it under and eaten it. Then suddenly it popped to the surface about twenty feet farther away. Link watched as the bird dived several times. It could disappear in a flash or sink slowly and then reappear fifteen or twenty feet away. He wished that he could swim like that underwater. Finally it disappeared for a much longer period of time. His eyes searched the surface of the pond looking for it. Then, entirely by chance, he saw its head slowly emerging in the reeds, not very far from where he sat. It came up slowly, its neck turning cautiously like a submarine periscope. Suddenly it hopped onto what seemed to be a floating pile of reeds. It scratched away some covering reeds and sat down on a nest.

Slowly and cautiously, Link raised his camera and took several pictures. He had been sitting within a few yards of the nest for some time without seeing it. He understood now what Harriet had meant when she said if he sat still long enough he would see things.

After ten minutes of thumbing through his book, he decided that the strange bird that could impersonate a submarine was a pied-bill grebe. He sat quietly for another hour. He saw blue jays and several songbirds that he could not identify and then—for a few hopeful minutes—he thought he saw a sandhill crane. An enormous bird flew high overhead on slow, flapping wings. Link looked at it through his camera lens. It was blue-gray, but it had no red crown on its head. His uncle Albert had warned him not to confuse the great blue heron with the sandhill crane.

"A crane flies with his neck stretched out straight and a heron curves his in an *S* curve," Albert had said.

He was growing stiff and restless, and buzzing insects continued to plague him, so he decided to call it a day, go back, and have a quick dip in the spring. He took a slightly different route and passed through a small natural clearing that he had not visited before. He was partway across when he realized that several birds, including a particularly noisy blue jay, were screaming excitedly about something. He stopped and looked around carefully, searching for the cause of all the fuss. He looked first at the ground and then at the lower branches of the trees. Suddenly he saw an animal about eighteen inches long up in a maple tree at the edge of the clearing. Whether it was the cause of the birds' alarm or not he had no idea, but it was so grotesque-looking that he forgot about the birds. He raised his camera to use the lens as his binoculars. The animal had sort of yellowish-tinged hair and a back and tail covered with white spikes. It was a porcupine! It seemed to be staring straight at him.

He moved slowly toward the tree. The porcupine made no move to run away or even to hide behind the tree trunk.

That would make quite a picture, he thought, as he watched the animal with its ratlike face and eyes. The trouble was that a branch partially blocked his view. He circled, trying to get a clear shot. Either maple leaves or the feathery branches of a nearby spruce kept him from getting a good picture. The porcupine still showed no sign of being afraid.

He looked at a low branch thoughtfully. If he climbed up about level with the animal he could get a beautiful shot. There would be nothing in the way, and he could take the picture from the correct angle as far as the light was concerned. What a story that would make when he got back home! "I was in the same tree as the porcupine when I took this shot," he would say casually.

He slung the camera over his shoulder so that it hung against his back. Then he reached up, grabbed the lowest limb, and began climbing. It was not difficult but he went slowly and cautiously, keeping a wary eye on the porcupine. He got up about ten feet, just slightly below the porcupine, propped himself in a reasonably secure position, and got his camera. He took several shots and then moved a trifle closer. The porcupine began to show the first signs of nervousness. It retreated along its branch, moving about three feet farther out. The fact that it seemed frightened of him gave Link more courage. He climbed one branch higher and leaned over to get at just the right angle. He snapped one picture and then leaned farther to the left. He was too intent on getting the picture, and his right foot slipped. He began to topple. He grabbed frantically for the nearest branch—which was the one on which the porcupine was perched. He caught it. The sudden weight on the small branch shook the porcupine off. Link was too busy to notice or care what happened to the porcupine. His right foot slipped off the branch completely, throwing most of his weight on his left foot. The branch on which it was resting was small, and it snapped. That left him with only his right hand grasping one branch. His left hand still held the precious camera. The branch was too big around to hold properly, and it was doubtful if he could have held himself by one hand anyway. He did manage to hold on long enough to allow his feet to swing over so that he was dangling upright. Then he let go and dropped.

It was not a long drop, and he landed on his feet on soft ground. Slightly off balance, he stumbled backward and sat down heavily. There was an instant searing pain. He let out a yelp of agony and dropped the camera. It fell only a few inches to the ground, which was carpeted with leaves and pine needles. Link was not much interested whether the camera was safe or not. He was in too much agony. He felt as though he were sitting on a red-hot stove. He rolled over until he was on his hands and knees. Then he reached back and felt the seat of his pants with his hand, half expecting to feel blood. Instead he felt what seemed to be stiff needles. He looked around suddenly for the porcupine. It was gone, but it had left plenty to remember it by. The entire seat of his pants was filled with quills! He had either landed on or beside the porcupine when he sat down.

Slowly and gingerly he got to his feet. Each movement was painful. He reached around and carefully took hold of the nearest quill he could see. He gave a yank. Nothing happened except he felt a sharp pain in his behind.

He picked up the camera and slowly started toward the cabin. Each step was torture. He paused every few feet, but he couldn't sit down. There was nothing to do but to plod onward, trying to move with the least amount of pain. About two thirds of the way he leaned against a tree, sort of half lying on his stomach, and examined the camera. It seemed unharmed. He blew away a few specks of dirt on the lens and got the lens cap from his pocket and put it on. At least he had got some good shots before he fell. And

what a story he would have to tell now when he showed the family those slides!

He reached the cabin, went to his room, and lay face down on his bed. Once more he tried pulling a quill. He had no more success than before. Those things were in there to stay! He could see himself being wheeled into a hospital, face down on the stretcher. The doctor would operate while the nurses and everyone stood around laughing.

He was wondering how he would ever get to the hospital when he heard his aunt drive in. He waited until she had entered the cabin.

"Would you come in here, Aunt Harriet?" he called. "I had an accident!"

Harriet came into the room. Link turned to look at her. She glanced at him without changing her expression and said, "Yes, you certainly did. And I'll bet it's painful! What did you do, sit on him?"

"I guess," he said. "I climbed a tree to take his picture and we both fell."

"Hurt yourself otherwise?" she asked.

"Nope. It was rough walking home, though."

"I'll bet it was," she said. "Well, we have to get those quills out. Each quill is covered with dozens of little barbs. That makes them hard to pull out. But if you don't pull them out they work deeper. You can't possibly take off your pants. I'll have to pull the quills out through the cloth. The best way is to take a pair of pliers and give a quick yank. I've got some antiseptic that has sort of a chilling effect, and I'll try to spray you thoroughly with that. Maybe it will soak through your trousers and deaden the pain a little. But I warn you it will hurt."

"Go ahead," Link said, relieved that he wouldn't have to go to the hospital.

Harriet left and returned a few minutes later with a pair of pliers from the car and a can of antiseptic spray. She sprayed Link's posterior thoroughly and then asked, "Ready?"

"I guess as ready as I'll ever be," Link said. He pressed his lips together.

There was a sudden stab of pain, and Harriet said, "That's one!

There's quite a few to go!"

"Don't count them," Link said. "I don't want to know how many until it's all over."

"The Indians dyed porcupine quills and used them to decorate deerskin shirts and pouches and moccasins," she said some time later as she yanked out the fifteenth quill.

"I'm going to save these and use them to decorate a poster that says 'Beware of Porcupines,' " Link said. He clenched his teeth as she gave another yank.

She pulled out twenty-two quills altogether. Link was sore and he knew he would be unable to sit comfortably for several days, but at least he could walk without pain.

"You'd better take off your clothes and examine yourself closely to be certain we haven't missed any. And then spray yourself with disinfectant again."

Link followed her suggestion and then dressed. "I'm going down to the spring," he announced as he walked into the main room of the cabin. "The other day when I waded in, my feet were numb by the time I'd gone three feet. Maybe if I sit down for fifteen minutes I can get the same results."

Harriet gave a slight chuckle. "I don't blame you." He had reached the door when she said, "Link."

He turned.

"I want you to know that I realize how painful that was," she said, almost shyly.

She was much more sympathetic than he had thought, he decided, as he went on toward the spring. But she didn't know how to express it. He was beginning to understand her a little, and the more he understood her the better he liked her. She was really quite a good egg.

What part of the story did you like best? Tell why.

What indications are there that Link will become interested in observing wildlife?

Write Would you like to spend the summer in an isolated cabin in the woods? Tell why.

Be Like the Bird

by Victor Hugo

Be like the Bird, who
Halting in his flight
On limb too slight
Feels it give way beneath him,
Yet sings
Knowing he hath wings.

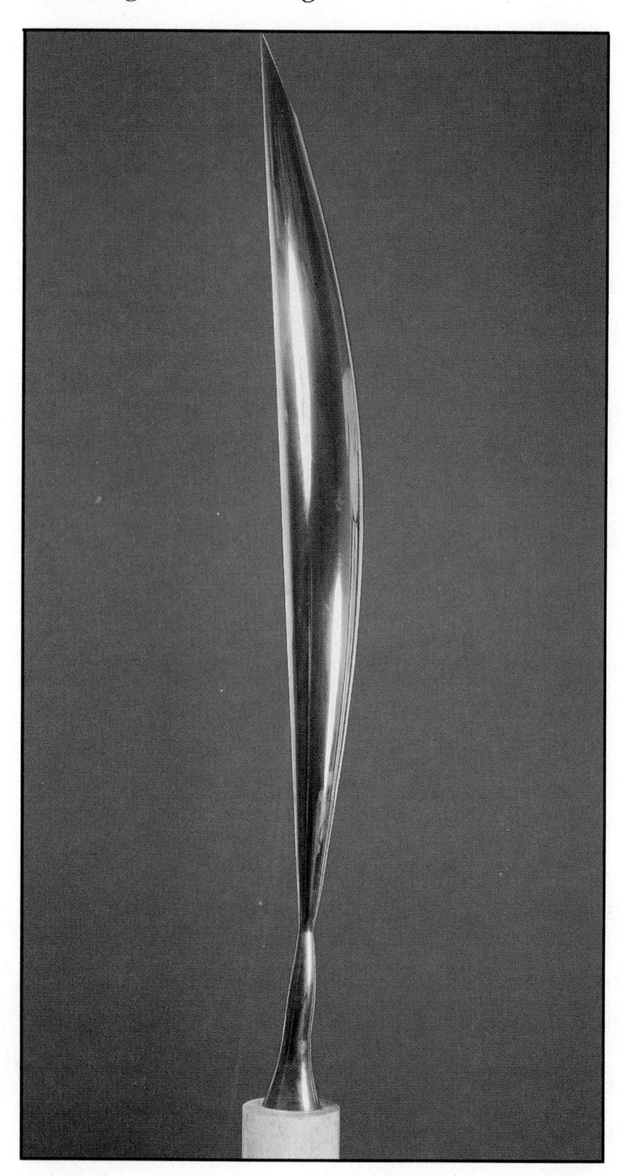

L'Oiseau, 1940, Constantin Brancusi, Musée National d'Art Moderne, Paris, France.

Watching Nature

Think about the different birds mentioned in each selection. Compare these birds to the description presented in Victor Hugo's poem "Be Like the Bird." What does Victor Hugo suggest that people can learn from birds? Do the selections support this belief?

Writer's Workshop

Reread Russell Hoban's poem "The Sparrow Hawk." Write a short essay describing one of the animals or birds from the selections or an animal or a bird that you have observed in nature.

Writer's Choice What can you learn by watching nature? Think about some of the things you have observed in nature. Choose an idea to write about and a writing form, such as a poem or a persuasive essay. Carry out a plan. Then find a fun way to share your work with others.

CONNECTIONS

MULTICULTURAL CONNECTION

YOUTHFUL ARTIST

When she was only three years old, Wang Yani amazed her family and friends with her wonderful pictures of animals. Born in Gongcheng, China, in 1975, this creative young woman has had her pictures in major exhibits and museums since she was four years old.

When she was young, her paintings were often of monkeys and cats. Now the landscape around her home and her family and friends are her favorite subjects.

Wang Yani has had little instruction in how to paint, but she has a wonderful imagination and a good memory, two important characteristics for an artist. When you look at her paintings, you can imagine the movements she made with her paint brushes when she was creating her delightful animals.

In 1985, thousands of visitors came to see her paintings at the Smithsonian Institution in Washington, D.C. Titled "Yani: The Brush of Innocence," the exhibition featured her paintings of animals, birds, and landscapes.

For many centuries, the Chinese have painted beautiful pictures of people, animals, and landscapes. They are also famous for intricate jade carvings and woven fabrics. Bring photographs of Chinese arts and crafts to class. Contrast the arts and crafts of China with those of the United States.

ART CONNECTION

PICTURES OF PICTURES

Create a poster about a painter whose work you admire. Design your poster any way you like, but be sure to include information about the painter's life, sample pictures of paintings with captions, and an analysis of his or her work. Display your poster on a wall or bulletin board in the classroom, and give a short presentation on the painter.

ART/SOCIAL STUDIES/SCIENCE CONNECTION

PAINTING PROJECT

Think of a feature of the natural world that you would like to paint. Then fill out a web or other graphic organizer, explaining why you would choose that subject, how you would paint the picture, and what impact you would like your painting to have on an audience. Summarize your thoughts in a short essay, and then explain your project to a small group.

Wang Yani

Unit Six

Solutions

Everyone faces problems—some large, some small—each requiring a different kind of solution. Learning to solve or overcome problems is a continuing process that enables us to grow. You will read how different people solved problems, from a young woman who helps people with disabilities to African Americans whose inventions have made all our lives easier. As you read this unit, think about ways *you* have helped people solve problems.

THEMES

BOOKSHELF

THE BROOKLYN BRIDGE: THEY SAID IT COULDN'T BE BUILT

BY JUDITH ST. GEORGE

This fascinating account describes the major contributions made by John A. Roebling and his son to the design and construction of one of the world's most famous bridges.

HARCOURT BRACE LIBRARY BOOK

OUTWARD DREAMS: BLACK INVENTORS AND THEIR INVENTIONS

BY JIM HASKINS

Few of the people in this book appear in history books, but all of these inventors were heroic in their struggles to overcome prejudice to gain patents and recognition.

The Wright Brothers: How They Invented the Airplane

BY RUSSELL FREEDMAN

Freedman tells how these self-taught bicycle mechanics solved problems that had baffled generations of scientists and engineers. Photographs illustrate this vivid account of the lives of these two young men.

ALA Notable Book

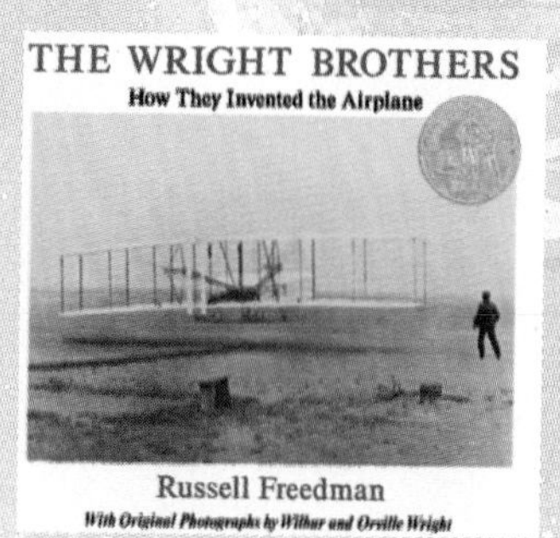

The Way Things Work

BY DAVID MACAULAY

This book is an overview of the technology of some of the inventions that shape our lives. Macaulay not only demonstrates how machines work...he also shows how inventions are linked to others.

ALA Notable Book, School Library Journal Best Book

The Astronaut Training Book for Kids

BY KIM LONG

This book will tell you all you need to know about preparing for an exciting career as an astronaut. Discover what space will be like when you get there.

THEME

LOOKING TOWARD OTHERS

For some people, finding solutions that help others is a lifetime goal. Discover how the people in the following selections use their skills and inventiveness to improve the lives of others.

CONTENTS

Raymond's Run

by Toni Cade Bambara

I don't have much work to do around the house like some girls. My mother does that. And I don't have to earn my pocket money by hustling; George runs errands for the big boys and sells Christmas cards. And anything else that's got to get done, my father does. All I have to do in life is mind my brother Raymond, which is enough.

Sometimes I slip and say my little brother Raymond. But as any fool can see he's much bigger and he's older too. But a lot of people call him my little brother cause he needs looking after cause he's not quite right. And a lot of smart mouths got lots to say about that too, especially when George was minding him. But now, if anybody has anything to say to Raymond, anything to say about his big head, they have to come by me. And I don't play the dozens or believe in standing around with somebody in my face doing a lot of talking. I much rather just knock you down and take my chances even if I am a little girl with skinny arms and a squeaky voice, which is how I got the name Squeaky. And if things get too rough, I run. And as anybody can tell you, I'm the fastest thing on two feet.

There is no track meet that I don't win the first place medal. I used to win the twenty-yard dash when I was a little kid in

illustrations by Jerry Pinkney

kindergarten. Nowadays it's the fifty-yard dash. And tomorrow I'm subject to run the quarter-meter relay all by myself and come in first, second, and third. The big kids call me Mercury cause I'm the swiftest thing in the neighborhood. Everybody knows that—except two people who know better, my father and me.

He can beat me to Amsterdam Avenue with me having a two fire-hydrant headstart and him running with his hands in his pockets and whistling. But that's private information. Cause can you imagine some thirty-five-year-old man stuffing himself into PAL shorts to race little kids? So as far as everyone's concerned, I'm the fastest and that goes for Gretchen, too, who has put out the tale that she is going to win the first place medal this year. Ridiculous. In the second place, she's got short legs. In the third place, she's got freckles. In the first place, no one can beat me and that's all there is to it.

I'm standing on the corner admiring the weather and about to take a stroll down Broadway so I can practice my breathing exercises, and I've got Raymond walking on the inside close to the buildings cause he's subject to fits of fantasy and starts thinking he's a circus performer and that the curb is a tightrope strung high in the air. And sometimes after a rain, he likes to step down off his tightrope right into the gutter and slosh around getting his shoes and cuffs wet. Or sometimes if you don't watch him, he'll dash across traffic to the island in the middle of Broadway and give the pigeons a fit. Then I have to go behind him apologizing to all the old people sitting around trying to get some sun and getting all upset with the pigeons fluttering around them, scattering their newspapers and upsetting the wax-paper lunches in their laps. So I keep Raymond on the inside of me, and he plays like he's driving a stagecoach, which is O.K. by me so long as he doesn't run me over or interrupt my breathing exercises, which I have to do on account of I'm serious about my running and don't care who knows it.

Now some people like to act like things come easy to them, won't let on that they practice. Not me. I'll high prance down 34th Street like a rodeo pony to keep my knees strong even if it does get my mother uptight so that she walks ahead like she's not with me, don't know me, is all by herself on a shopping trip, and I am somebody else's crazy child.

Now you take Cynthia Procter for instance. She's just the opposite. If there's a test tomorrow, she'll say something like, "Oh I guess I'll play handball this afternoon and watch television tonight," just to let you know she ain't thinking about the test. Or like last week when she won the spelling bee for the millionth time, "A good thing you got 'receive,' Squeaky, cause I would have got it wrong. I completely forgot about the spelling bee." And she'll clutch the lace on her blouse like it was a narrow escape. Oh, brother.

But of course when I pass her house on my early morning trots around the block, she is practicing the scales on the piano over and over and over and over. Then in music class, she always lets herself get bumped around so she falls accidently on purpose onto the piano stool and is so surprised to find herself sitting there, and so decides just for fun to try out the ole keys and what do you know—Chopin's waltzes just spring out of her fingertips and she's the most surprised thing in the world. A regular prodigy. I could kill people like that.

I stay up all night studying the words for the spelling bee. And you can see me anytime of day practicing running. I never walk if I can trot and shame on Raymond if he can't keep up. But of course he does, cause if he hangs back someone's liable to walk up to him and get smart, or take his allowance from him, or ask him where he got that great big pumpkin head. People are so stupid sometimes.

So I'm strolling down Broadway breathing out and breathing in on counts of seven, which is my lucky number, and here comes Gretchen and her sidekicks—Mary Louise, who used to be a friend of mine when she first moved to Harlem from Baltimore and got beat up by everybody till I took up for her on account of her mother and my mother used to sing in the same choir when they were young girls, but people ain't grateful, so now she hangs out with the new girl Gretchen and talks about me like a dog; and Rosie, who is as fat as I am skinny and has a big mouth where Raymond is concerned and is too stupid to know that there is not a big deal of difference between herself and Raymond and that she can't afford to throw stones. So they are steady coming up Broadway and I see right away that it's going to be one of those Dodge City scenes cause the street ain't that big and they're close to the buildings just as we are. First I think I'll step into the candy store and look over the new comics and let them pass. But that's chicken and I've got a reputation to consider. So then I think I'll just walk straight on through them or over them if necessary. But as they get to me, they slow down. I'm ready to fight, cause like I said I don't feature a whole lot of chit-chat, I much prefer to just knock you down right from the jump and save everybody a lotta precious time.

"You signing up for the May Day races?" smiles Mary Louise, only it's not a smile at all.

A dumb question like that doesn't deserve an answer. Besides, there's just me and Gretchen standing there really, so no use wasting my breath talking to shadows.

"I don't think you're going to win this time," says Rosie, trying to signify with her hands on her hips all salty, completely forgetting that I have whupped her many times for less salt than that.

"I always win cause I'm the best," I say straight at Gretchen, who is, as far as I'm concerned, the only one talking in this ventriloquist-dummy routine.

Gretchen smiles but it's not a smile and I'm thinking that girls never really smile at each other because they don't know how and don't want to know how and there's probably no one to teach us how cause grown-up girls don't know either. Then they all look at Raymond, who has just brought his mule team to a standstill. And they're about to see what trouble they can get into through him.

"What grade you in now, Raymond?"

"You got anything to say to my brother, you say it to me, Mary Louise Williams of Raggedy Town, Baltimore."

"What are you, his mother?" sasses Rosie.

"That's right, Fatso. And the next word out of anybody and I'll be *their* mother too." So they just stand there and Gretchen shifts from one leg to the other and so do they. Then Gretchen puts her hands on her hips and is about to say something with her freckle-face self but doesn't. Then she walks around me looking me up and down but keeps walking up Broadway, and her sidekicks follow her. So me and Raymond smile at each other and he says "Gidyap" to his team and I continue with my breathing exercises, strolling down

Broadway toward the ice man on 145th with not a care in the world cause I am Miss Quicksilver herself.

I take my time getting to the park on May Day because the track meet is the last thing on the program. The biggest thing on the program is the May Pole dancing, which I can do without, thank you, even if my mother thinks it's a shame I don't take part and act like a girl for a change. You'd think my mother'd be grateful not to have to make me a white organdy dress with a big satin sash and buy me new white baby-doll shoes that can't be taken out of the box till the big day. You'd think she'd be glad her daughter ain't out there prancing around a May Pole getting the new clothes all dirty and sweaty and trying to act like a fairy or a flower or whatever you're supposed to be when you should be trying to be yourself, whatever that is, which is, as far as I am concerned, a poor black girl who really can't afford to buy shoes and a new dress you only wear once a lifetime cause it won't fit next year.

I was once a strawberry in a Hansel and Gretel pageant when I was in nursery school and didn't have no better sense than to dance on tiptoe with my arms in a circle over my head doing umbrella steps and being a perfect fool just so my mother and father could come dressed up and clap. You'd think they'd know better than to encourage that kind of nonsense. I am not a strawberry. I do not dance on my toes. I run. That is what I am all about. So I always come late to the May Day program, just in time to get my number pinned on and lay in the grass till they announce the fifty-yard dash.

I put Raymond in the little swings, which is a tight squeeze this year and will be impossible next year. Then I look around for Mr. Pearson, who pins the numbers on. I'm really looking for Gretchen if you want to know the truth, but she's not around. The park is jam-packed. Parents in hats and corsages and breast-pocket handkerchiefs peeking up. Kids in white dresses and light-blue suits. The parkees unfolding chairs and chasing the rowdy kids from Lenox as if they had no right to be there. The big guys with their caps on backwards, leaning against the fence swirling the basketballs on the tips of their fingers, waiting for all these crazy people to clear out the park so they can play. Most of the kids in my class are carrying bass drums and glockenspiels and flutes. You'd think they'd put in a few bongos or something for real like that.

Then here comes Mr. Pearson with his clipboard and his cards and pencils and whistles and safety pins and fifty million other things he's always dropping all over the place with his clumsy self. He sticks out in a crowd cause he's on stilts. We used to call him Jack and the Beanstalk to get him mad. But I'm the only one that can outrun him and get away, and I'm too grown for that silliness now.

"Well, Squeaky," he says checking my name off the list and handing me number seven and two pins. And I'm thinking he's got no right to call me Squeaky, if I can't call him Beanstalk.

"Hazel Elizabeth Deborah Parker," I correct him and tell him to write it down on his board.

"Well, Hazel Elizabeth Deborah Parker, going to give someone else a break this year?" I squint at him real hard to see if he is seriously thinking I should lose the race on purpose just to give someone else a break.

"Only six girls running this time," he continues, shaking his head sadly like it's my fault all of New York didn't turn out in sneakers. "That new girl should give you a run for your money." He looks around the park for Gretchen like a periscope in a submarine movie. "Wouldn't it be a nice gesture if you were . . . to ahhh . . ."

I give him such a look he couldn't finish putting that idea into words. Grownups got a lot of nerve sometimes. I pin number seven to myself and stomp away—I'm so burnt. And I go straight for the track and stretch out on the grass while the band winds up with "Oh the Monkey Wrapped His Tail Around the Flag Pole," which my teacher calls by some other name. The man on the loudspeaker is calling everyone over to the track and I'm on my back looking at the sky trying to pretend I'm in the country, but I can't, because even grass in the city feels hard as sidewalk and there's just no pretending you are anywhere but in a "concrete jungle" as my grandfather says.

The twenty-yard dash takes all of the two minutes cause most of the little kids don't know no better than to run off the track or run the wrong way or run smack into the fence and fall down and cry. One little kid, though, has got the good sense to run straight for the white ribbon up ahead, so he wins. Then the second-graders line up for the thirty-yard dash and I don't even bother to turn my head to watch cause Raphael Perez always wins. He wins before he even begins by psyching the runners, telling them they're going to trip on their shoelaces and fall on their faces or lose their shorts or something, which he doesn't really have to do since he is very fast, almost as fast as I am. After that is the forty-yard dash, which I used to run when I was in first grade. Raymond is hollering from the swings cause he knows I'm about to do my thing cause the man on the loudspeaker has just announced the fifty-yard dash, although he might just as well be giving a recipe for angel food cake cause you can hardly make out what he's saying for the static. I get up and slip off my sweat pants and then I see Gretchen standing at the starting line kicking her legs out like a pro. Then as I get into place I see that ole Raymond is in line on the other side of the fence, bending down with his fingers on the ground just like he knew what he was doing. I was going to yell at him but then I didn't. It burns up your energy to holler.

Every time, just before I take off in a race, I always feel like I'm in a dream, the kind of dream you have when you're sick with fever and feel all hot and weightless. I dream I'm flying over a sandy beach in the early morning sun, kissing the leaves of the trees as I fly by. And there's always the smell of apples, just like in the country when I was little and use to think I was a choo-choo train, running through the fields of corn and chugging up the hill to the orchard. And all the time I'm dreaming this, I get lighter and lighter until I'm flying over the beach again, getting blown through the sky like a feather that weighs nothing at all. But once I spread my fingers in the dirt and crouch over for the Get on Your Mark, the dream goes and I am solid again and am telling myself, Squeaky, you must win, you must win, you are the fastest thing in the world, you can even beat your father up Amsterdam if you really try. And then I feel my weight coming back just behind my knees then down to my feet then into the earth and the pistol shot explodes in my blood and I am off and weightless again, flying past the other runners, my arms pumping up and down and the whole world is quiet except for the crunch as I zoom over the gravel in the track. I glance to my left and there is no one. To the right a blurred Gretchen, who's got her chin jutting out as if it would win the race all by itself. And on the other

side of the fence is Raymond with his arms down to his side and the palms tucked up behind him, running in his very own style and the first time I ever saw that and I almost stop to watch my brother Raymond on his first run. But the white ribbon is bouncing toward me and I tear past it racing into the distance till my feet with a mind of their own start digging up footfuls of dirt and brake me short. Then all the kids standing on the side pile on me, banging me on the back and slapping my head with their May Day programs, for I have won again and everybody on 151st Street can walk tall for another year.

"In first place . . ." the man on the loudspeaker is clear as a bell now. But then he pauses and the loudspeaker starts to whine. Then static. And I lean down to catch my breath and here comes Gretchen walking back for she's overshot the finish line too, huffing and puffing with her hands on her hips taking it slow, breathing in steady time like a real pro and I sort of like her a little for the first time. "In first place . . ." and then three or four voices get all mixed up on the loudspeaker and I dig my sneaker into the grass and stare at Gretchen, who's staring back, we both wondering just who did win. I can hear old Beanstalk arguing with the man on the loudspeaker and then a few others running their mouths about what the stop watches say.

Then I hear Raymond yanking at the fence to call me and I wave to shush him, but he keeps rattling the fence like a gorilla in a cage like in them gorilla movies, but then like a dancer or something he starts climbing up nice and easy but very fast. And it occurs to me, watching how smoothly he climbs hand over hand and remembering how he looked running with his arms down to his side and with the wind pulling his mouth back and his teeth showing and all, it occurred to me that Raymond would make a very fine runner. Doesn't he always keep up with me on my trots? And he surely knows how to breathe in counts of seven cause he's always doing it at the dinner table, which drives my brother George up the wall. And I'm smiling to beat the band cause if I've lost this race, or if me and Gretchen tied, or even if I've won, I can always retire as a runner and begin a whole new career as a coach with Raymond as my champion. After all, with a little more study I can beat Cynthia and her phony self at the spelling bee. And if I bugged my mother,

I could get piano lessons and become a star. And I have a big rep as the baddest thing around. And I've got a roomful of ribbons and medals and awards. But what has Raymond got to call his own?

So I stand there with my new plan, laughing out loud by this time as Raymond jumps down from the fence and runs over with his teeth showing and his arms down to the side, which no one before him has quite mastered as a running style. And by the time he comes over I'm jumping up and down so glad to see him—my brother Raymond, a great runner in the family tradition. But of course everyone thinks I'm jumping up and down because the men on the loudspeaker have finally gotten themselves together and compared notes and are announcing "In first place—Miss Hazel Elizabeth Deborah Parker." (Dig that.) "In second place—Miss Gretchen P. Lewis." And I look over at Gretchen wondering what the P stands for. And I smile. Cause she's good, no doubt about it. Maybe she'd like to help me coach Raymond; she obviously is serious about running, as any fool can see. And she nods to congratulate me and then she smiles. And I smile. We stand there with this big smile of respect between us. It's about as real a smile as girls can do for each other, considering we don't practice real smiling every day you know, cause maybe we too busy being flowers or fairies or strawberries instead of something honest and worthy of respect . . . you know . . . like being people.

Do you think Squeaky will be a good coach for Raymond? Give several reasons to support your opinion.

At the end of the story, why does Squeaky feel that winning the race isn't the most important thing anymore? What is important to her? Why?

How does Squeaky feel about Raymond? Explain, using examples from the story.

WRITE What do you like best about Squeaky? Write a paragraph explaining whether you would want to be like her.

NCTE TEACHER'S CHOICE

People Who Make A Difference

by Brent Ashabranner

You are thirsty. A cold drink is in the refrigerator ten feet away, but it might as well be ten miles away. You can't move a muscle to reach it. Your nose itches until your eyes water, but you can't lift a hand to scratch. You want to watch a videotape, but all you can do is look helplessly at your VCR across the room and wait until someone comes to put in the cassette.

Your name is Mitch Coffman, and you are a prisoner in your own body. Your mind is clear and sharp; you can talk and move your head, but you can't move any other part of your body. Like almost a hundred thousand other men and women in the United States, you are a quadriplegic, totally paralyzed from the neck down.

Mitch Coffman's entry into the world of the quadriplegic came on a day that should have been a happy one. He was returning from a party to celebrate his thirtieth birthday when his car skidded on a bridge and went into a spin. Mitch was thrown out with an impact that broke his neck.

When Mitch regained consciousness, he came instantly face-to-face with a terrible reality: he had suffered permanent damage to his spine between the third and fifth cervical vertebrae. He would be paralyzed for the rest of his life.

After months of physical therapy, Mitch regained enough movement in his left hand to operate the control for an electric wheelchair. And he was more fortunate than most quadriplegics because he was able to move into a government-subsidized apartment building especially equipped for people with severe physical disabilities. The building has ramps instead of stairs, roll-in showers, light switches and other electrical and kitchen equipment that are easy to reach and operate. Attendants are also on duty at all times. Still, there were endless hours every day and night when Mitch was alone in his apartment waiting, waiting for the simplest tasks to be performed for him.

And then one day a stranger arrived in Mitch's little apartment. She was only eighteen inches tall, weighed but a furry six pounds, and communicated in excited squeaks and endless trills. But she could open the refrigerator door and bring Mitch a cold drink or a sandwich. She could scratch his nose with a soft cloth when it itched. She could put a videotape in the VCR. She could do dozens of other things for him that he could not do for himself.

The stranger was a black and brown capuchin[1] monkey, and her improbable name was Peepers. Almost as important as what she could do for him was the fact that she was there, a companion, a constant presence in the apartment where, for most of the long hours of long days, there had been only Mitch.

"It took us months to learn to live together," Mitch explains as Peepers sits quietly in his lap. "Now I can't imagine living without her."

The modest quarters of Helping Hands: Simian Aides for the Disabled are on the fourth floor of an office building on Commonwealth Avenue in Boston. On my first visit there I could hear monkeys chattering in the training room. I was eager to watch the training, but before that I wanted to talk to Mary Joan Willard, the educational psychologist who started and is director of Helping Hands.

Quantum leaps of the imagination have always fascinated me, and I opened our conversation on that point. "How did you get the idea that monkeys might be trained to do things for paralyzed human beings?" I asked. "What made you think it was possible?"

Mary Joan explained that after receiving her doctorate in educational psychology from Boston University, she began a postdoctoral fellowship in 1977 at Tufts New England Medical Center in Boston. The fellowship was for rehabilitative study and work with persons who had suffered severe physical injury. In her daily rounds she soon came to know Joe, a patient at the center. One minute he had been a happy, healthy twenty-three-year-old. The next minute, because of a diving accident, he was a quadriplegic, paralyzed from the neck down. His story was an all-too-familiar one, but he was the first quadriplegic Mary Joan had ever known.

"I was shocked," she said. "I found it inconceivable that someone so young, so full of life was going to spend the rest of his days completely dependent on other people, dependent for a drink of water, for a bite of food, dependent on someone to bring him a book or turn out a light. I am a psychologist, and I kept thinking, there has to be some way to make him more independent.

"I couldn't get him out of my mind. I would sit in my room and

---

[1]capuchin [kap'yə · shən]

Mary Joan Willard enjoys her capuchin friend.

think about him lying there in his room, helpless. And then one night it hit me out of the blue. Chimps! Why couldn't chimpanzees be trained to do things for quadriplegics like Joe? I kept thinking about it, and I didn't get much sleep that night."

The next day Mary Joan went to see B. F. Skinner, the famous Harvard psychologist who has done extensive pioneering research with animals, using reward and punishment techniques to alter their behavior. Mary Joan had worked three years for Skinner as a part-time assistant. He might not think her idea was workable, but she knew he would not scoff at it.

Skinner was amused at his assistant's excitement over her new idea; he pointed out that chimpanzees grow to be almost as big as humans, are stronger than humans, and often are bad-tempered. Chimpanzees would be too risky. But Mary Joan was right; Skinner did not laugh. The idea intrigued him.

Why not, he asked, think about using capuchins, the little creatures traditionally known as organ-grinder monkeys? They are small, usually no more than six or seven pounds and seldom more than eighteen inches tall. They are intelligent, easy to train, and form strong bonds of loyalty to their human masters. Furthermore, they have a long life expectancy, an average of about thirty years.

That was all the encouragement Mary Joan needed. She did some reading about capuchins, found out where they could be purchased, then went to the director of postdoctoral programs at Tufts and asked for money to start an experimental capuchin training program.

"He nearly fell off his chair laughing," Mary Joan said, remembering the director's first reaction to her proposal.

But Mary Joan was persistent and persuasive. When the director stopped laughing, he came through with a grant and some training space. The grant was just two thousand dollars, but it was enough for Mary Joan to buy four monkeys, some cages, and hire student trainers at one dollar an hour.

"I thought we could train them in eight weeks," Mary Joan recalled. "I had never touched a monkey! It took us eight weeks just to coax them out of their cages. The monkeys I was able to buy had had some pretty hard treatment. They weren't in a mood to trust any human being."

But a beginning had been made, and patience and dedication paid off in training the monkeys in an astonishing variety of tasks: taking food from a refrigerator and putting it in a microwave oven; turning lights on and off; doing the same with a television set, stereo, heater, air conditioner; opening and closing curtains; setting up books, magazines, and computer printouts on a reading stand.

One piece of equipment essential to most quadriplegics is a mouthstick, which is used for turning pages, dialing a phone, typing, working a computer, and many other actions which improve the quality of a quadriplegic's life. One problem is that the mouthstick often falls to the floor or onto the wheelchair tray. The monkey helper is quickly taught to pick up the stick and replace it correctly in its master's mouth.

"The capuchins have great manual dexterity, greater than a human adult's," Mary Joan said, "and they're very bright. But we don't try to train them to do tasks where they have to think."

Judi Zazula, an occupational therapist, has been with Helping Hands almost from the beginning. Her title is program director, but Mary Joan describes her as a partner. Judi makes the same point about not putting a monkey in a situation where it has to think about the right way to do something. "Everything," she says, "is planned so that the monkey has just one way to respond if it does the task right."

The basic motivation for a monkey to perform a task correctly is a simple reward system. When it carries out a command as it is supposed to—turning on a VCR or bringing a drink—the trainer, and later the quadriplegic owner, praises the monkey for doing a good job and at the same time gives it a treat, usually a few drops of strawberry-flavored syrup. The quadriplegic releases the syrup by means of a wheelchair control.

There is also a system of punishment because capuchins are endlessly curious and occasionally mischievous. One monkey, for example, began dimming the lights when its owner was reading so that it would get a reward when it was told to turn them up again. More often, however, misbehavior is likely to be opening a drawer without being asked to or throwing paper out of a wastebasket in the hope of finding something interesting.

The monkeys are taught that anything with a white circular sticker pasted on it—such as a medicine cabinet—is off limits. If a monkey violates the off-limits rule, it is warned with a buzz from a small battery-operated device that it wears on a belt around its waist. If it doesn't obey the warning, the quadriplegic master can use remote controls to give the monkey a tiny electric shock. The warning buzz is usually sufficient.

Late in 1979 Robert Foster, a twenty-five-year-old quadriplegic living near Boston, became the first person to take part in a pilot project to test the feasibility of using a capuchin monkey aide. Robert, paralyzed from the shoulders down as the result of an automobile accident at the age of eighteen, had been living by himself for several years with the help of a personal care attendant. The attendant lived in the apartment with Robert but worked full time in a nearby hospital. That meant that Robert was alone in the apartment for nine hours or more at least five days a week.

Robert's new helper, a six-pound capuchin female named Hellion, helped to fill the long hours and continues to do so eight years after the experiment began. Robert communicates with Hellion—who deserves a nicer name—by aiming a small laser pointer at what he wants the monkey to bring or do. The laser is mounted on the chin control mechanism of his wheelchair. He also gives her a voice command such as "Bring" or "Open."

Hellion feeds Robert, brushes his hair, tidies up his wheelchair tray, brings him books, and carries out a whole range of other helpful tasks. For his part Robert dispenses strawberry-syrup rewards and tells Hellion how nice she is. Hellion is close by Robert's wheelchair all day, but when he tells her it is time for bed, she will go into her cage and lock the door.

As publicity about simian aides has spread across the country, Helping Hands has been swamped with requests for monkeys. Mary Joan and Judi are proceeding slowly with placements, however, still treating each case as an experiment. A number of additional capuchins have been placed with quadriplegics, and there have been no failures.

Mary Joan has had to spend an increasing amount of her time in fund raising and in administrative details of making Helping Hands a smoothly functioning nonprofit organization. "For the first two years we had to get along on three thousand dollars a year," Mary Joan said. "Fortunately, we don't have to pay student trainers much, and they love the experience."

Several major organizations and agencies concerned with severely disabled persons were interested, but all were skeptical. In the early stages Mary Joan wrote thirty-nine grant proposals and sent them to philanthropic foundations and government agencies, but not one was approved. But she persisted and, as evidence mounted that the capuchins could do the job, a trickle of financial support began. Now the Veterans Administration, National Medical Enterprises, the Educational Foundation of America, and the Paralyzed Veterans of America give some financial help to Helping Hands. Money is also received through private contributions, but fund raising still requires time that Mary Joan would rather be giving to other parts of the program.

Lack of money was not the only problem in the early days of the program. Some critics said that the idea of monkeys serving as helpers was demeaning to the quadriplegics as human beings. Some medical authorities said that mechanical equipment—robotics is the technical term—could be developed to do a better job than monkeys.

To the first criticism, Mary Joan points out that no one thinks it is beneath the dignity of a blind person to have a dog serve as a guide. As to robotic equipment, she agrees that for some quadriplegics mechanical tools may be best. But she points out that no piece of equipment can provide the companionship and sheer pleasure that an affectionate capuchin can.

"A robot won't sit in your lap and put its arms around you," Mary Joan said.

Trial-and-error testing proved to the Helping Hands crew that early socialization was necessary to train a monkey that would be affectionate and happy when it became part of a human household. The answer has been the creation of a foster home program. When the monkeys are young babies, six to eight weeks old, they are placed with foster families. These volunteer families agree to raise the monkeys in their homes for about three years and then turn them over to Helping Hands to be trained as aides to quadriplegics.

The carefully selected volunteer families agree to spend ten hours a day with their primate babies for the first six months—ten

Judi Zazula teaches one of her bright pupils to place a tape in a cassette player.

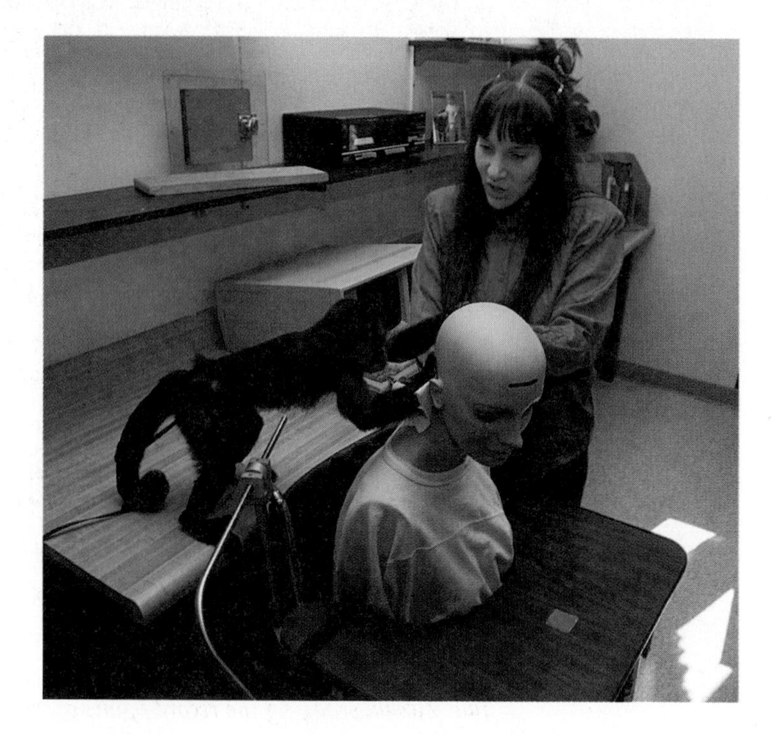

Practice makes perfect. Someday this monkey will gently rub a quadriplegic's itching nose or cheek.

Judi Zazula studying the record of one of the monkeys in training.

hours with the monkey outside its cage. This means that the foster mother and father and older children are actually carrying the baby monkey as they go about their household routines. Older monkeys require less time, but members of the household still must spend at least four hours daily with the young capuchin if it is to become a truly "humanized" primate.

Being a foster parent to a young monkey may sound like fun, and in many ways it can be a delightful experience. But it is time-consuming and demanding, and the time inevitably comes when the monkey must be given over to Helping Hands. "Everyone knows this moment of parting is coming, and most people handle it well," Mary Joan said, "but for some it is very hard. We have been offered as much as five thousand dollars to let a family keep a monkey. But, of course, we can't do that."

If for any reason a monkey does not successfully complete its training at Helping Hands, it is offered to its foster care family as a pet. Should the foster care family be unable to take it, Helping Hands maintains a carefully screened list of other families who have applied for a monkey pet. The "unsuccessful" monkey will be placed in the kind of human home environment to which it is accustomed.

Over sixty-five monkeys are now living with foster families. More than a hundred additional families have passed the screening test and are waiting to receive their foster "children."

Judi Zazula is a rehabilitation engineer. Together with Doug Ely, a solar research specialist for Arthur D. Little, Inc., she has designed most of the special equipment needed in the Helping Hands program: the laser pointer, chin and other wheelchair controls, and equipment that the capuchin's tiny hands can hold and manipulate.

"One of the first things I was asked to design was the nose scratcher," Judi told me and added, "The monkeys helped design a lot of the equipment."

She explained that by watching the monkeys as they carried out their tasks, she and Doug Ely could tell when a piece of equipment needed changing or when some new device was necessary.

The training of a monkey usually takes about eight months. A session with the student trainer may last from half an hour to an hour, but it might be as short as ten minutes depending upon the monkey's personality. There may be several training sessions a day.

"Every monkey is different," Judi said. "Every one has her own personality and her own strengths and weaknesses."

Judi's biggest job within Helping Hands is to match the right monkey with the right quadriplegic who is being considered to receive one. A training log is kept on each monkey, and Judi pores over every page until she knows everything that can be known about a particular capuchin's personality and about her strengths and weaknesses.

Then Judi visits the quadriplegic. She stays at least two days and gets to know as much about the person as she can and about the environment where the monkey is going to live and work for the rest of her life. Judi even makes a video of the quadriplegic's living quarters so that they can be duplicated in the final training of the monkey the quadriplegic will receive.

"I am totally consumed with getting the right monkey in the right place," Judi said to me. "By the time they leave this training room, they are my children. I always think, what kind of life will they have out there? I want to make sure it will be the best and most useful life possible."

Judi has come to know dozens of quadriplegics very well, and she has thought a great deal about the total loss of hope that they suffer. "A spinal cord injury is an especially terrible thing," Judi said, "because it usually happens to young people, and it usually occurs at a happy moment in life—a car accident after a junior-senior prom or having fun diving into a swimming pool or playing football. Then everything is lost in a split second. The person comes to and his or her world has collapsed and a nightmare begins.

"Most people thinking about something like that happening to them say, 'I wouldn't want to live; I'd rather be dead.' But these people aren't dead. Slowly, if they begin to believe that they can do things and affect things, they begin to think that it is worth hanging around."

Both Mary Joan and Judi know very well that the success of Helping Hands depends upon how effective simian aides are in performing tasks that help quadriplegics lead better and more productive lives. But they also believe passionately that having a capuchin helper adds an interest and spice to quadriplegics' lives

Judi Zazula rewards a capuchin trainee.

that can make a huge psychological difference. The companionship is important, but beyond that their ability to control the monkey makes them special. They can do something few other people can do.

As part of her master's degree work, Judi made a study of how people react to a quadriplegic with and without a monkey helper. When one quadriplegic she was using in her study was at a shopping center without his monkey, only two strangers stopped to talk with him in the course of an hour. When the monkey was sitting beside him on the wheelchair, seventy-one people took time from their shopping to speak to the quadriplegic during the same amount of time.

"The quadriplegic who can control a monkey is an expert in a very unusual way," Judi said, "and that makes him interesting to other people."

One quadriplegic had this to say: "When I go outdoors in my wheelchair, all that people see is the wheelchair. But when I go out with my monkey, the only thing they see is the monkey. Nobody notices the chair at all."

Mary Joan Willard has a sense of history and a vision of the future. In terms of need and demand, Helping Hands may seem slow in getting trained monkeys to the thousands of quadriplegics who want them. But she points out that the possibility of training dogs to guide the blind had been debated and advocated for a century before the Seeing Eye program began early in this century.

"Compared to that, we are doing all right," Mary Joan said to me.

Mary Joan's immediate goal for Helping Hands is to place forty simian aides a year and to move beyond that as fast as the job can be done properly. Costs for training, equipment, and placement are approximately nine thousand dollars for each Helping Hands monkey. If a recipient is able to meet these costs from insurance payments or other personal resources, he or she is expected to do so; however, no one selected to receive a monkey is refused for inability to pay. For most quadriplegics, costs are met from U.S. Veterans Administration and state rehabilitation program funds or from private research or charitable organizations.

Of one thing Mary Joan Willard is sure. "I see this as a life's work," she told me.

Judi Zazula feels the same way. "I can't imagine getting the satisfaction out of anything else that I get from this work," she said.

Judi was recently married to Doug Ely, her long-time partner in equipment development. Instead of a flower girl, Judi decided to have a flower primate. Hellion, the first monkey to become a simian aide in the Helping Hands program, carried a little bouquet of flowers.

What is the most interesting thing that you learned from reading this selection? Explain your answer.

What motivated Mary Joan Willard to begin training capuchin monkeys?

What do you think of the methods of training used with the capuchins? Support your opinion with examples from the selection.

WRITE One quadriplegic man said that when his monkey is with him in public, no one notices his wheelchair. Imagine that you see this person while shopping in your town. Write a conversation that the two of you might have.

Words from Brent Ashabranner

Everything I write flows out of my life interests. Many of my books deal with the interaction of different cultures. That interest came from my years of living in Ethiopia, Libya, and India when I was in the Peace Corps. One of the reasons I've written so frequently about the immigrant experience is that, to a small extent, I have been an immigrant myself, trying to adjust to a different culture, a different world. Also, I've seen those people—the ones who become immigrants here—in their native lands, and so I have a special interest in watching how they make the adjustment to a new culture.

One of the purposes of writing nonfiction is to correct distorted ideas by letting a person examine an issue or an idea more fully. By the same token, nonfiction also gives the reader new ideas. Imagine that you see something on television that interests you. A news clip is only a minute or two long, so if you want to learn more about that topic, you go to a book on the subject. You can really pursue your interests with nonfiction.

I think a great deal about my readers when I write. Based on my own experience, I've been firmly convinced for a long time that the most important reading we do is when we're young. The experiences that I had overseas, what I was learning about other cultures and how they relate to each other, seemed important to share with my young readers.

I understand from many teachers and librarians that there is a special interest in nonfiction these days. That gratifies me, even though I started my career as a fiction writer. For many years I just wrote short stories, and I've written two fiction books for young people. It's funny, though, I still think of myself as a storyteller. I've never lost the tools I learned writing fiction. I always look for the "story," and until I find it, I can't write a word. I see everything as a story or a series of stories.

In an odd way, the idea for my book *People Who Make a Difference* came out of my other books. My photographer, Paul Conklin, and I are constantly

the Author:
ranner

traveling around, gathering information. In our journeys, we've heard of or met people who in one way or another have made a difference. We decided someday we would do a book about these people.

Mary Joan Willard, the woman in "Helping Hands," came to my attention while I was in Boston working on another book. I was reading the newspaper and saw a small feature about her work. I called her, and she was happy to become a part of the book. It was an affecting experience to interview her. I've always been fascinated by quantum leaps of the human imagination, and her idea of using monkeys to aid the disabled certainly is one. She told me that it took one hundred years for the idea of guide dogs for the blind to gain any credence, but I hope monkeys for the disabled will take off faster than that.

I May, I Might, I Must

by Marianne Moore

If you will tell me why the fen
appears impassable, I then
will tell you why I think that I
can get across it if I try.

I Watched an Eagle Soar

by Virginia Driving Hawk Sneve

Grandmother, I watched an eagle soar
high in the sky
until a cloud covered him up.
Grandmother,
I still saw the eagle
behind my eyes.

Plains tribes eagle dancer

LOOKING TOWARD OTHERS

Reread "I May, I Might, I Must." How does the poem fit in with what you read in the other selections?

WRITER'S WORKSHOP

What do you think might happen to Squeaky after the May Day race in "Raymond's Run"? Write a play about one event in which Squeaky applies the lessons she learned that day. You can use characters and a setting from the story. You may also want to create your own new characters.

Writer's Choice The poet John Donne wrote, "No man is an island." Do you agree? The people you read about in this theme showed some of the ways that people rely on each other. How do you look toward others? Write about your own ideas on this theme. Your writing can take any form you choose. When you are ready, share your project with an audience.

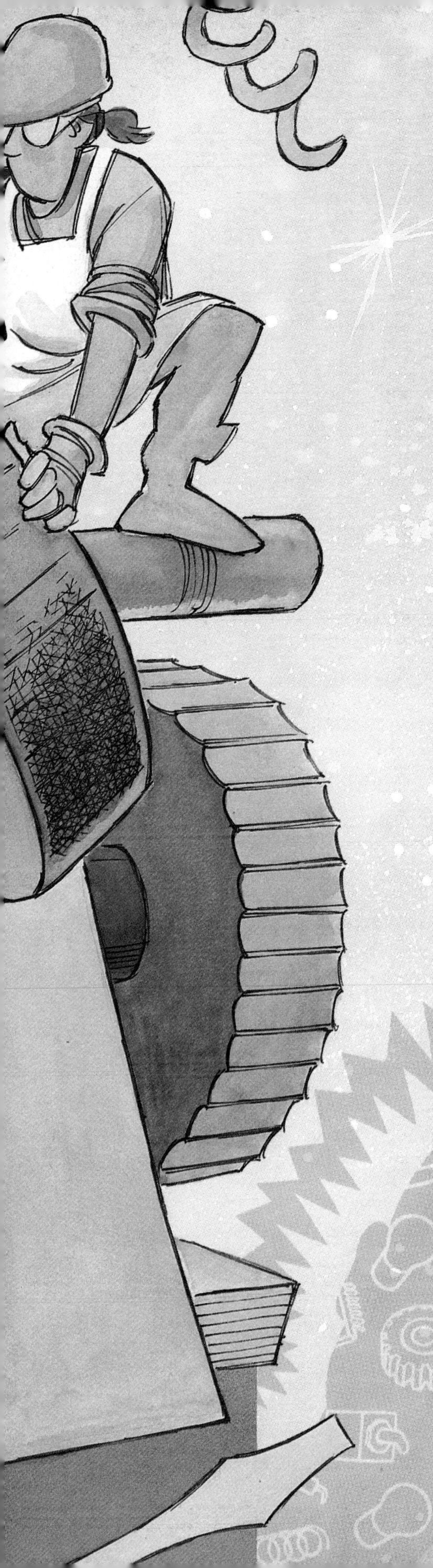

THEME

INNOVATIONS

Have you ever picked up a simple gadget and wondered how it came to be invented? Keep your inventive mind alert as you read about a variety of inventions and their creators.

CONTENTS

▼▼▼▼▼▼▼▼ BE AN ▼▼▼▼▼▼▼▼

INVENTOR

BY BARBARA TAYLOR

WHAT MAKES A PERSON INVENTIVE?

When many people hear the word *inventor,* they picture a mad scientist with fuzzy hair surrounded by bubbling test tubes and generators crackling with electricity.

But, in fact, inventors are very much like the rest of us. They may be old or young, male or female, postgraduate students or kindergartners. They may work in multimillion-dollar laboratories or in family kitchens.

Yet inventors do have qualities in common that set them apart from other people. They are curious about the world around them. They have active imaginations. They are willing to work at solving problems. They have the confidence to make their inventions successful, regardless of what others think or say.

Let's take a closer look at some well-known inventors of the past and present to see what role these four factors played in their work.

illustrations by Clarence Porter

INVENTORS ARE CURIOUS

Ever hear the saying "Necessity is the mother of invention"? If that's true, then curiosity might well be the father of invention. It is curiosity that sets the spark of creativity in the inventor's mind and starts him or her on the path to a new invention.

Think about Velcro®, the popular, lightweight, washable fastener that keeps your coat and book bag closed.

George de Mestral had just returned from a walk with his dog in the Swiss mountains near his home when he noticed his pet's fur was thick with burrs.

As de Mestral struggled to pull off the burrs, he wondered what made them cling so stubbornly to his dog. He looked at the burrs under a microscope and saw that they had tiny hooks that snagged onto the dog's fur. It suddenly occurred to de Mestral that if he could copy the hooks of the burr, he could invent the perfect fastener.

It wasn't until years later that the inventor got around to working on his fastener. After many experiments with different materials, de Mestral found a way to copy nature's hooks and loops and attach them to strips of cloth. In 1957 he patented his invention.

Today the Velcro fastener is used on everything from children's shoes to spacecraft supplies. It can withstand the heat of the tropics and the freezing cold of the Arctic. And we can thank a curious man out for a stroll for this popular product.

INVENTORS ARE IMAGINATIVE

It takes imagination to find the answer to a puzzling problem, even though that answer may be right under the inventor's nose.

In 1960, scientist Theodore Marton was looking for a way to bring an astronaut in space back safely into a spacecraft. A safety line to do the job had to be both flexible and rigid. It had to be flexible so that the astronaut could move about freely in space. But it also had to be rigid to keep the weightless person from drifting about while being drawn back into the spacecraft.

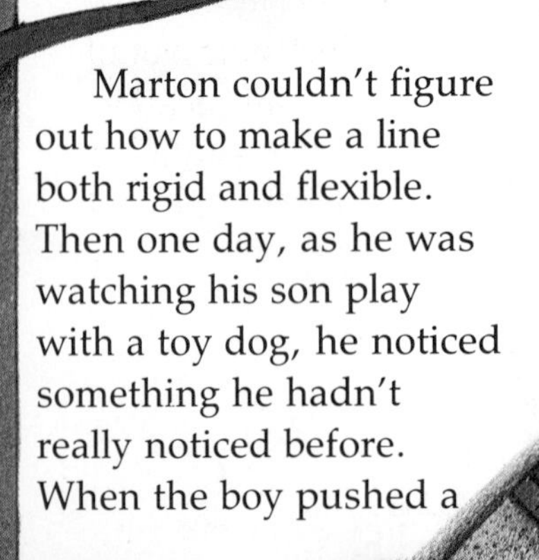

Marton couldn't figure out how to make a line both rigid and flexible. Then one day, as he was watching his son play with a toy dog, he noticed something he hadn't really noticed before. When the boy pushed a button on the toy, the dog collapsed.

Examining the toy, Marton saw that the dog was made of small segments and was kept erect by a tight string inside it. When the button was pushed, the string relaxed and the dog collapsed.

Marton used this idea in designing his safety line. The line is relaxed and flexible when an astronaut walks in space but it can be tightened, or made rigid, when the astronaut is towed back into the spacecraft. By using his imagination, Marton was able to apply the workings of a simple children's toy to create an important tool for space travel.

INVENTORS ARE PROBLEM SOLVERS

While working on a new invention, an inventor may face a number of different problems. The inventor's success or failure depends on how hard he or she is willing to work at solving these problems.

Jack St. Clair Kilby, an engineer working for Texas Instruments, is one inventor whose solution to a tough problem resulted in a revolution in the field of electronics.

Kilby's problem was parts—tens of thousands of them. In the mid-1950s, he and other electrical engineers were struggling to build an electric circuit. This circuit would have to perform the big jobs needed in the new electronic age of communications and space travel.

An electric circuit for such tasks had to hold hundreds of thousands of transistors, resistors, and capacitors. All these parts had to be connected in one unbroken path along which current could flow. To wire and solder all these parts together would be a nightmare. One mistake, and the path would be broken; current would not flow. And even if such a circuit could be designed, it would be so gigantic it could never fit in a newsroom or a rocket going to the moon.

Many engineers believed such a circuit could never be built, but Jack Kilby disagreed. He took fresh approaches to solving this difficult problem. One approach was to think in miniature. Why not put an entire electric circuit together on a single chip of silicon? The silicon would conduct electric charges to all parts of the circuit at once so there would be no need to wire or solder the parts. And the parts could be squeezed onto a space no larger than a fingernail.

In 1958 Kilby made his idea a reality. He built the first integrated circuit, or chip, as it came to be called. Today, the chip is the heart of every computer.

Some inventions are so much a part of our lives that we cannot imagine being without them. Think what your life would be like without light bulbs, television, or telephones.

On the other hand, some inventions have very particular and special uses. You might consider many of these inventions strange, but the United States government grants their inventors protection, called a patent, because the inventions are new and different, and because some people might find them useful.

Here are five unusual patented products. See if you can guess their uses. Then check the description of each invention on page 556.

B. *Patented November 18, 1879*
Patent Number 221, 855

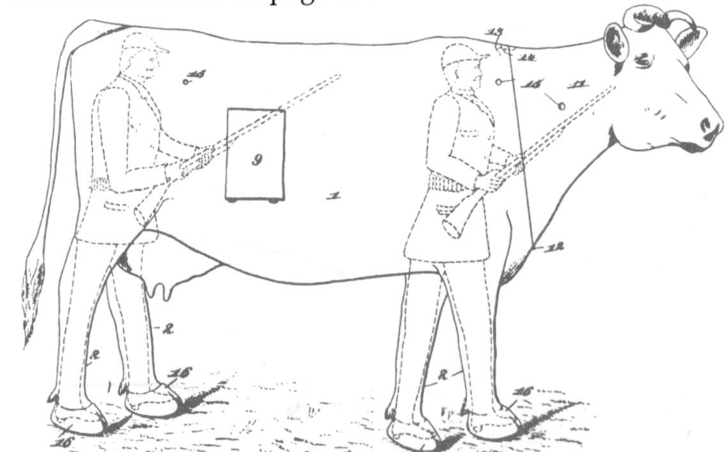

A. *Patented July 13, 1897*
Patent Number 586, 145

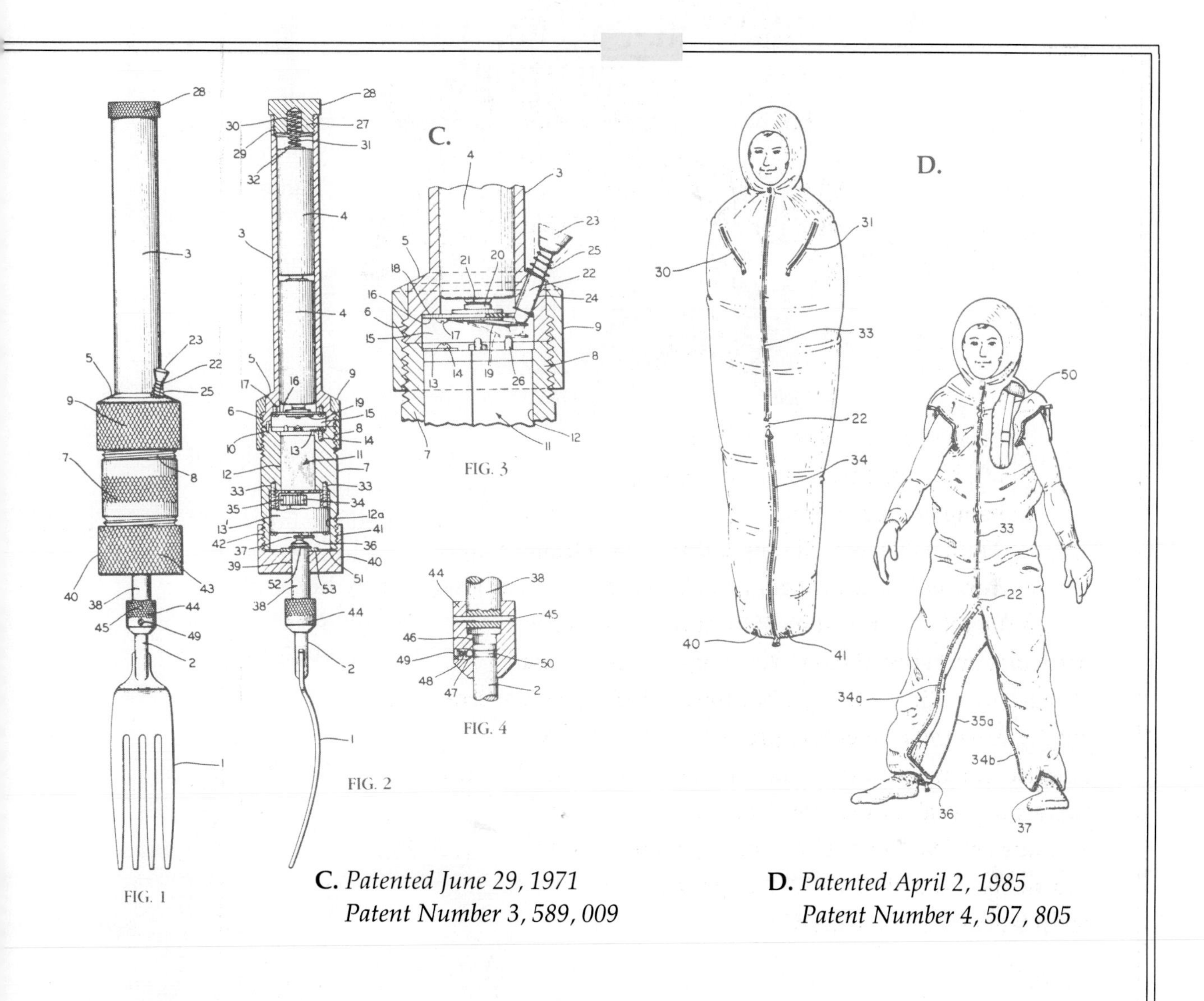

C. *Patented June 29, 1971*
Patent Number 3, 589, 009

D. *Patented April 2, 1985*
Patent Number 4, 507, 805

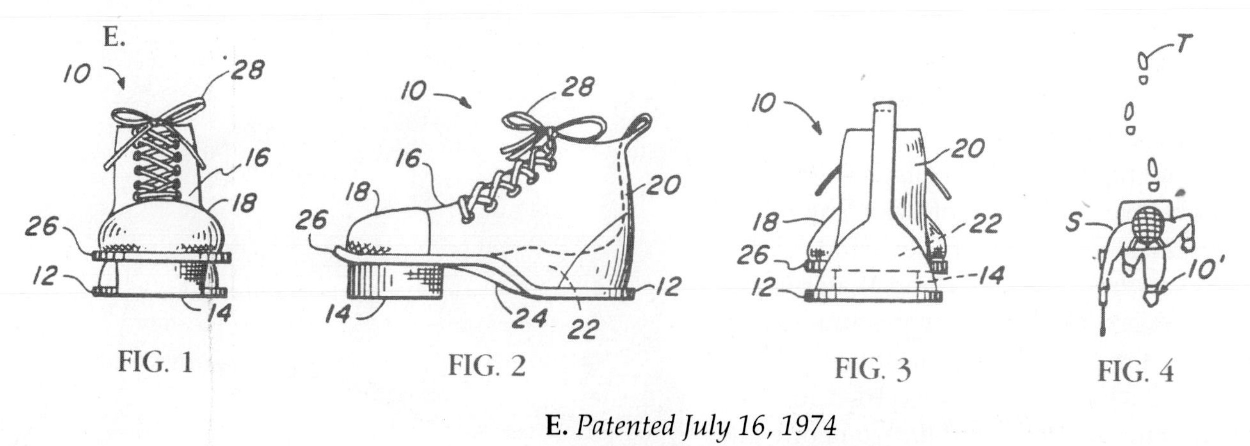

E. *Patented July 16, 1974*
Patent Number 3, 823, 494

A BEHIND-THE-SCENES LOOK AT SOME INVENTIONS

Why does one person think of the idea for an invention before anyone else does? Let's take a behind-the-scenes look at how some inventions came to be. There may be lessons to learn from these stories.

HERO OF THE SAFETY HOOD

Some people create inventions that make life safer for others. They get their ideas by thinking of other people's welfare instead of their own needs or comforts.

Garrett Morgan was granted a patent in 1912 for the Morgan Safety Hood, a special breathing helmet that pumped air directly into a mask that fitted over a person's face. The air was stored in a bag attached to the mask. There was enough air in the bag for 15 to 20 minutes of breathing—enough time for a firefighter to enter a smoke-filled burning building and rescue people inside.

Morgan was awarded the grand prize at the Industrial Exposition of Safety in New York in 1914, but it wasn't until an unexpected disaster in 1916 that Morgan and his invention became famous.

One night a tunnel collapsed 250 feet below the surface of Lake Erie in Morgan's hometown of Cleveland, Ohio. Workers from the Cleveland Waterworks were overcome by deadly gas fumes and trapped in the tunnel. Poisonous gas drove back firefighters who tried to reach the trapped men. But someone at the scene of the disaster remembered seeing Morgan give a demonstration of his safety hood some weeks before.

Police quickly located the inventor and asked him to come to their aid. Morgan, accompanied by his brother, arrived at the scene of the disaster with safety hoods. The two entered the clouded tunnel to rescue the helpless workers inside.

Garrett Morgan, pioneer in safety

Morgan and his brother succeeded in carrying all 32 trapped workmen from the tunnel. Fortunately, many were still alive and the inventor was proclaimed a hero. As news spread of the daring rescue, his safety hood became a great success. Soon it was standard equipment in fire departments across the nation.

When the United States entered World War I, Morgan adapted his safety hood into a gas mask that was worn by American soldiers fighting in Europe. The masks protected them from deadly chlorine fumes on the battlefield.

Garrett Morgan continued to invent, keeping other people's welfare in mind. He designed the first three-way traffic signal, making roadways safer for millions of motorists. Before he died in 1963 at the age of 86, Garrett Morgan had lived to see the United States a safer country, thanks to his inventions.

INVENTOR'S IDEA BOX

Getting an Idea

- What products do I or my friends use that could work better? Be more appealing? Be made to do more? Be made for less?
- Is there something that would make a person's job easier?
- What particular problem would I like solved?

The FABULOUS FRISBEE

Some inventors take a common item already in existence and find an entirely new use for it. That's how the popular toy the Frisbee came to be.

One day in 1948, Walter Fred Morrison happened to be driving past the Frisbie Pie Company in Bridgeport, Connecticut, when he saw two truck drivers tossing empty pie pans back and forth in the parking lot.

It reminded Morrison of his childhood, when he'd thrown pie pans with his playmates. Returning home to Los Angeles, California, Morrison went to work designing a disc that could be thrown back and forth like the pie pans. The disc had to be light enough not to hurt someone who got in its flight path and still heavy enough to fly a good distance. He found the right material for his toy—a soft plastic that was bouncy but tough. He called his invention "Morrison's Flyin' Saucer" and took two cartons of his toys to a nearby county fair to sell.

Morrison thought of a gimmick to make people want to buy his flying saucers. He told the crowds at the fair that there was an "invisible wire" stretched between him and a friend. When Morrison threw the saucer, he

claimed it flew along the wire directly to his friend's waiting hand. Morrison charged one cent per foot for the invisible wire and threw in a "free" Flyin' Saucer with every 100 feet of wire a customer bought. The gimmick worked and soon Morrison had sold out his supply of saucers and invisible wire.

But Morrison still wasn't satisfied. He improved the design and gave the toy a new name—the Pluto Platter. In 1957, the Wham-O Toy Company of San Gabriel, California, saw the Pluto Platter, liked it, and bought it from Morrison.

Sales of Pluto Platters were steady among beachgoers, who loved playing catch with them, but were slow among the general public. Then one day, Wham-O owner Rich Knerr saw some college students throwing the Platters at Harvard University in Cambridge, Massachusetts. The students told him how they used to throw pie pans from the Frisbie Pie Company. Knerr remembered Morrison's story about the same pie company and decided that a change of name would make the toy more popular. The Pluto Platter became the Frisbee (an unintentional misspelling) and the rest is history.

The Frisbee remains popular with people of all ages and athletic abilities. And it all started with an empty pie pan and an inventor with imagination.

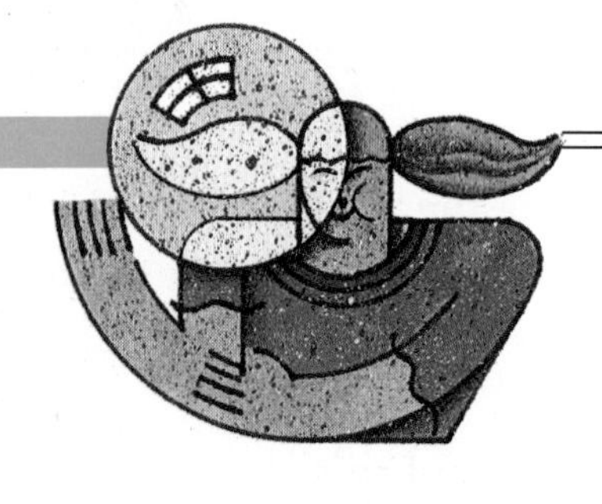

From Chicle ▾▾▾▾ to ▾▾▾▾ Chewing Gum

What is worthless to one person may be valuable to someone else. And when that someone else happens to be an inventor, the results can be spectacular.

Take the case of Thomas Adams of New Jersey. Adams turned a supply of apparently useless tree sap sitting in his warehouse into a new product—chewing gum.

The dried sap Adams had is called *chicle.* It comes from the wild sapodilla tree of Central America. Adams had spent two years trying to make a substitute for rubber from the chicle but his efforts had failed. Then Adams noticed his young son chewing chicle in imitation of the Indians who had chewed it for over a thousand years. What was good for the Indians, thought Adams, might just be enjoyable to the folks at home. At that time, Americans were chewing less tasty materials such as spruce resin and paraffin.

So Adams and his sons, Horatio and Thomas, went to work. They mixed chicle with water, rolled it into balls, and sold it to druggists along the East Coast. Customers welcomed the flavorless chewing gum and, by 1872, Adams was operating his own chewing-gum factory with 250 workers.

Despite teachers who outlawed it in schools and doctors who mistakenly warned that it would make the intestines stick together if swallowed, chewing gum became a worldwide success.

Adams constantly improved his product. He changed the packaging, sold it in vending machines, and added numerous flavors. You can still buy his licorice-flavored Black Jack in stores today.

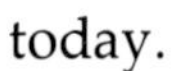

Some inventors adapt their inventions to meet the needs of others.

Rebecca Schroeder was only nine when she invented the glow sheet. She went for a drive with her mother and sat in the car doing homework while her mother went shopping. Soon it began to grow dark and Rebecca could no longer see well enough to write. As the light grew dimmer, another kind of light lit up in Rebecca's brain. Why not make a board or panel, she thought, that would light up so that people could write in the dark?

It was a great idea, but how was she going to turn it into a practical invention? Rebecca asked her father, a patent attorney and an inventor himself, to buy her some luminous paint. Then one night, after experimenting with the paint in her bedroom, she came running out to tell her surprised parents, "It works! It works!"

Rebecca's invention, which she calls the "Glow Sheet," consists of a sheet of special luminous paper embedded in a plastic clipboard. When a sheet of writing paper is placed over the clipboard, it lights up. The darker it is, the brighter the paper glows. When she found that the glow sheet began to lose its glow after 15 minutes, Rebecca found a way to lengthen the glow's life. She wired the clipboard with electricity and attached a battery-operated button. To "turn" the glow sheet on, a person only had to push the button.

Today, in her mid-20s, Rebecca heads her own company. She works at trying to get her glow sheets produced as inexpensively as possible so that many people will be able to afford to buy them.

And she's busy promoting her glow sheet idea to various groups and individuals. She is always thinking up new ways to make her invention useful. For example, with the glow sheet, hospital nurses could write their reports without turning on the lights and disturbing a sleeping patient. Police officers could fill out reports in emergencies or at the darkened scene of a crime. Radiologists and photographers, who must develop their X rays and photographs in darkened rooms, could take notes without damaging their work. And customers in dimly lit restaurants could read the menu more easily.

Finally, Rebecca's invention could help other inventors. When an idea for a new invention comes in the middle of the night, an inventor could just reach for the glow sheet on the bedside table and jot down the idea. In the morning, the inventor would be ready to start working on that midnight inspiration!

If you're inspired by the example of other inventors and you think you have what it takes to join their ranks, how do you get started? Every invention begins with an idea. But where does the all-important idea come from? It comes from you or the people you know.

Ask Around.

Every successful invention fulfills a need. Sometimes it's a personal need, sometimes it's a need shared by many people.

You know what you need. The way to find out about the needs of others is to ask questions. Talk to your friends, neighbors, classmates, and family members. Ask them what would make their jobs easier or their lives more fun.

Clarence Birdseye, a member of a U.S. government survey team in Labrador in 1915, asked the local people what they needed most. The answer he got was fresh foods. Few vegetables or meats could be produced in such a cold, northern land and there was no way to transport foods there without spoilage.

Frozen foods had been available commercially in the United States since 1865, but they had little flavor when they were thawed. Birdseye noticed that fish frozen very quickly by the Labradorean natives retained all its flavor after being thawed. It occurred to him that the problem with commercial freezing was that it was done too slowly. The food spoiled partially during the long freezing process and food cells were damaged.

After several years of experimenting, Birdseye developed a process to quick-freeze foods and came to be known as the "Father of Frozen Foods."

But Clarence Birdseye never stopped asking questions. He surveyed his customers regularly to see what new kinds of frozen foods they wanted. Today you can still buy Birds Eye® frozen foods, named after the inventor of modern quick-freezing.

Birdseye did not only ask questions; he set out to improve something that already existed—frozen foods. Not every invention needs to be new. There's always room for taking an old idea and making it better.

INVENTOR'S IDEA BOX

Getting the Facts

- What subject areas should I read about and study before going ahead with my invention?
- What specific information will I need to know to make my invention work?
- What books or periodicals might add to my knowledge of my subject?
- What persons or organizations might be of help?

Inventors need more than original ideas to develop an invention. They need to learn everything they can about the subject areas related to their ideas. This information helps them plan, design, and refine their inventions. Clarence Birdseye had to learn all about ice crystals before he could successfully freeze food. Marconi took physics courses to find out how sound travels. George Eastman learned about chemicals and early photography before he invented film and the Kodak camera. And Melville Bissell, inventor of the carpet sweeper, had to become an expert on a subject as simple as brushes to help him with his famous invention.

You, too, will need to become an expert on your subject. Read all you can about it—in books, magazines, and journals—and add constantly to your collection of information. If possible, contact manufacturers and organizations specializing in your subject.

TAKE YOUR TIME

You've probably heard the old saying "Rome wasn't built in a day." The same could be said for a successful invention. Asking questions, researching facts, and thinking your invention through in every detail all take time. If you rush past any step, you may overlook something important.

Gail Borden spent years inventing a way to preserve milk. In the 1800s, there was no refrigeration, and milk often went bad before consumers drank it. Many people became sick drinking this contaminated milk; some even died.

Borden believed that if he could remove the water from milk—condense it—it could be canned and remain safe for long periods of time. He tested and retested many methods for condensing. He checked and rechecked each step in his process. But when he succeeded and applied for a patent on his condensing method, the U.S. Patent Office turned him down. They claimed his process showed "nothing new."

But Gail Borden did not give up. He kept working at his invention. Finally, in 1856, he proved his condensing method new and workable and was granted a patent.

He was soon operating the world's first condensed-milk factory. Today the Borden Company still turns out millions of cans of condensed milk, as well as many other dairy products, for people everywhere.

Borden had a saying that was later engraved on his tombstone, words that every inventor should keep in mind, especially when things are going wrong: *I tried and failed; I tried again and again, and succeeded.*

ANSWERS to "STRANGE and UNUSUAL INVENTIONS"

PAGES 546-547

A. Hunting Decoy. Designed to help hunters outsmart ducks and other flying game, this grazing cow is actually camouflage for two hunters. When the hunters are ready to fire, they lower the neck of the decoy or open a panel on its side.

B. Improvement in Fire Escapes. This invention helps people save themselves from burning buildings. A person attaches the five-foot-wide parachute to his or her head, neck, or arms before leaping from the burning building. With the parachute, the person can land safely, while pads on the soles of the shoes cushion the shock.

C. Spaghetti Fork. This spinning fork is intended to make a favorite food easier to eat. The diner turns on the switch and a motor spins the tines, wrapping strands of spaghetti neatly around the fork.

D. Ambulatory Sleeping Bag. This unique sleeping bag is called ambulatory because it lets a camper move about. It has openings for arms and legs, allowing a camper, while snug inside the bag, to scratch an itchy nose or to take off in a hurry from a wandering bear.

E. Footwear with Heel and Toe Positions Reversed. The toes of these soldier's boots point in the opposite direction from that in which they're actually moving. Because the boots point backward when the soldier walks forward, they give the enemy the impression that its foe is headed another way.

Make a Notebook

Before you go to work on your invention, get a notebook and keep it handy. Inventors say their notebooks are their most valuable tools. They fill them with notes on their ideas and the materials they use, test results, progress reports, and things they learn while working on their inventions.

As you fill up your notebook, get witnesses—friends or family members—to sign some dated entries. This is valuable proof that your invention is your idea and no one else's. You might need to present these witnessed records to the U.S. Patent Office if someone else claims to have invented the same invention before you did.

Daniel Drawbaugh learned this lesson the hard way. If he had kept a notebook containing witnesses' signatures, he might today be honored as the inventor of the telephone. Witnesses claimed they had heard him talk over his telephone long before Alexander Graham Bell even filed a patent application for the same invention in 1876. But their words weren't good enough in a court of law. The law wanted written, dated testimony and that was the one thing Drawbaugh couldn't produce.

To avoid cases like Drawbaugh's, patent officials stress the importance to inventors of notebooks to show when their work on an invention began and how they followed through on the idea.

Thomas Edison, inventor of the phonograph, the electric lamp, and the kinetoscope, among other things, called the work he did in his notebooks "thinking on paper." He filled hundreds of notebooks and sketchbooks with notes, diagrams, and drawings. For the electric lamp alone, he wrote more than 40,000 pages of notes!

You, too, will come to value your notebooks. These written records of your invention's progress will help you plan, think through your ideas, and solve problems. You will want to share them with experts and fellow inventors.

Which of the stories about an invention interested you the most? Explain what made that story so interesting.

What characteristics did the inventors in the selection have in common? Why are these qualities important for inventors?

Name an invention that you could not live without. Tell why.

Write Describe an invention that you would like to create to make your life easier.

The Microscope

by Maxine Kumin

Anton Leeuwenhoek was Dutch.
He sold pincushions, cloth and such.
The waiting townsfolk fumed and fussed
As Anton's dry goods gathered dust.

He worked instead of tending store,
At grinding special lenses for
A microscope. Some of the things
He looked at were:
                                        mosquitoes' wings,
the hairs of sheep, the legs of lice,
the skin of people, dogs and mice;
ox eyes, spiders' spinning gear,
fishes' scales, a little smear
of his own blood.
                                        and best of all,
the unknown, busy, very small
bugs that swim and bump and hop
inside a simple water drop.

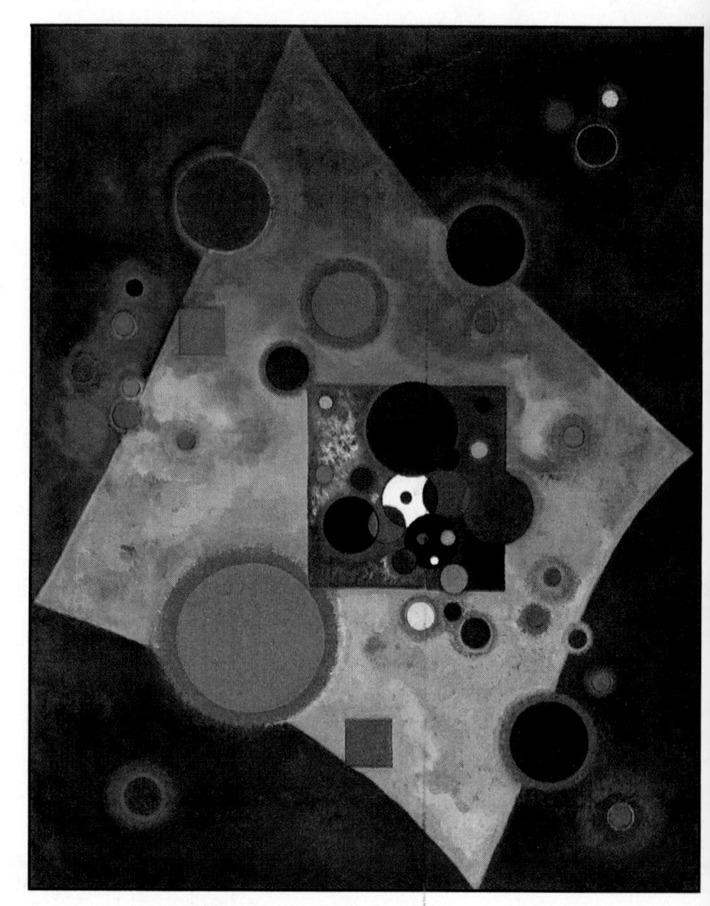

Accent in Rose, Wassily Kandinsky, 1926. Musée National d'Art Moderne, Paris, France.

Impossible! Most Dutchmen said.
This Anton's crazy in the head.
We ought to ship him off to Spain.
He says he's seen a housefly's brain.
He says the water that we drink
Is full of bugs. He's mad, we think!

They called him dumkopf, which means dope.
That's how we got the microscope.

INNOVATIONS

How can reading "Be an Inventor" help you understand Anton Leeuwenhoek from "The Microscope"? Do you think Anton might have had some of the qualities that "Be an Inventor" says are important?

Writer's Workshop

What do you think is the most important modern invention? Who invented it and why? One good source of information about an invention is a business that makes the product. Write a letter to a maker of your favorite product, asking for information about the invention. Make sure your request is clear, specific, and polite.

Writer's Choice Innovations mean progress. You have read about the origins of several inventions. Did reading "Be an Inventor" change the way you think about progress? Write a response to the theme Innovations in any form you choose. Discuss your writing strategies with a partner.

THEME

SPACE

When you look up at the stars, do you ever wonder whether someone out there is looking back at you? For generations, people have been wondering about life elsewhere in the universe. Now we have the capacity to send people into space to explore its possibilities. The following selections offer two very different perspectives on space travel.

CONTENTS

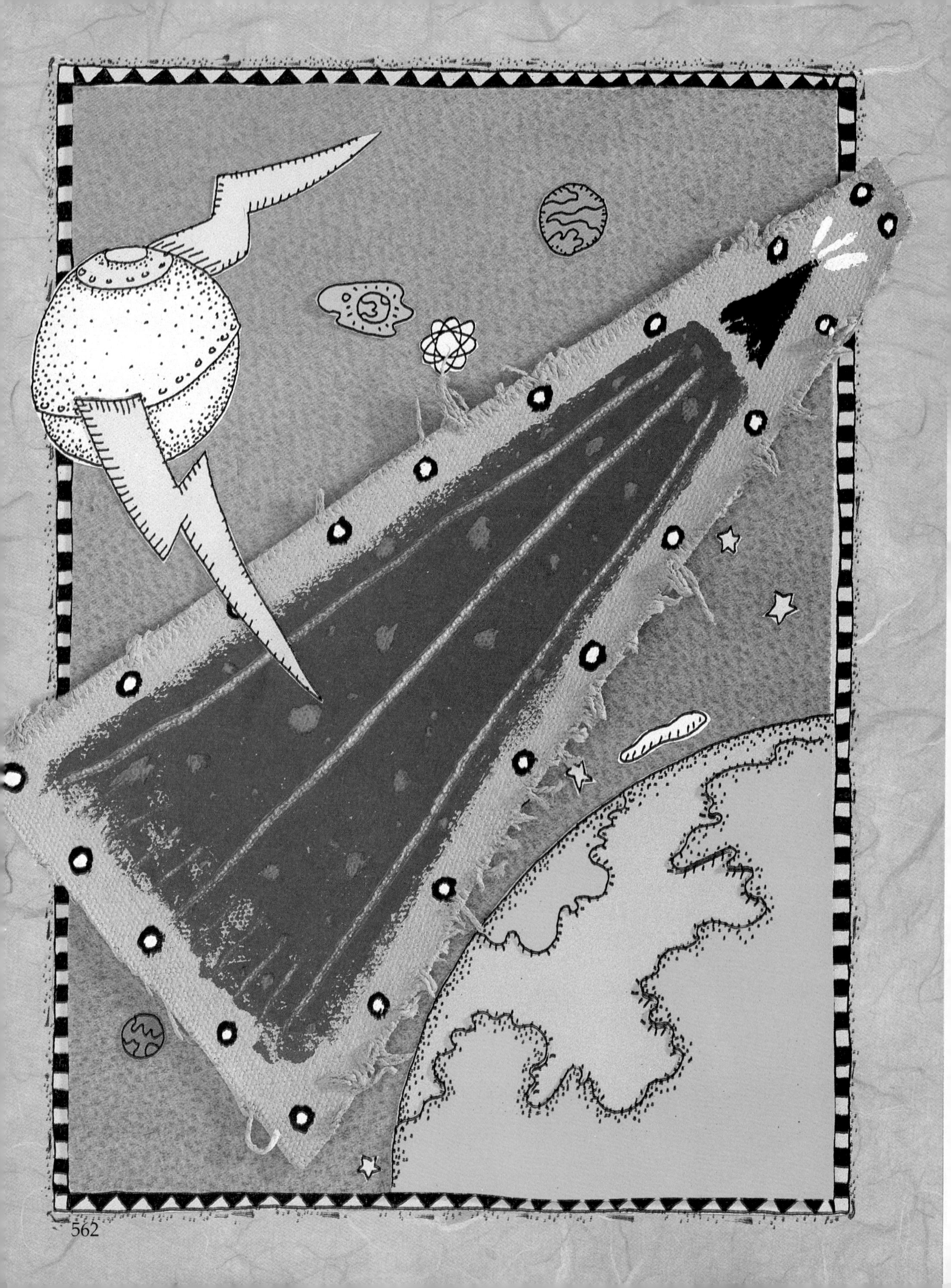

Little Green Men

BY BARRY B. LONGYEAR

Jhanni caught his breath and rested in the shade of a boulder; he had found nothing. His father had forbidden him to search with the other Star Scouts for the UFO reported three days ago, and he wouldn't think of disobeying his father. Still, I said nothing about searching on my own, thought Jhanni.

"All this about 'invaders from outer space' is nonsense." His father had been unshakable on the subject, and nearly everybody thought the same way since the probe to Venus had reported no detectable life on the planet. *Adventurer 7* had met with a mishap on its way to Saturn, and Jhanni's father had been furious. "More taxpayers' money thrown away on foolishness! We should spend the money to take care of problems here." Evidently the government felt the same way. When Jhanni turned thirteen the space program was canceled. Along with the program, the Star Scouts were officially scrapped.

Still, Jhanni's friends, and Star Scouts from all over, kept their squadrons alive to search for evidence—proof that would rekindle the space program and put them back on their road to the stars. Every time a UFO was reported, the squadron in that area would turn out and search for evidence—disturbed soil, burn marks, abandoned equipment—anything. But two years of searching had turned up nothing.

ILLUSTRATIONS BY FRANKLIN HAMMOND

"Someday," Jhanni had told his squadron, "someday we'll find the proof we need, but until then we have to keep on trying." Nevertheless, one by one, the Star Scouts were leaving the squadron. Some, like Jhanni, were forbidden to waste good study time on such foolishness; others were discouraged; and still more had come to believe as their parents believed: Space travel costs too much to spend for uncertain returns. Jhanni's father had pulled him out of the squadron when his grades began to drop.

"We've had UFO reports for years. Spaceships, death rays and little green men from outer space, and it's always been something that could be explained. I don't want you ruining your education by wasting your time with it."

Jhanni loved his father, but he had argued with him for the first time in his life. "How do you know there's no life on other planets? Isn't it possible?"

"No one knows for sure, Jhanni, but I'll tell you this: Before I believe it, someone's going to have to show me one of those little green men."

And that's what we're looking for, thought Jhanni, one of those little green men. He pushed away from the boulder and stepped into the sunlight. Shielding his eyes, he looked around. The squadron was searching the hills north of the development where the "object" was reported to have come down during the dust storm three days ago. His father wouldn't give his permission to join the search in the hills, and Jhanni was so angry it took him three tries to properly cycle the airlock on his home before stepping out into the desert.

He went south from the development to search the boulder field, although the "object" was reported north. The wind storm was blowing south that day, thought Jhanni. It's possible; not probable, but possible.

As he looked out over the boulder-strewn desert floor, the evening shadows grew long. Soon it would be dark and the desert cold. He checked the light buckle and heater in his belt and headed for his favorite boulder. At every turn he strained to glimpse the spaceship he hoped would be there. He knew he could get a better view from his boulder, the largest one in the field. It was pockmarked with great holes bored there by the action of the wind and sand, and Jhanni hadn't been there since he was a child playing with the friends who later became his mates in the Star Scouts.

Sometimes he would take one of his mother's blankets and some extra power cells and spend most of an icy night on his boulder, looking at the stars and dreaming of traveling among them. But the dreams became fewer as he grew older. There was no official interest anymore in moons, planets, stars or anything else that might cost the taxpayers more money.

As the sun dropped below the horizon, the stars appeared, and Jhanni watched them as he reached his boulder and climbed to the top. As he watched the countless pinpricks of light from unknown and unexplored stars, he let himself dream again of flying among them. His eyes glistened and he looked down. Maybe it is childish, he thought. The road to the stars is closed unless people can see the little green men in the flesh. And maybe . . . maybe the little green men don't exist after all.

Jhanni thought he heard a sound, and he looked over his shoulder. Seeing nothing unusual, he crawled over and around the boulder, looking into the tiny, wind-blown caves. There was nothing. He shrugged and stood atop the boulder, looking toward the development and his home. The outside light was on at his house, and his mother would scold him if he were late for dinner. He shook his head when he remembered he still had a tough stretch of homework to do and a math test in the morning. He knew he'd better pass this one. Too much imagination and not enough perspiration, his father would say if he failed. Taking one last look at the stars, Jhanni sighed and began to climb down from the boulder.

PING.

Jhanni froze. Slowly he turned his head in the direction of the sound. Deep in the shadow of a wind hole, a tiny light danced back and forth. Warily he crept toward the hole.

"HEY!"

Jhanni picked himself off the ground, knocked there by the suddenness of the sound. He reached to his belt and turned on his light buckle, aiming it at the hole. Inside there was a small, white cylinder propped up on spindly legs supported by round pads. The cylinder was dented, and its legs looked bent and battered.

"Turn off the light! I can't see."

Jhanni turned off his light buckle, and as his widening eyes adjusted again to the dark, tiny lights on the cylinder appeared and illuminated the hole. On one side of the object a tiny door opened, and a small, white-clad creature emerged, looked around and climbed down a tiny built-in ladder to the bottom of the wind hole. Jhanni peered closely as the creature lifted something and aimed it in Jhanni's direction.

"Can you hear me?"

"Uh . . ."

"Hold it." The creature adjusted a knob on its chest. "Had to lower the volume a bit. Good thing you dropped by; I only have a day's life support left."

"Uh . . .," Jhanni tried to untie his tongue, a million questions in his mind competing for the first answer. "Are you . . . are you from up there?" He pointed up. "How can you talk to me, and where . . . ?"

"One thing at a time. That's where I come from, and I'm talking to you through a universal translator. I rigged it up with a speaker from the lander console in case anyone came by."

"What happened?"

The creature threw up its tiny arms. "What didn't? I've been out of touch with my base ever since the wind blew me into this hole three days ago, damaging my oxygen regulator and radio. I'm running a little short. Can you get me to an oxygen-enriched atmosphere?"

"Well . . . there's my gas box. I raise tropical insects, and they're oxygen absorbing. I did it for a school project in biochem once, and . . ."

"Do the bugs eat meat?"

"Oh. Well, I can put them in another container. Can you fly or anything? My home's quite a walk from here."

"I guess you better carry me, but take it easy."

"I will." Jhanni picked up the little creature and held it in his hand, surprised at its weight. It was only as tall as one of Jhanni's fingers. He could just barely see the creature shaking his head inside his tiny helmet.

"I can't get over how big you Martians are. Wait until Houston hears about this!"

Jhanni laughed. "If you think I'm big, wait until you see my father!" And wait until my father gets a load of you, thought Jhanni. "By the way, creature, what color are you under that suit?"

"My name's Frank Gambino, Captain, United States Air Force. I'm sort of brown; why?"

"No special reason." Jhanni slipped the tiny creature into his pocket and began climbing down from the boulder. The little man isn't green, thought Jhanni, but he'll do. As he reached the desert floor and started to run home, he stopped himself just in time from patting his pocket.

What questions would you like to ask an alien if you were to meet one?

Once you found out that Frank Gambino is a human being, how did your image of Jhanni change? Describe what you think Jhanni looks like.

What are some of the clues the author uses to reveal the identities of Jhanni and the alien?

WRITE Do you believe there is life on other planets? Explain your answer in a paragraph, giving several reasons to support your opinion.

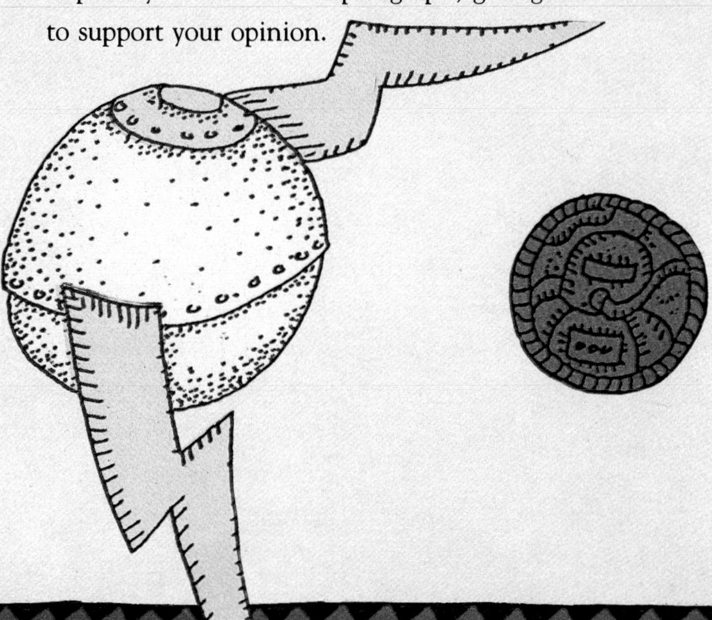

Richard J. Hieb, Thomas D. Akers, and Pierre J. Thuot work together to move the 4.5 ton communications satellite, Intelsat VI, into the space shuttle Endeavour's *cargo bay.*

ASTRONAUTS IN TRAINING

By Kim Long

Nobody knew exactly what to expect when the first astronauts were chosen to go into space. These astronauts were picked very carefully for their excellent physical condition, ability to work under unknown conditions and stress, and their past experience in piloting aircraft.

Many of the tests for selecting astronauts are no longer used. Although an astronaut-candidate must still be in good physical and mental condition, extreme physical tests have proven to be unnecessary.

The first astronauts were chosen only from candidates who were test pilots. The experience of being a test pilot was thought to be a good measure for conditioning, working under stress, and reacting quickly to new situations. Test pilots were also familiar with technical and engineering work, so they could be valuable in understanding and helping to modify the then new space vehicles.

NASA still requires candidates for the positions of astronaut pilot and commander to have flying experience. Mission specialists and payload specialists do not have to be pilots. As space exploration becomes more sophisticated, the astronaut's role will grow more specialized. Even now, a shuttle mission will include the following special kinds of astronauts:

Astronaut pilot. The astronaut who actually flies the shuttle. Most shuttle missions have an experienced astronaut pilot and a rookie pilot on board.

Mission specialist. An astronaut who is trained to carry out scientific experiments. Most mission specialists are expected to fly on twenty to thirty shuttle missions.

Payload specialist. An astronaut who is trained to carry out specific tasks or scientific experiments on a special flight. Because the payload specialist has specialized training only for certain flights, he or she may only fly on a few shuttle missions. Most payload

The crew of STS-45 makes astronaut training look easy on the KC-135 zero-gravity-simulating aircraft.

NASA

specialists are already experts in a particular scientific area before they go through a short astronaut-training course to prepare for a mission. Since they do not have to learn how to fly the shuttle or operate its systems (except for the life-support systems such as the zero-gravity toilet), their astronaut training may last only a few months.

Manned spaceflight engineer (MSE). An astronaut who is also a military officer, trained to participate in the design, testing, and deployment of military payloads. MSEs do not apply to NASA for this job but are picked by a special group of military personnel according to their qualifications. Like other astronauts, MSEs have studied different sciences in college, and most have more than one college degree. Unlike the other military astronauts, MSEs do not have to be pilots.

Civilian astronaut. A passenger on board a shuttle mission who has gone through the minimum training program from NASA. Usually, this person is part of a private, nongovernment project that is trying to develop profitable manufacturing techniques in zero-gravity.

Physical Condition

An astronaut-candidate has to be in good physical condition. Medical problems could make a space mission ineffective and even dangerous. Medical tests of candidates identify those physiological problems that are considered unsuitable for astronauts. Such problems as hearing loss, defective vision, asthma, heart murmurs or irregularities, liver malfunctions, ulcers, and life-threatening diseases can prevent a candidate from becoming an astronaut. It is not necessary, however, to have perfect hearing or vision to be acceptable.

Many of the dangers that were anticipated for humans in space turned out not to be problems after all. The G-forces[1] that the rocket boosters created were minor compared to what pilots were used to experiencing. Spacesickness, also called space adaptation syndrome (SAS), has created the most problems, but these are not serious.

So far, NASA has been unable to devise a test that can predict who will suffer from spacesickness. Flying in the special KC-135 plane, also known as the "vomit comet," produces periods of weightlessness for as long as thirty seconds. This experience makes many people sick, but some of them do not have the same reaction in the weightlessness of space itself. Some people who got sick on the KC-135 did not suffer from spacesickness in orbit, but other people who did not get sick on the KC-135 did. In most cases, however, spacesickness goes away in a few days.

Many astronauts who were not chosen after taking NASA's tests the first time applied again and were accepted. Sometimes this was because they learned more when they went back to college or worked on scientific projects. NASA also changes its tests and requirements from time to time, and

---

[1] G-forces: a unit of gravity. One *g* equals the normal gravitational force on the earth's surface.

Astronaut Mae C. Jemison examines a model of the shuttle escape pole as part of emergency bailout training.

something that keeps a candidate from passing the first time may no longer be a problem the second time around.

Floating around inside a space shuttle in zero-gravity does not require much effort. In fact, almost everything that is done in space requires little effort, yet astronauts must be in very good physical shape. Why? Because being in good shape helps prevent sickness, makes people more alert, and allows the body to stay busier for longer periods without tiring. One aspect of space travel that does require a great deal of endurance is extravehicular activity (EVA)—spacewalking. Astronauts who have experienced EVA have described it as very physically tiring.

Almost all astronaut-candidates have participated in sports and exercise activities. These include swimming, skiing, jogging, basketball, football, baseball, racquetball, scuba diving, and bicycling. What is important is regular exercise that builds cardiovascular conditioning and develops coordination. What is not important is

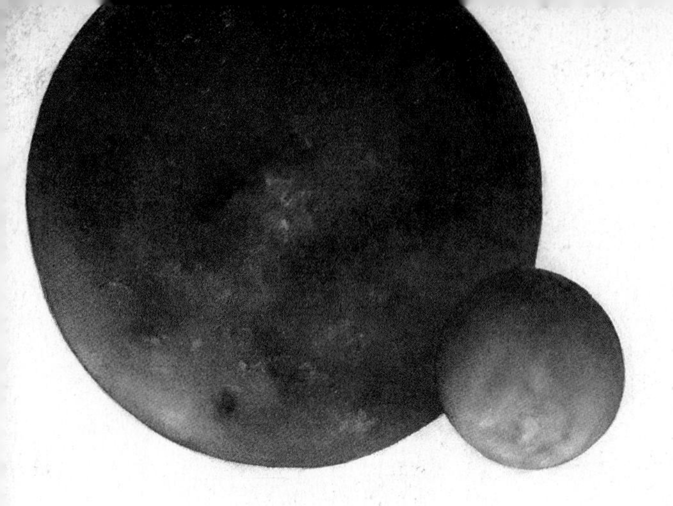

being a weight-lifting champion or being the fastest runner on the track team.

Psychological Condition

An astronaut must not have an unstable mental condition that could endanger a mission or the lives of a crew. Nor can an astronaut have trouble working with other people, because the success of a mission depends upon the mutual cooperation of its members. NASA looks for astronaut-candidates who are well-balanced people who get along with others and can adapt to the sometimes stressful conditions of space travel.

Astronaut-candidates are interviewed by psychologists and psychiatrists during the testing program. They also take written tests. Although this type of testing seems relatively simple, cheating is not possible, because the interviews and the tests don't have right and wrong answers. The goal is to weed out those who may not react quickly and safely in emergencies or during dull, routine work in the hostile environment of space.

Since NASA began testing candidates for the astronaut program, very few have been turned down because of psychological concerns. About the only problem that has kept candidates from being accepted is claustrophobia, the fear of enclosed spaces.

Pilot Training

It is no longer necessary for all astronauts to be pilots. Some candidates might be sent to flight school after selection if they do not already have piloting experience. Flight training has proven to be effective in preparing space shuttle passengers for the sensations of riding in a vehicle that is maneuvered into many unusual positions.

In the past, NASA gave preference to scientists who had valuable skills if they were also pilots. This situation is changing, however, as the space program becomes more complex and more people are needed to carry out new assignments. For instance, the simulator for the MMU[2] is a complex machine that requires dexterity and good hand-eye coordination. But experienced pilots who have good dexterity and coordination usually take longer to get the hang of this device than nonfliers.

Survival Training

The U.S. astronaut corps uses the space shuttle as its only form of transportation to space and back. Because something could go wrong during the launch or reentry

---

[2] MMU (manned maneuvering unit): the backpack power device that astronauts use when they need to maneuver away from the shuttle

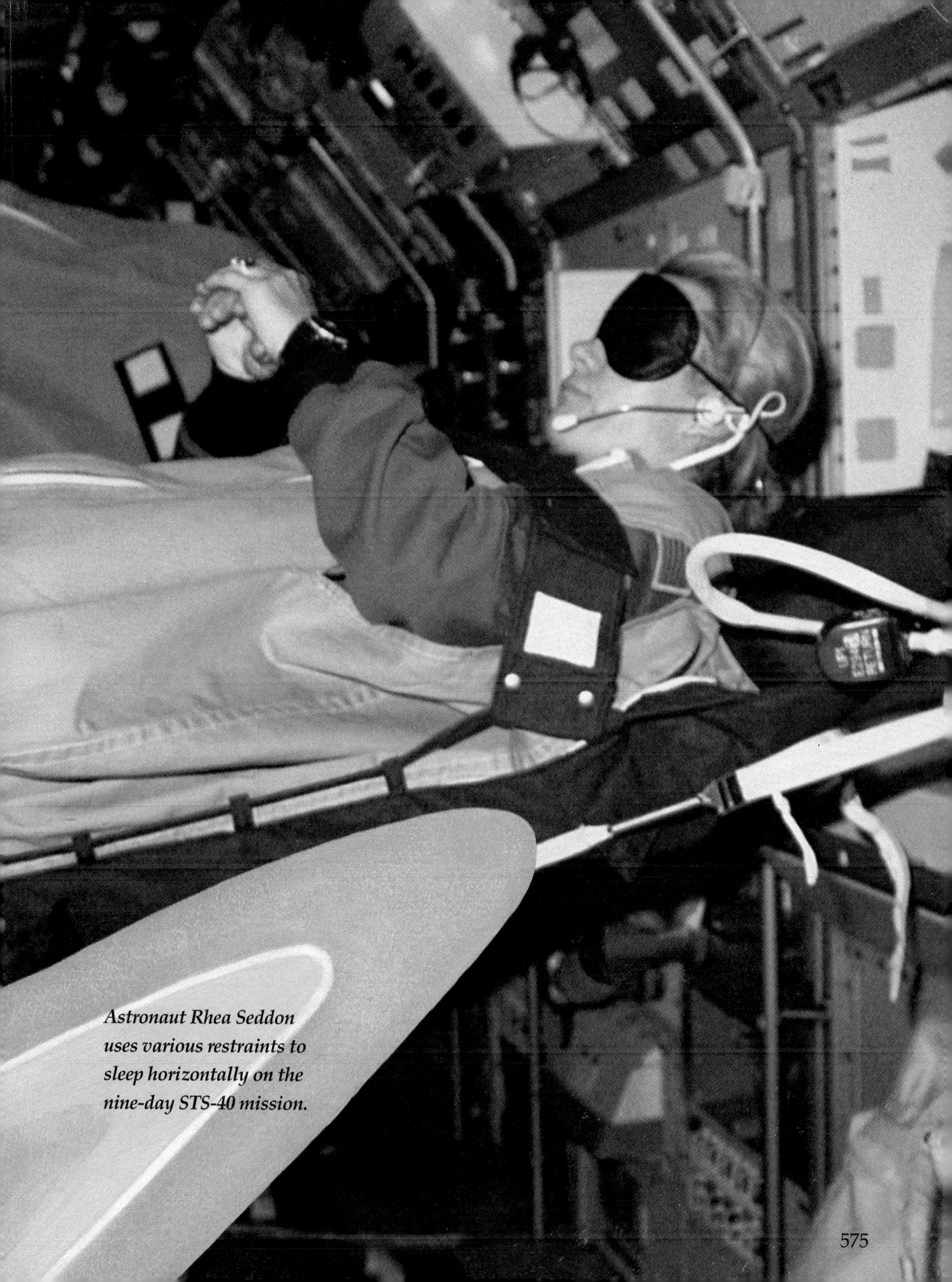

Astronaut Rhea Seddon uses various restraints to sleep horizontally on the nine-day STS-40 mission.

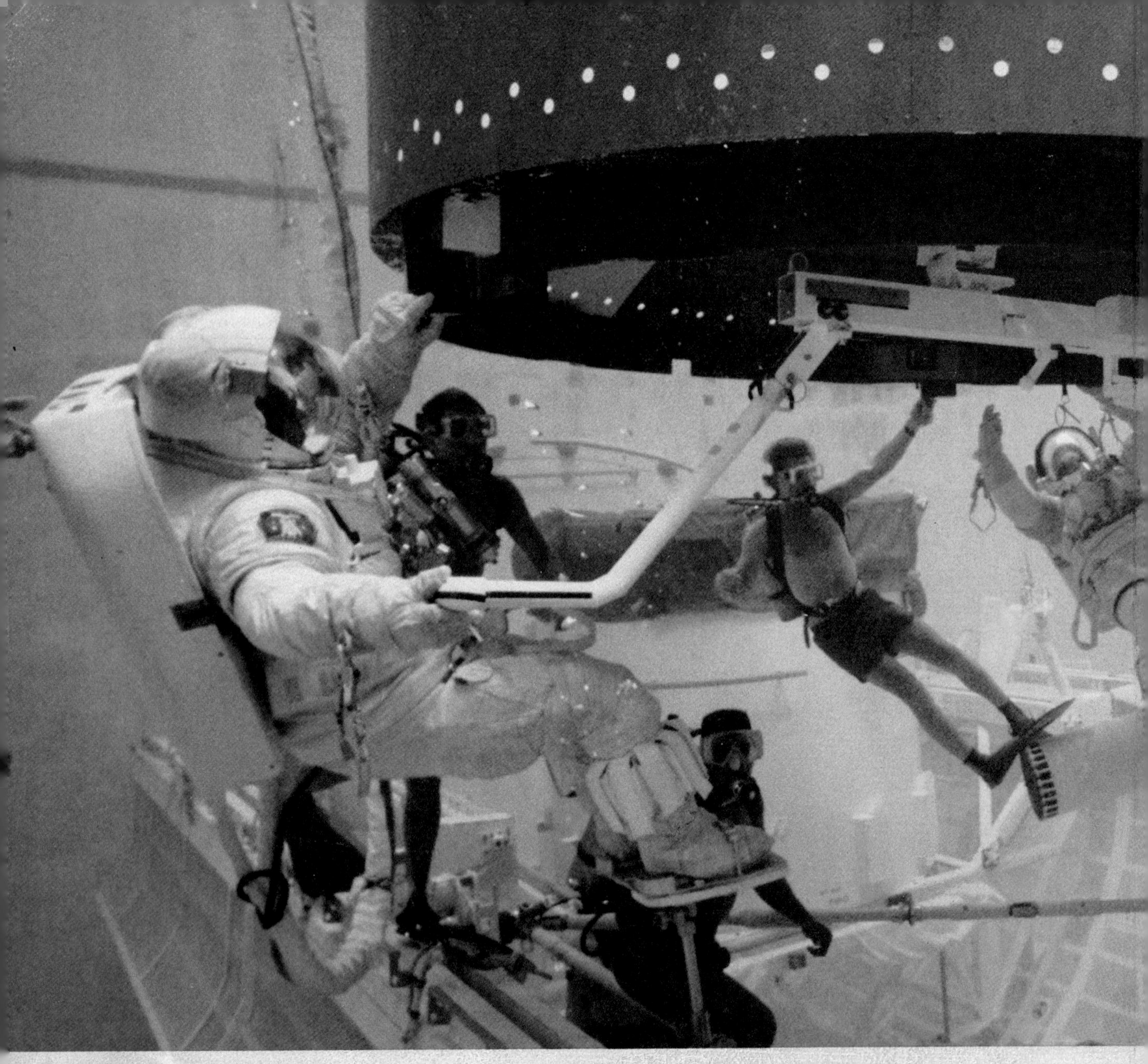

phase of a mission, the space shuttle might not be able to land at its designated spot. A forced landing at sea or in a remote area makes survival training a necessity for all astronauts.

This training involves demonstrations and practice. Emergency exits from shuttle mock-ups are practiced on dry land and in the water. Methods of using rafts and helicopter retrievals are part of this program. Astronauts who take flight instruction must also learn ejection techniques and the use of parachutes.

Classroom Training

Most of the astronaut's time during the first year is spent in classrooms, learning new material. Astronauts must learn how

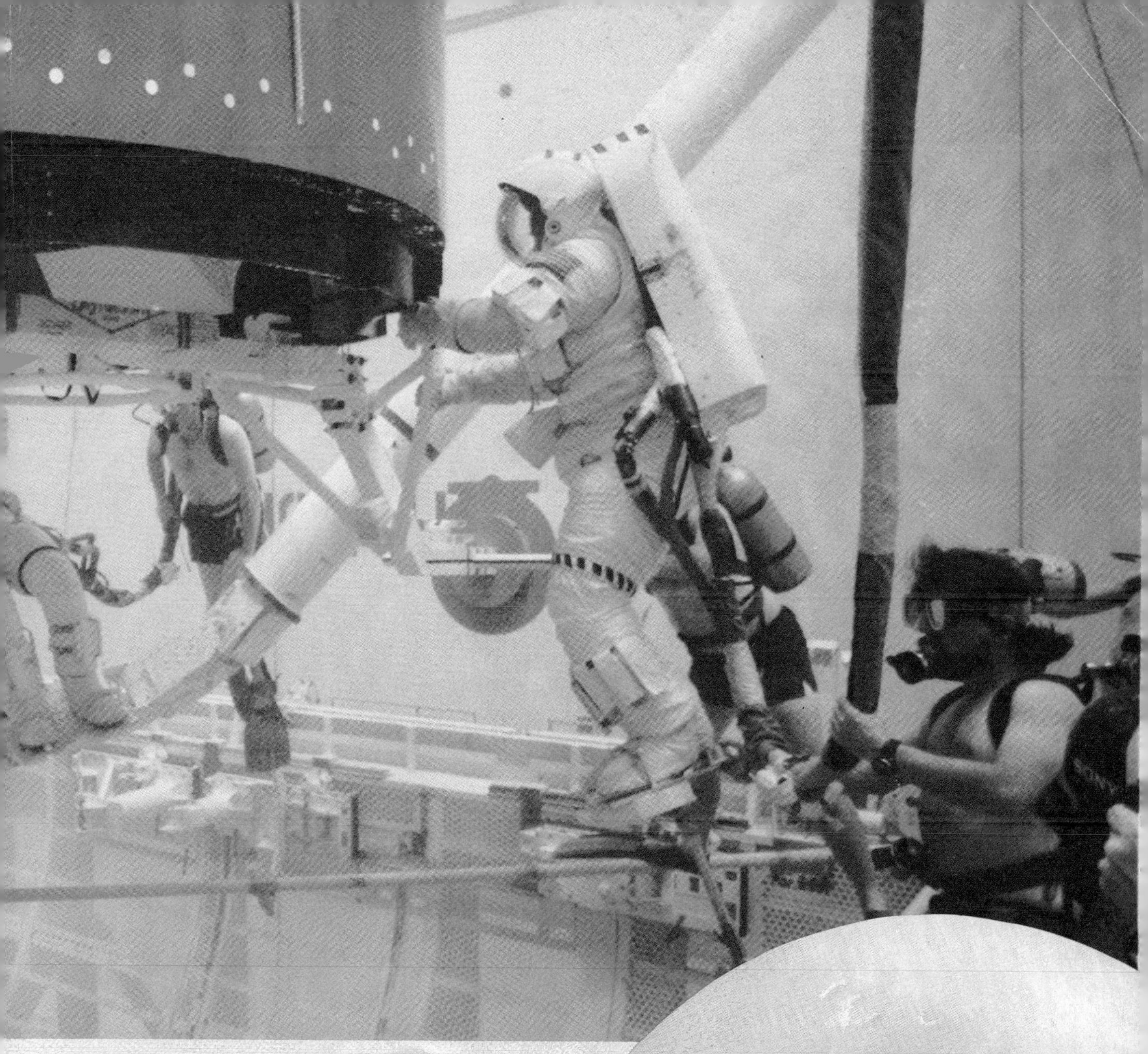

the shuttle is constructed, how it works, and how to operate the life-support systems, as well as the complex flight controls and many console monitors, equipment controls, and computers. They must also study ground-control operations.

Astronauts must be familiar with every aspect of the system that runs each spaceflight. Even though

Three astronauts wearing extravehicular mobility units (EMUs) practice techniques for capturing Intelsat in the Weightless Environment Training Facility.

astronauts have already become experts in specialized fields before being accepted into the space program, they must also learn about other subjects. In space, astronauts have to do many things, and understanding different sciences and procedures ensures that they will be able to do the job.

Technical Training

After a year of classroom study, astronauts begin several years of specialized assignments, in which they work alongside scientists, technicians, and engineers who are putting together the shuttle system. This work is necessary as the shuttles are constantly being upgraded, modified, and studied to improve their performance.

Other assignments include learning about mission control, testing new procedures in the KC-135 plane, and advanced pilot training. Shuttle pilots must become familiar with the complex controls of this high-tech spacecraft. Many different simulators are used to duplicate the effects of flying the shuttle. These include a shuttle training aircraft, navigation simulator, systems engineering simulator, shuttle mission simulator, and motion-base simulator.

Some special assignments for astronauts involve working for companies that NASA has paid to design shuttle equipment. Astronauts provide valuable information, because they are the ones who will be using this equipment. Satellites or other shuttle payloads may also require special astronaut assignments.

Mission control always uses an astronaut during missions to relay voice communications to the orbiting crew. This astronaut has completed the same training as the crew and can therefore respond more quickly if a problem develops. Working at mission control also gives astronauts more information about how the ground-support system helps the crew during a mission.

Astronauts who will be wearing spacesuits and space walking must have advanced training. Much of this is accomplished in a large swimming pool called a weightless environment training facility. An astronaut wearing a spacesuit in this tank is not completely weightless, but being in the tank feels almost like being in space.

Other advanced training is done with the remote manipulator arm simulator and the manned maneuvering unit simulator. These gadgets can be fun, but most of the work that astronauts do to prepare for missions is less exciting and more tedious. Astronauts must have good study skills and be motivated enough to stay attentive during their training.

Future Training

Astronauts today can only fly missions that use the space shuttle. In the future, space stations, other space vehicles, and bases on the moon and other planets will require a different kind of astronaut and different kinds of training.

Spacecraft pilots will need the most specialized training. But because fewer activities in space will be carried out on board the transport vehicle, the pilots will have less involvement with other space operations and will spend less time in orbit. Their jobs will resemble those of airline pilots, delivering and returning people and payloads from orbit.

In the future, astronauts who remain in space for longer periods aboard the space station or other spacecraft will need less training than today's astronauts. Their jobs will require more in-depth scientific and engineering skills, not detailed knowledge of the operating systems of the vehicle they live on.

These space workers will spend most of their time doing work in their specialized fields. As scientists, they must be good at what they do, but they will also have to know a little about living in space. Their preflight training will take only a few weeks or months, just long enough to familiarize them with the life-support systems, emergency procedures, and exercise programs necessary for zero-gravity conditions.

The space station and other space habitations will include some crew members with advanced knowledge about the systems and operations. These astronauts must be able to monitor, adjust, and repair equipment that isn't working properly. There must also be someone in charge. This person will be the most knowledgeable about the space structure and will have the training and leadership abilities to command its crew.

Would you like to be an astronaut? Why or why not?

If you were an astronaut assigned to a space flight, which specialized role would you most enjoy? What qualities or interests do you have that made you choose that role?

What part of the training would you enjoy most? What part would you enjoy least? Explain your answers.

WRITE Write a letter to NASA telling why you would like to be considered as a candidate for a space mission.

The First

by Lilian Moore

Moon,
remember
how men left their
planet
in streams of
flame,
rode weightless
in the skies
till you pulled
them down,
and then
in the blinding sunlight
how the first shadow
of an
Earthling
lay
on your
bleak dust?

"Little Green Men" and "Astronauts in Training" both tell about exploring space, but they have very different points of view. Do you think that Jhanni would enjoy reading "Astronauts in Training"? Explain your answer.

Writer's Workshop

What is interesting about space? Choose a topic that fascinates you, and investigate it. Gather information from books, magazines, and other sources, and then write a research report.

Writer's Choice You have read two very different pieces on space exploration. What do you think about the universe beyond Earth? Write about the theme Space. Use any form you think will work with your ideas. Carry out your plan, and publish your writing to share it with others.

CONNECTIONS

MULTICULTURAL CONNECTION

MAJOR CONTRIBUTORS

African American scientists and inventors have made many contributions to American life. For example, mathematician and inventor Benjamin Banneker helped create the urban plan for Washington, D.C., and chemist Percy Lavon Julian developed drugs that saved thousands of lives. Few inventors or scientists accomplished more, however, than Granville T. Woods (1856–1910).

Woods, a self-taught inventor and electrical engineer, was once called "the greatest electrician in the world." He secured more than fifty patents during his lifetime for inventions ranging from a telephone transmitter to an electrified "third rail" for subway systems.

Woods also helped revolutionize the railroad system with his invention of air brakes and a telegraph system that allowed moving trains to communicate with train stations. The overall scope and brilliance of his inventions led some to compare Woods with fellow inventor and contemporary, Thomas Alva Edison.

Think of a current need or problem, and design an invention to meet that need. Share your invention with classmates, explaining how it works and why it is useful or necessary.

SCIENCE/SOCIAL STUDIES CONNECTION

AFRICAN AMERICAN SCIENTISTS

Research the life and achievements of an important African American scientist or inventor, such as Benjamin Banneker, Daniel Hale Williams, Garrett A. Morgan, or Charles Richard Drew. Prepare a written report on that person, and present an oral summary of your report to classmates.

SCIENCE CONNECTION

THE ORIGINS OF THINGS

With a partner or in a small group, investigate the origins of three innovations or inventions. They may be small, simple things or great, important developments. Make a chart listing the invention or innovation, its origins or inventor, and how it solved a problem or met a need. Add pictures or drawings to your chart, and display it for your classmates.

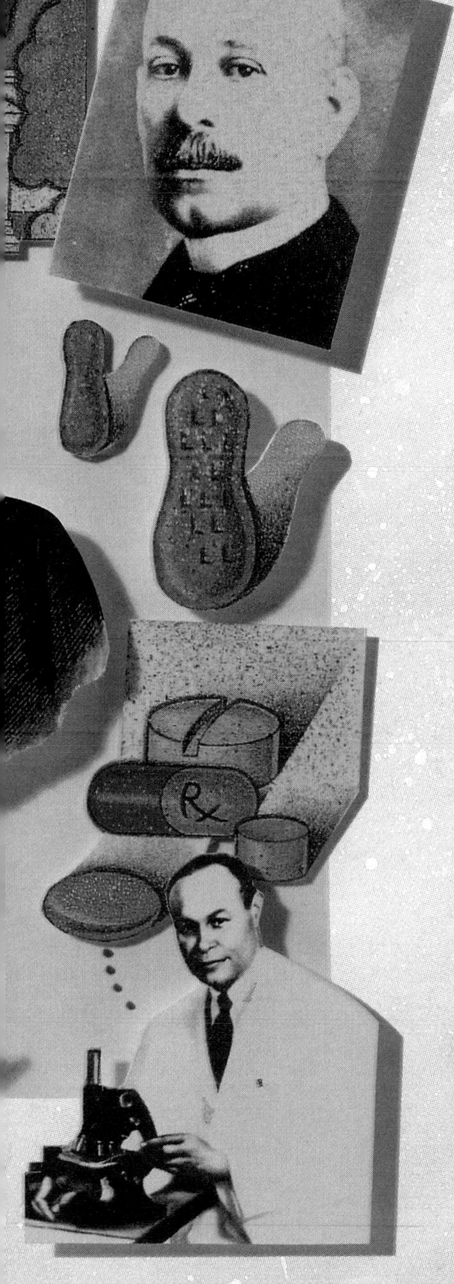

Clockwise from left: Granville T. Woods, Daniel Hale Williams, Charles Richard Drew

GLOSSARY

The **pronunciation** of each word in this glossary is shown by a phonetic respelling in brackets—for example, [ab′ə·rā′shən]. An accent mark (′) follows the syllable with the most stress: [kə·līd′]. A secondary, or lighter, accent mark (′) follows a syllable with less stress: [di·tir′ē·ə·rāt′]. The key to other pronunciation symbols is below. You will find a shortened version of this key on alternate pages of the glossary.

Pronunciation Key*

a	add, map	m	move, seem	u	up, done
ā	ace, rate	n	nice, tin	û(r)	burn, term
â(r)	care, air	ng	ring, song	yo͞o	fuse, few
ä	palm, father	o	odd, hot	v	vain, eve
b	bat, rub	ō	open, so	w	win, away
ch	check, catch	ô	order, jaw	y	yet, yearn
d	dog, rod	oi	oil, boy	z	zest, muse
e	end, pet	ou	pout, now	zh	vision, pleasure
ē	equal, tree	o͝o	took, full	ə	the schwa, an
f	fit, half	o͞o	pool, food		unstressed
g	go, log	p	pit, stop		vowel representing
h	hope, hate	r	run, poor		the sound spelled
i	it, give	s	see, pass		a in *above*
ī	ice, write	sh	sure, rush		e in *sicken*
j	joy, ledge	t	talk, sit		i in *possible*
k	cool, take	th	thin, both		o in *melon*
l	look, rule	~~th~~	this, bathe		u in *circus*

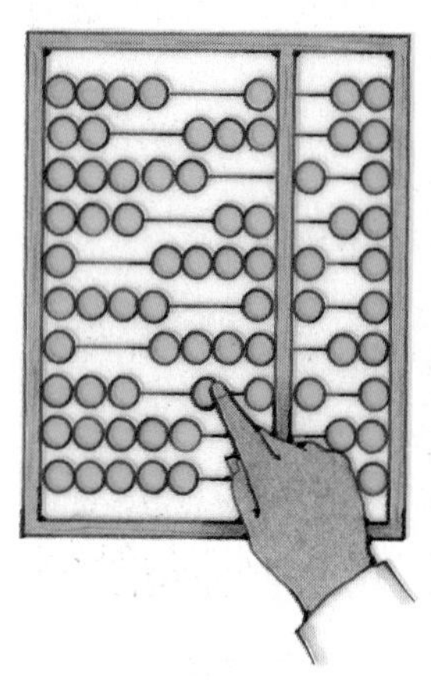

abacus

aftermath *Math* in this word comes from the Old English *maeth,* which meant "mowing." In Britain the growing season was short. When farmers harvested two crops of hay in the same season, the second mowing or harvest was often inferior to the first. So an *aftermath* is often an outcome of a bad event.

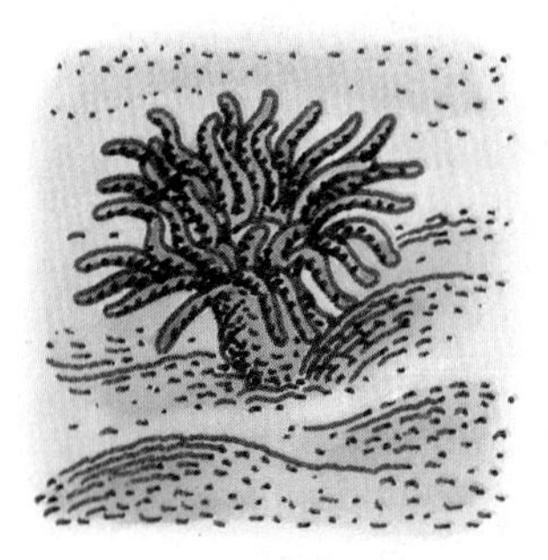

anemone

A

ab·a·cus [ab′ə·kəs] *n.* An instrument for computation made of a frame, rods, and movable beads: **Huang's *abacus* had been used by his grandfather when he was a schoolboy.**

ab·a·lo·ne [ab′ə·lō′nē] *n.* A type of shellfish enclosed in a flat shell: **The diver searched underwater for *abalone.***

ab·er·ra·tion [ab′ə·rā′shən] *n.* **1** Any departure from what is correct or natural. **2** The failure of a lens or a mirror to focus light rays on a single point.

ac·a·dem·ic [ak′ə·dem′ik] *adj.* Scholarly, as opposed to commercial or artistic: **Sophia had always enjoyed sculpting and oil painting, but she disliked her *academic* art history course.**

ac·cord [ə·kôrd′] *v.* **ac·cord·ed, ac·cord·ing** To give or grant what is due or earned: **When she became the mayor, she was *accorded* a city car and a spacious office.**

ac·cost [ə·kôst′ *or* ə·kost′] *v.* **ac·cost·ed, ac·cost·ing** To stop a person and talk to him or her in an aggressive way. *syn.* approach

ad·ren·a·line [ə·dren′ə·lin] *n.* A substance produced in the body to prepare a person to respond to difficult situations: **Victor felt his *adrenaline* rush when he saw a barking dog running toward him.**

ad·vo·cate [ad′və·kāt′] *v.* **ad·vo·cat·ed, ad·vo·cat·ing** To say or write that one supports or is in favor of something. *syns.* endorse, recommend

af·ter·math [af′tər·math] *n.* An effect or result of a traumatic or disastrous event. *syn.* consequence

a·loof [ə·lo͞of′] *adj.* Uninterested or distant in behavior or character; not warm or friendly: **Many parents at the school picnic were offended by the *aloof* new principal.**

an·a·lyt·i·cal [an′ə·lit′ə·kəl] *adj.* Having the tendency to examine issues, events, or objects critically, by breaking them into their separate elements: **Harry enjoys science lab where he can solve problems in an *analytical* way.**

a·nem·o·ne [ə·nem′ə·nē] *n.* A brightly colored sea animal whose body is shaped like a flower: **At the aquarium, Toyo saw *anemones* and other sea creatures with unusual shapes.**

ap·pre·ci·a·tion [ə·prē′shē·ā′shən] *n.* Awareness or sensitivity; recognition of value and significance: **After watching the group, Josef has an *appreciation* of the discipline of ballet.**

a·que·duct [ak′wə·dukt′] *n.* A human-made channel for transporting water over a great distance.

arc [ärk] *n.* A section of a curve, particularly of a circle: **The path of the rising airplane was an *arc.***

ar·cade [är·kād′] *n.* A row of arches and columns: **The director of the play decided to limit the set to two *arcades* and a fountain.**

a·stride [ə·strīd′] *adv.* With one leg on each side.

B

bal·last [bal′əst] *n.* Heavy material placed in a ship or boat to keep it steady: **The sacks of grain in the hold provided *ballast* for the sailing ship.**

bard [bärd] *n.* A poet; a singer of poems: **His folk songs were so poetic that he gained fame as a *bard* at Madison Junior High.**

bar·na·cle [bär′nə·kəl] *n.* A shellfish that attaches to docks and the bottoms of ships.

bat·ten [bat′(ə)n] *n.* A strip of wood used to stiffen the edge of a canvas sail: **The sailor inserted *battens* along the edge of the sail.**

ba·zaar [bə·zär′] *n.* A marketplace; a row of shops.

be·calm [bi·käm′] *v.* **be·calmed, be·calm·ing** To make motionless due to a lack of wind: **Elena was unable to return to the harbor before dark because her sailboat had been *becalmed* for several hours.**

bod·ice [bod′is] *n.* The upper portion of a dress: **The skirt of the unusual dress was black with white polka dots, and the *bodice* was pink with red stripes.**

boom [bo͞om] *n.* A pole that extends horizontally from a mast and is used to expand a sail: **When the wind turned, the *boom* swung and knocked him off the boat.**

bow·sprit [bou′sprit′] *n.* A pole that extends from the front of a sailboat and is used to brace the mast: **During the storm, the *bowsprit* of one boat pierced the hull of another.**

bron·co or **bron·cho** [brong′kō] *n.* A wild horse of the western U.S.: **Dale wanted to ride a *bronco* in the rodeo.**

C

ca·coph·o·ny [kə·kof′ə·nē] *n.* A harsh combination of sounds: **The small child was frightened by the *cacophony* of police sirens and beeping car horns.**

can·o·py [kan′ə·pē] *n.* An overhead covering: **Because it was about to rain, Carlos made a *canopy* with plastic to protect the food for the picnic.**

car·niv·o·rous [kär·niv′ə·rəs] *adj.* Meat-eating: **All members of the cat family, from lions to house cats, are *carnivorous.***

ca·vort [kə·vôrt′] *v.* **ca·vort·ed, ca·vort·ing** To prance about.

cha·os [kā′os] *n.* Complete disorder and confusion: **The news reporter described the *chaos* following the earthquake.** *syn.* disorder

chi·val·ric [shə·val′rik] *adj.* Demonstrating the qualities of ideal knighthood—gallantry, courtesy, bravery, and kindness.

chlo·rine [klôr′ēn′] *n.* A poisonous gaseous element with a strong odor; sometimes used as a disinfectant: **The workers coughed when they breathed in some *chlorine.***

chron·i·cle [kron′i·kəl] *n.* A record of historical events.

cir·cum·vent [sûr′kəm·vent′] *v.* **cir·cum·vent·ed, cir·cum·vent·ing** To avoid or to find a way around.

clam·ber [klam′bər] *v.* **clam·bered, clam·ber·ing** To climb up or down using hands and feet: **Mr. Vazquez *clambered* up the tree to rescue the howling cat.**

cock·pit [kok′pit′] *n.* The sunken part of a boat deck, where the boat is steered: **From inside the *cockpit,* he didn't see the rock that damaged the ship's hull.**

co·he·sion [kō·hē′zhən] *n.* A logical connection among parts. *syn.* unity

co·hort [kō′hôrt] *n.* A follower or a group of companions: **Juan faced the bully on the playground with several of his *cohorts* for support.**

bronco

chaos Today the word *chaos* means "extreme disorder." In Greek mythology, however, it apparently meant the emptiness that existed before the creation of the universe. Our word *chasm,* a deep, gaping canyon in the earth, is related to *chaos.* In the seventeenth century a chemist made up the word *gas* from *chaos* to name the form of matter that lacks a definite shape and volume.

a	add	**o͝o**	took
ā	ace	**o͞o**	pool
â	care	**u**	up
ä	palm	**û**	burn
e	end	**yo͞o**	fuse
ē	equal	**oi**	oil
i	it	**ou**	pout
ī	ice	**ng**	ring
o	odd	**th**	thin
ō	open	**t̶h̶**	this
ô	order	**zh**	vision

ə = a in *above*, e in *sicken*, i in *possible*, o in *melon*, u in *circus*

co·in·cide [kō′in·sīd′] *v.* **co·in·cid·ed, co·in·cid·ing** To happen at the same time: **Kiko's business trip here *coincided* with my vacation, so we spent several days together.**

co·in·ci·dence [kō·in′sə·dens] *n.* A chance occurrence of two similar or related events at the same time: **By *coincidence,* Aunt Luzanne telephoned from Europe just as we opened her letter.**

colander

col·an·der [kul′ən·dər *or* kol′ən·dər] *n.* A bowl-like utensil with holes in it; used to drain liquids from foods: **Lemuel drained the noodles in the *colander* before he served them.** *syn.* strainer

col·lide [kə·līd′] *v.* **col·lid·ed, col·lid·ing** To crash together violently: **We saw the train *colliding* with the truck as it went through the crossing.** *syn.* crash

com·mer·cial [kə·mûr′shəl] *adj.* Pertaining to business as opposed to scholarly or artistic: **In the *commercial* program, Esteban studied word processing, banking, and retailing.**

com·mer·cial·ly [kə·mûr′shəl·ē] *adv.* For sale to the public in stores: **Soda pop is a *commercially* available product that can be bought in many stores.**

com·part·ment [kəm·pärt′mənt] *n.* A separate section of an enclosed area: **The small child ran up the aisle to the front *compartment* of the plane.**

com·pound [kom′pound′] *n.* A group of buildings inside a wall or fence.

concave

con·cave [kon·kāv′ *or* kon′kāv′] *adj.* Curved inward like the inside of a bowl: **The warrior held the shield so that its *concave* side was against his body.** *syn.* hollowed

con·ceit·ed [kən·sē′tid] *adj.* Overly impressed with oneself: **Rudy was so *conceited* that he thought his friends were admiring his clothes when actually they were laughing at his vanity.** *syn.* vain

con·di·tion·ing [kən·dish′ən·ing] *n.* Fitness; good physical and mental health: **Her *conditioning* helped her to prepare for the meet.**

con·fig·u·ra·tion [kən·fig′yə·rā′shən] *n.* The shape, form, or arrangement of something: **The *configuration* of the parking area made it impossible for more than three cars to fit comfortably.**

con·firm [kən·fûrm′] *v.* **con·firmed, con·firm·ing** To verify; to eliminate all doubt about something.

con·form·i·ty [kən·fôr′mə·tē] *n.* Acceptance of the ideas, behaviors, and rules established by others; going along with the wishes of others.

con·gen·ial [kən·jēn′yəl] *adj.* Getting along well; having the same nature: **The *congenial* co-workers often went out to lunch together.**

con·sole [kon′sōl′] *n.* The part of a spacecraft that contains the knobs, meters, speakers, and other equipment to operate the ship: **During a rocket launch, an astronaut must pay careful attention to all the dials on the *console.***

con·tempt [kən·tempt′] *n.* A feeling of disrespect or revulsion for another person, act, or object. *syns.* disdain, scorn

con·tour [kon′to͝or] *n.* The shape of something: **The *contour* of the mountains was extremely jagged.** *syns.* outline, shape

craft [kraft] *n.* Skill, occupation, or trade: **The *craft* of jewelry making is one of the world's oldest trades.**

crest [krest] *v.* **crest·ed, crest·ing** To reach the top or highest point.

crev·ice [krev′is] *n.* A narrow crack or opening in a rock or wall: **The black snake slid through the *crevice* in the wall, escaping from the garden.**

cruis·er [kro͞o′zər] *n.* A motorboat with a cabin: **The captain carefully steered her *cruiser* into the harbor.**

cur·ric·u·lum [kə·rik′yə·ləm] *n.* All of the courses taught in a school or particular grade: **The summer school *curriculum* included classes in waterskiing, cooking, flower arranging, and pet grooming.**

cyn·i·cal·ly [sin′i·klē] *adv.* In a way that doubts the goodness of others: **When I said that I was mowing Mrs. Alvarez's lawn to help her and not just to make money, my sister laughed *cynically*.** *syn.* sarcastically

D

dan·der [dan′dər] *n.* Temper; anger.

de·ceit·ful [di·sēt′fəl] *adj.* Conniving; misleading or lying.

def·er·en·tial·ly [def′ə·ren′shəl·ē] *adv.* With respect and consideration.

de·for·es·ta·tion [dē·fôr′is·tā′shən] *n.* The destruction and clearing of forests: **If *deforestation* continues at the current rate, soon there will be few birds in this area.**

de·hy·drate [dē·hī′drāt′] *v.* **de·hy·drat·ed, de·hy·drat·ing** To remove the water from: **Elena's high fever *dehydrated* her body, so the doctor told her to drink lots of liquids.**

de·mean·ing [di·mēn′ing] *adj.* Making someone feel inferior: **Domingo was shorter than the other boys, and they sometimes said cruel, *demeaning* things about his height.** *syns.* degrading, insulting

de·ploy·ment [di·ploi′mənt] *n.* The process of moving into appropriate positions: **Careful planning by the officers resulted in the successful *deployment* of the soldiers.**

de·ri·sion [di·rizh′ən] *n.* Mocking laughter; ridicule: **The class clown was greeted with *derision* from his classmates.**

des·ig·nate [dez′ig·nāt′] *v.* **des·ig·na·ted, des·ig·nat·ing** To point out; to indicate for a specific purpose: **The school gym was *designated* the location for the senior prom.**

de·tect·a·ble [di·tekt′ə·bəl] *adj.* Able to be measured with instruments: **Scientists do not believe that life exists on Mars because there is no *detectable* evidence.** *syns.* noticeable, measurable

de·te·ri·o·rate [di·tir′ē·ə·rāt′] *v.* **de·te·ri·o·rat·ed, de·te·ri·o·rat·ing** To diminish in value, condition, or quality: **The old photos may *deteriorate* if we leave them in the moldy trunk in the basement.**

de·vour [di·vour′] *v.* **de·voured, de·vour·ing** To consume eagerly.

dex·ter·i·ty [dek·ster′ə·tē] *n.* The ability to use one's hands or body skillfully. *syn.* agility

dig·i·tal [dij′i·təl] *adj.* Presenting information with numerals: **According to the *digital* sign on the roof of the bank, it was 101°F this afternoon.**

dig·ni·tar·y [dig′nə·ter′ē] *n.* An official in a high government or church position: **The town held a parade in honor of the foreign *dignitary*.**

curriculum The Latin word meaning "to run" is *currere.* From this word developed *curriculum,* a "small chariot" that the sports-loving Romans used for races. Later the word came to be used for the track where the races took place. Finally, the word was taken over by scholars to mean the "path" or "course of education" that students follow.

dander

a	add	**o͝o**	took
ā	ace	**o͞o**	pool
â	care	**u**	up
ä	palm	**û**	burn
e	end	**yo͞o**	fuse
ē	equal	**oi**	oil
i	it	**ou**	pout
ī	ice	**ng**	ring
o	odd	**th**	thin
ō	open	**th̶**	this
ô	order	**zh**	vision

ə = a in *above*, e in *sicken*, i in *possible*, o in *melon*, u in *circus*

eaves

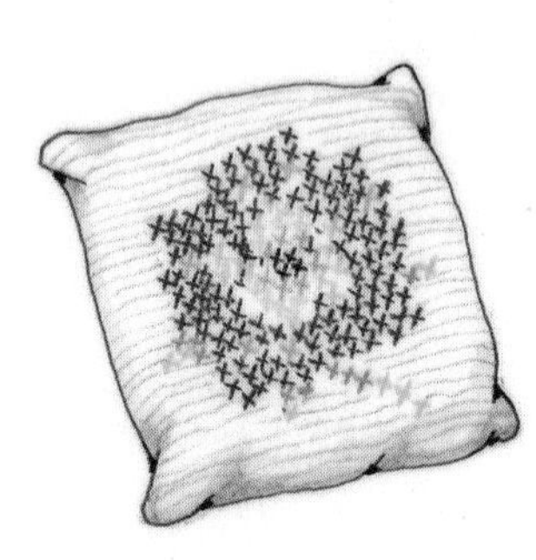
embroidery

erosion

dis·a·bil·i·ty [dis′ə·bil′ə·tē] *n.* A physical condition that prevents a person from being able to do certain things in a typical way: **Rolando was born blind, so he attended a special school for people with *disabilities.*** *syn.* impairment

dis·lo·cate [dis′lō·kāt′] *v.* **dis·lo·cat·ed, dis·lo·cat·ing** To put out of position: **Anita *dislocated* her knee when she scored the winning goal.**

di·verge [di·vûrj′ *or* dī·vûrj′] *v.* **di·verged, di·verg·ing** To branch off in different directions: **We all hiked together at first, but then we broke into two groups at a fork in the trail where two paths *diverged.*** *syn.* split

di·vert [di·vûrt′] *v.* **di·vert·ed, di·vert·ing** To turn something away: **Joe thought he could steal the ball by *diverting* my attention.** *syn.* distract

doc·tor·ate [dok′tər·it] *n.* An advanced degree from a university: **Most college professors have earned *doctorates* in their fields of study.**

do·mes·tic [də·mes′tik] *adj.* Pertaining to the home or family or to one's own country.

down·cast [doun′kast′] *adj.* Depressed; sad. *syn.* dejected

drone [drōn] *v.* **droned, dron·ing** To speak in a boring way, without variation in inflection: **Pat *droned* on about his favorite baseball game until his listeners started yawning.**

dys·lex·ic [dis·lek′sik] *adj.* Having a condition that makes it difficult to learn to read: **The woman is a good student, even though she is *dyslexic.***

E

eaves [ēvz] *n. pl.* On a roof, the lower part that hangs over or extends beyond the walls of the building.

ec·sta·sy [ek′stə·sē] *n.* Great happiness; rapture: **Isabel is in *ecstasy* about her high score on the math test.**

ec·stat·ic [ek·stat′ik] *adj.* Full of great joy or happiness. *syns.* joyful, rapturous

ee·ri·ness [ir′ē·nis] *n.* A feeling of fear or strangeness.

e·lude [i·lo͞od′] *v.* To escape or avoid through speed or cleverness.

em·broi·der·y [im·broi′dər·ē] *n.* Needlework decoration: **Carlita has beautiful *embroidery* on her blouse.**

en·deav·or [in·dev′ər] *n.* An attempt or struggle: **The fact that Larry is blind made his *endeavor* to climb Mt. Washington even more admirable.**

en·trance [in·trans′] *v.* **en·tranced, en·tranc·ing** To fill with wonder. *syns.* fascinate, charm

ere [âr] *prep.* Before.

e·ro·sion [i·rō′zhən] *n.* A wearing away or destruction of something by the action of wind or water.

ex·ca·vate [eks′kə·vāt′] *v.* **ex·ca·vat·ed, ex·ca·vat·ing** To uncover; to dig out carefully.

ex·er·tion [ig·zûr′shən] *n.* Great effort.

ex·po·sure [ik·spō′zhər] *n.* **1** The act of displaying or uncovering. **2** A section of film for one photograph.

ex·tra·ve·hic·u·lar [ek′strə·vē·hik′yə·lər] *adj.* Taking place outside a vehicle.

F

fac·tor [fak′tər] *n.* One element of a situation or one cause of a result. *syn.* consideration

fal·low [fal′ō] *adj.* Left unplanted to increase soil fertility.

fe·ro·cious [fə·rō′shəs] *adj.* Extremely intense or violent. *syns.* fierce, savage

fi·ber·glass [fī′bər·glas′] *n.* Thin, light, flexible building material made of glass fibers: **Her new *fiberglass* surfboard was much lighter than her old wooden one.**

flail [flāl] *v.* **flailed, flail·ing** To swing or beat: **The baby *flailed* his arms in the swimming pool like a bird flapping its wings.**

flak [flak] *n. informal* Criticism; verbal opposition: **The committee received a lot of *flak* for inviting the boring speaker to the meeting.**

for·ag·ing [fôr′ij·ing] *n.* A search for food or supplies.

forge [fôrj] *v.* **forged, forg·ing** To shape hot metal; to create objects out of unformed metal.

fur·row [fûr′ō] *n.* A long trench dug in the ground by a plow.

fu·tile [fyōō′təl] *adj.* Useless. *syn.* ineffective

G

gen·er·a·tor [jen′ə·rā′tər] *n.* A machine that produces electricity.

ge·ner·ic [ji·ner′ik] *adj.* Occurring everywhere; not specific: **Palm trees are *generic* in Florida and on many tropical islands.** *syns.* universal, general

gim·mick [gim′ik] *n.* A feature that makes people want to buy a product: **Putting small toys in cereal boxes is a *gimmick* that influences people to buy certain kinds of cereal.**

gin·ger·ly [jin′jər·lē] *adv.* In a cautious manner. *syn.* carefully

glock·en·spiel [glok′ən·spēl′] *n.* A musical instrument made up of metal bars that are hit with a small hammer: **At the German festival, we heard musicians play cheerful songs on *glockenspiels.***

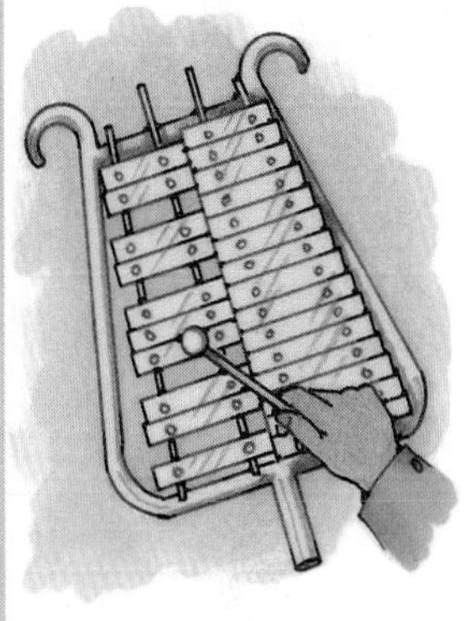

glockenspiel

gnarled [närld] *adj.* Knotty, lumpy, and twisted: **The veins on the old man's hands were *gnarled.***

gro·tesque [grō·tesk′] *adj.* Very ugly or strange looking. *syn.* distorted

gyre [jīr] *n.* A spiraling motion: **The water in the whirlpool moved in a *gyre.***

H

hal·yard [hal′yərd] *n.* A rope used to hoist a sail up the mast: **Both of the *halyards* snapped when the sails were halfway up the masts.**

hatch [hach] *n.* The door that covers an opening in a ship's deck: **The divers expected to find gold beneath the *hatch* of the sunken ship.**

ha·ven [hā′vən] *n.* A safe place. *syns.* shelter, refuge

heart·rend·ing [härt′ren′ding] *adj.* Causing great sadness. *syn.* heartbreaking

helm [helm] *n.* A device used for steering a ship: **The wind was so strong that two crew members had to hold the *helm* to keep the ship on course.**

a	add	**ŏŏ**	took
ā	ace	**ōō**	pool
â	care	**u**	up
ä	palm	**û**	burn
e	end	**yōō**	fuse
ē	equal	**oi**	oil
i	it	**ou**	pout
ī	ice	**ng**	ring
o	odd	**th**	thin
ō	open	**th**	this
ô	order	**zh**	vision

ə = a in *above*, e in *sicken*, i in *possible*, o in *melon*, u in *circus*

hieroglyphics

immerse *Immerse* comes from the Latin prefix *in-*, "into," and *mergere*, "to plunge." When you see the prefix *in-* or its variations *im-*, *il-*, and *ir-*, don't plunge to the conclusion that it means "in," "into," or "on." It certainly has this sense in words like *illuminated*, *indoctrinated*, and *inspired*. However, Latin has another prefix *in-* that means "not." This meaning appears in *improbable*, *inaudible*, and *irresistible*. *In-* meaning "in" goes back even farther than Latin to the ancient root *en*. *In-* that means "not," however, has its origins in *ne*, which is seen in *never* and *neither*.

her·cu·le·an [hûr·kyo͞o′lē·ən *or* hûr′kyə·lē′ən] *adj.* Requiring superhuman strength or endurance: **Removing the fallen tree was a *herculean* task.**

hi·er·o·glyph·ics [hī′ər·ə·glif′iks *or* hī′rə·glif′iks] *n. pl.* A method of writing using pictures or symbols.

hutch [huch] *n.* A fenced place where small animals are kept: **At the farm, Pat watched the rabbits playing in the *hutches*.** *syns.* pen, coop

hy·brid [hī′brid] *n.* Something of mixed or blended origin or composition: **A beefalo is a *hybrid* animal bred from cattle and American buffaloes.**

I

il·lu·mi·nate [i·lo͞o′mə·nāt′] *v.* **il·lu·mi·nat·ed, il·lu·mi·nat·ing** To light up: **When the electricity went out, Kenji *illuminated* the room with candles.**

im·merse [i·mûrs′] *v.* **im·mersed, im·mers·ing** To involve or absorb oneself in an idea or activity completely.

im·pen·e·tra·ble [im·pen′ə·trə·bəl] *adj.* Not able to be solved or understood: **The complicated code was to remain an *impenetrable* mystery.**

im·pro·vise [im′prə·vīz′] *v.* **im·pro·vised, im·pro·vis·ing** **1** To create on the spur of the moment without rehearsal: **Because Nadjee had forgotten to prepare her oral report, she *improvised* one.** **2** To create out of any available materials: **Marta *improvised* a spoon out of a piece of plastic so that we could eat the yogurt.**

im·pu·dent [im′pyə·dənt] *adj.* Rude and disrespectful. *syn.* insolent

in·ad·e·qua·cy [in·ad′ə·kwə·sē] *n.* **in·ad·e·qua·cies** Being unsuccessful or lacking certain skills: **Sumi's *inadequacies* in reading music and staying on key made singing in the choir a challenge for her.**

in·au·di·ble [in·ô′də·bəl] *adj.* Unable to be heard.

in·can·des·cent [in′kən·des′ənt] *adj.* Very bright; glowing; shining: **Teresa had spent so much time waxing the car that it appeared *incandescent*.**

in·doc·tri·nate [in·dok′trə·nāt′] *v.* **in·doc·tri·nat·ed, in·doc·tri·nat·ing** To teach behavior or attitudes. *syns.* train, instruct

in·dul·gent·ly [in·dul′jənt·lē] *adv.* Giving in to someone else's wishes. *syn.* leniently

in·ef·fec·tive [in′i·fek′tiv] *adj.* Not capable of performing as expected: **Josh learned quickly that his plan for the party was *ineffective* when there were not enough seats for the guests.**

in·ev·i·ta·bil·i·ty [in·ev′ə·tə·bil′ə·tē] *n.* An event that is certain to happen: **The senator's victory in the election was an *inevitability* because she was so popular with the voters.** *syn.* certainty

in·i·ti·ate [in·ish′ē·āt′] *v.* **in·i·ti·at·ed, in·i·ti·at·ing** To introduce a person to an activity, status, or stage of life; to welcome a person to membership through a special ceremony.

in·spire [in·spīr′] *v.* **in·spired, in·spir·ing** To fill with hope, energy, or motivation: **Seeing the movie *inspired* Assunta to finish her screenplay.**

in·stan·ta·ne·ous [in′stən·tā′nē·əs] *adj.* Occurring in an instant: **Her *instantaneous* reaction to the whizzing ball was to duck.** *syn.* immediate

in·stinc·tu·al [in·stingk′chōō·əl] *adj.* Pertaining to inborn impulses and natural abilities: **She had never received any formal instruction in tennis; her playing was purely *instinctual.*** *syns.* instinctive, innate

in·sur·gent [in·sûr′jənt] *adj.* Rebelling; in opposition to authority.

in·ten·sive·ly [in·ten′siv·lē] *adv.* In a thorough and complete manner: **Coach Rodriguez *intensively* prepared her field hockey team for the state championship.**

in·ter·cept [in′tər·sept′] *v.* **in·ter·cept·ed, in·ter·cept·ing** To seize; to prevent from passing by or getting through: **The Bulldogs' halfback *intercepted* the pass, ran it down the field, and scored a touchdown.**

in·ter·mit·tent·ly [in′tər·mit′ənt·lē] *adv.* In a way that stops and starts or occurs from time to time. *syn.* occasionally

in·ter·stel·lar [in′tər·stel′ər] *adj.* Between stars: **The scientist was working on a spacecraft that could make an *interstellar* journey.**

in·tim·i·date [in·tim′ə·dāt′] *v.* **in·tim·i·dat·ed, in·tim·i·dat·ing** To frighten; to scare into submission: **The powerful current of the Colorado River can *intimidate* boaters into heading for shore.**

in·trep·id [in·trep′id] *adj.* Courageous; without fear.

in·trigue [in·trēg′] *v.* **in·trigued, in·tri·guing** To spark someone's interest: **Because Vasco enjoyed baking so much, he was *intrigued* by the idea of taking a night class in cooking.** *syn.* fascinate

in·trin·sic [in·trin′sik] *adj.* Pertaining to the real nature of something.

in·tru·sion [in·trōō′zhən] *n.* An action that invades a person's privacy.

in·vol·un·tar·i·ly [in′vol′ən·ter′ə·lē] *adv.* Done without intention or control. *syns.* accidentally, unintentionally

ir·re·sis·ti·ble [ir′i·zis′tə·bəl] *adj.* Impossible to oppose or refuse.

i·so·late [ī′sə·lāt′] *v.* **i·so·lat·ed, i·so·lat·ing** To separate from others.

J

jib [jib] *n.* A triangular sail set in front of the mast of a boat: **We could always spot the Tangs' boat on the horizon because it had a bright orange *jib* blowing in the breeze.**

jounce [jouns] *v.* **jounced, jounc·ing** To bounce; to shake: **The baby *jounced* along in her stroller as her mother jogged behind.**

K

knot [not] *n.* A unit of measurement, equal to 1 nautical mile per hour, used to describe the speed of boats or wind: **The ship was traveling at a speed of 20 *knots*.**

L

lac·er·ate [las′ər·āt′] *v.* **lac·er·at·ed, lac·er·at·ing** To wound by tearing.

la·goon [lə·gōōn′] *n.* A shallow body of water separated from the sea by a reef: **The pirates rowed the boat around the reef to the largest of the *lagoons*, where they dumped the trunk.**

intercept

jib

a	add	**ŏŏ**	took
ā	ace	**ōō**	pool
â	care	**u**	up
ä	palm	**û**	burn
e	end	**yōō**	fuse
ē	equal	**oi**	oil
i	it	**ou**	pout
ī	ice	**ng**	ring
o	odd	**th**	thin
ō	open	**th̶**	this
ô	order	**zh**	vision

ə = a in *above*, e in *sicken*, i in *possible*, o in *melon*, u in *circus*

lingo Our word *language* developed from the Latin word for "tongue," *lingua.* This makes sense because the tongue is an important organ of speech. *Lingo* usually refers to speech or language that we can't understand.

locust

meander In the western part of Asia Minor settled by the early Greeks was a river called Maiandros. It didn't seem to know where it was going, but it wound aimlessly back and forth as it flowed toward the ocean. That is why people who wander around without a clear destination are said to *meander.*

lev·er·age [lev′ər·ij *or* lē′vər·ij] *n.* The extra power or help a person gets from using an object to lift something: **To gain *leverage,* Yumiko pulled on a tree branch to climb the steep bank.**

li·cense [lī′səns] *v.* **li·censed, li·cens·ing** To issue legal permission to do, be, or own something.

line [līn] *n.* A rope used to fasten a boat to a dock: **One of the *lines* was loose, so the boat slipped away from the dock.**

lin·e·age [lin′ē·ij] *n.* All of a person's ancestors. *syn.* ancestry

lin·go [ling′gō] *n.* A language used in a particular field of interest or by a specific group of individuals; jargon.

lin·guis·tics [ling·gwis′tiks] *n.* The study of language: **In a lesson about *linguistics,* David learned that many English words were borrowed from Greek.**

lo·cus [lō′kəs] *n.* A specific area, especially one being focused on: **A patch of white sand covered with bread scraps was the *locus* of the seagulls' diving and swooping.**

lo·cust [lō′kəst] *n.* An insect that is similar to a grasshopper and travels in swarms, destroying crops: **After the *locusts* devoured our entire crop of corn, they moved on to the next farm.** *syn.* cicada

lor·ry [lôr′ē] *n.* A sideless wagon pulled by a horse: **The farmer hitched up the horse to the *lorry* stacked with bales of hay.**

low re·lief [lō ri·lēf′] *n.* A form of sculpture in which figures are only partially carved out from the background.

lu·mi·nous [lo͞o′mə·nəs] *adj.* Glowing.

M

mal·le·a·ble [mal′ē·ə·bəl] *adj.* Able to be hammered, rolled, or bent without breaking. *syn.* flexible

ma·neu·ver [mə·n(y)o͞o′vər] *n.* A procedure or a planned movement.

ma·noeu·vre [mə·n(y)o͞o′vər] *n.* A maneuver.

ma·ri·na [mə·rē′nə] *n.* A docking site for sailboats and yachts: **The sailors refueled the yacht and picked up supplies at the *marina.***

mas·o·chism [mas′ə·kiz′əm *or* maz′ə·kiz′əm] *n.* The abnormal finding of pleasure in a situation that causes pain or discomfort to oneself.

mast [mast] *n.* A vertical pole from which the sails on a boat hang: **He climbed up the *mast* to try to repair the torn sail.**

mas·tiff [mas′tif] *n.* A breed of large hunting dog with strong jaws, used chiefly as watchdogs or guard dogs.

me·an·der [mē·an′dər] *v.* **me·an·dered, me·an·der·ing** To move in a winding path: **Some rivers flow in an almost straight line, but this one *meanders* through the fields to the sea.** *syns.* wind, wander

mes·quite [mes·kēt′] *n.* A shrub or tree common to the southwestern U.S. and Central America: **Manolo started a roaring fire with *mesquite* branches.**

mete [mēt] *v.* **met·ed, met·ing** To dole out; to distribute according to a measure or judgment: **The Red Cross volunteer carefully *meted* out three gallons of water to each family.**

mi·cro·or·gan·ism [mī′krō·ôr′gən·iz′əm] *n.* A living thing that is so small that it can only be seen by using a microscope: **The scientist was studying bacteria and other *microorganisms* by looking through her microscope.**

mi·cro·wave [mī′krə·wāv′] *n.* An electromagnetic wave with a short wavelength: ***Microwaves* are used in radar, in communication over moderate distances, and for cooking.**

mis·de·mean·or [mis′di·mē′nər] *n.* A legal offense that is not as serious as a felony: **The lawyer tried to convince the judge to rule that his client's offense was only a *misdemeanor*.**

mis·sion [mish′ən] *n.* One's role, task, or purpose.

mon·o·cle [mon′ə·kəl] *n.* An eyeglass for one eye.

mo·sa·ic [mō·zā′ik] *n.* Art consisting of tiny pieces of colored stone or glass carefully arranged: **The artist was asked to create a large *mosaic* on the side wall of the national museum.**

mo·ti·va·tion [mō′tə·vā′shən] *n.* Something that causes someone to act in a certain way. *syn.* incentive

mu·ral [myŏŏr′əl] *n.* A painting done on a wall.

muse [myōōz] *v.* **mused, mus·ing** To ponder in a thoughtful way. *syns.* consider, contemplate

mus·keg [mus′keg] *n.* A soft, moist area of land. *syns.* bog, marsh

N

ne·go·ti·ate [ni·gō′shē·āt′] *v.* **ne·go·ti·at·ed, ne·go·ti·at·ing** To give and take in order to reach an agreement: **My family spent a week *negotiating* vacation plans before everyone agreed to go on a camping trip.** *syn.* bargain

non·cha·lant [non′shə·länt′] *adj.* Unaffected; casual and calm.

O

ob·scu·ri·ty [əb·skyŏŏr′ə·tē] *n.* The condition of not being well known: **No one had heard of the artist, who lived in *obscurity*.**

ob·ses·sion [əb·sesh′ən] *n.* A thought or an idea that constantly occupies a person's mind: **Elvira was always reading books about science because her interest in the subject had become an *obsession*.**

o·ce·an·og·ra·pher [ō′shən·og′rə·fər] *n.* A scientist who studies the physical features, chemistry, and life forms of oceans.

op·tion [op′shən] *n.* A choice: **Tracy had two *options*—to join the choir or to play on the volleyball team.** *syn.* alternative

P

pag·eant [paj′ənt] *n.* A show that is put on for an audience: **Masako was not nervous about being in the play because she had been in a *pageant* last year.**

pa·lav·er [pə·lav′ər] **1** *v.* **pa·lav·ered, pa·lav·er·ing** To talk idly. **2** *n.* A discussion or conference in public, sometimes including idle chatter.

pal·i·sade [pal′ə·sād′] *n.* A barrier made of stakes set upright in the ground: **The explorers surrounded their camp with a *palisade* to keep out animals.** *syns.* fence, barricade

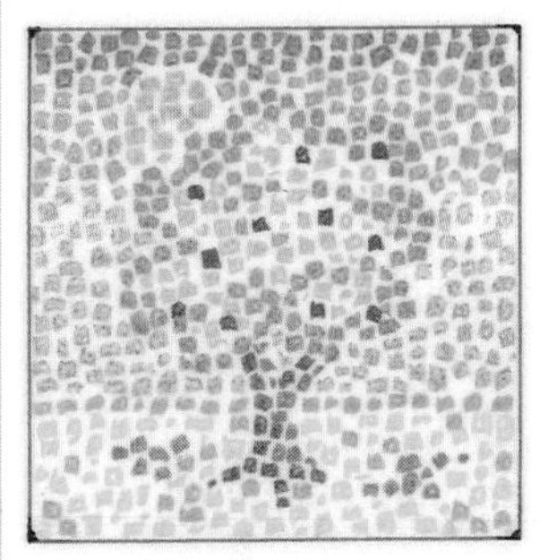

mosaic

mural

a	add	**ŏŏ**	took
ā	ace	**ōō**	pool
â	care	**u**	up
ä	palm	**û**	burn
e	end	**yōō**	fuse
ē	equal	**oi**	oil
i	it	**ou**	pout
ī	ice	**ng**	ring
o	odd	**th**	thin
ō	open	**th̶**	this
ô	order	**zh**	vision

ə = a in *above*, e in *sicken*, i in *possible*, o in *melon*, u in *circus*

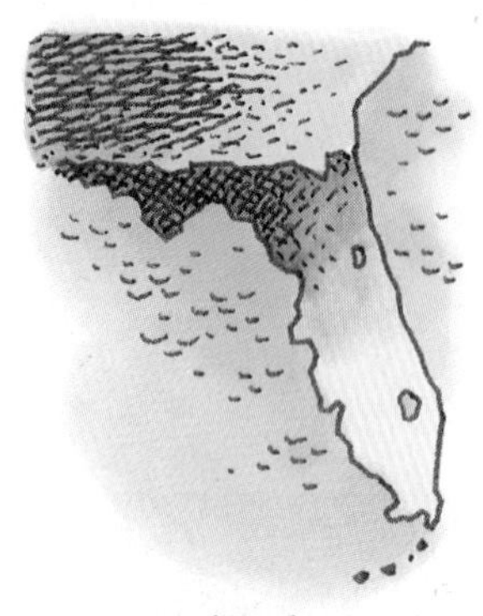

peninsula

periscope

plagiarism The word *plagiarism* goes all the way back to the ancient Greek *plagios,* meaning "crooked." Like our word *crooked, plagios* also had the figurative sense "treacherous." The word passed into Latin as *plagium,* which signified a special kind of treachery — "kidnapping." People who *plagiarize* aren't just using someone else's words; they are guilty of kidnapping them!

pal·let [pal′it] *n.* A thin mattress filled with straw: **The *pallets* the explorers slept on did not prevent the arctic ground from chilling them.**

pas·sion·ate [pash′ən·it] *adj.* Filled with intense emotion: **Sam was so *passionate* about his writing that he got a job in order to buy a word processor.**

pay·load [pā′lōd] *n.* In a spacecraft, the load that consists of people and things directly related to the purpose of the flight, as opposed to things necessary for routine operation of the spacecraft.

pen·in·su·la [pə·nin′s(y)ə·lə] *n.* A section of land that juts out and is almost completely surrounded by water: **The Iberian *Peninsula* is bordered by the Atlantic Ocean and the Mediterranean Sea.**

Pen·ta·teuch [pen′tə·t(y)o͞ok′] *n.* The first five books of the Old Testament in the Bible: **Lola's grandmother read parts of the *Pentateuch* to her every night at bedtime.**

per·e·stroi·ka [per·i·stroi′kə] *n.* A restructuring of society in what was the Soviet Union; being connected with the time of that restructuring: **The citizens cheered the speaker when he described the effects of *perestroika.***

per·il·ous [per′əl·əs] *adj.* Very dangerous.

per·i·scope [per′ə·skōp′] *n.* A tube that someone who is underwater in a submarine can look through to see things on the surface of the water: **When Clara looked through the *periscope,* she could see an island in the distance.**

per·jure [pûr′jər] *v.* **per·jured, per·jur·ing** To make (oneself) guilty of lying: **That woman will *perjure* herself if she claims that she did not witness the accident.**

per·sis·tent [pər·sis′tənt] *adj.* Being able to stick to doing something: **Alonso wrote poetry every day, and this *persistent* practice helped him develop into a great poet.** *syn.* persevering

per·sua·sive [pər·swā′siv] *adj.* Being able to make someone do something: **Before the lecture, we didn't agree with Teresa, but she is such a *persuasive* speaker that we signed her petition.**

phar·ma·co·poe·ia [fär′mə·kō·pē′(y)ə] *n.* A book containing a list of drugs, with directions for their preparation and identification.

phil·an·throp·ic [fil′ən·throp′ik] *adj.* Having to do with giving money to help people or organizations. *syn.* charitable

pho·net·ic [fə·net′ik] *adj.* Relating to the way words sound when spoken: **Poets appreciate the *phonetic* qualities of words.**

phys·i·cal ther·a·py [fiz′i·kəl ther′ə·pē] *n.* External treatment, such as massage or exercise, for disease or injury: **After the car accident, Lonnie had to have *physical therapy* in order to use his hand again.**

pin·na·cle [pin′ə·kəl] *n.* A tapering spire, often of rock. *syns.* turret, peak

pla·gia·rism [plā′jə·riz′əm] *n.* Stealing and presenting as one's own the ideas, writings, or work of another.

pla·toon [plə·to͞on′] *n.* A unit within a company or troop: **Each counselor at Camp Redwood led a *platoon* of seven campers.**

plumb [plum] *adv. informal* Completely; entirely: **After pruning all the trees in the yard, Rick was *plumb* exhausted.**

pneu·mo·nia [n(y)o͞o·mōn′yə] *n.* A disease causing inflammation of one or both lungs.

pock·mark [pok′märk′] *v.* **pock·marked, pock·mark·ing** To cover with holes or scars: **In archery class, the targets are *pockmarked* with holes from our arrows.**

prance [prans] *v.* **pranced, pranc·ing** To walk in a very lively, bouncy way.

pre·cau·tion [pri·kô′shən] *n.* A measure taken to prevent injury or harm.

pre·dic·a·ment [pri·dik′ə·mənt] *n.* A difficult, embarrassing, or dangerous situation.

pre·mon·i·to·ry [pri·mon′ə·tôr′ē] *adj.* Giving a warning.

pres·tig·ious [pres·tē′jəs *or* pres·tij′əs] *adj.* Well-known and well-respected: **Ms. Benitez, a *prestigious* mathematician from Mexico, spoke to the students about careers in mathematics.** *syn.* esteemed

pre·sum·a·bly [pri·zo͞o′mə·blē] *adv.* Probably; according to what is believed to be true: ***Presumably,* the pep rally will be in the gym, where it was last year.**

pri·mate [prī′māt′] *n.* Any of an order of mammals that includes apes, monkeys, lemurs, and human beings.

pri·va·tion [prī·vā′shən] *n.* The lack of essential or everyday things that make people comfortable. *syn.* deprivation

probe [prōb] *n.* A mission or a measurement device for gaining specific information: **The main purpose of the space *probe* is to get photographs of the planet's surface.** *syn.* investigation

prod·i·gy [prod′ə·jē] *n.* A child who is very talented at doing something.

prom·i·nent·ly [prom′ə·nənt·lē] *adv.* In a manner that is highly visible: ***Prominently* displayed on her mother's desk was the trophy she had won in fourth grade.** *syn.* conspicuously

prov·en·der [prov′ən·dər] *n.* Food, especially dry food for cattle.

psych [sīk] *v. informal* **psyched, psych·ing** To outguess, analyze, or make someone uneasy.

psy·chi·a·trist [sī·kī′ə·trist] *n.* A doctor who treats mental illness: **The *psychiatrist* asked Luis when his depression began.**

ptar·mi·gan [tär′mə·gən] *n.* A plump bird with feathered legs that lives in North America: **The bird watchers spotted a *ptarmigan* in the brush.** *syn.* grouse

Q

quaint [kwānt] *adj.* Pleasantly odd, unusual, or old-fashioned: **The old Victorian-style house had been turned into a *quaint* little hotel.**

quan·tum [kwon′təm] *adj.* Abrupt or sudden; totally different or new: **The discovery was a *quantum* leap in our knowledge of disease.**

quill [kwil] *n.* A stiff, barbed spine from the hide of an animal: **The poor dog came whimpering back from its romp in the forest with a nose full of porcupine *quills*.**

quo·tient [kwō′shənt] *n.* **1** The answer to a division problem. **2** The key to solving a mystery or an unfamiliar problem: **In the 1800s, a scientist found that the presence of bacteria in milk was the *quotient* for understanding the cause of certain diseases.**

R

ra·di·ol·o·gist [rā′dē·ol′ə·jist] *n.* Someone who uses X-rays to study diseases: **The *radiologists* looked concerned after having viewed the patient's X-rays.**

primate

ptarmigan

a	add	**o͝o**	took
ā	ace	**o͞o**	pool
â	care	**u**	up
ä	palm	**û**	burn
e	end	**yo͞o**	fuse
ē	equal	**oi**	oil
i	it	**ou**	pout
ī	ice	**ng**	ring
o	odd	**th**	thin
ō	open	**th̶**	this
ô	order	**zh**	vision

ə = a in *above*, e in *sicken*, i in *possible*, o in *melon*, u in *circus*

reciprocal If you have a *reciprocal* agreement with someone, it is a give-and-take arrangement. The word itself contains the Latin roots meaning both "back" and "forward," *re* and *pro.*

reef

rag·time [rag′tīm′] *n.* An early form of jazz, using rhythms that are syncopated (having accents on normally unaccented beats).

ram·i·fi·ca·tion [ram′ə·fə·kā′shən] *n.* A result. *syns.* outgrowth, consequence

ran·dom [ran′dəm] *adj.* Without a plan or a system; chance; in any order.

rap·port [ra·pôr′] *n.* A warm or close relationship.

rav·i·o·li [rav′ē·ō′lē] *n.* Pasta filled with cheese or meat and usually smothered in tomato sauce: **Antonio's family loved his homemade *ravioli* because he stuffed it with anchovies instead of cheese.**

re·cip·i·ent [ri·sip′ē·ənt] *n.* Someone who receives something: **Marta was the *recipient* of several gifts on her birthday.** *syn.* receiver

re·cip·ro·cal [ri·sip′rə·kəl] *adj.* Given by two sides in mutual exchange. *syn.* mutual

rec·og·ni·tion [rek′əg·nish′ən] *n.* Public acknowledgment; fame: **Suzanne didn't expect to make a fortune from her car-part sculptures, but she did hope for some *recognition.***

re·con·noi·ter [rē′kə·noi′tər *or* rek′ə·noi′tər] *v.* To survey one's position.

reef [rēf] *n.* A ridge made of sand, rocks, or coral near the surface of the water.

re·for·es·ta·tion [rē′fôr·is·tā′shən] *n.* The replanting of trees and regenerating of forest: **A great deal of *reforestation* is needed in Brazil, where huge areas of rain forest have been destroyed.**

re·ha·bil·i·ta·tive [rē′hə·bil′ə·tāt′iv] *adj.* Having to do with helping people recover or get better at doing things.

re·ju·ve·nate [ri·jo͞o′və·nāt′] *v.* **re·ju·ve·nat·ed, re·ju·ve·nat·ing** To cause to feel younger or more lively. *syn.* enliven

re·kin·dle [ri·kin′dəl] *v.* To make active again: **Carmen noticed that her father hardly played the piano anymore, and she wanted to *rekindle* his interest in playing.** *syn.* reactivate

re·luc·tance [ri·luk′təns] *n.* Lack of eagerness: **Our cat Mabel showed her *reluctance* to go out in the rain by hiding in a closet.** *syn.* unwillingness

rem·i·nisce [rem′ə·nis′] *v.* **rem·i·nisced, rem·i·nisc·ing** To think fondly about the past. *syns.* remember, recollect

re·nal [rē′nəl] *adj.* Involving or relating to the kidneys: **When Yoko felt pain in her kidneys, she called a doctor who treats people with *renal* problems.**

res·ig·na·tion [rez′ig·nā′shən] *n.* Calm acceptance: **When she was asked to serve on another school committee, Lois smiled with *resignation.***

re·sis·tor [ri·zis′tər] *n.* An object that provides resistance to an electric current.

rés·u·mé [rez′o͞o·mā′ *or* rez′o͞o·mā′] *n.* A summary of one's job or educational experience and accomplishments: **Todd forgot to include his summer job on his *résumé,* so he had to type it all over again.**

rev·er·y [rev′ər·ē] *n. Also spelled* **reverie.** A daydream.

rid·dle [rid′(ə)l] *v.* **rid·dled, rid·dling** To affect throughout; to permeate.

rig [rig] *v.* **rigged, rig·ging** To equip a boat with sails: **She learned to *rig* a boat correctly before she ever went sailing.**

riv·et·ing [riv′it·ing] *adj.* Attracting and holding attention completely. *syns.* spellbinding, fascinating

S

sat·u·rat·ed [sach′ə·rā′tid] *adj.* Completely soaked. *syn.* drenched

saun·ter [sôn′tər] *v.* **saun·tered, saun·ter·ing** To walk slowly and casually. *syn.* stroll

schol·ar·ship [skol′ər·ship′] *n.* A money award given to a student to pay for tuition.

sec·ond·hand [sek′ənd·hand′] *adj.* Previously owned; not new.

sed·en·tar·y [sed′ən·ter′ē] *adj.* **1** Requiring or accustomed to sitting. **2** Not movable or portable. *syn.* settled

sem·blance [sem′bləns] *n.* Outward appearance; display. *syn.* impression

ser·rat·ed [ser′ā·tid] *adj.* Having edges that are notched or toothed like a saw blade: **Only a *serrated* knife would cut the tough meat.**

sheer [shir] **1** *v.* To veer off course. **2** *adj.* Very steep; straight up.

short·hand·ed [shôrt′han′did] *adj.* Having too few employees or workers: **Because the doughnut factory was *shorthanded,* all employees had to work overtime.**

siege [sēj] *n.* A military operation against a fortified town or city: **The city was surrounded by the enemy and remained under *siege* for three months.**

sil·i·con [sil′ə·kən] *n.* An element found in the earth′s crust and often used for computer circuits.

sim·i·an [sim′ē·ən] *adj.* Having to do with monkeys or apes.

sim·u·lat·or [sim′yə·lāt′ər] *n.* A device that imitates events that are likely to occur naturally: **Student pilots practice landing in a *simulator* before trying it in an airplane.**

sin·ew·y [sin′yōō·ē] *adj.* Strong or firm. *syns.* tough, muscular

smite [smīt] *v.* **smote, smit·ten, smit·ing** To affect powerfully and unexpectedly.

smit·ten [smit′(ə)n] *Past participle of* **smite.**

so·cial·i·za·tion [sō′shəl·ī·zā′shən] *n.* Experience that helps a person or an animal get along with others.

so·lic·i·tous·ly [sə·lis′ə·təs·lē] *adv.* In a way that shows concern, worry, or interest: **The doctor asked her *solicitously* about her symptoms.**

sol·stice [sol′stis] *n.* Each of the two periods of time during the year when the sun is at its farthest north or south of the equator: **Rita was always glad when the winter *solstice* came because the days would begin to get longer.**

so·phis·ti·cat·ed [sə·fis′tə·kā′tid] *adj.* Having complex equipment: **Instead of buying a basic model, Eva bought a *sophisticated* car with a stereo, air conditioning, and a burglar alarm.** *syn.* advanced

sou·ve·nir [sōō′və·nir′] *n.* An object that serves to remind someone about the past: **Mom bought a picture of a seagull as a *souvenir* of her trip to Cape Cod.** *syn.* memento

spay [spā] *v.* **spayed, spay·ing** To perform an operation on a female animal to prevent it from having offspring: **Joe's father insisted on *spaying* the dog because he didn't want her to have puppies.**

squad·ron [skwod′rən] *n.* An organized group of people: **Every pilot in the *squadron* returned safely from the mission.** *syn.* unit

saturated

siege *Siege* came into English from the French *sieger,* "to sit." That is exactly what an army does when it *besieges* a town or city. It surrounds the city and sits down to wait for the inhabitants to surrender. *Sieger* itself goes back to the Latin word *sedere,* "to sit." English words such as *sedentary* bypassed French and came to us directly from this Latin root.

a	add	**ŏŏ**	took
ā	ace	**ōō**	pool
â	care	**u**	up
ä	palm	**û**	burn
e	end	**yōō**	fuse
ē	equal	**oi**	oil
i	it	**ou**	pout
ī	ice	**ng**	ring
o	odd	**th**	thin
ō	open	**t͟h**	this
ô	order	**zh**	vision

ə = a in *above*, e in *sicken*, i in *possible*, o in *melon*, u in *circus*

stern

stoicism Zeno was a Greek philosopher who claimed that people should lead their lives unmoved by either pleasure or pain. Zeno and his pupils used to gather in the marketplace of ancient Athens at the *poikile stoa,* or "painted porch." This covered portico supported by columns was decorated with famous paintings. From this *stoa,* Zeno's philosophy was named *stoicism* and his followers, *stoics.*

terraced

staff [staf] *n.* A pole used as a cane, weapon, or symbol of authority: **Queen Valda used her golden *staff* to keep her subjects from touching her.**

stalk [stôk] *v.* **stalked, stalk·ing** To track; to sneak up on.

stam·i·na [stam′ə·nə] *n.* Strength: **Ballerinas take several dance classes each day to build up their *stamina.*** *syns.* vitality, endurance

stern [stûrn] *n.* The back end of a boat: **The captain told the seasick passengers that the boat would feel calmer at the *stern.***

sto·i·cism [stō′ə·siz′əm] *n.* A calm mood without happiness, pain, or other feelings.

stren·u·ous [stren′yo͞o·əs] *adj.* Requiring a great deal of effort and energy: **The climb up the steps of the ancient temple was too *strenuous* for Nell's grandfather.** *syn.* rigorous

stride [strīd] *v.* **strode, strid·den, strid·ing** To take long steps.

strode [strōd] *Past tense* of **stride.**

stuc·co [stuk′ō] *adj.* Made of a fine plaster or cement: **The *stucco* walls kept the house cool in the summer and warm in the winter.**

sub·si·dized [sub′sə·dīzd′] *adj.* Aided by gifts of money: **Gloria attended a *subsidized* school, which was given money by the city.** *syn.* funded

suc·cumb [sə·kum′] *v.* **suc·cumbed, suc·cumb·ing** To give in to something: **Ana *succumbed* to her exhaustion and fell asleep.** *syn.* yield

suede [swād] *adj.* Made of soft, velvety leather: **Her new brown *suede* shoes were ruined in the rain.**

suf·fi·cient [sə·fish′ənt] *adj.* Enough: **Elena thought it was *sufficient* to study only half an hour for her test.**

swell [swel] *n.* The long roll of a wave: **The *swells* slowly lifted the ship, carrying it farther from the coast.**

T

tac·i·turn [tas′ə·tûrn′] *adj.* Not given to speaking; silent; reserved: **When she heard about Chuck's visit, the usually *taciturn* Eloisa suddenly couldn't stop talking.**

tech·ni·cal [tek′ni·kəl] *adj.* Of or having to do with mechanical, industrial, or scientific skills: **The *technical* adviser for the space shuttle determines whether it is ready for launch.**

te·lep·a·thy [tə·lep′ə·thē] *n.* Communication through thoughts alone: **Martha found a book about the *telepathy* between identical twins who seemed to sense each other's thoughts.**

ten·der·foot [ten′dər·fo͝ot′] *n.* An inexperienced person; a beginner. *syn.* rookie

ter·raced [ter′ist] *adj.* Consisting of a series of raised, level areas, one on top of the other, creating steps: **Many of the hills in southeast China are *terraced,* so that crops can easily be grown on their leveled surfaces.**

teth·er [teth′ər] *v.* **teth·ered, teth·er·ing** To tie or fasten something with a rope or chain so it can't get away: **The man *tethered* his horse to the tree.** *syns.* attach, hitch

ther·a·py [ther′ə·pē] *n.* Treatment that helps someone recover from an illness or injury. *syn.* treatment

there·up·on [thâr′ə·pon′] *adv.* Then; right afterward.

the·sis [thē′sis] *n.* A statement or an opinion that can be supported with evidence.

throng [throng] *v.* **thronged, throng·ing** To move as a crowd: **Teenagers were *thronging* to the theater to hear their favorite rock star.** *syn.* crowd

tor·til·la [tôr·tē′yä] *n.* Circular, flat Mexican bread made of cornmeal or wheat flour: **Conchita and Eduardo made 300 *tortillas* for the wedding reception.**

tot·ter [tot′ər] *v.* **tot·tered, tot·ter·ing** To walk weakly and unsteadily. *syn.* wobble

tran·scend [tran·send′] *v.* **tran·scended, tran·scend·ing** To go beyond the limits of everyday experience: **Bernardo feels that no other experience *transcends* the thrill of mountain climbing.** *syn.* exceed

tran·sis·tor [tran·zis′tər] *n.* An electronic object made of a semiconductor with at least three electrodes.

trans·lu·cent [trans·lo͞o′sənt] *adj.* Allowing light to pass through without allowing objects to be identified: **Through the cloudy, *translucent* glass of the door, I could see that someone was there, but I couldn't tell who it was.**

trough [trôf] *n.* A narrow valley or a depression between the swells of waves: **The Coast Guard lost sight of the sinking boat every time it dipped into a *trough.***

trudge [truj] *v.* **trudged, trudg·ing** To walk heavily and with great effort: **Loren was *trudging* across the flooded field toward home, in his boots weighted down with mud.** *syn.* plod

tu·i·tion [t(y)o͞o·ish′ən] *n.* The charge for school instruction.

tur·bu·lence [tûr′byə·ləns] *n.* The choppy movement of water or air. *syn.* agitation

tur·moil [tûr′moil] *n.* Confusion and agitation: ***Turmoil* erupted in the auditorium when the principal announced that the school board was closing the school.** *syns.* tumult, upheaval

U

un·de·ci·phered [un′di·sī′fərd] *adj.* Not translated or interpreted: **The detective thought the *undeciphered* message was the key to solving the mystery.** *syns.* uninterpreted, unexplained

un·ex·pur·gat·ed [un′eks′pər·gāt′əd] *adj.* Published whole as written, with parts that might offend some readers.

un·ob·tru·sive·ly [un′əb·tro͞o′siv·lē] *adv.* In a way that cannot be noticed. *syn.* unnoticeably

V

var·mint [vär′mənt] *n. informal* A rascal or scoundrel; a person or animal that is mischievous or troublesome.

ve·loc·i·ty [və·los′ə·tē] *n.* Rate of speed: **The car was traveling at a *velocity* of 55 miles per hour.**

ven·dor [ven′dər] *n.* A seller: **At the Boston market, there was one *vendor* selling food next to another selling leather goods.**

ven·geance [ven′jəns] *n.* Punishment given with extreme power.

ven·tril·o·quist [ven·tril′ə·kwist] *n.* A person who can speak and make it appear that his or her voice is coming from something or someone else.

tortilla

ventriloquist
Ventriloquists are people who can make their voices appear to come from somewhere else. The name derives from the Latin words for "belly," *venter,* and "to speak," *loqui.*

a	add	**o͝o**	took
ā	ace	**o͞o**	pool
â	care	**u**	up
ä	palm	**û**	burn
e	end	**yo͞o**	fuse
ē	equal	**oi**	oil
i	it	**ou**	pout
ī	ice	**ng**	ring
o	odd	**th**	thin
ō	open	**t̶h̶**	this
ô	order	**zh**	vision

ə = a in *above*, e in *sicken*, i in *possible*, o in *melon*, u in *circus*

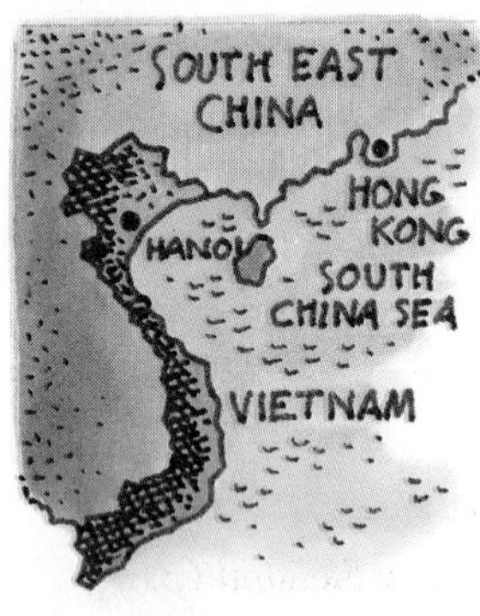

Vietnam

Vi·et·nam [vē·et′näm′] *n.* A southeast Asian country bordering on the South China Sea: **Hue located his native *Vietnam* on the world map.**

vi·tal [vīt′(ə)l] *adj.* Very important. *syn.* essential

W

war·i·ly [wâr′ə·lē] *adv.* Suspiciously; cautiously. *syn.* carefully

warp [wôrp] *v.* **warped, warp·ing** To bend or twist out of shape.

whee·dle [(h)wēd′(ə)l] *v.* **whee·dled, whee·dling** To persuade someone by using flattery. *syn.* coax

wield [wēld] *v.* **wield·ed, wield·ing** To hold and use; to handle: **The carpenter skillfully *wielded* his hammer and saw.**

wince [wins] *v.* **winced, winc·ing** To recoil or to draw back from something painful or unpleasant. *syn.* flinch

with·drawn [wi~~th~~·drôn′ *or* with·drôn′] *adj.* Lost in thought; quiet and reserved. *syn.* unsociable

Y

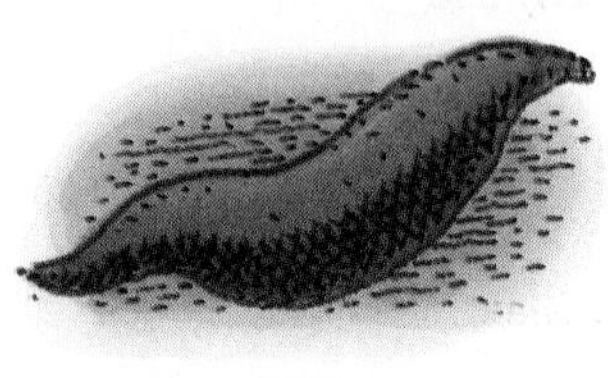
yam

yam [yam] *n.* A type of sweet potato; a root vegetable.

Z

zeph·yr [zef′ər] *n.* A soft, gentle wind.

INDEX OF TITLES AND AUTHORS

Page numbers in light type refer to biographical information.

Acknowledgments continued

HarperCollins Publishers: Cover illustration by John Schoenherr from *Julie of the Wolves* by Jean Craighead George. Illustration copyright © 1972 by John Schoenherr. Cover illustration from *Jodie's Journey* by Colin Thiele. Illustration copyright © 1988 by HarperCollins Publishers. From pp. 63–86 in *Sea Glass* by Laurence Yep. Text copyright © 1979 by Laurence Yep.

Hastings House Publishers, New York, Ltd.: "Advice to Travelers" from *Come As You Are* by Walker Gibson. © 1958 by Walker Gibson.

Holiday House: Cover photograph from *The Wright Brothers: How They Invented the Airplane* by Russell Freedman. Photograph courtesy of The Smithsonian Institution. "I Watched an Eagle Soar" by Virginia Driving Hawk Sneve from *Dancing Teepees: Poems of American Indian Youth.* Text copyright © 1989 by Virginia Driving Hawk Sneve.

Houghton Mifflin Company: Cover illustration from *The Way Things Work* by David Macaulay. Illustration copyright © 1988 by David Macaulay. From pp. 70–95 in *Trial by Wilderness* by David Mathieson. Text copyright © 1985 by David Mathieson. From pp. 25–39 in *Carlota* by Scott O'Dell. Text copyright © 1977 by Scott O'Dell. "How Winter Man's Power Was Broken" from *Tales of the Cheyennes* by Grace Jackson Penney. Text copyright 1953 by Grace Jackson Penney; copyright © renewed 1981 by Grace Jackson Penney.

Daniel F. Jaffe: "The Forecast" by Daniel F. Jaffe from *Prairie Schooner*. Text © 1964 by Dan Jaffe.

Alfred A. Knopf, Inc.: "Long Trip" from *Selected Poems* by Langston Hughes. Text copyright 1926 by Alfred A. Knopf, Inc., renewed 1954 by Langston Hughes. Cover illustration by Leo and Diane Dillon from *Anthony Burns: The Defeat and Triumph of a Fugitive Slave* by Virginia Hamilton. Illustration copyright © 1988 by Leo and Diane Dillon.

Little, Brown and Company: Cover illustration from *Jingo Django* by Sid Fleischman. Copyright © 1971 by Albert S. Fleischman.

Lodestar Books, an affiliate of Dutton Children's Books, a division of Penguin Books USA Inc.: From *The Astronaut Training Book for Kids* (Retitled: "Astronauts in Training") by Kim Long. Copyright © 1990 by Kim Long.

Barry B. Longyear: "Little Green Men" by Barry B. Longyear. Text © 1987 by Barry B. Longyear.

Los Angeles Times: From "At Home with the Titan of the Trail" by Paul Dean from the *Los Angeles Times*, April 29, 1990. Text copyright 1990 by Los Angeles Times.

Margaret K. McElderry Books, an imprint of Macmillan Publishing Company: Cover illustration by James Watts from *Back in the Beforetime: Tales of the California Indians*, retold by Jane Louise Curry. Illustration copyright © 1987 by James Watts. Cover illustration from *Frozen Fire* by James Houston. Copyright © 1977 by James Houston. From pp. 53–76 in *The Mystery of the Ancient Maya* by Carolyn Meyer and Charles Gallenkamp. Text copyright © 1985 by Carolyn Meyer and Charles Gallenkamp.

Morrow Junior Books, a division of William Morrow & Company, Inc.: From "The Platoon System" in *A Girl from Yamhill* by Beverly Cleary. Copyright © 1988 by Beverly Cleary.

Alan Nahigian: Cover illustration by Alan Nahigian from *Benjamin Banneker* by Kevin Conley.

Harold Ober Associates Incorporated: "The Sparrow Hawk" from *The Pedaling Man and Other Poems* by Russell Hoban. Text copyright © 1968 by Russell Hoban.

Orchard Books, New York: From *Seeing Earth from Space* by Patricia Lauber. Text copyright © 1990 by Patricia Lauber. "Lost at Sea," a version of *The Voyage of the Frog* by Gary Paulsen. Text copyright © 1989 by Gary Paulsen. Originally published in *Boys' Life* Magazine.

Prentice-Hall, a Division of Simon & Schuster, New York: Cover illustration from *Kon-Tiki* by Thor Heyerdahl. Copyright © 1950, 1960, 1984 by Thor Heyerdahl.

Puffin Books, a division of Penguin Books USA Inc.: Cover illustration by Robert Barrett from *Rascal* by Sterling North. Illustration copyright © 1990 by Robert Barrett.

G. P. Putnam's Sons: Cover illustration by Margot Tomes from *Homesick: My Own Story* by Jean Fritz. Illustration copyright © 1982 by Margot Tomes. Cover illustration from *The Brooklyn Bridge: They Said It Couldn't Be Built* by Judith St. George. Copyright © 1982 by Judith St. George.

The Putnam Publishing Group/Jeremy P. Tarcher, Inc.: From "The Flood" in *The Beauty of the Beasts* by Ralph Helfer. Text copyright © 1990 by Ralph Helfer.

R studio T: Cover design by R studio T from *Outward Dreams: Black Inventors and Their Inventions* by Jim Haskins. © by R studio T, New York.

Random House, Inc.: From *Gorilla, My Love* (Retitled: "Raymond's Run") by Toni Cade Bambara. Text copyright © 1970 by Toni Cade Bambara. From "The Bird and the Machine" in *The Immense Journey* by Loren Eiseley. Text copyright © 1955 by Loren Eiseley. Cover illustration by Domenick D'Andrea from *The Black Stallion* by Walter Farley. Illustration copyright © 1991 by Domenick D'Andrea. From *Chesapeake* by James Michener. Text copyright © 1978 by Random House, Inc.

Marian Reiner, on behalf of Lilian Moore: "The First" from *Something New Begins* by Lilian Moore. Text copyright © 1980, 1982 by Lilian Moore.

Barrett Root: Cover illustration by Barrett Root from *Baseball in April and Other Stories* by Gary Soto.

Scholastic, Inc.: "The Golden Apples, the Story of Atalanta and Hippomenes" from *Favorite Greek Myths*, retold by Mary Pope Osborne. Text copyright © 1989 by Mary Pope Osborne.

Charles Scribner's Sons, an imprint of Macmillan Publishing Company: Cover illustration by N.C. Wyeth from *The Yearling* by Marjorie Kinnan Rawlings. Illustration copyright 1939 by Charles Scribner's Sons; copyright renewed © 1967 by Charles Scribner's Sons.

The Society of Authors, as the literary representative of the Estate of John Masefield: "Sea Fever" from *Poems* by John Masefield. Text copyright 1912 by Macmillan Publishing Company, Inc., renewed 1940 by John Masefield.

The University of Chicago Press and Walter Blair: From "Pecos Bill, King of Texas Cowboys" in *TALL TALE AMERICA: A Legendary History of Our Humorous Heroes* by Walter Blair. Text © 1944, 1987 by Walter Blair.

Viking Penguin, a division of Penguin Books USA Inc.: "I May, I Might, I Must" from *The Complete Poems of Marianne Moore* by Marianne Moore. Text copyright © 1959 by Marianne Moore. "Trombones and Colleges" from *Fast Sam, Cool Clyde and Stuff* by Walter Dean Myers, cover illustration by Jerry Pinkney. Text copyright © 1975 by Walter Dean Myers; cover illustration copyright © 1988 by Viking Penguin Inc. *If You Say So, Claude* by Joan Lowery Nixon. Text copyright © 1980 by Joan Lowery Nixon. Cover illustration from *The Twenty-One Balloons* by William Pene du Bois. Copyright 1947 by William Pene du Bois, renewed © 1975 by William Pene du Bois. From *In Search of a Sandhill Crane* by Keith Robertson. Text copyright © 1973 by Keith Robertson. *Three Strong Women* by Claus Stamm. Text copyright © 1962 by Claus Stamm and Kazue Mizumura, renewed © 1990 by Claus Stamm and Kazue Mizumura.

Tricia Zimic: Cover illustration by Tricia Zimic from *The Ordinary Princess* by M. M. Kaye. Illustration copyright © 1986 by Tricia Zimic.

Illustration Credits
KEY: (t) top, (b) bottom, (l) left, (r) right, (c) center.

Theme Opening Art

Chris Armstrong, 332–333; Tim Bodendistel, 114–115; Charles Cashwell, 214–215; Britt Taylor Collins, 238–239, 404–405; Cheryl Cooper, 300–301; Dave Gaadt, 360–361, 436–437; Ken Hobson, 266–267; Marilyn King, 508–509; Kurt Krebs, 148–149; Jackie Pittman, 540–541; Drew Rose, 46–47, 70–71, 474–475; Dean St. Clair, 560–561

Theme Closing Art

Chris Armstrong, 331; Dave Bates, 397; Lindy Burnett, 539; Charles Cashwell, 69, 265; Britt Taylor Collins, 181; Dave Gaadt, 107, 237; Ken Hobson, 473; Dick Larson, 147; Jackie Pittman, 581; Drew Rose, 45; Dean St. Clair, 435; Don Wieland, 559

Connections Art

Lindy Burnett, 108–109, 398–399; R.M. Schneider, 294–295, 582–583; Karen Strelecki, 208–209, 502–503

Unit Opener, Bookshelf, & Connections Border Art (4/c)

Chris Armstrong, 16–17; Charles Cashwell, 210–211; Garth Glazier, 504-505; Ed Klautky, 110–111; Hank Kolodziej, 296–297; Drew Rose, 400–401

Selection Art

Dan Andreasen, 252–264; Edson Campos, 134–141, 384–396; Charles Cashwell, 198–205; Richard Cook, 484–499; Greg Correll, 94–106; Manuel Garcia, 268–283; Richard Garcia, Jr., 284–292; Ken Goldammer, 48–57; Cheryl Greisbach & Stanley Martucci, 176–180; Franklin Hammond, 562–567; David McCall Johnston, 170–175; Ross McDonald, 184–197; Francisco Mora, 84–91; Paul Morin, 162–169; David Moses, 116–133; Brian Pinkney, 62–68; Jerry Pinkney, 510–521; Clarence Porter, 334–347, 542–557; Muns Quan, 362–381; Scott Scheidly, 143–146, 348–349, 568–579; S.D. Schindler, 458–467; Patrick Soper, 438–455; J.A. White, 22–41; Leslie Wu, 362–381